PETER GRILL
AND THE PHILOSOPHER'S TIME

03

Story & Art by
DAISUKE HIYAMA

CONTENTS

Chapter **11** Peter Grill and the **Secret Treaty** 003

Chapter **12** Peter Grill and the **Fate of the Treaty** 029

Chapter **13** Peter Grill and the **Megaton Axe of Rage** 069

Chapter **14** Peter Grill and the **Principles of Battle** 105

Chapter **15** Peter Grill and the **Warrior who Cried Love** 133

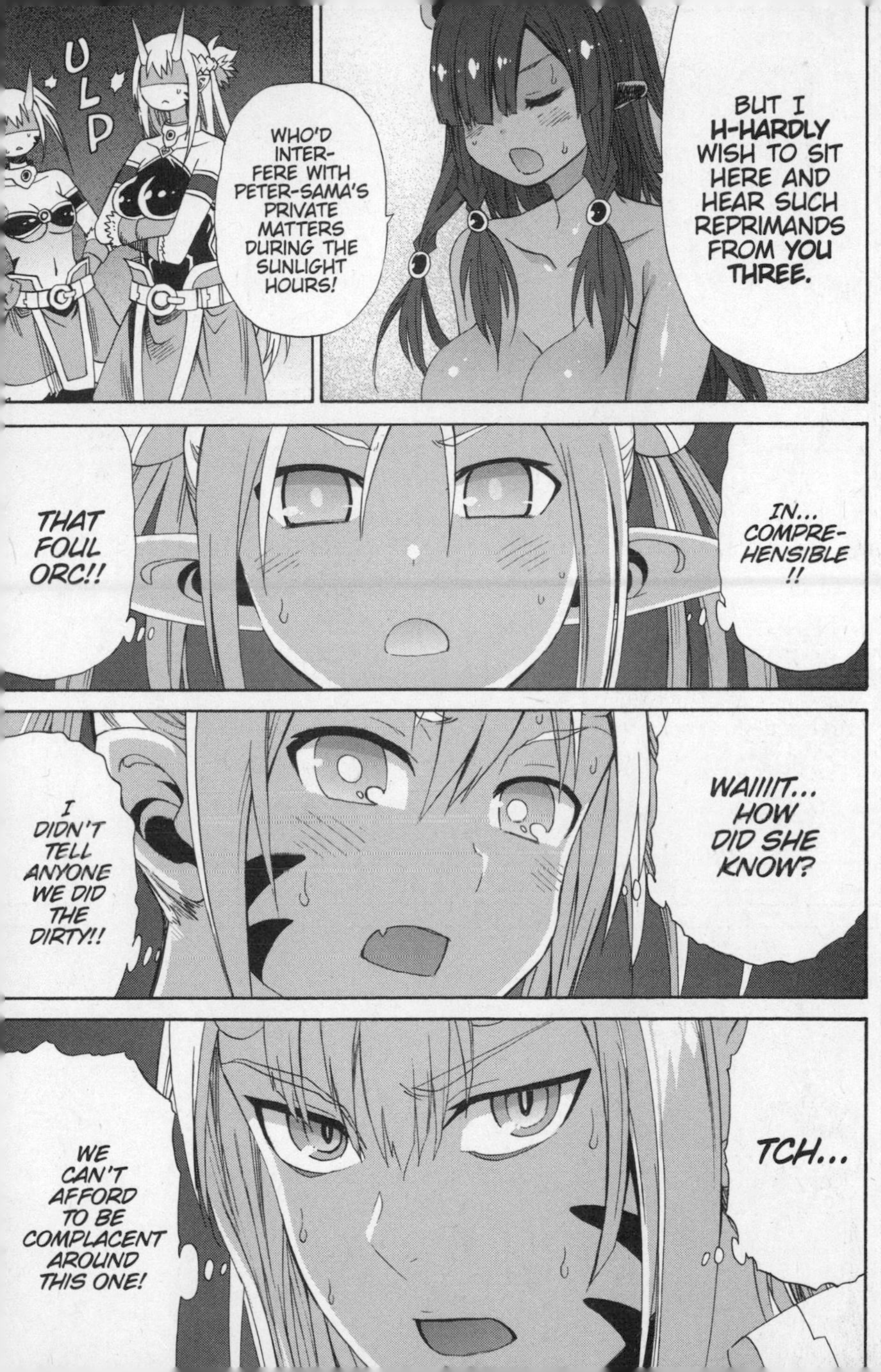
BUT I H-HARDLY WISH TO SIT HERE AND HEAR SUCH REPRIMANDS FROM YOU THREE.
WHO'D INTER-FERE WITH PETER-SAMA'S PRIVATE MATTERS DURING THE SUNLIGHT HOURS!
ULP
IN... COMPRE-HENSIBLE!!
THAT FOUL ORC!!
WAIIIIT... HOW DID SHE KNOW?
I DIDN'T TELL ANYONE WE DID THE DIRTY!!
TCH...
WE CAN'T AFFORD TO BE COMPLACENT AROUND THIS ONE!

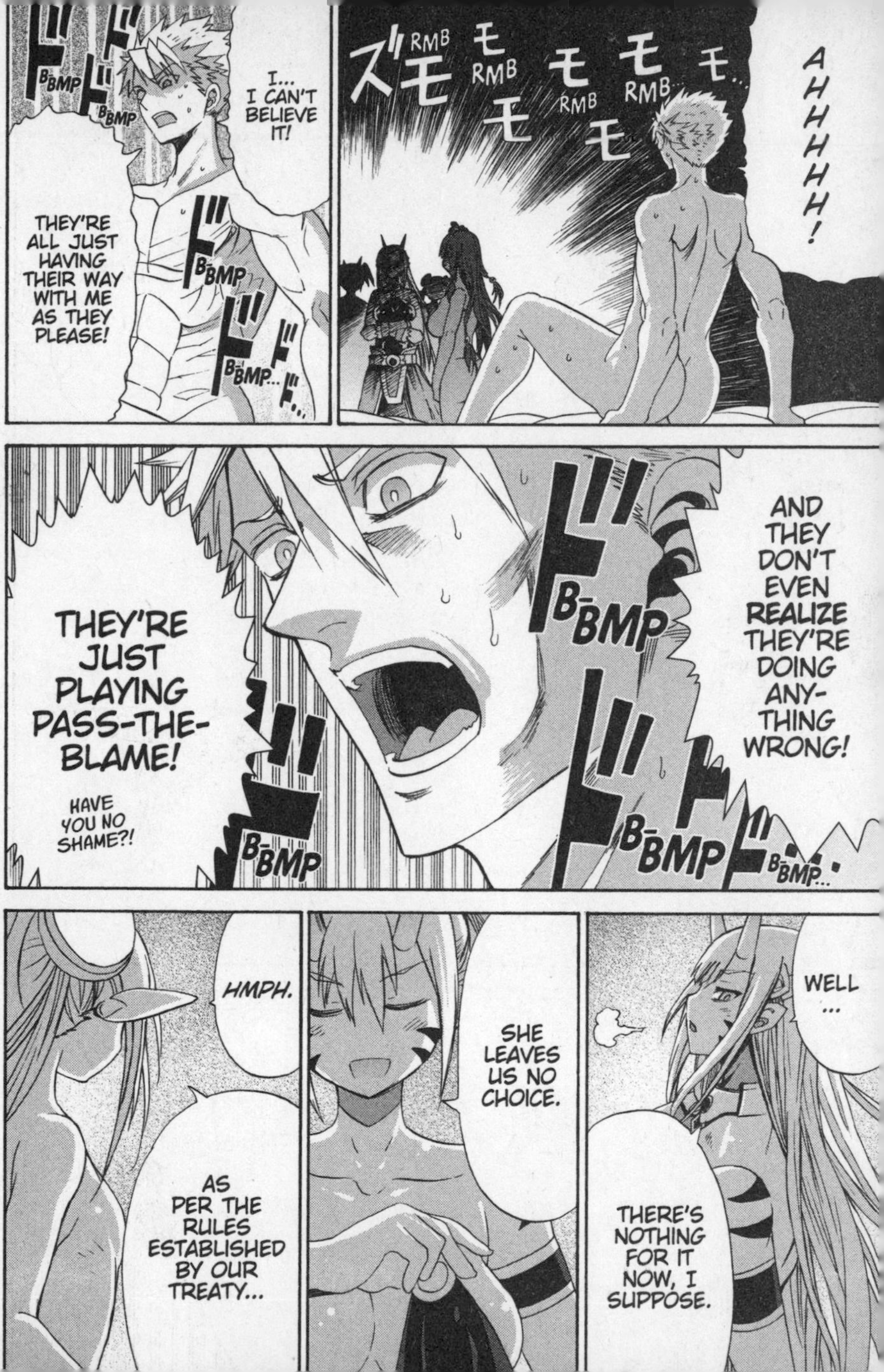
ズモ RMB モ RMB モ RMB モ RMB モ モ... モ
AHHHHHH!
I... I CAN'T BELIEVE IT!
B-BMP B-BMP
THEY'RE ALL JUST HAVING THEIR WAY WITH ME AS THEY PLEASE!
B-BMP B-BMP...
AND THEY DON'T EVEN REALIZE THEY'RE DOING ANY-THING WRONG!
B-BMP B-BMP B-BMP...
THEY'RE JUST PLAYING PASS-THE-BLAME!
HAVE YOU NO SHAME?!
B-BMP
WELL ...
THERE'S NOTHING FOR IT NOW, I SUPPOSE.
SHE LEAVES US NO CHOICE.
HMPH.
AS PER THE RULES ESTABLISHED BY OUR TREATY...

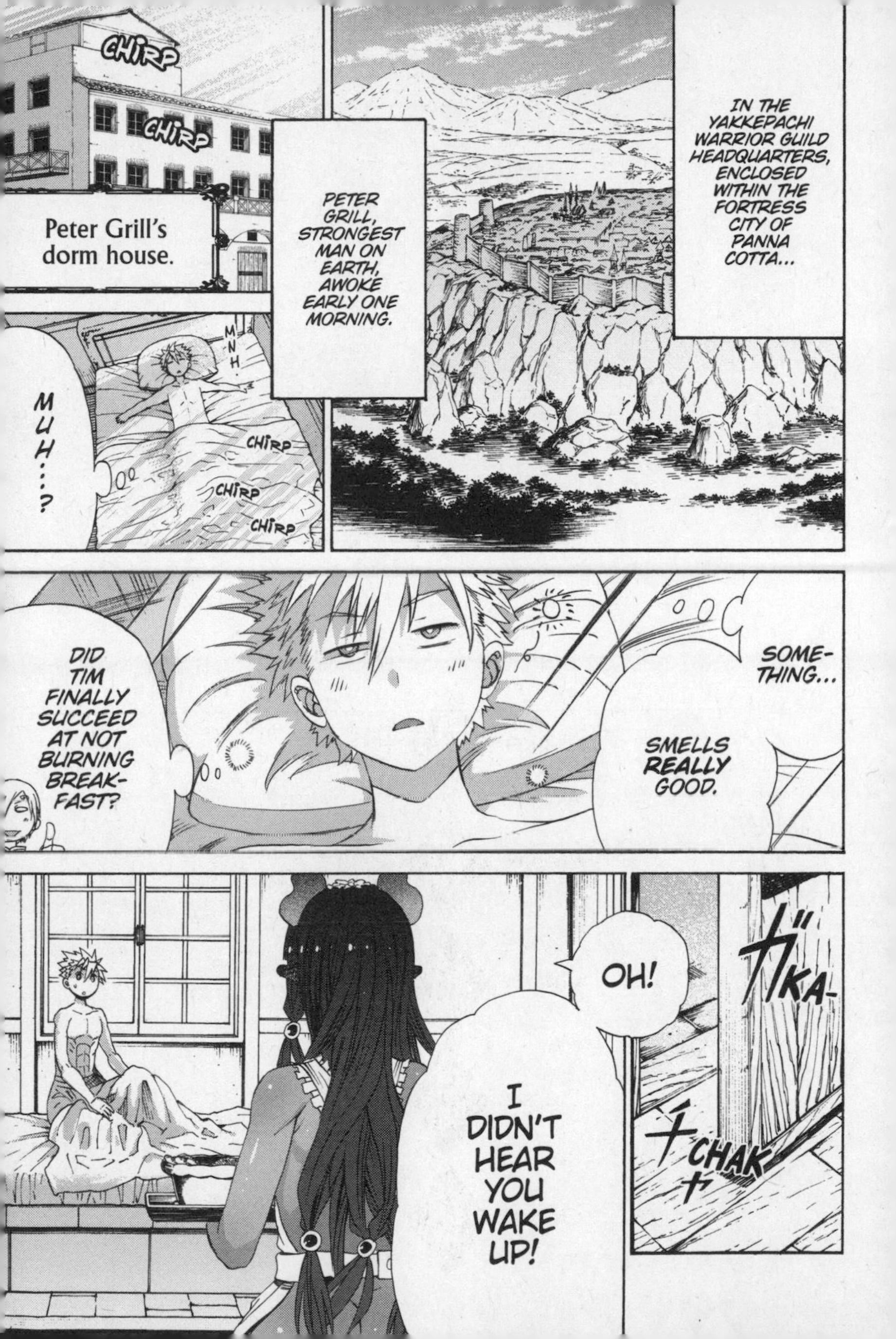
IN THE YAKKEPACHI WARRIOR GUILD HEADQUARTERS, ENCLOSED WITHIN THE FORTRESS CITY OF PANNA COTTA...
PETER GRILL, STRONGEST MAN ON EARTH, AWOKE EARLY ONE MORNING.
CHIRP
CHIRP
Peter Grill's dorm house.
MNH
CHIRP
CHIRP
CHIRP
MUH...?
SOME-THING...
SMELLS REALLY GOOD.
DID TIM FINALLY SUCCEED AT NOT BURNING BREAK-FAST?
KA-
CHAK
OH!
I DIDN'T HEAR YOU WAKE UP!

Chapter 11 Peter Grill and the Secret Treaty

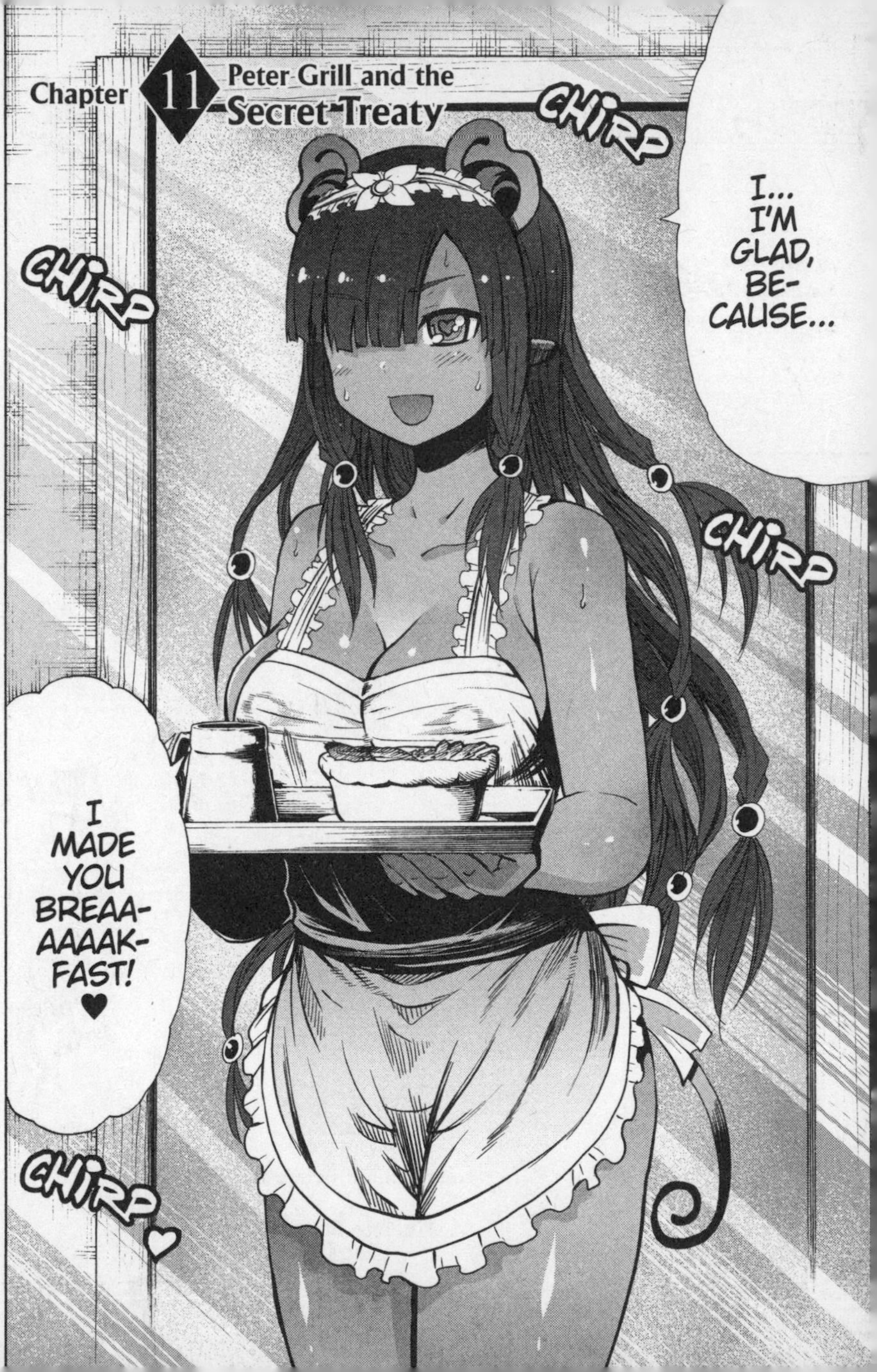
CHIRP
I... I'M GLAD, BE-CAUSE...
CHIRP
CHIRP
I MADE YOU BREAAAAAAK-FAST! ♥
CHIRP ♥

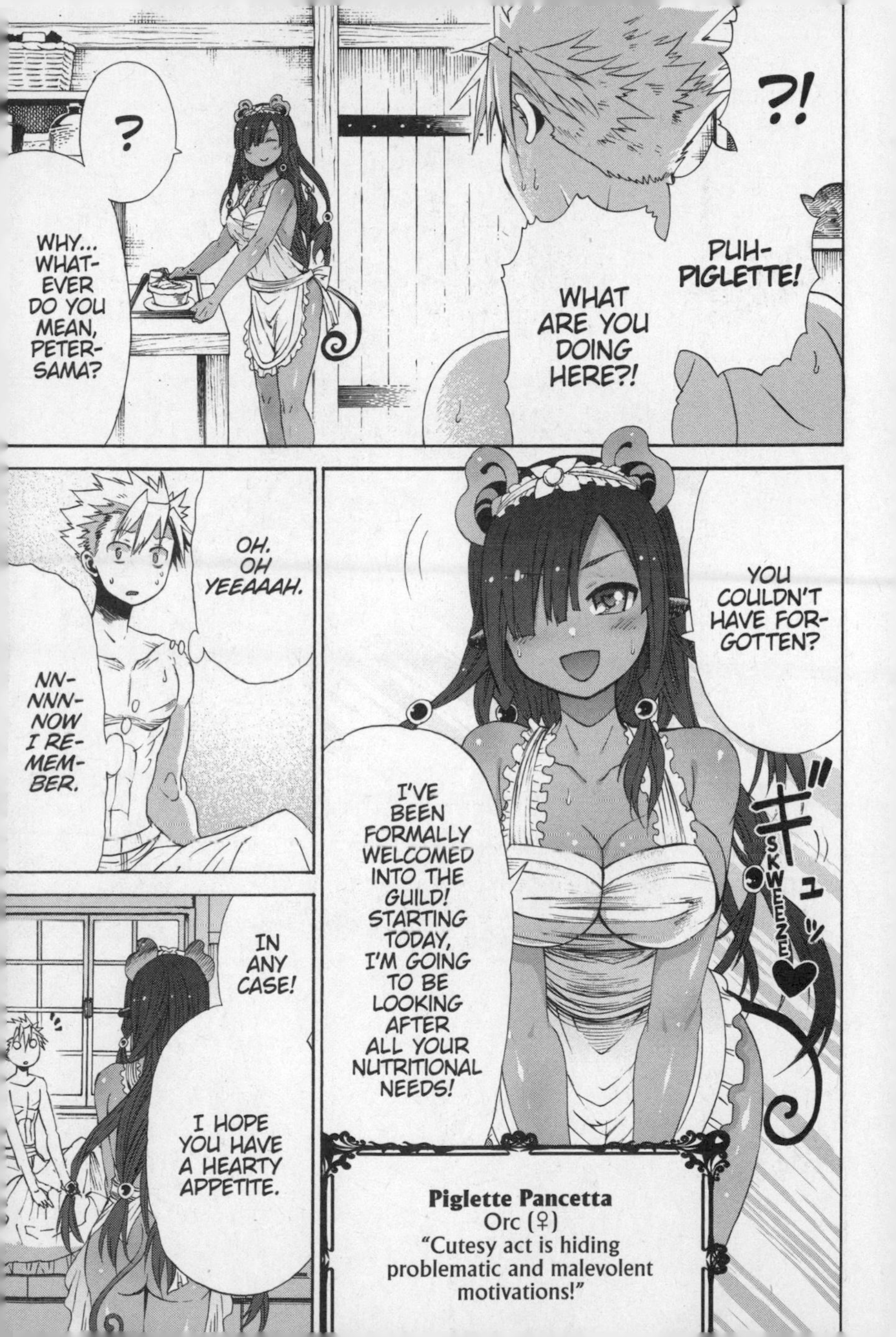
?!
PUH-PIGLETTE!
WHAT ARE YOU DOING HERE?!
?
WHY... WHAT-EVER DO YOU MEAN, PETER-SAMA?
YOU COULDN'T HAVE FOR-GOTTEN?
SKWEEZE
I'VE BEEN FORMALLY WELCOMED INTO THE GUILD! STARTING TODAY, I'M GOING TO BE LOOKING AFTER ALL YOUR NUTRITIONAL NEEDS!
Piglette Pancetta
Orc (♀)
"Cutesy act is hiding problematic and malevolent motivations!"
OH. OH YEEAAAH.
NN-NNN-NOW I RE-MEM-BER.
IN ANY CASE!
I HOPE YOU HAVE A HEARTY APPETITE.

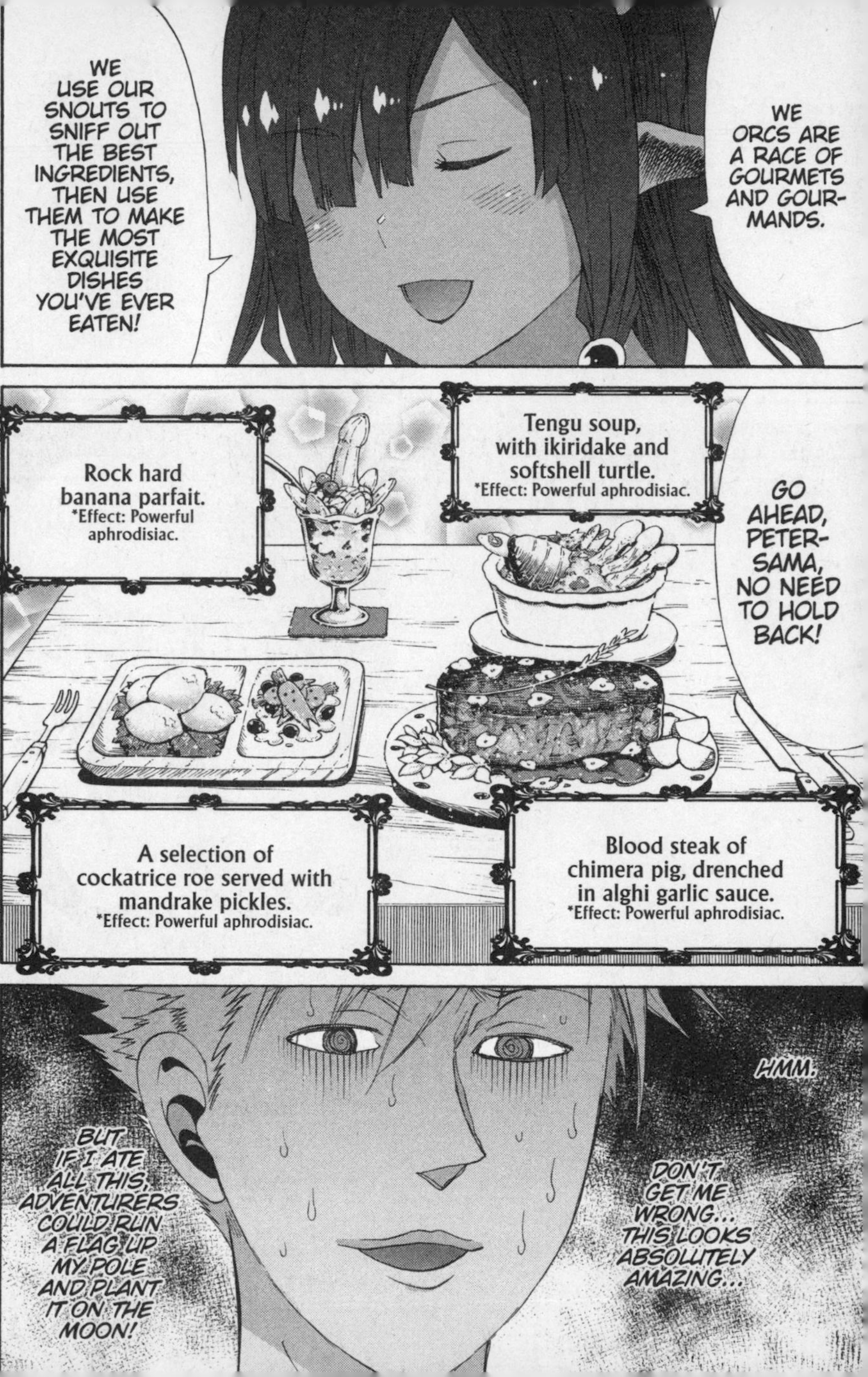
WE ORCS ARE A RACE OF GOURMETS AND GOURMANDS.
WE USE OUR SNOUTS TO SNIFF OUT THE BEST INGREDIENTS, THEN USE THEM TO MAKE THE MOST EXQUISITE DISHES YOU'VE EVER EATEN!
GO AHEAD, PETER-SAMA, NO NEED TO HOLD BACK!
Tengu soup, with ikiridake and softshell turtle. *Effect: Powerful aphrodisiac.
Rock hard banana parfait. *Effect: Powerful aphrodisiac.
Blood steak of chimera pig, drenched in alghi garlic sauce. *Effect: Powerful aphrodisiac.
A selection of cockatrice roe served with mandrake pickles. *Effect: Powerful aphrodisiac.
HMM.
DON'T GET ME WRONG... THIS LOOKS ABSOLUTELY AMAZING...
BUT IF I ATE ALL THIS, ADVENTURERS COULD RUN A FLAG UP MY POLE AND PLANT IT ON THE MOON!

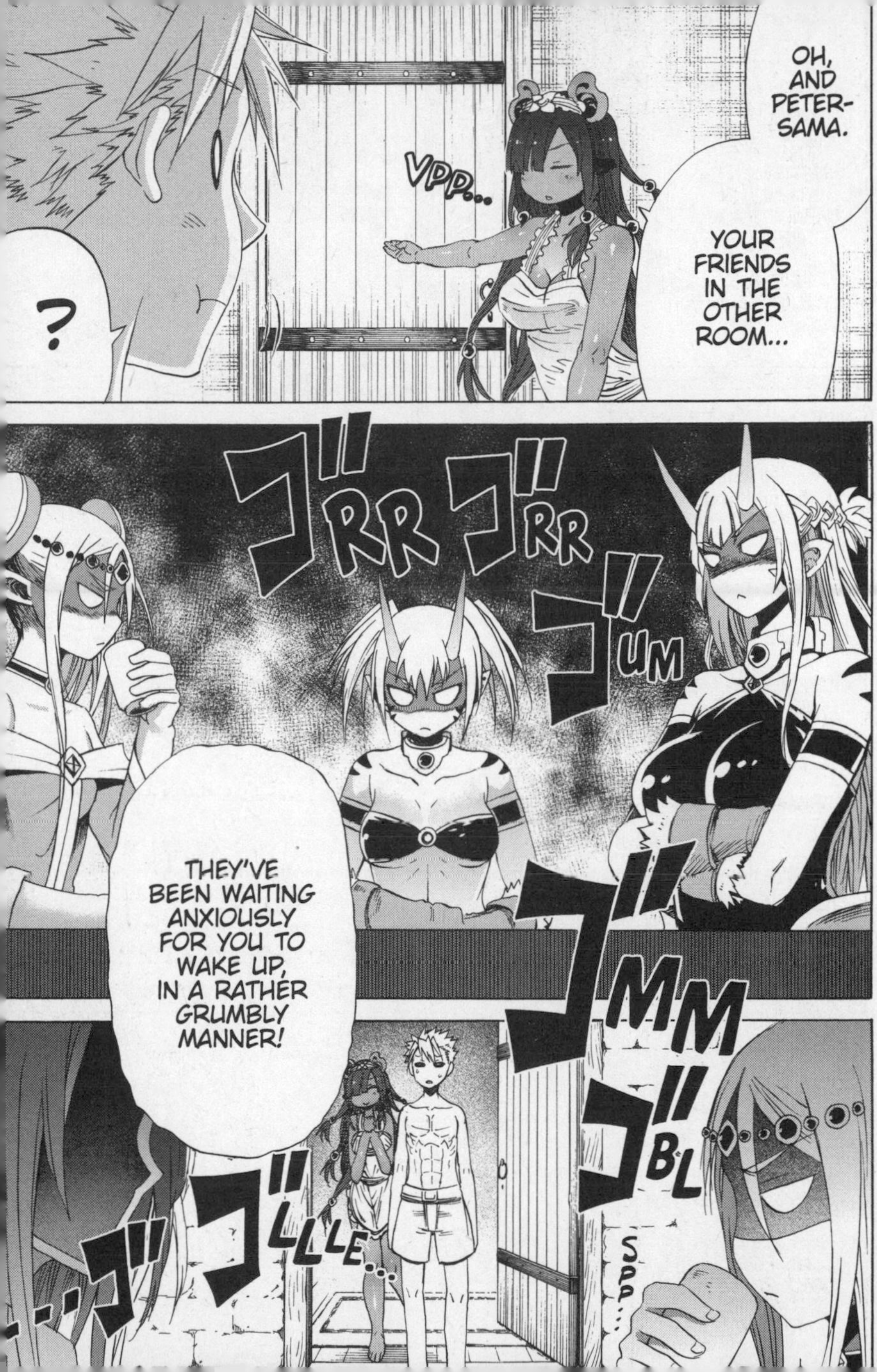
OH, AND PETER-SAMA.
YOUR FRIENDS IN THE OTHER ROOM...
VPP...
?
ゴRR
ゴRR
ゴUM
THEY'VE BEEN WAITING ANXIOUSLY FOR YOU TO WAKE UP, IN A RATHER GRUMBLY MANNER!
ゴMM
ゴBL
SPP...
...ゴ
ゴLLLE...

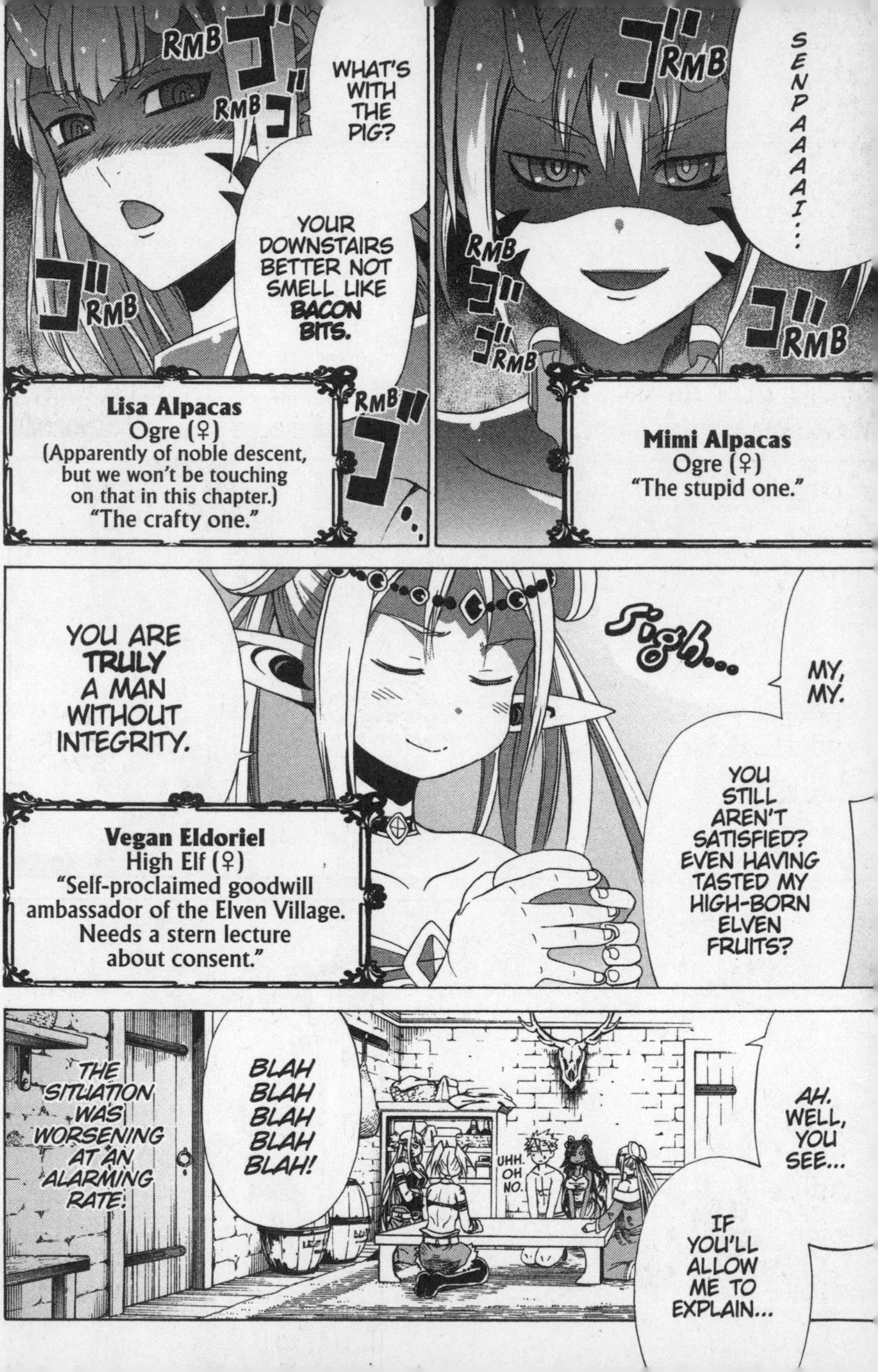
SENPAAAAAI...
ゴ RMB
ゴ RMB
ゴ RMB
ゴ RMB
Mimi Alpacas
Ogre (♀)
"The stupid one."
RMB ゴ
RMB ゴ
WHAT'S WITH THE PIG?
YOUR DOWNSTAIRS BETTER NOT SMELL LIKE BACON BITS.
ゴ RMB
RMB ゴ
...
Lisa Alpacas
Ogre (♀)
(Apparently of noble descent, but we won't be touching on that in this chapter.)
"The crafty one."
MY, MY.
Sigh...
YOU STILL AREN'T SATISFIED? EVEN HAVING TASTED MY HIGH-BORN ELVEN FRUITS?
YOU ARE TRULY A MAN WITHOUT INTEGRITY.
Vegan Eldoriel
High Elf (♀)
"Self-proclaimed goodwill ambassador of the Elven Village. Needs a stern lecture about consent."
AH. WELL, YOU SEE...
IF YOU'LL ALLOW ME TO EXPLAIN...
UHH. OH NO.
BLAH BLAH BLAH BLAH BLAH!
THE SITUATION WAS WORSENING AT AN ALARMING RATE.

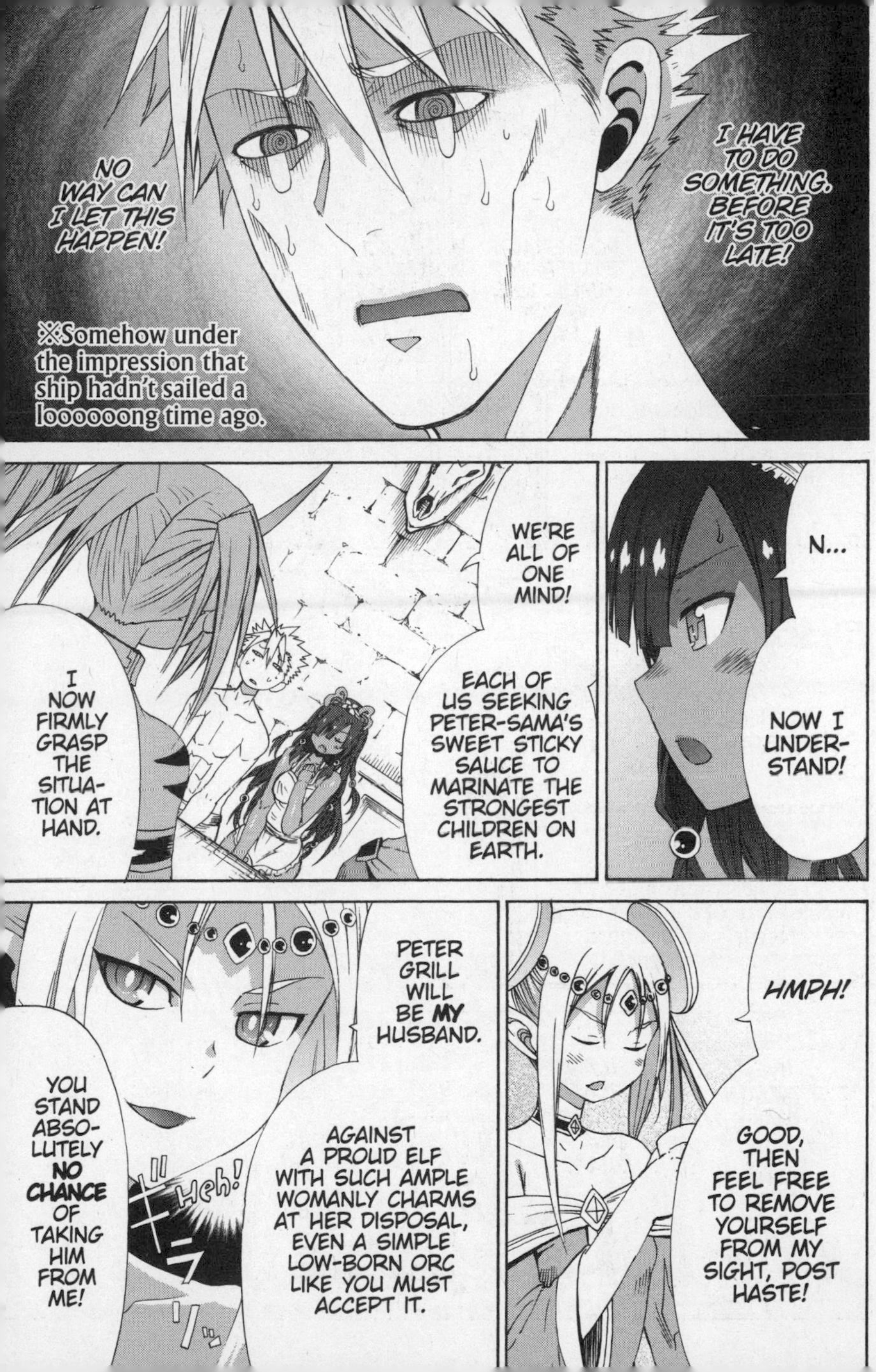
I HAVE TO DO SOMETHING. BEFORE IT'S TOO LATE!
NO WAY CAN I LET THIS HAPPEN!
※Somehow under the impression that ship hadn't sailed a loooooong time ago.
N...
NOW I UNDERSTAND!
WE'RE ALL OF ONE MIND!
EACH OF US SEEKING PETER-SAMA'S SWEET STICKY SAUCE TO MARINATE THE STRONGEST CHILDREN ON EARTH.
I NOW FIRMLY GRASP THE SITUATION AT HAND.
HMPH!
GOOD, THEN FEEL FREE TO REMOVE YOURSELF FROM MY SIGHT, POST HASTE!
PETER GRILL WILL BE **MY** HUSBAND.
AGAINST A PROUD ELF WITH SUCH AMPLE WOMANLY CHARMS AT HER DISPOSAL, EVEN A SIMPLE LOW-BORN ORC LIKE YOU MUST ACCEPT IT.
YOU STAND ABSOLUTELY **NO CHANCE** OF TAKING HIM FROM ME!
Heh!

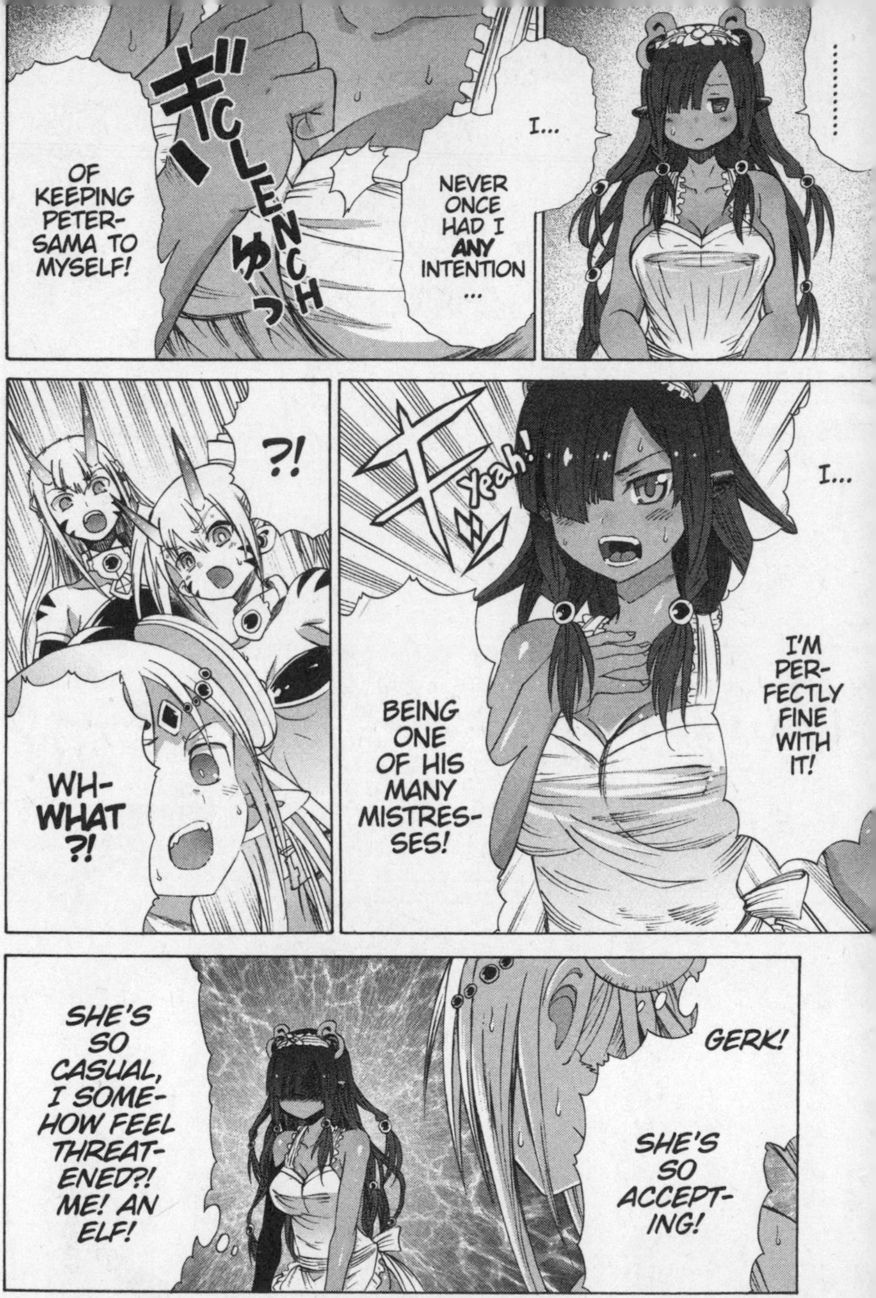
......
I...
NEVER ONCE HAD I ANY INTENTION ...
OF KEEPING PETER-SAMA TO MYSELF!
CLENCH
I...
I'M PER-FECTLY FINE WITH IT!
Yeah!
BEING ONE OF HIS MANY MISTRES-SES!
?!
WH-WHAT?!
GERK!
SHE'S SO ACCEPT-ING!
SHE'S SO CASUAL, I SOME-HOW FEEL THREAT-ENED?! ME! AN ELF!

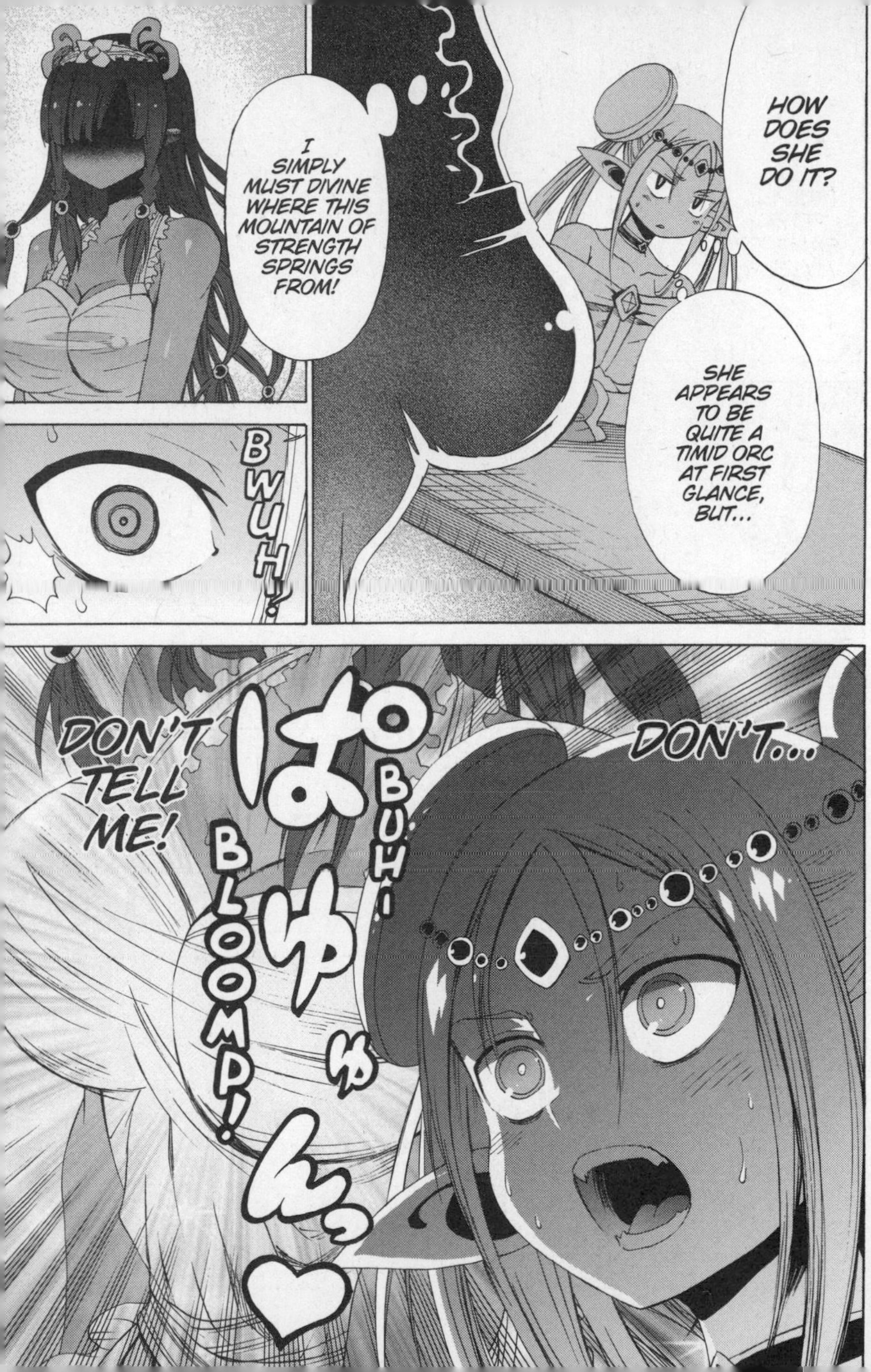
HOW DOES SHE DO IT?
SHE APPEARS TO BE QUITE A TIMID ORC AT FIRST GLANCE, BUT...
I SIMPLY MUST DIVINE WHERE THIS MOUNTAIN OF STRENGTH SPRINGS FROM!
BWUH!?
DON'T...
BUH!
ぽゆゆんっ
BLOOMP!
DON'T TELL ME!

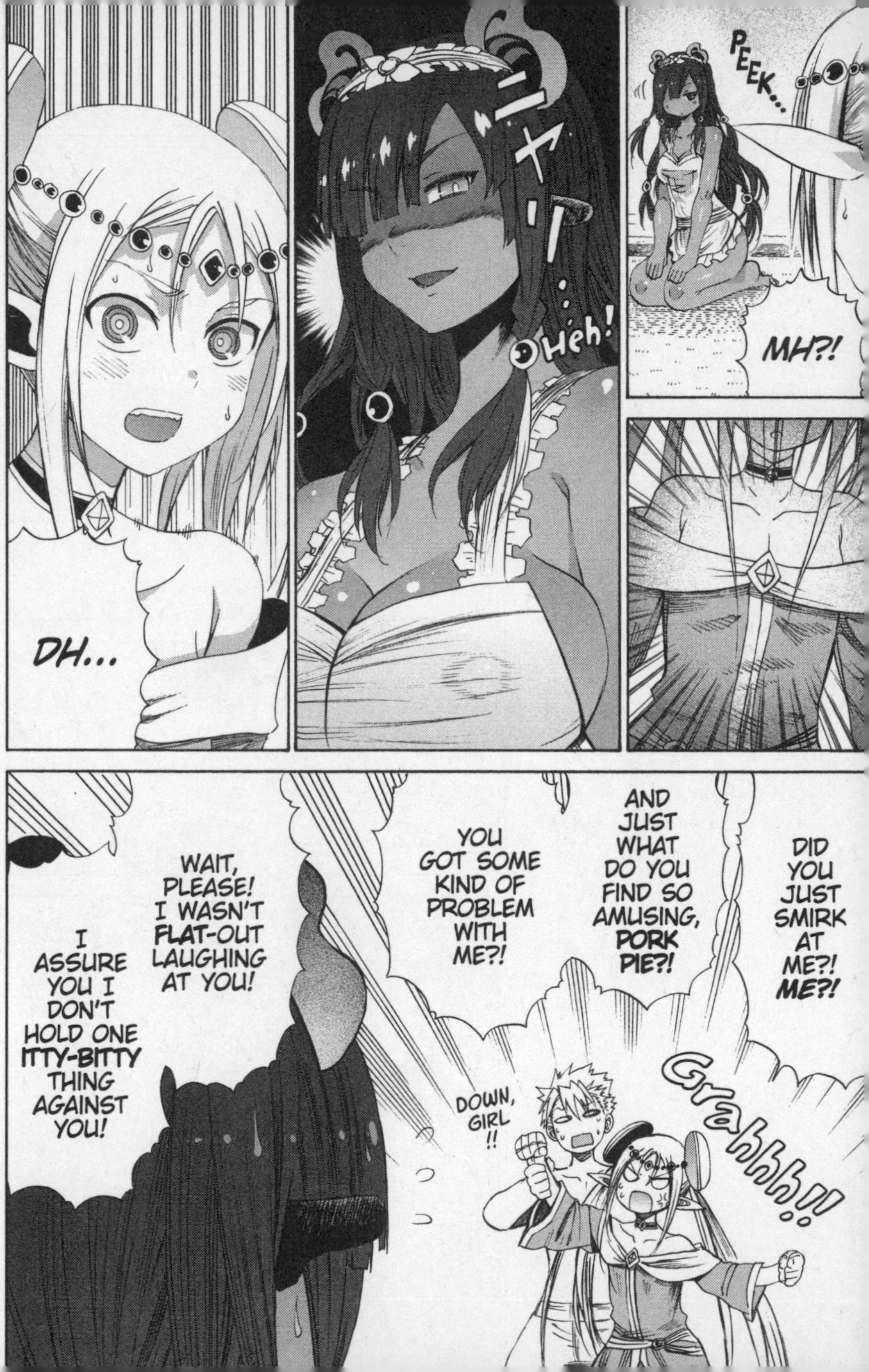
PEEK...
MH?!
Heh!
DH...
DID YOU JUST SMIRK AT ME?! ME?!
AND JUST WHAT DO YOU FIND SO AMUSING, PORK PIE?!
YOU GOT SOME KIND OF PROBLEM WITH ME?!
Grahhh!!
DOWN, GIRL!!
WAIT, PLEASE! I WASN'T FLAT-OUT LAUGHING AT YOU!
I ASSURE YOU I DON'T HOLD ONE ITTY-BITTY THING AGAINST YOU!

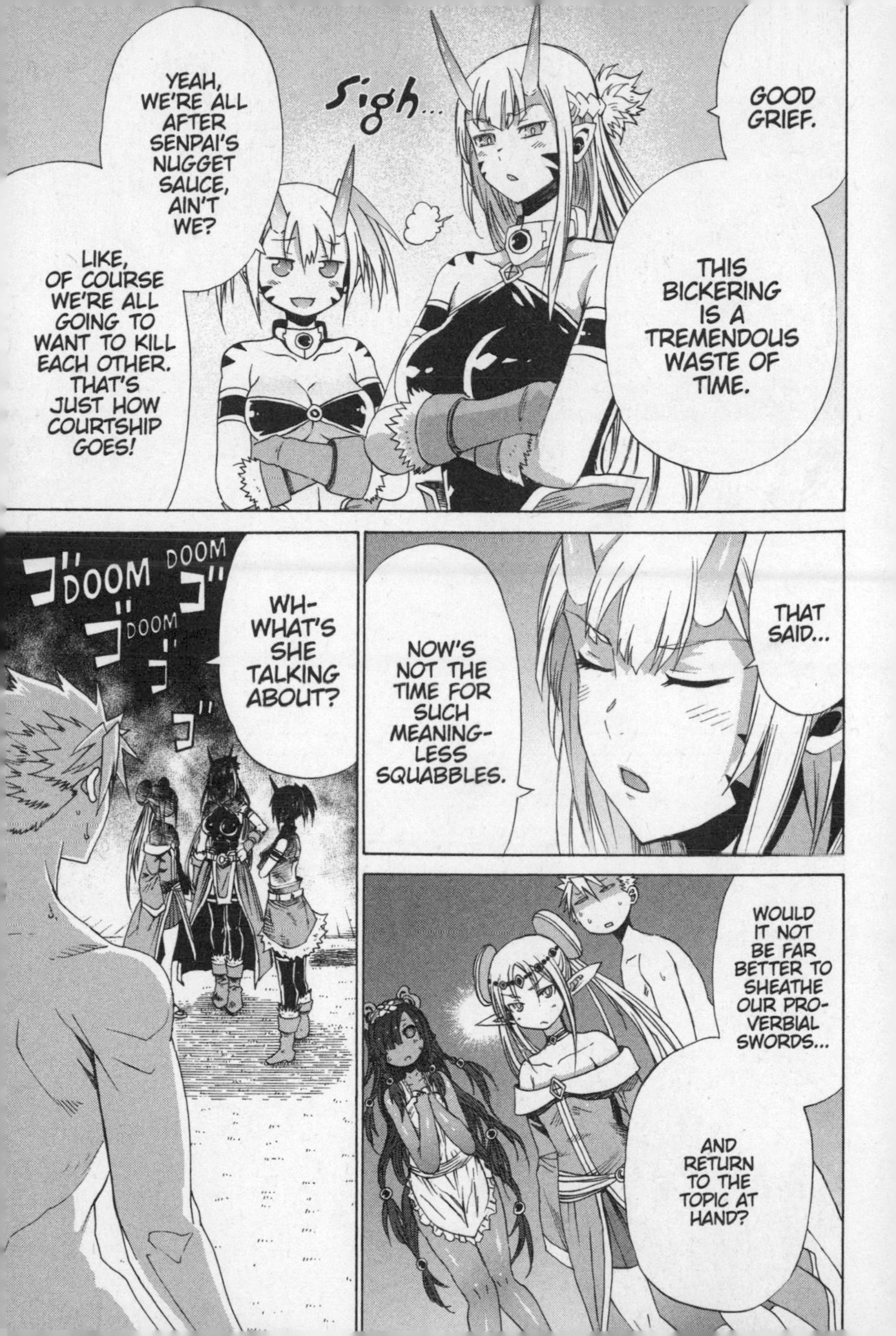
GOOD GRIEF.
THIS BICKERING IS A TREMENDOUS WASTE OF TIME.
Sigh...
YEAH, WE'RE ALL AFTER SENPAI'S NUGGET SAUCE, AIN'T WE?
LIKE, OF COURSE WE'RE ALL GOING TO WANT TO KILL EACH OTHER. THAT'S JUST HOW COURTSHIP GOES!
THAT SAID...
NOW'S NOT THE TIME FOR SUCH MEANING-LESS SQUABBLES.
WOULD IT NOT BE FAR BETTER TO SHEATHE OUR PRO-VERBIAL SWORDS...
AND RETURN TO THE TOPIC AT HAND?
DOOM
DOOM
DOOM
WH-WHAT'S SHE TALKING ABOUT?

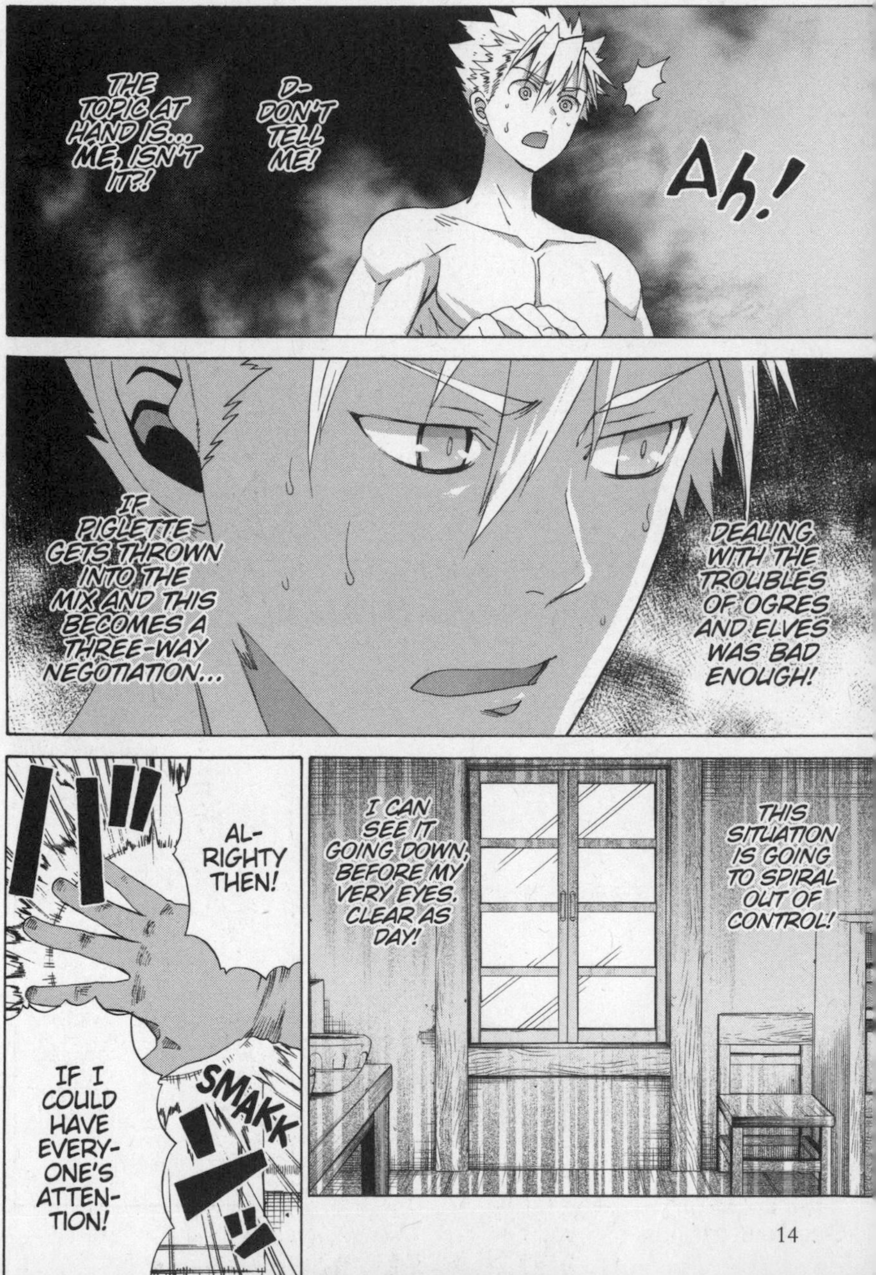
Ah!
D- DON'T TELL ME!
THE TOPIC AT HAND IS... ME, ISN'T IT?!
DEALING WITH THE TROUBLES OF OGRES AND ELVES WAS BAD ENOUGH!
IF PIGLETTE GETS THROWN INTO THE MIX AND THIS BECOMES A THREE-WAY NEGOTIATION...
THIS SITUATION IS GOING TO SPIRAL OUT OF CONTROL!
I CAN SEE IT GOING DOWN, BEFORE MY VERY EYES. CLEAR AS DAY!
AL-RIGHTY THEN!
SMAKK
IF I COULD HAVE EVERY-ONE'S ATTEN-TION!

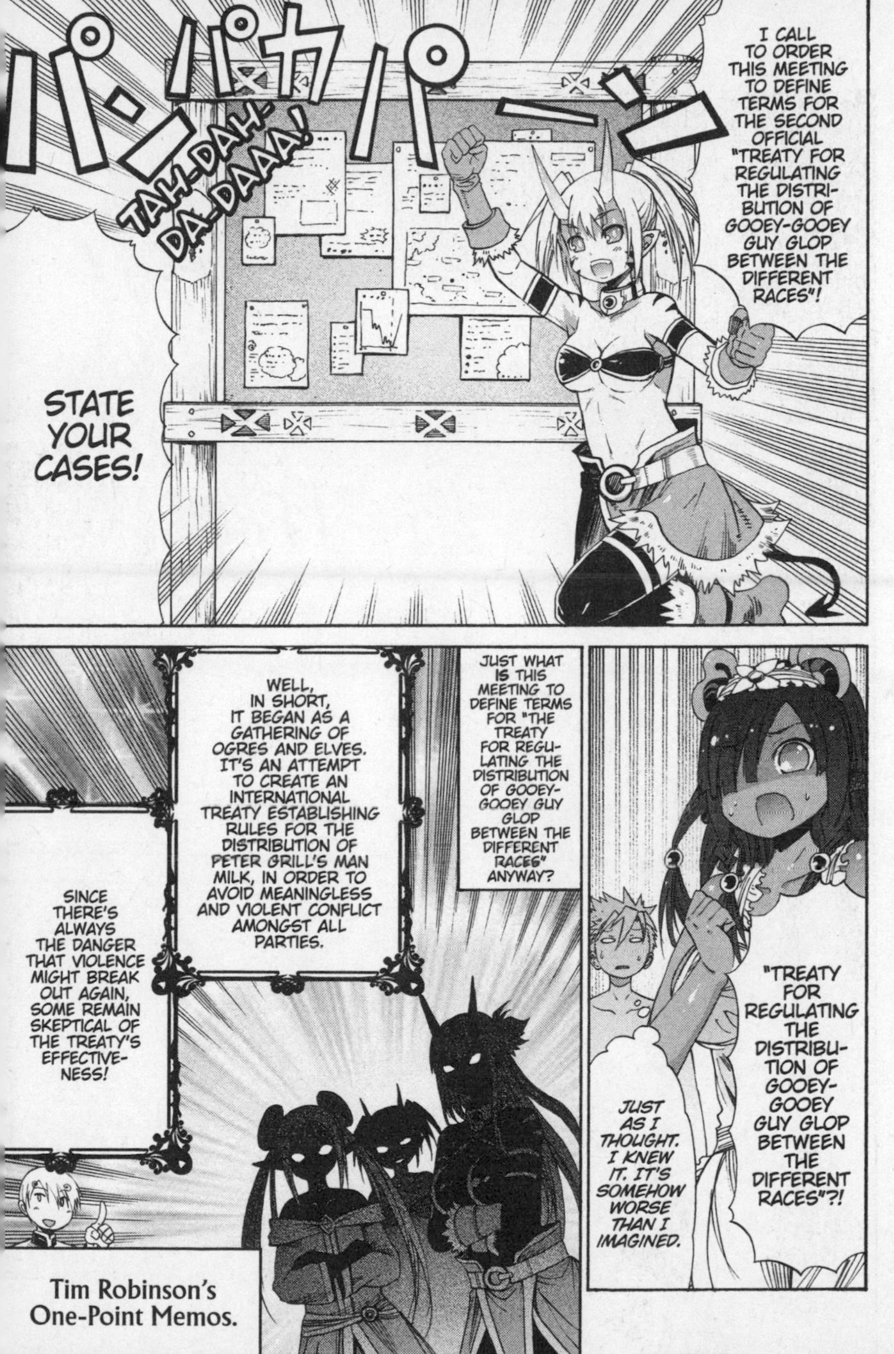
I CALL TO ORDER THIS MEETING TO DEFINE TERMS FOR THE SECOND OFFICIAL "TREATY FOR REGULATING THE DISTRIBUTION OF GOOEY-GOOEY GUY GLOP BETWEEN THE DIFFERENT RACES"!
パ・パパパ パー
TAH-DAH-DAH-DA-DAAA!
STATE YOUR CASES!
"TREATY FOR REGULATING THE DISTRIBUTION OF GOOEY-GOOEY GUY GLOP BETWEEN THE DIFFERENT RACES"?!
JUST AS I THOUGHT. I KNEW IT. IT'S SOMEHOW WORSE THAN I IMAGINED.
JUST WHAT IS THIS MEETING TO DEFINE TERMS FOR "THE TREATY FOR REGULATING THE DISTRIBUTION OF GOOEY-GOOEY GUY GLOP BETWEEN THE DIFFERENT RACES" ANYWAY?
WELL, IN SHORT, IT BEGAN AS A GATHERING OF OGRES AND ELVES. IT'S AN ATTEMPT TO CREATE AN INTERNATIONAL TREATY ESTABLISHING RULES FOR THE DISTRIBUTION OF PETER GRILL'S MAN MILK, IN ORDER TO AVOID MEANINGLESS AND VIOLENT CONFLICT AMONGST ALL PARTIES.
SINCE THERE'S ALWAYS THE DANGER THAT VIOLENCE MIGHT BREAK OUT AGAIN, SOME REMAIN SKEPTICAL OF THE TREATY'S EFFECTIVENESS!
Tim Robinson's One-Point Memos.

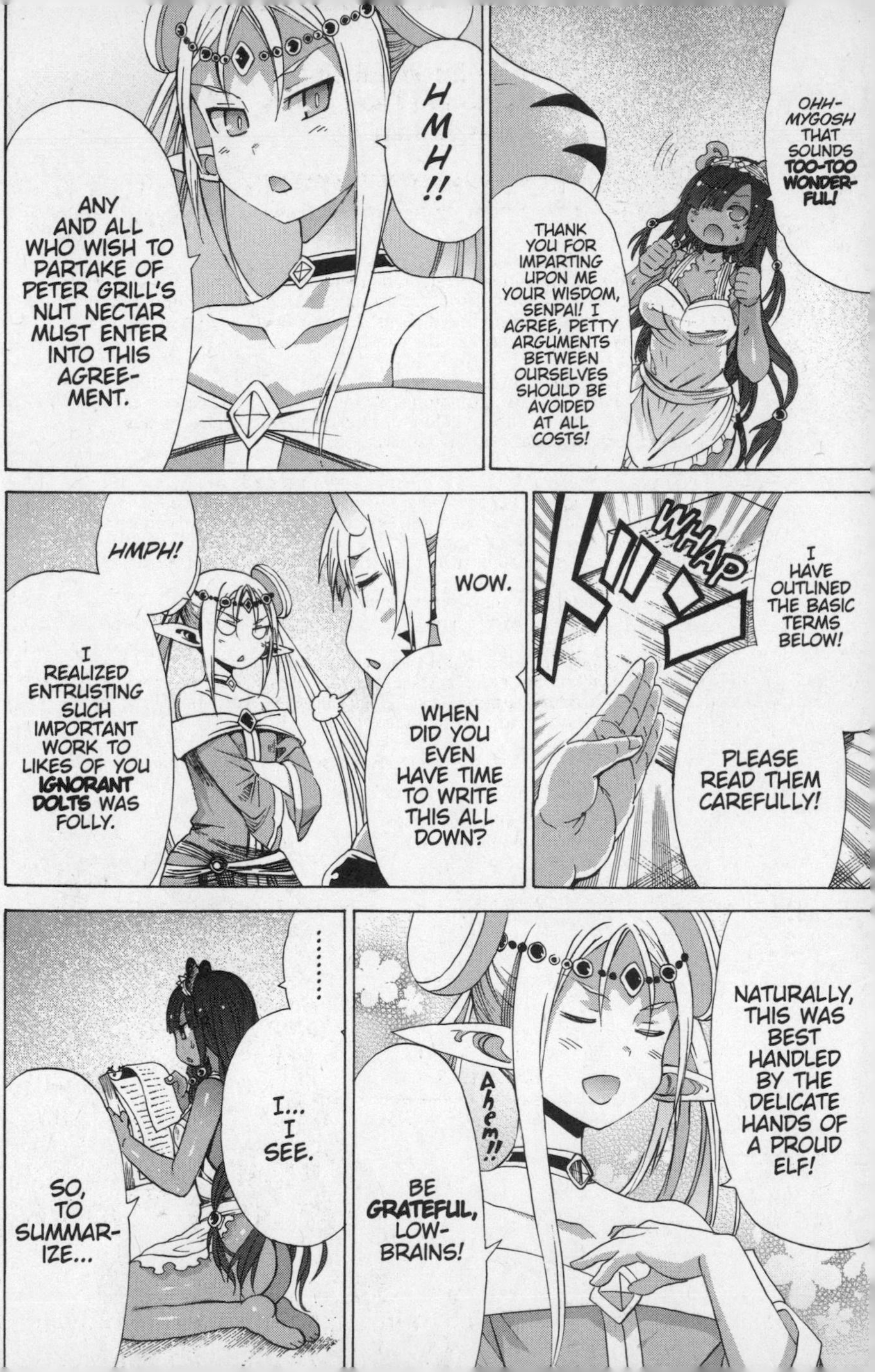

OHH-MYGOSH THAT SOUNDS **TOO-TOO WONDERFUL!**
THANK YOU FOR IMPARTING UPON ME YOUR WISDOM, SENPAI! I AGREE, PETTY ARGUMENTS BETWEEN OURSELVES SHOULD BE AVOIDED AT ALL COSTS!
HMH!!
ANY AND ALL WHO WISH TO PARTAKE OF PETER GRILL'S NUT NECTAR MUST ENTER INTO THIS AGREEMENT.
WHAP
I HAVE OUTLINED THE BASIC TERMS BELOW!
PLEASE READ THEM CAREFULLY!
WOW.
WHEN DID YOU EVEN HAVE TIME TO WRITE THIS ALL DOWN?
HMPH!
I REALIZED ENTRUSTING SUCH IMPORTANT WORK TO LIKES OF YOU **IGNORANT DOLTS** WAS FOLLY.
NATURALLY, THIS WAS BEST HANDLED BY THE DELICATE HANDS OF A PROUD ELF!
Ahem!!
BE **GRATEFUL,** LOW-BRAINS!
......
I... I SEE.
SO, TO SUMMARIZE...

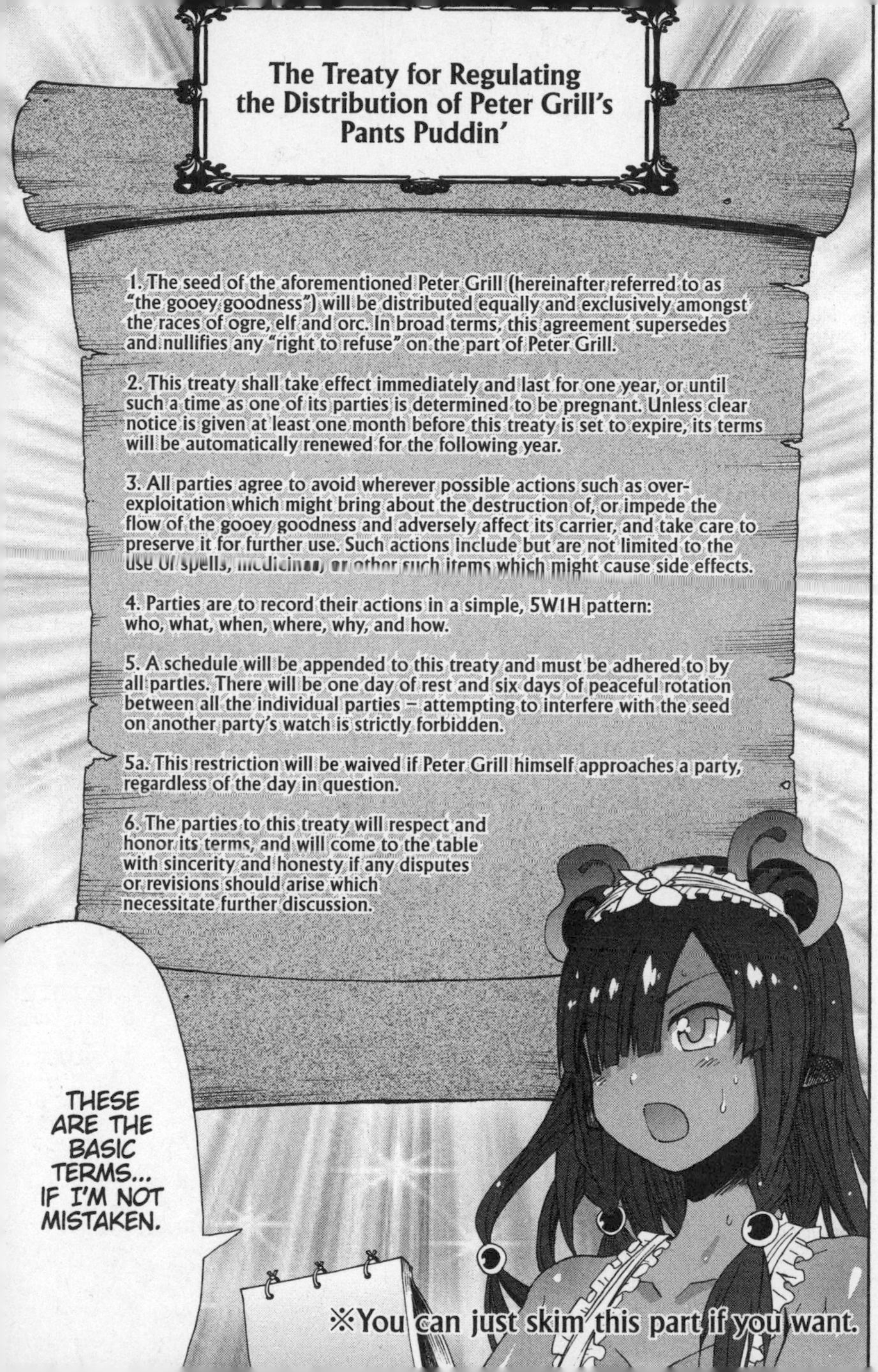
The Treaty for Regulating the Distribution of Peter Grill's Pants Puddin'
1. The seed of the aforementioned Peter Grill (hereinafter referred to as "the gooey goodness") will be distributed equally and exclusively amongst the races of ogre, elf and orc. In broad terms, this agreement supersedes and nullifies any "right to refuse" on the part of Peter Grill.
2. This treaty shall take effect immediately and last for one year, or until such a time as one of its parties is determined to be pregnant. Unless clear notice is given at least one month before this treaty is set to expire, its terms will be automatically renewed for the following year.
3. All parties agree to avoid wherever possible actions such as over-exploitation which might bring about the destruction of, or impede the flow of the gooey goodness and adversely affect its carrier, and take care to preserve it for further use. Such actions include but are not limited to the use of spells, medicines, or other such items which might cause side effects.
4. Parties are to record their actions in a simple, 5W1H pattern: who, what, when, where, why, and how.
5. A schedule will be appended to this treaty and must be adhered to by all parties. There will be one day of rest and six days of peaceful rotation between all the individual parties – attempting to interfere with the seed on another party's watch is strictly forbidden.
5a. This restriction will be waived if Peter Grill himself approaches a party, regardless of the day in question.
6. The parties to this treaty will respect and honor its terms, and will come to the table with sincerity and honesty if any disputes or revisions should arise which necessitate further discussion.
THESE ARE THE BASIC TERMS... IF I'M NOT MISTAKEN.
※You can just skim this part if you want.

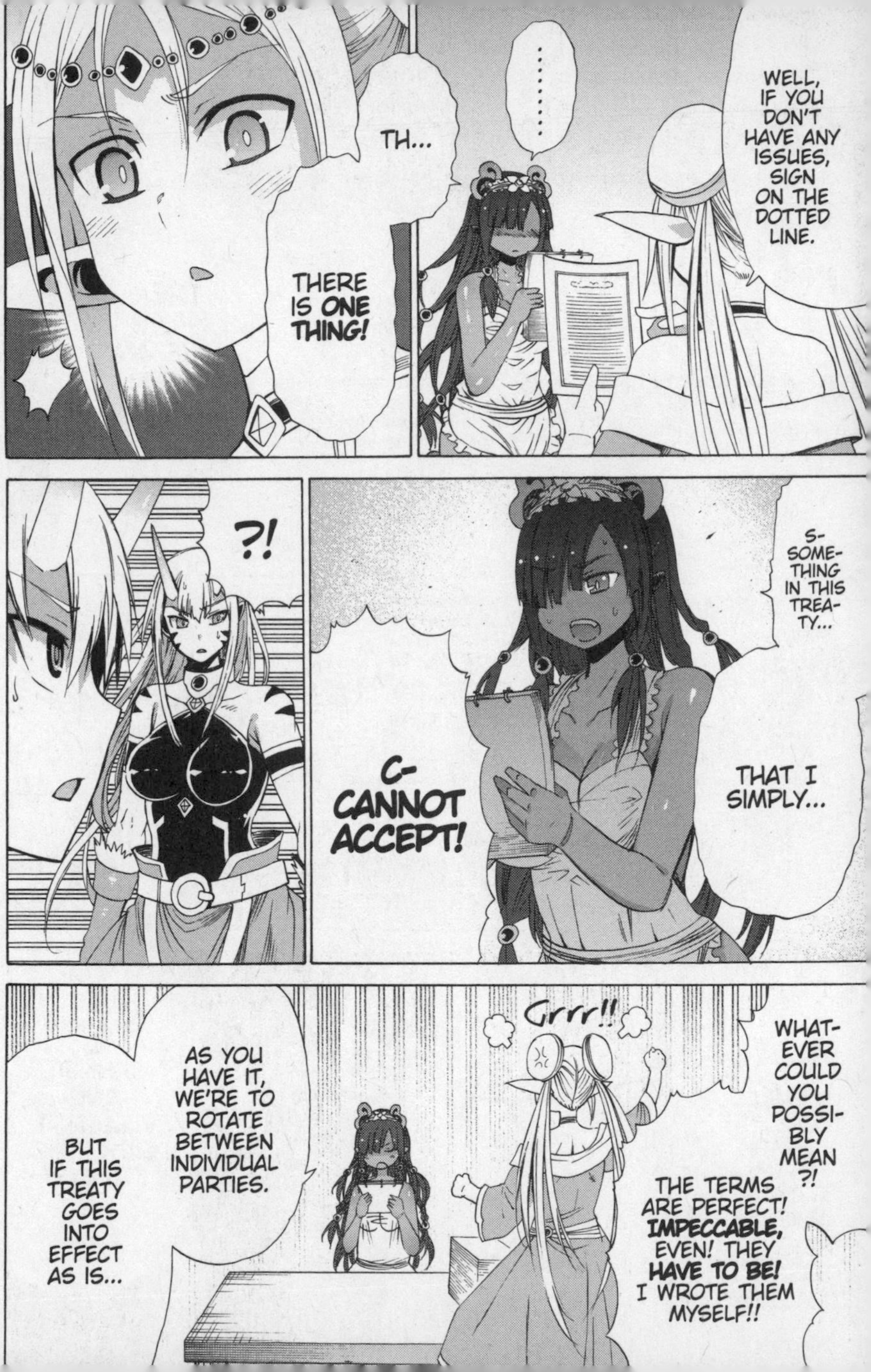
WELL, IF YOU DON'T HAVE ANY ISSUES, SIGN ON THE DOTTED LINE.
......
TH...
THERE IS ONE THING!
S-SOMETHING IN THIS TREATY...
THAT I SIMPLY...
C-CANNOT ACCEPT!
?!
Grrr!!
WHATEVER COULD YOU POSSIBLY MEAN?!
THE TERMS ARE PERFECT! IMPECCABLE, EVEN! THEY HAVE TO BE! I WROTE THEM MYSELF!!
AS YOU HAVE IT, WE'RE TO ROTATE BETWEEN INDIVIDUAL PARTIES.
BUT IF THIS TREATY GOES INTO EFFECT AS IS...

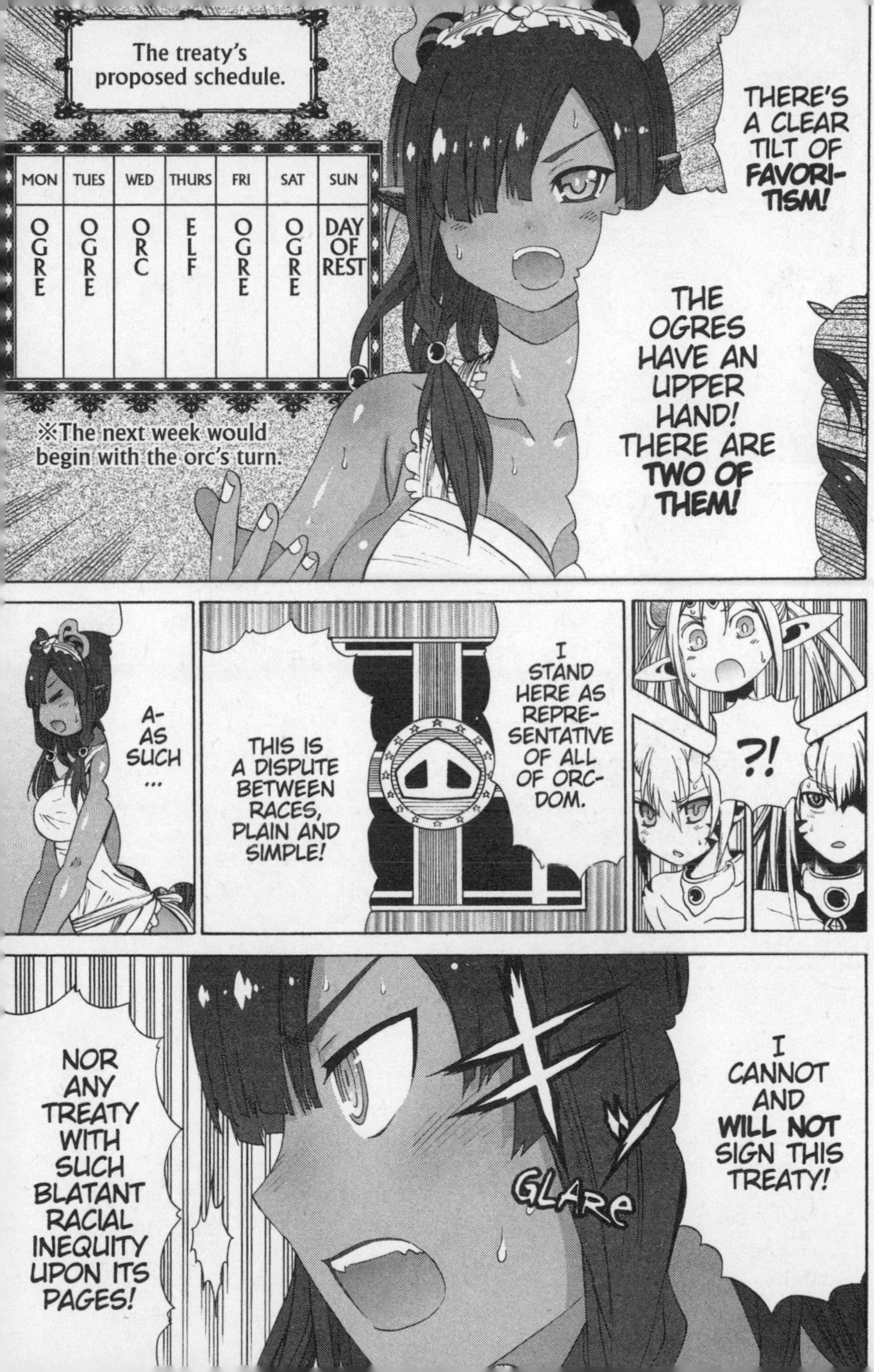
THERE'S A CLEAR TILT OF FAVORITISM!
THE OGRES HAVE AN UPPER HAND! THERE ARE TWO OF THEM!
The treaty's proposed schedule.

MON	TUES	WED	THURS	FRI	SAT	SUN
OGRE	OGRE	ORC	ELF	OGRE	OGRE	DAY OF REST

※The next week would begin with the orc's turn.
?!
I STAND HERE AS REPRESENTATIVE OF ALL OF ORCDOM.
THIS IS A DISPUTE BETWEEN RACES, PLAIN AND SIMPLE!
A- AS SUCH ...
I CANNOT AND WILL NOT SIGN THIS TREATY!
GLARE
NOR ANY TREATY WITH SUCH BLATANT RACIAL INEQUITY UPON ITS PAGES!

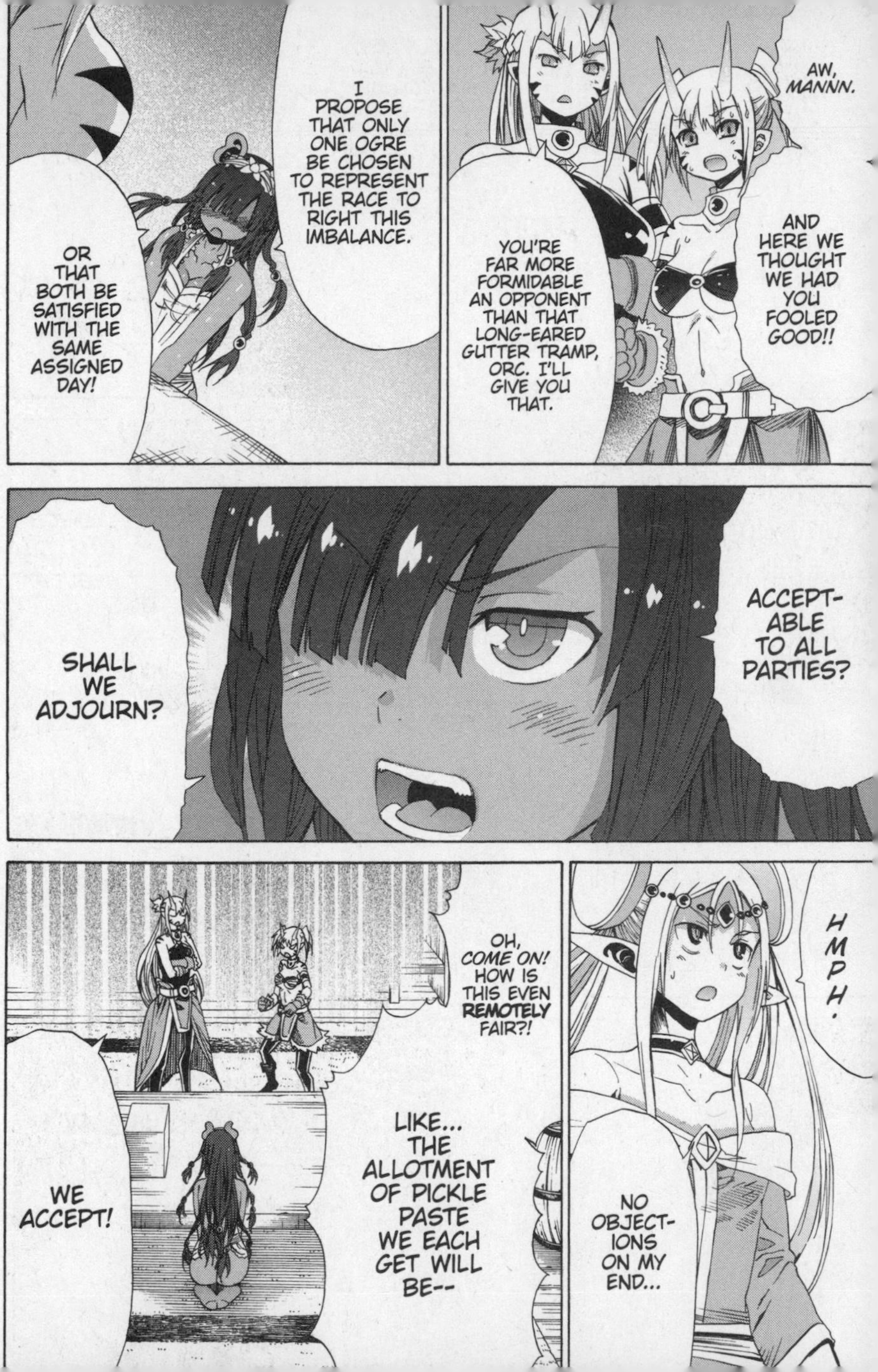
AW, MANNN.
AND HERE WE THOUGHT WE HAD YOU FOOLED GOOD!!
YOU'RE FAR MORE FORMIDABLE AN OPPONENT THAN THAT LONG-EARED GUTTER TRAMP, ORC. I'LL GIVE YOU THAT.
I PROPOSE THAT ONLY ONE OGRE BE CHOSEN TO REPRESENT THE RACE TO RIGHT THIS IMBALANCE.
OR THAT BOTH BE SATISFIED WITH THE SAME ASSIGNED DAY!
ACCEPT-ABLE TO ALL PARTIES?
SHALL WE ADJOURN?
HMPH.
NO OBJECT-IONS ON MY END...
OH, *COME ON!* HOW IS THIS EVEN **REMOTELY** FAIR?!
LIKE... THE ALLOTMENT OF PICKLE PASTE WE EACH GET WILL BE--
WE ACCEPT!

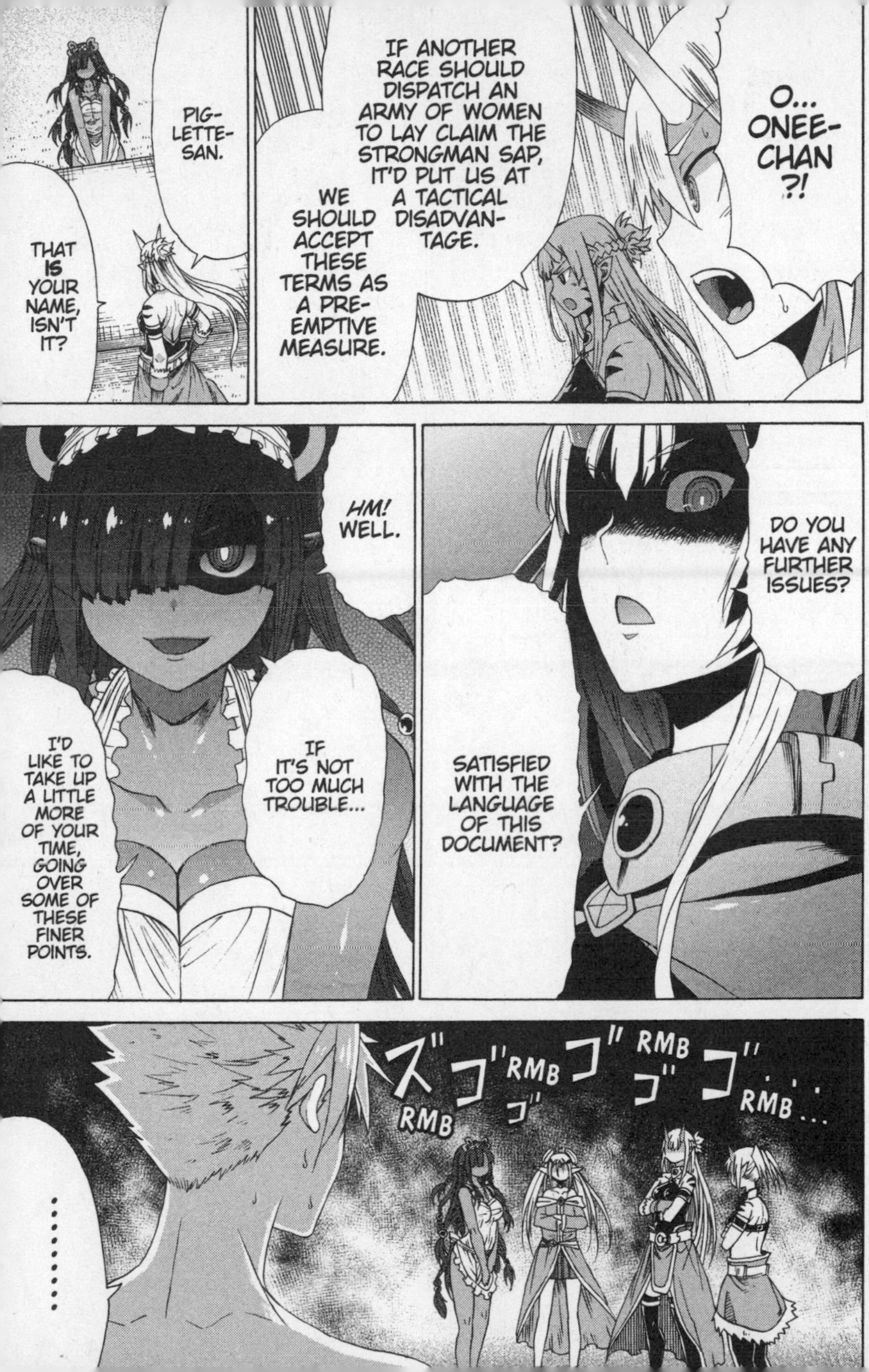
O... ONEE-CHAN?!
IF ANOTHER RACE SHOULD DISPATCH AN ARMY OF WOMEN TO LAY CLAIM THE STRONGMAN SAP, IT'D PUT US AT A TACTICAL DISADVANTAGE.
WE SHOULD ACCEPT THESE TERMS AS A PREEMPTIVE MEASURE.
PIG-LETTE-SAN.
THAT IS YOUR NAME, ISN'T IT?
DO YOU HAVE ANY FURTHER ISSUES?
SATISFIED WITH THE LANGUAGE OF THIS DOCUMENT?
HM! WELL.
IF IT'S NOT TOO MUCH TROUBLE...
I'D LIKE TO TAKE UP A LITTLE MORE OF YOUR TIME, GOING OVER SOME OF THESE FINER POINTS.
ズゴ゛ゴ゛ゴ゛ゴ゛ゴ゛...
RMB RMB RMB RMB...
....

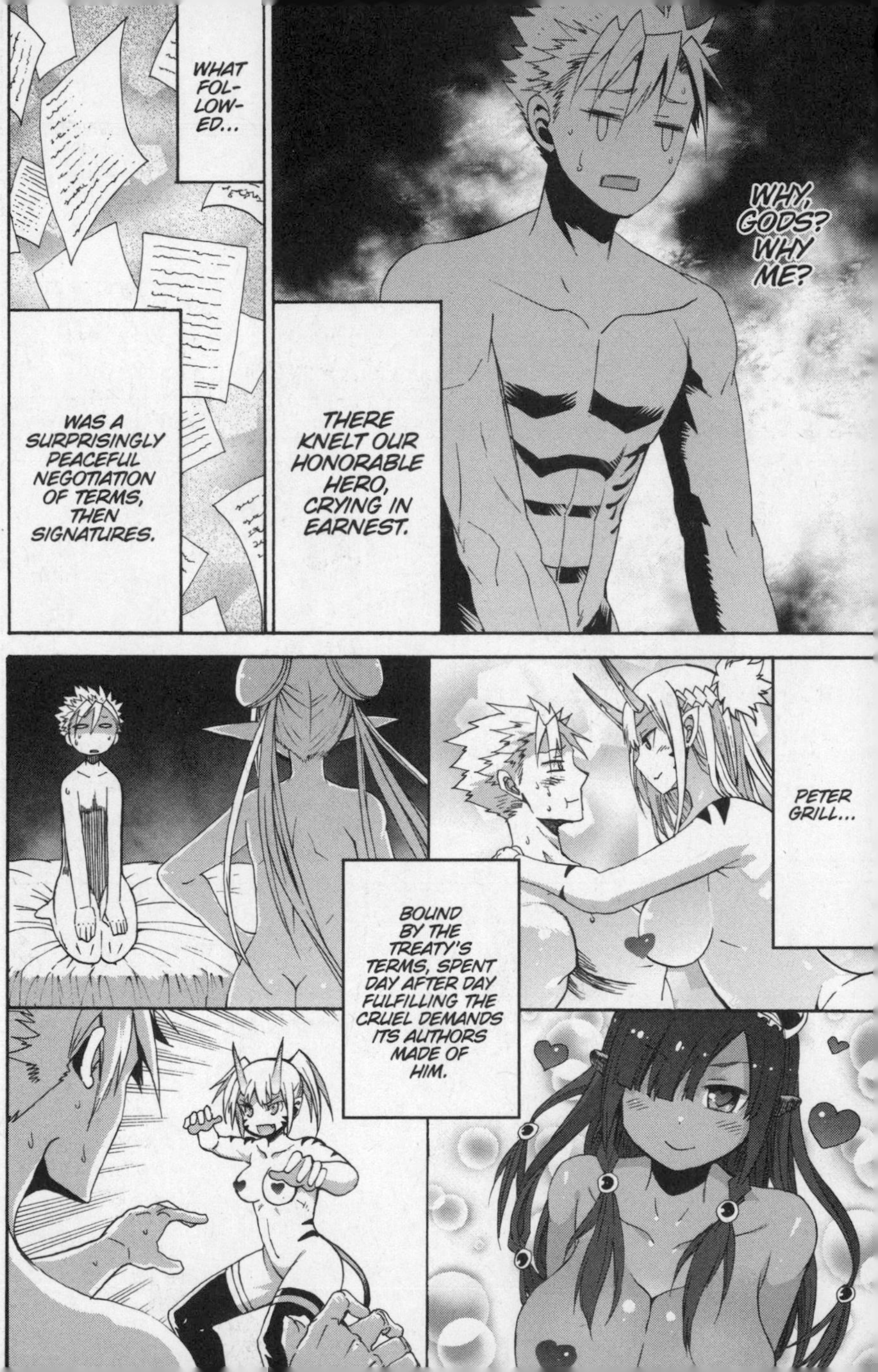
WHY, GODS? WHY ME?
THERE KNELT OUR HONORABLE HERO, CRYING IN EARNEST.
WHAT FOL-LOW-ED...
WAS A SURPRISINGLY PEACEFUL NEGOTIATION OF TERMS, THEN SIGNATURES.
PETER GRILL...
BOUND BY THE TREATY'S TERMS, SPENT DAY AFTER DAY FULFILLING THE CRUEL DEMANDS ITS AUTHORS MADE OF HIM.

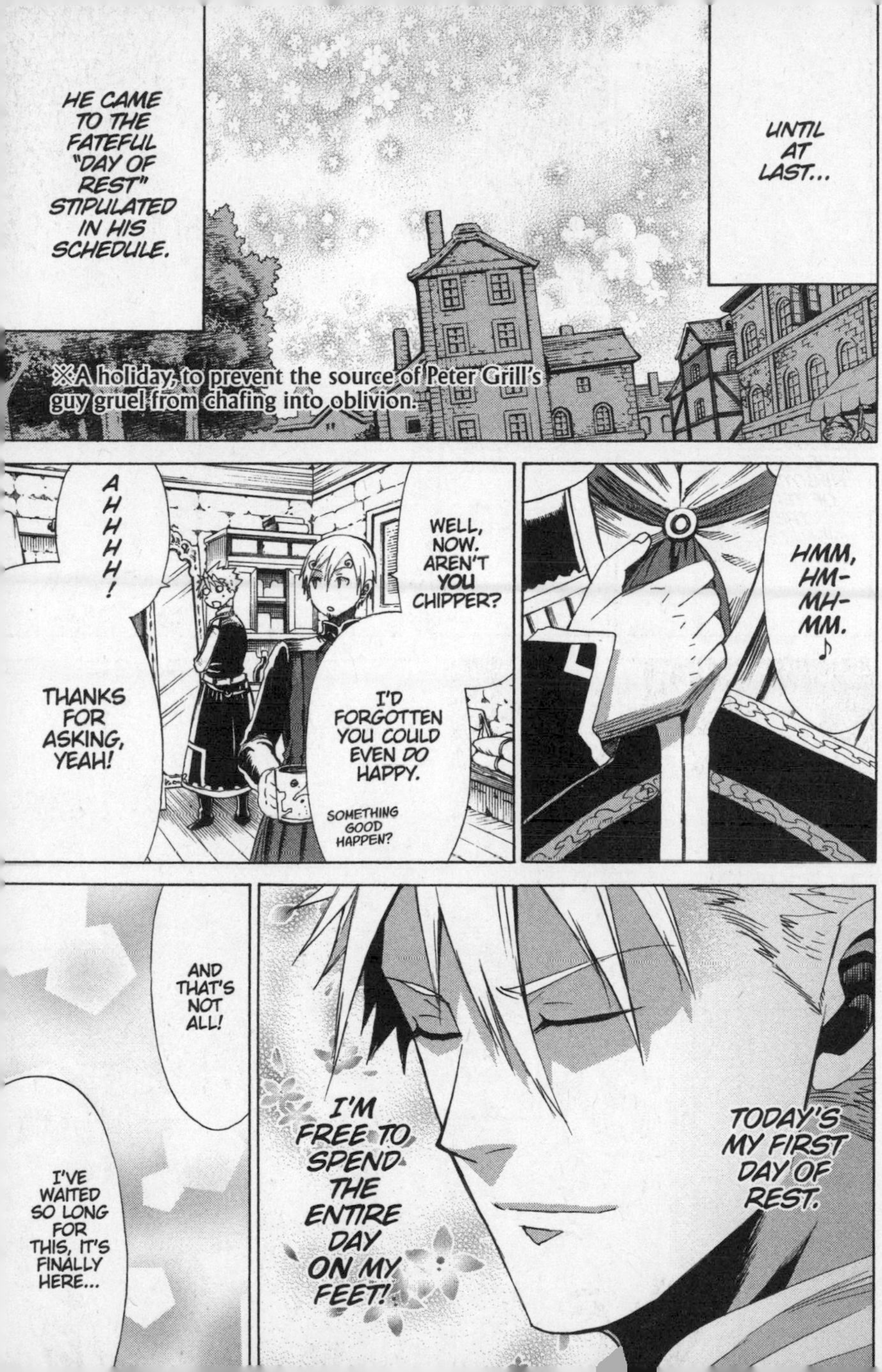

UNTIL AT LAST...
HE CAME TO THE FATEFUL "DAY OF REST" STIPULATED IN HIS SCHEDULE.
※A holiday, to prevent the source of Peter Grill's guy gruel from chafing into oblivion.
HMM, HM-MH-MM. ♪
WELL, NOW. AREN'T YOU CHIPPER?
I'D FORGOTTEN YOU COULD EVEN DO HAPPY.
SOMETHING GOOD HAPPEN?
AHHHH!
THANKS FOR ASKING, YEAH!
TODAY'S MY FIRST DAY OF REST.
I'M FREE TO SPEND THE ENTIRE DAY ON MY FEET!
AND THAT'S NOT ALL!
I'VE WAITED SO LONG FOR THIS, IT'S FINALLY HERE...

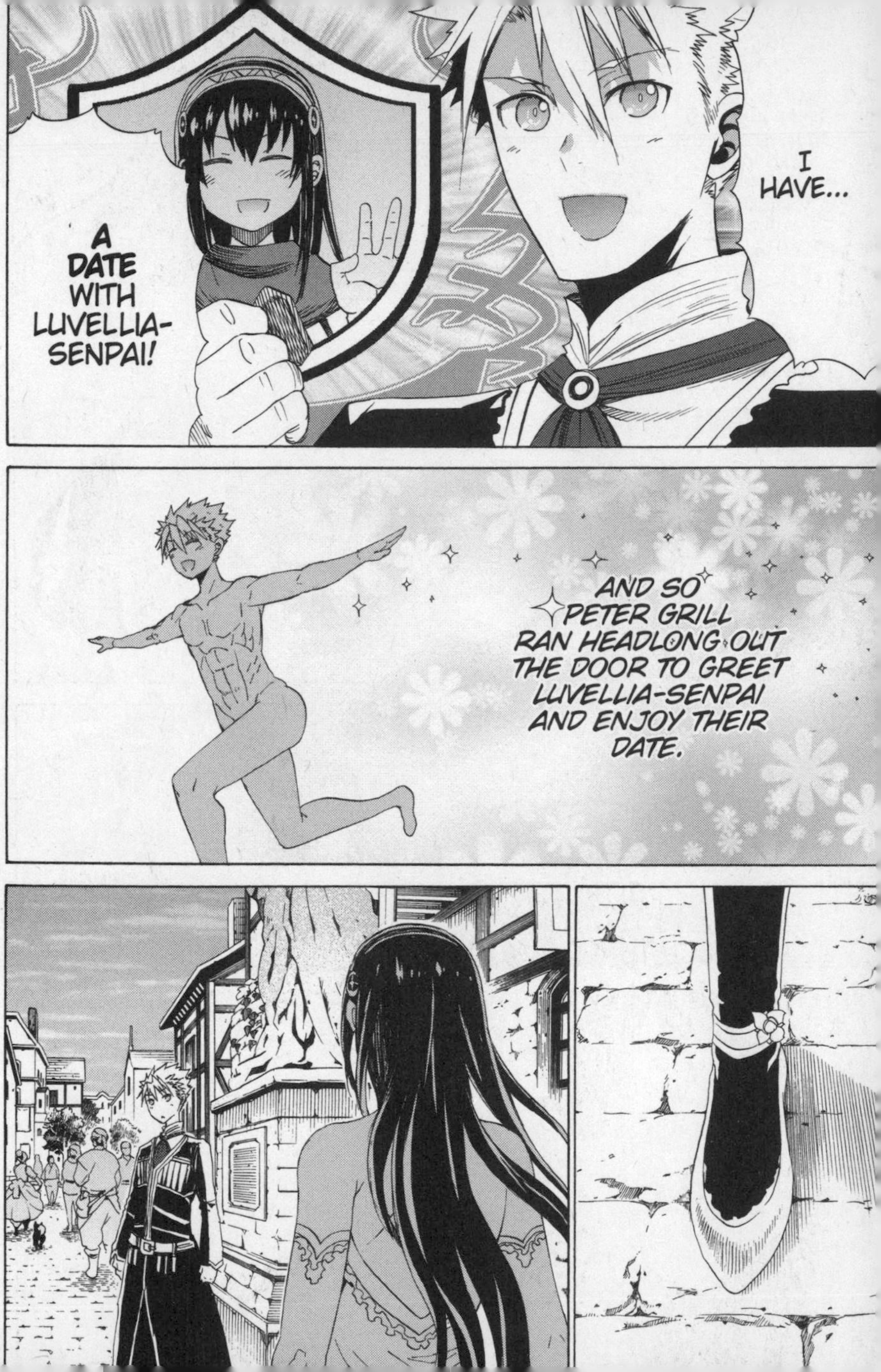
I HAVE...
A DATE WITH LUVELLIA-SENPAI!
AND SO PETER GRILL RAN HEADLONG OUT THE DOOR TO GREET LUVELLIA-SENPAI AND ENJOY THEIR DATE.

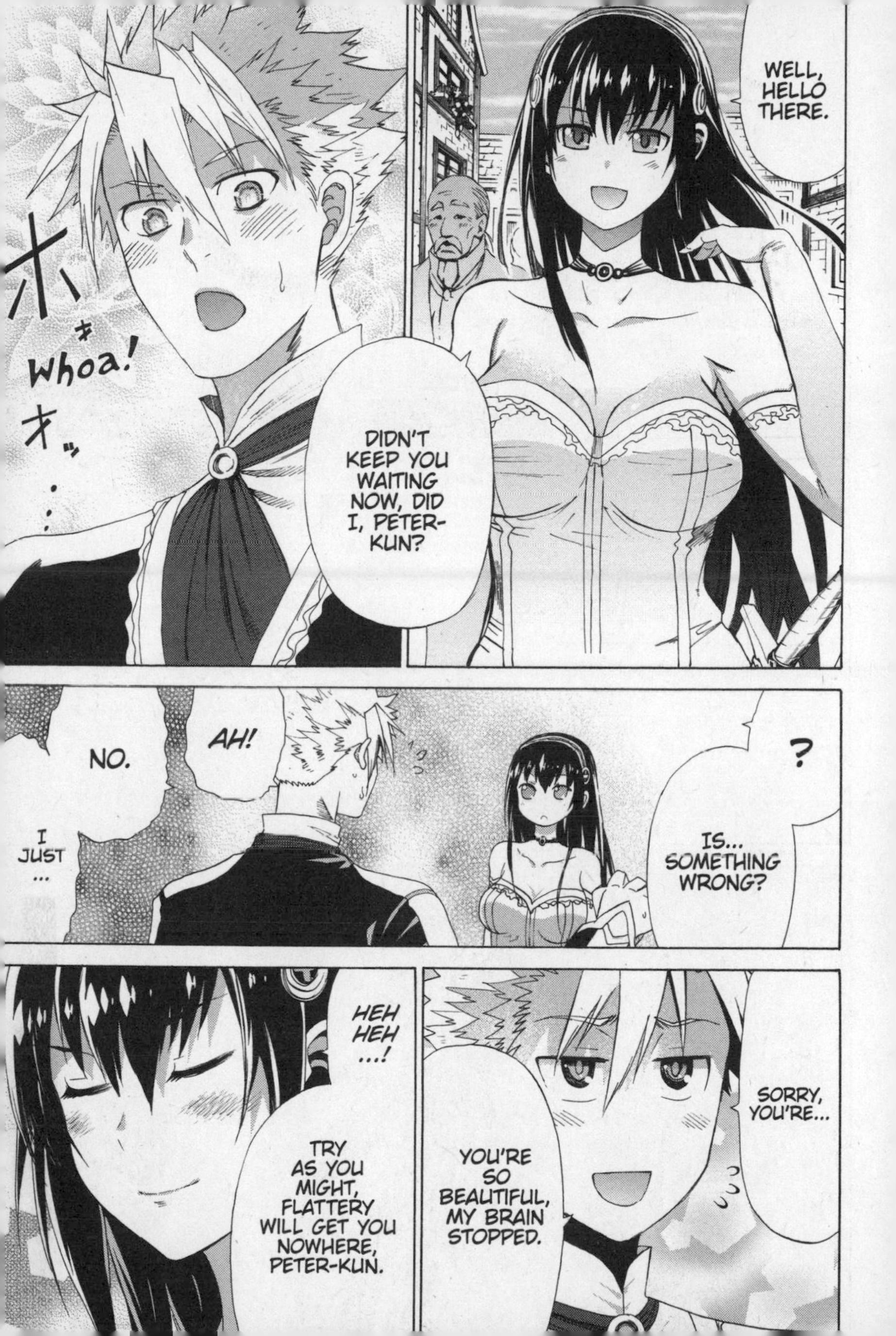
WELL, HELLO THERE.
DIDN'T KEEP YOU WAITING NOW, DID I, PETER-KUN?
Whoa!
?
IS... SOMETHING WRONG?
AH!
NO.
I JUST ...
SORRY, YOU'RE...
YOU'RE SO BEAUTIFUL, MY BRAIN STOPPED.
HEH HEH ...!
TRY AS YOU MIGHT, FLATTERY WILL GET YOU NOWHERE, PETER-KUN.

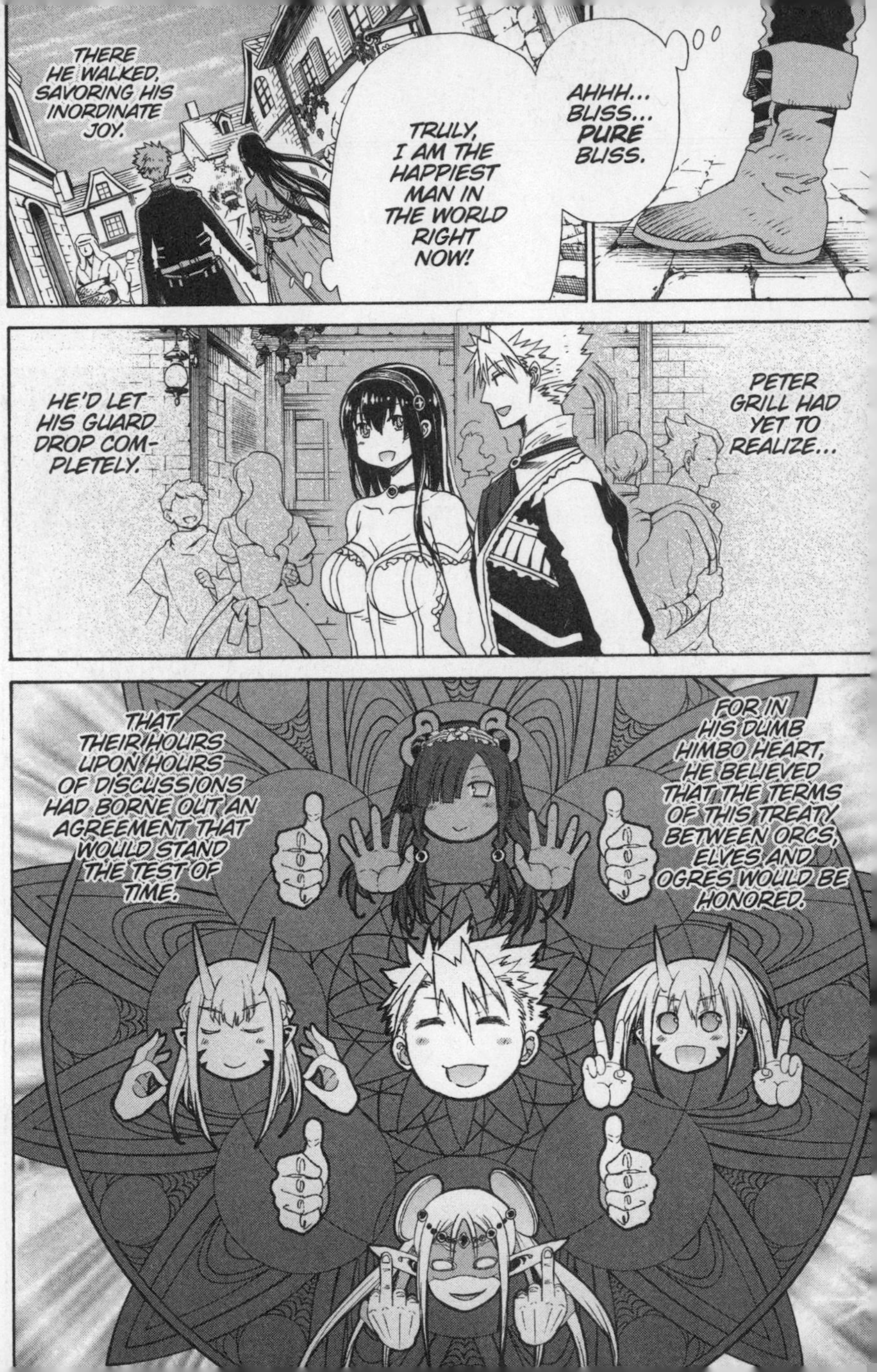
THERE HE WALKED, SAVORING HIS INORDINATE JOY.
TRULY, I AM THE HAPPIEST MAN IN THE WORLD RIGHT NOW!
AHHH... BLISS... PURE BLISS.
HE'D LET HIS GUARD DROP COMPLETELY.
PETER GRILL HAD YET TO REALIZE...
THAT THEIR HOURS UPON HOURS OF DISCUSSIONS HAD BORNE OUT AN AGREEMENT THAT WOULD STAND THE TEST OF TIME.
FOR IN HIS DUMB HIMBO HEART, HE BELIEVED THAT THE TERMS OF THIS TREATY BETWEEN ORCS, ELVES AND OGRES WOULD BE HONORED.

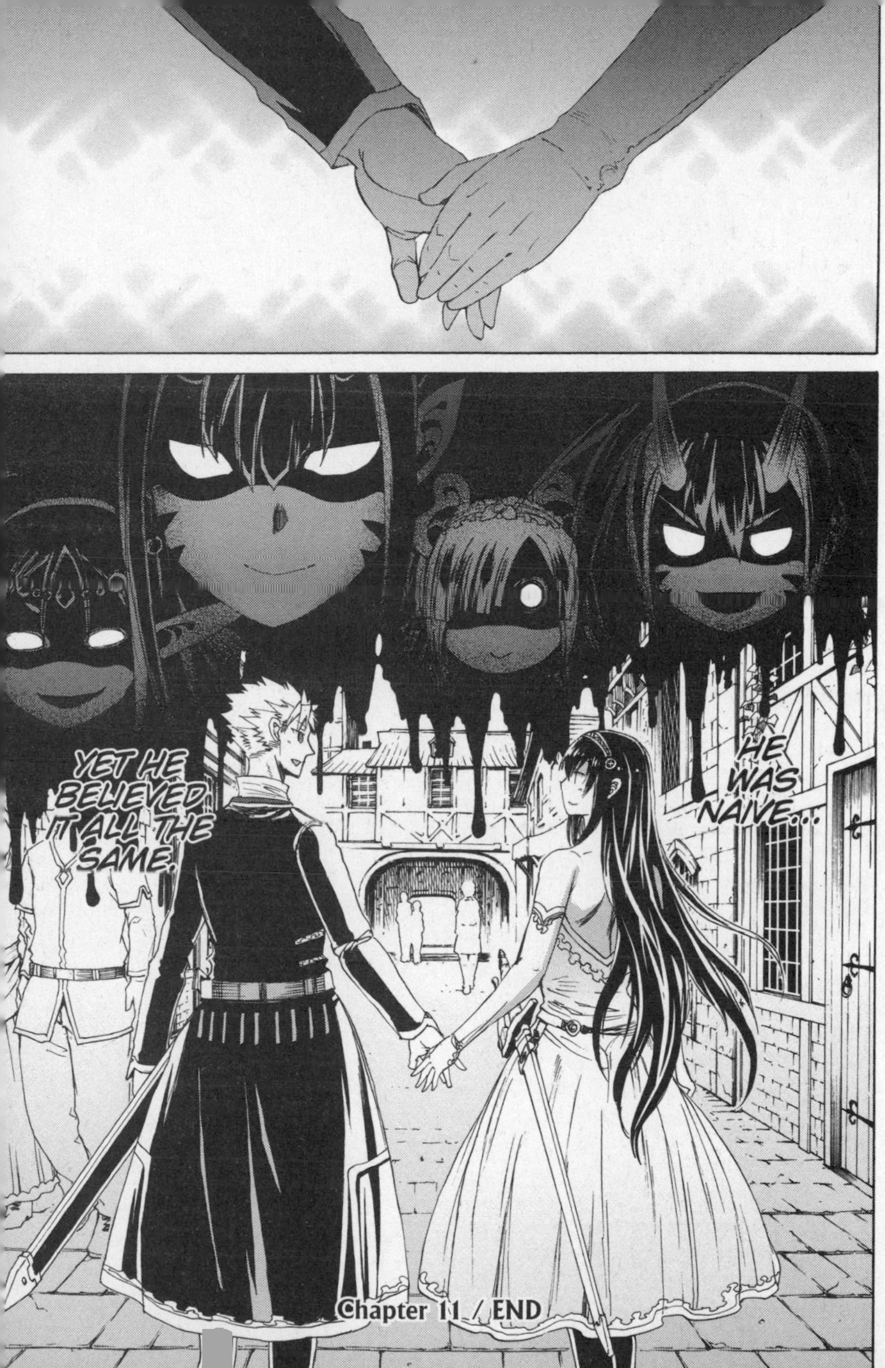
HE WAS NAIVE...
YET HE BELIEVED IT ALL THE SAME.

Chapter 11 / END

PETER GRILL
AND THE PHILOSOPHER'S TIME

Previously, on *Peter Grill*...

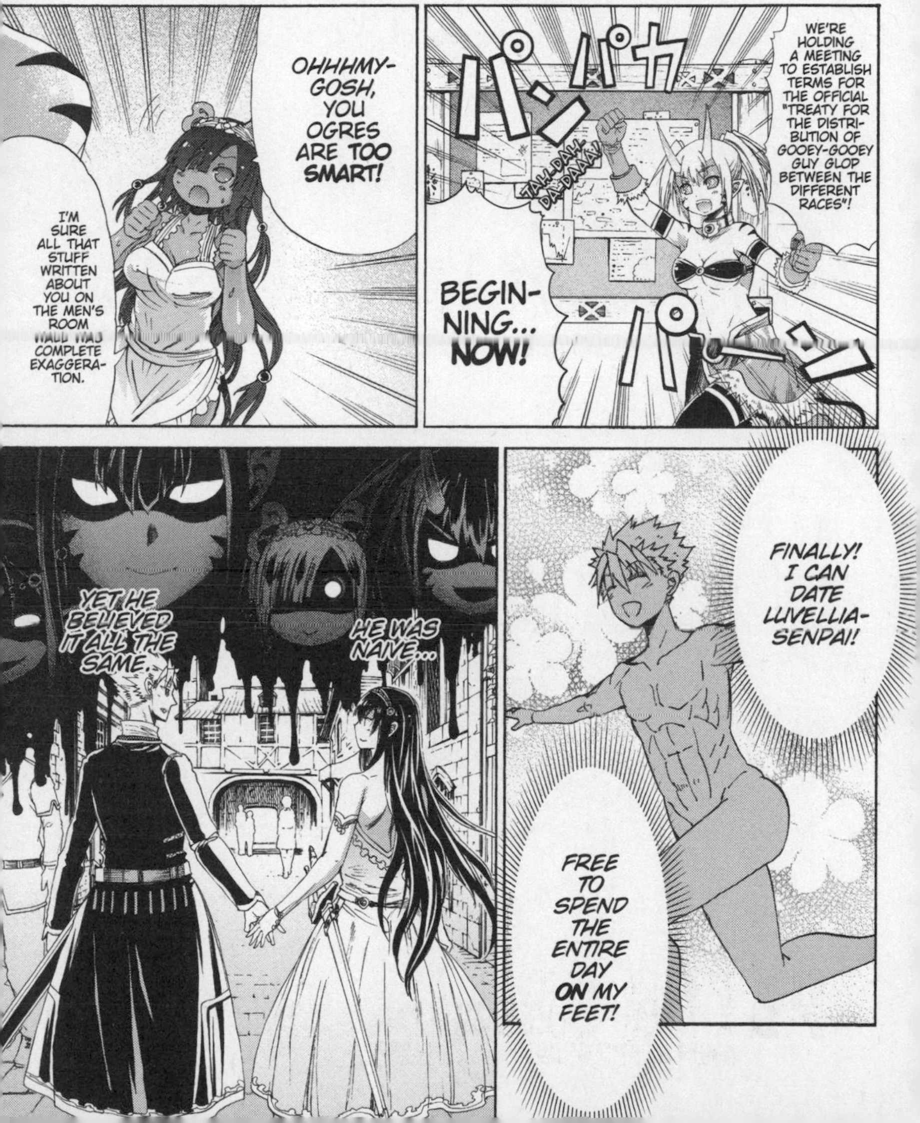
WE'RE HOLDING A MEETING TO ESTABLISH TERMS FOR THE OFFICIAL "TREATY FOR THE DISTRIBUTION OF GOOEY-GOOEY GUY GLOP BETWEEN THE DIFFERENT RACES"!
TAH-DAH DA-DAAA!
BEGINNING... NOW!
OHHHMY-GOSH, YOU OGRES ARE TOO SMART!
I'M SURE ALL THAT STUFF WRITTEN ABOUT YOU ON THE MEN'S ROOM WALL WAS COMPLETE EXAGGERATION.
FINALLY! I CAN DATE LUVELLIA-SENPAI!
FREE TO SPEND THE ENTIRE DAY ON MY FEET!
HE WAS NAIVE...
YET HE BELIEVED IT ALL THE SAME.

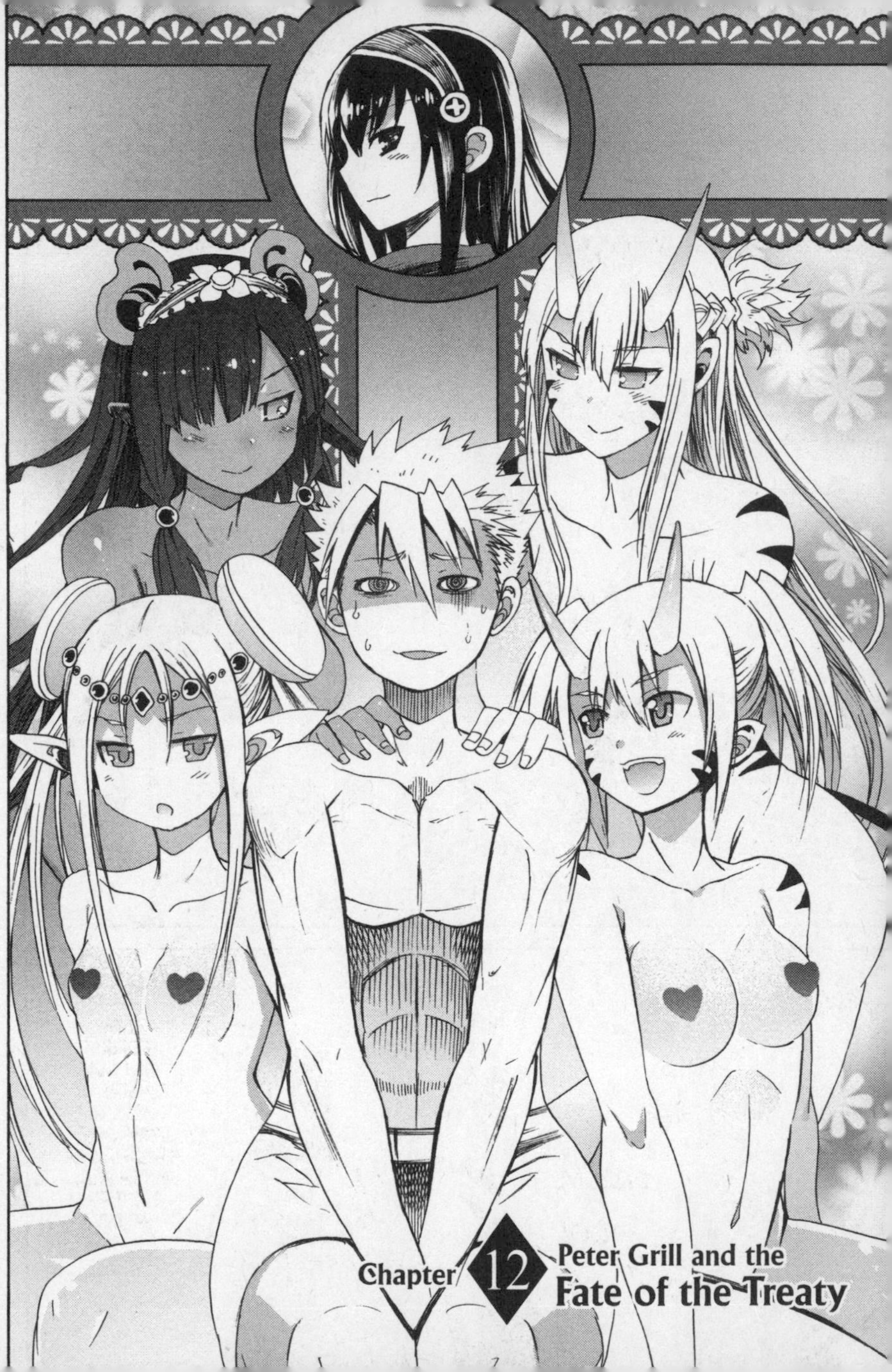
Chapter 12 Peter Grill and the Fate of the Treaty

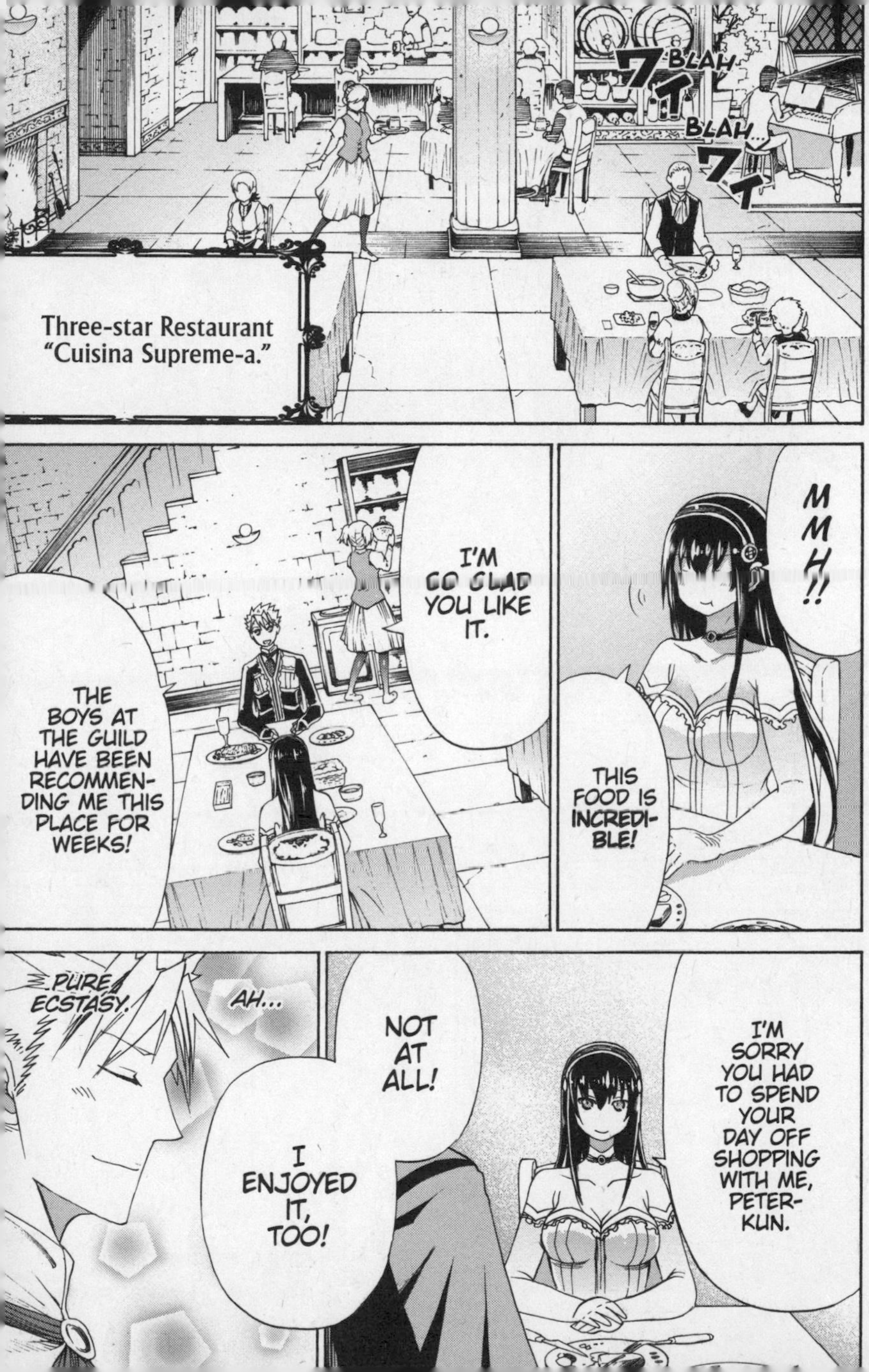

ワイ BLAH
BLAH... ワイ
Three-star Restaurant "Cuisina Supreme-a."
MMH!!
THIS FOOD IS INCREDIBLE!
I'M SO GLAD YOU LIKE IT.
THE BOYS AT THE GUILD HAVE BEEN RECOMMENDING ME THIS PLACE FOR WEEKS!
I'M SORRY YOU HAD TO SPEND YOUR DAY OFF SHOPPING WITH ME, PETER-KUN.
NOT AT ALL!
I ENJOYED IT, TOO!
AH...
PURE ECSTASY.

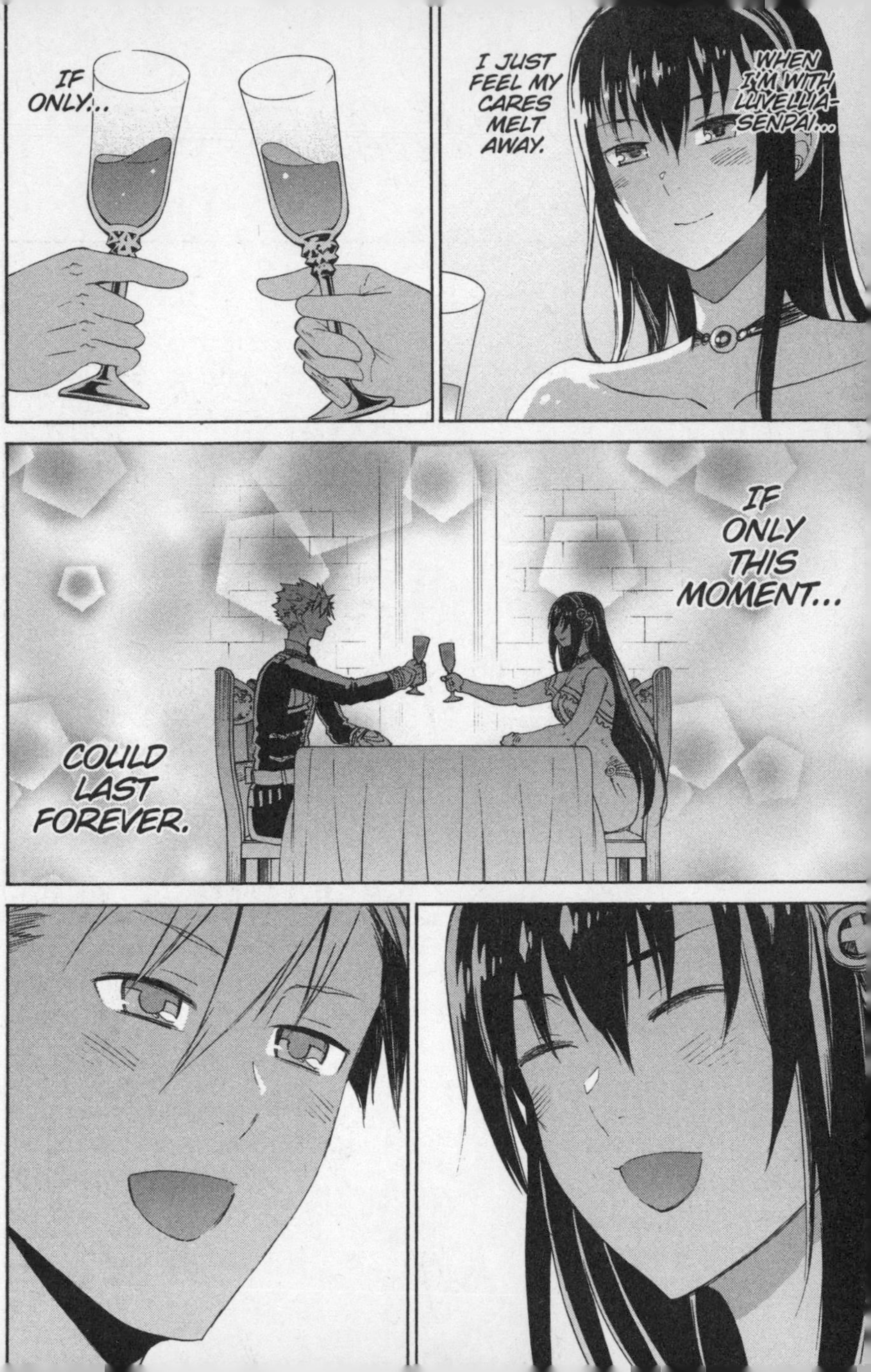
WHEN I'M WITH LUVELLIA-SENPAI...
I JUST FEEL MY CARES MELT AWAY.
IF ONLY...
IF ONLY THIS MOMENT...
COULD LAST FOREVER.

YOU DIDN'T THINK IT WOULD GO THAT EASY FOR OUR HERO, DID YOU?

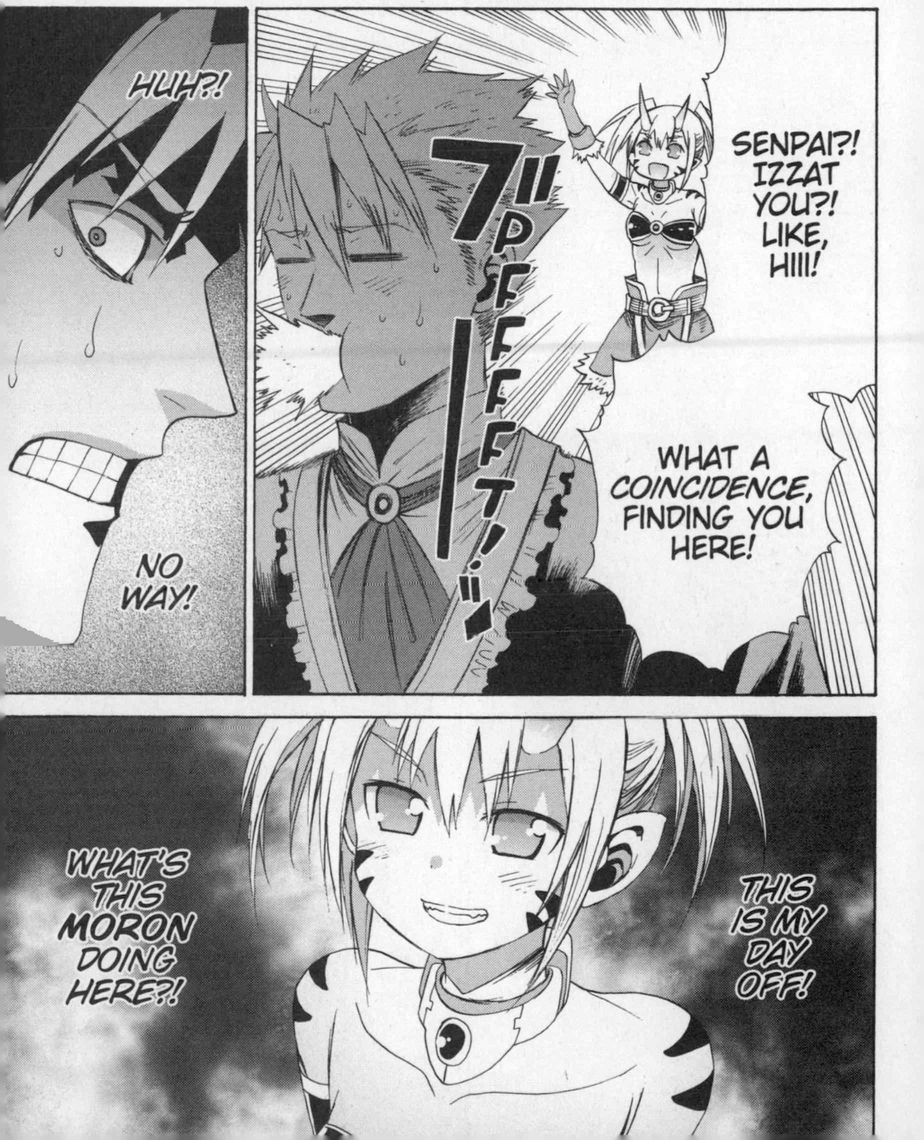
SENPAI?! IZZAT YOU?! LIKE, HIII!
WHAT A COINCIDENCE, FINDING YOU HERE!
PFFFFT!!
HUH?!
NO WAY!
THIS IS MY DAY OFF!
WHAT'S THIS MORON DOING HERE?!

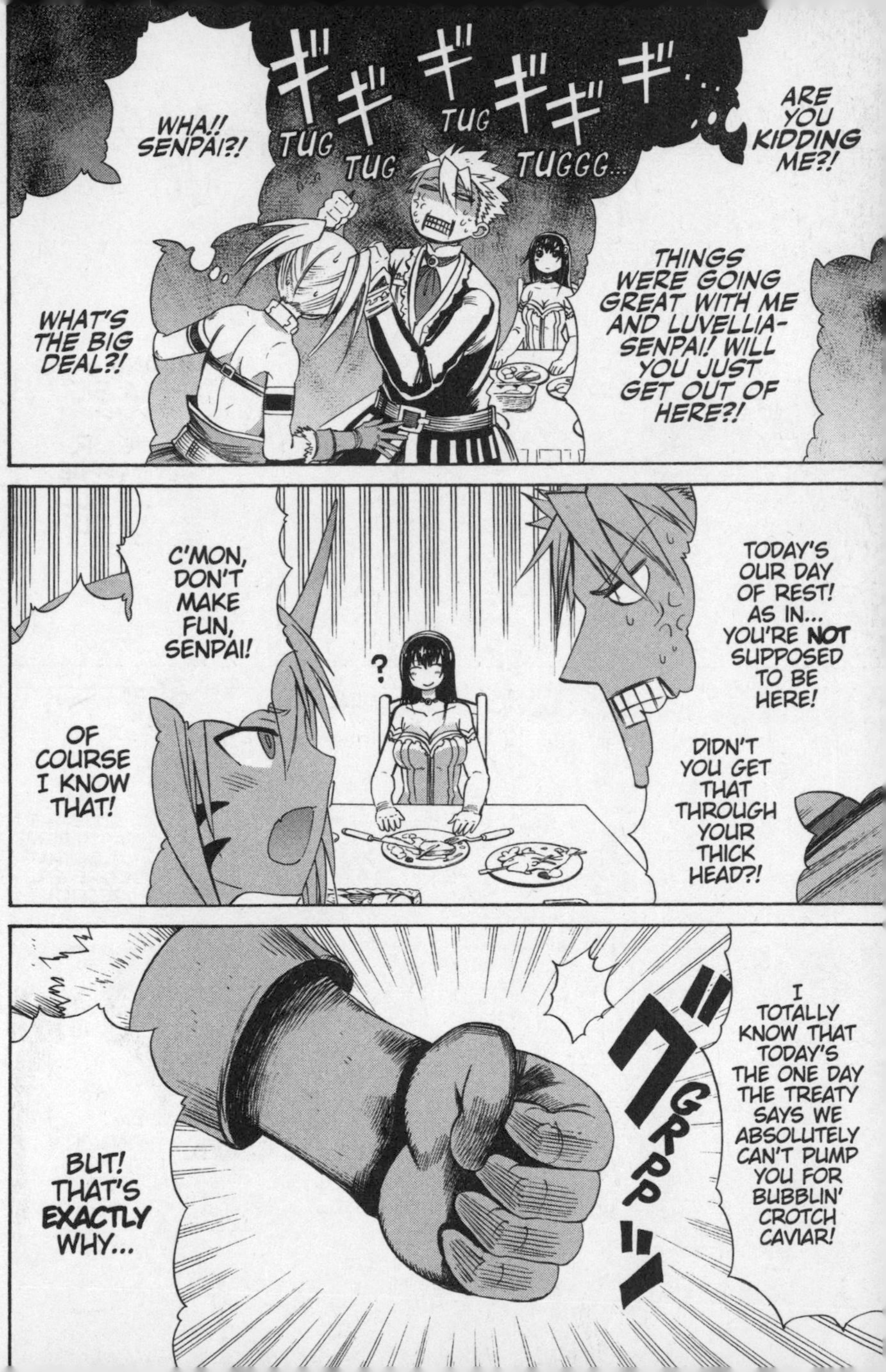
ARE YOU KIDDING ME?!
ギギギギギギ...
TUG TUG TUG TUGGG...
WHA!! SENPAI?!
THINGS WERE GOING GREAT WITH ME AND LUVELLIA-SENPAI! WILL YOU JUST GET OUT OF HERE?!
WHAT'S THE BIG DEAL?!
TODAY'S OUR DAY OF REST! AS IN... YOU'RE **NOT** SUPPOSED TO BE HERE!
C'MON, DON'T MAKE FUN, SENPAI!
?
DIDN'T YOU GET THAT THROUGH YOUR THICK HEAD?!
OF COURSE I KNOW THAT!
ゴ
GRPP
I TOTALLY KNOW THAT TODAY'S THE ONE DAY THE TREATY SAYS WE ABSOLUTELY CAN'T PUMP YOU FOR BUBBLIN' CROTCH CAVIAR!
BUT! THAT'S **EXACTLY** WHY...

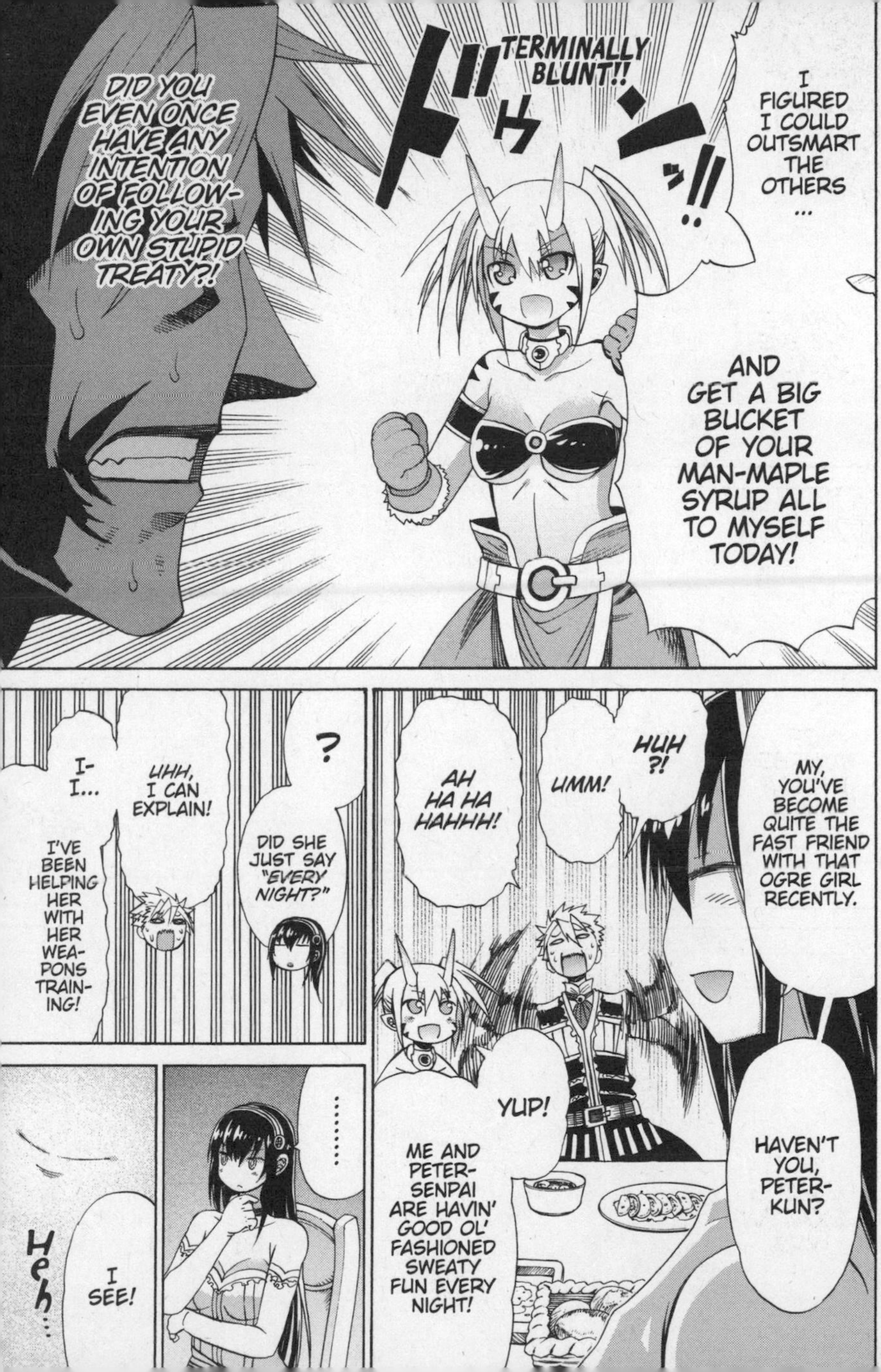
I FIGURED I COULD OUTSMART THE OTHERS ...
AND GET A BIG BUCKET OF YOUR MAN-MAPLE SYRUP ALL TO MYSELF TODAY!
TERMINALLY BLUNT!!
DID YOU EVEN ONCE HAVE ANY INTENTION OF FOLLOWING YOUR OWN STUPID TREATY?!
MY, YOU'VE BECOME QUITE THE FAST FRIEND WITH THAT OGRE GIRL RECENTLY.
HAVEN'T YOU, PETER-KUN?
HUH ?!
UMM!
AH HA HA HAHHH!
YUP!
ME AND PETER-SENPAI ARE HAVIN' GOOD OL' FASHIONED SWEATY FUN EVERY NIGHT!
?
DID SHE JUST SAY "EVERY NIGHT?"
UHH, I CAN EXPLAIN!
I- I...
I'VE BEEN HELPING HER WITH HER WEAPONS TRAINING!
......
I SEE!
Heh...

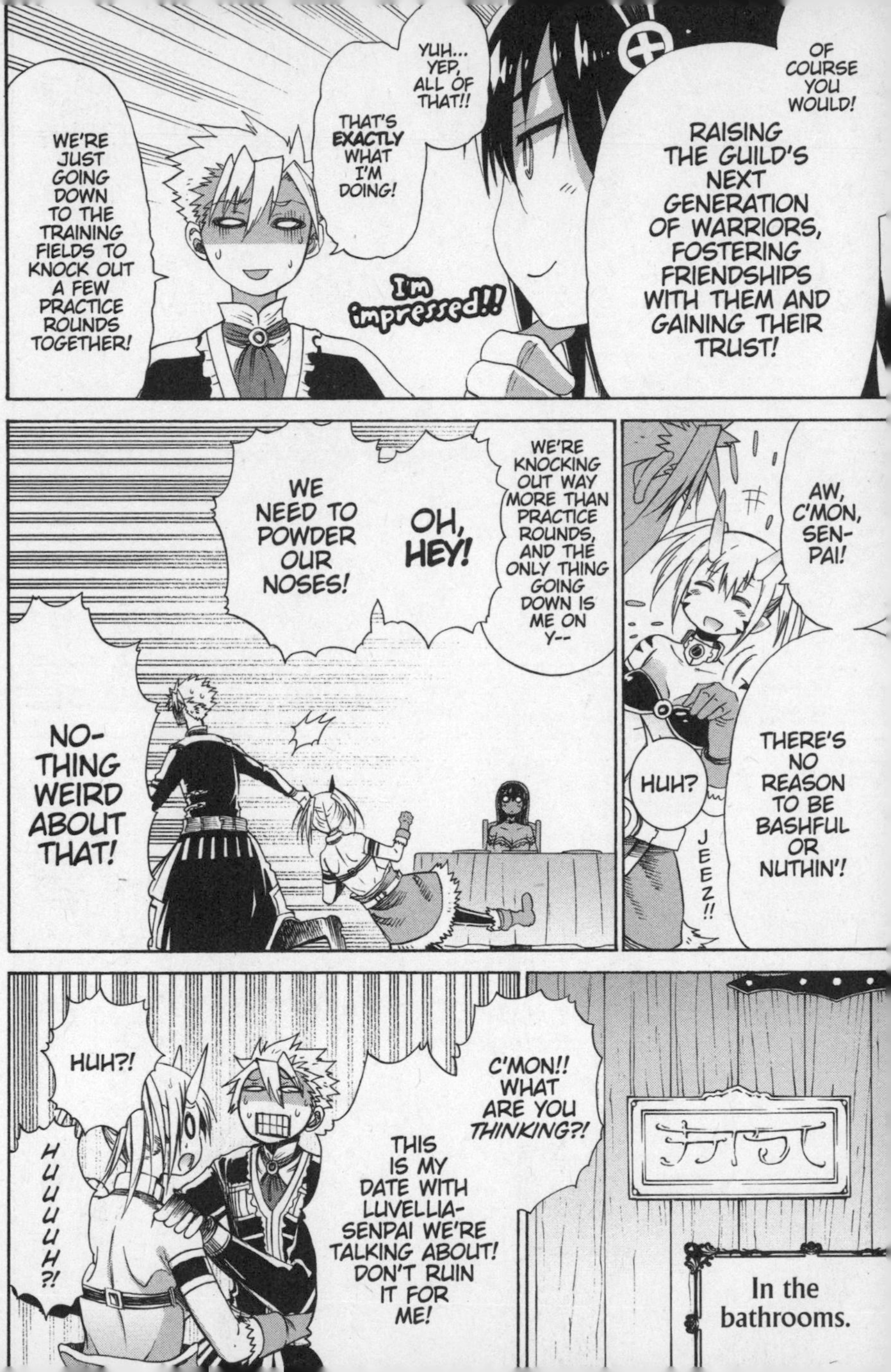
OF COURSE YOU WOULD!
RAISING THE GUILD'S NEXT GENERATION OF WARRIORS, FOSTERING FRIENDSHIPS WITH THEM AND GAINING THEIR TRUST!
YUH... YEP, ALL OF THAT!!
THAT'S EXACTLY WHAT I'M DOING!
I'm impressed!!
WE'RE JUST GOING DOWN TO THE TRAINING FIELDS TO KNOCK OUT A FEW PRACTICE ROUNDS TOGETHER!
AW, C'MON, SEN-PAI!
THERE'S NO REASON TO BE BASHFUL OR NUTHIN'!
HUH?
JEEZ!!
WE'RE KNOCKING OUT WAY MORE THAN PRACTICE ROUNDS, AND THE ONLY THING GOING DOWN IS ME ON Y--
OH, HEY!
WE NEED TO POWDER OUR NOSES!
NO-THING WEIRD ABOUT THAT!
In the bathrooms.
C'MON!! WHAT ARE YOU THINKING?!
THIS IS MY DATE WITH LUVELLIA-SENPAI WE'RE TALKING ABOUT! DON'T RUIN IT FOR ME!
HUH?!
HUUUUUH?!

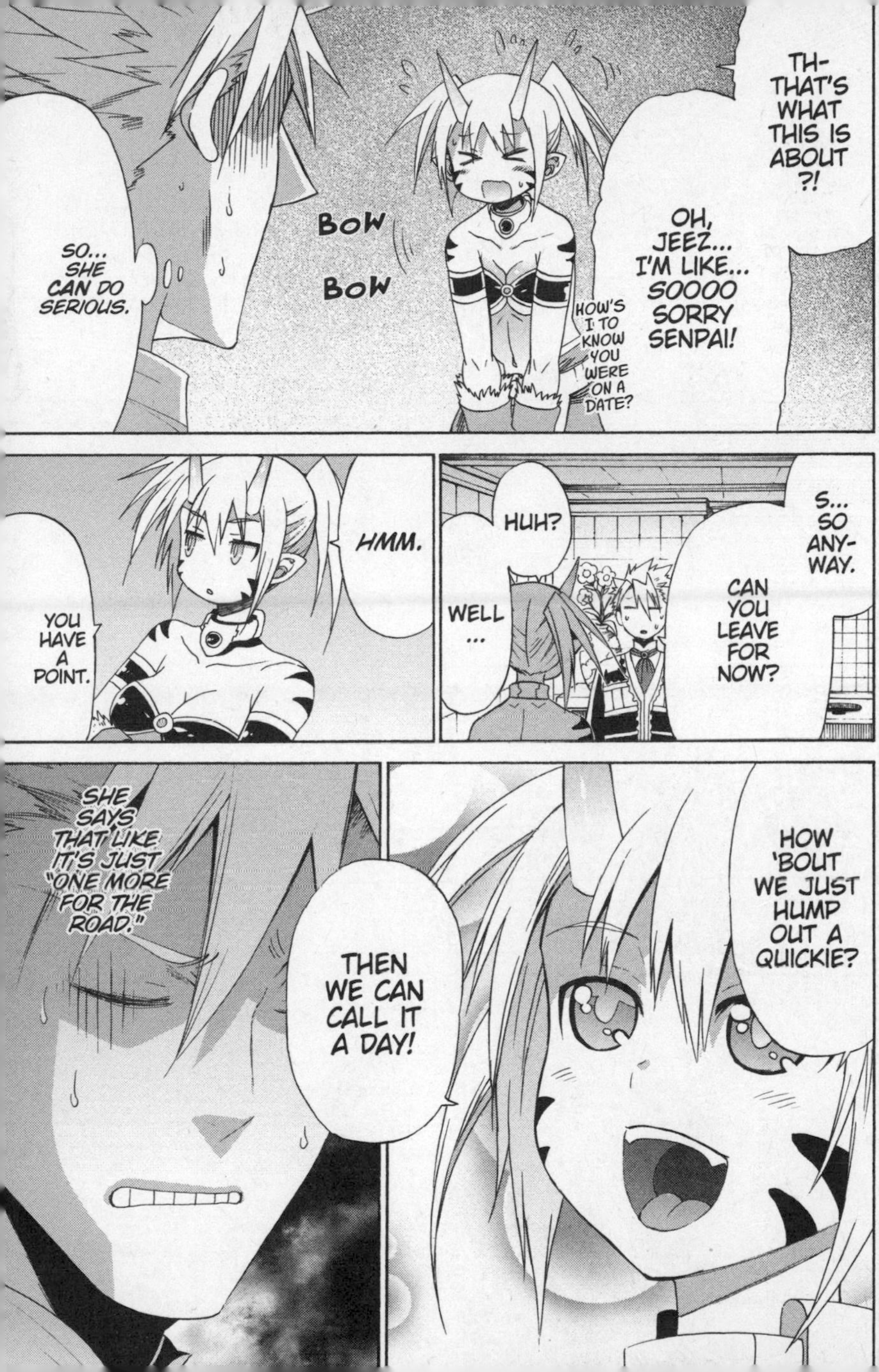
TH- THAT'S WHAT THIS IS ABOUT?!
OH, JEEZ... I'M LIKE... SOOOO SORRY SENPAI!
HOW'S I TO KNOW YOU WERE ON A DATE?
BOW
BOW
SO... SHE CAN DO SERIOUS.
S... SO ANY-WAY.
CAN YOU LEAVE FOR NOW?
HUH?
WELL ...
HMM.
YOU HAVE A POINT.
HOW 'BOUT WE JUST HUMP OUT A QUICKIE?
THEN WE CAN CALL IT A DAY!
SHE SAYS THAT LIKE IT'S JUST "ONE MORE FOR THE ROAD."

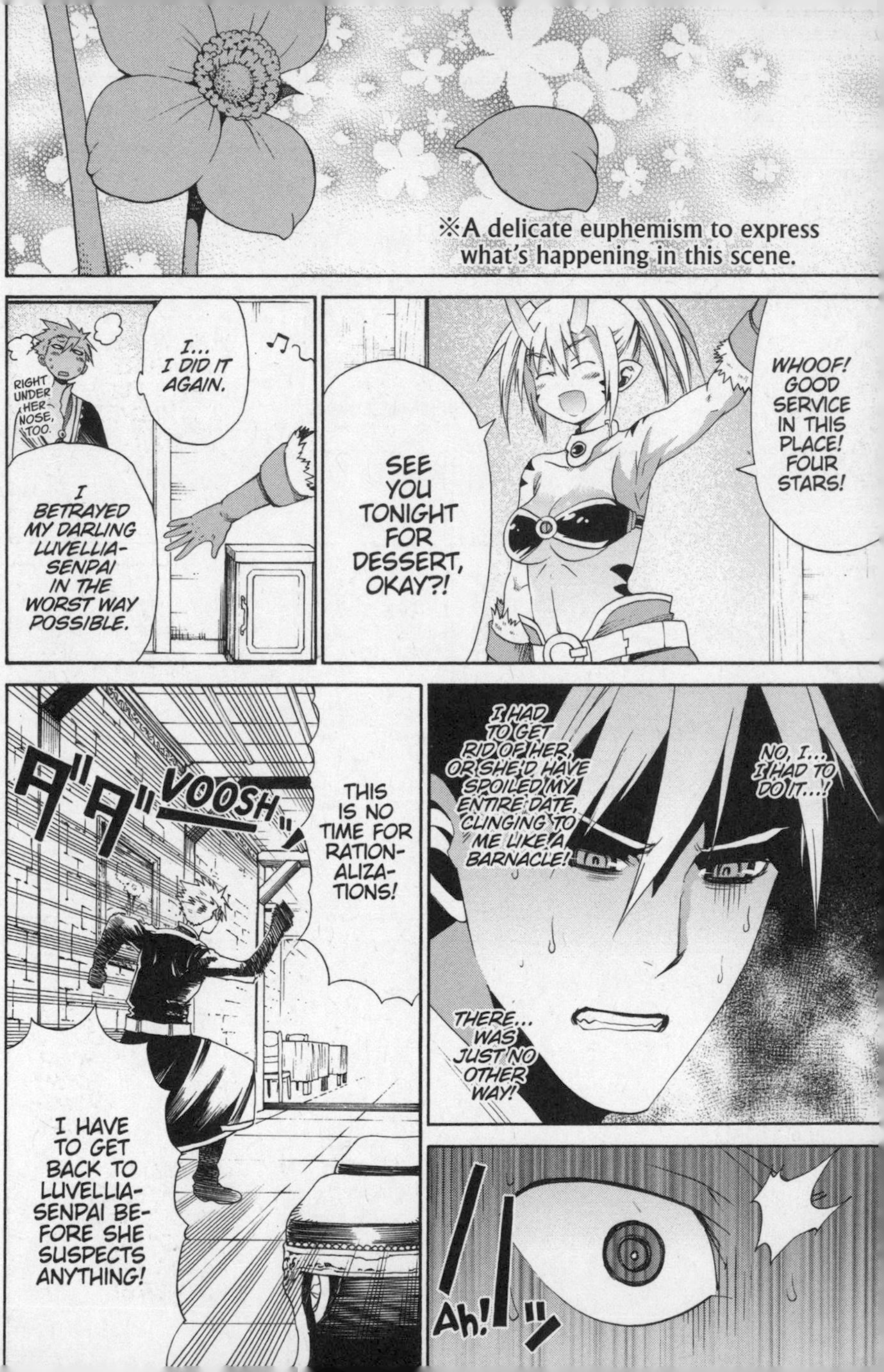
※A delicate euphemism to express what's happening in this scene.
WHOOF! GOOD SERVICE IN THIS PLACE! FOUR STARS!
SEE YOU TONIGHT FOR DESSERT, OKAY?!
I... I DID IT AGAIN.
RIGHT UNDER HER-NOSE, TOO.
I BETRAYED MY DARLING LUVELLIA-SENPAI IN THE WORST WAY POSSIBLE.
NO, I... I HAD TO DO IT...!
I HAD TO GET RID OF HER, OR SHE'D HAVE SPOILED MY ENTIRE DATE, CLINGING TO ME LIKE A BARNACLE!
THERE... WAS JUST NO OTHER WAY!
Ah!!
VOOSH
THIS IS NO TIME FOR RATION-ALIZA-TIONS!
I HAVE TO GET BACK TO LUVELLIA-SENPAI BE-FORE SHE SUSPECTS ANYTHING!

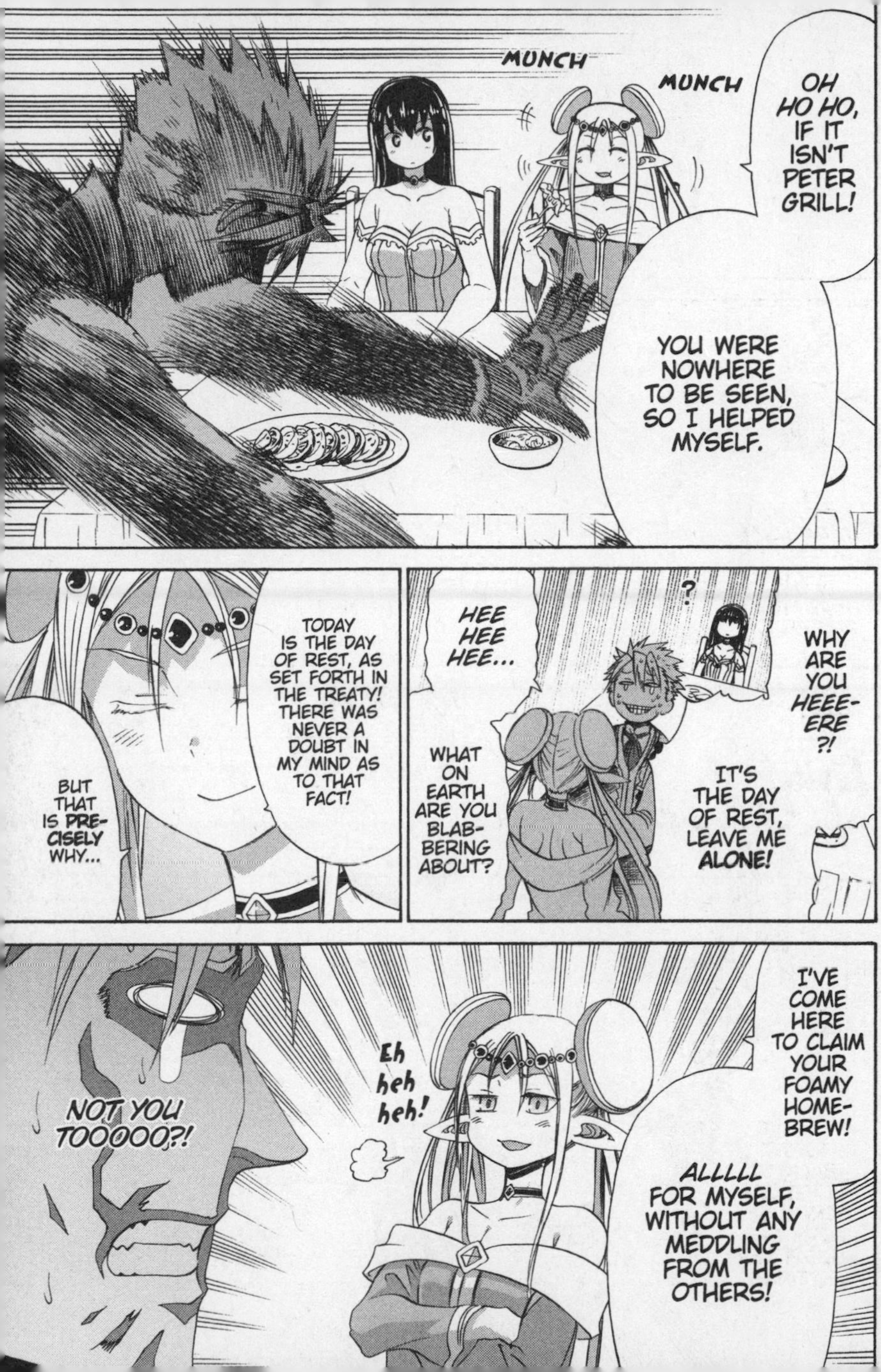
OH HO HO, IF IT ISN'T PETER GRILL!
YOU WERE NOWHERE TO BE SEEN, SO I HELPED MYSELF.
MUNCH
MUNCH
WHY ARE YOU HEEEE-ERE?!
IT'S THE DAY OF REST, LEAVE ME ALONE!
?
HEE HEE HEE...
WHAT ON EARTH ARE YOU BLABBERING ABOUT?
TODAY IS THE DAY OF REST, AS SET FORTH IN THE TREATY! THERE WAS NEVER A DOUBT IN MY MIND AS TO THAT FACT!
BUT THAT IS PRECISELY WHY...
I'VE COME HERE TO CLAIM YOUR FOAMY HOMEBREW!
ALLLLL FOR MYSELF, WITHOUT ANY MEDDLING FROM THE OTHERS!
Eh heh heh!
NOT YOU TOOOOOO?!

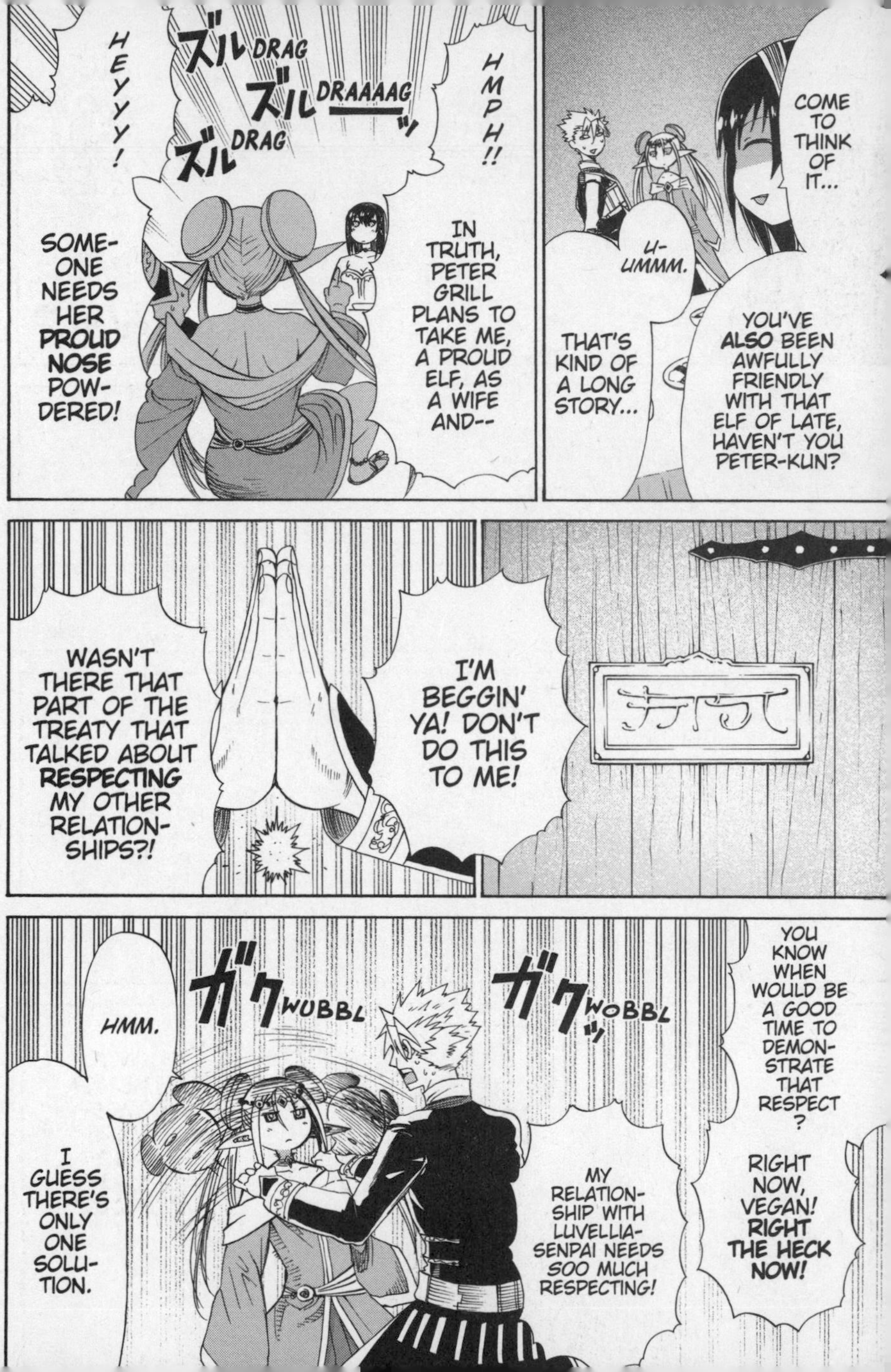
COME TO THINK OF IT...
YOU'VE ALSO BEEN AWFULLY FRIENDLY WITH THAT ELF OF LATE, HAVEN'T YOU PETER-KUN?
U-UMMM.
THAT'S KIND OF A LONG STORY...
HMPH!!
ズル DRAG
ズルーッ DRAAAAG
ズル DRAG
HEYYY!
IN TRUTH, PETER GRILL PLANS TO TAKE ME, A PROUD ELF, AS A WIFE AND--
SOME-ONE NEEDS HER PROUD NOSE POW-DERED!
I'M BEGGIN' YA! DON'T DO THIS TO ME!
WASN'T THERE THAT PART OF THE TREATY THAT TALKED ABOUT RESPECTING MY OTHER RELATION-SHIPS?!
YOU KNOW WHEN WOULD BE A GOOD TIME TO DEMON-STRATE THAT RESPECT?
RIGHT NOW, VEGAN! RIGHT THE HECK NOW!
MY RELATION-SHIP WITH LUVELLIA-SENPAI NEEDS SOO MUCH RESPECTING!
ガクッ WOBBL
ガク WUBBL
HMM.
I GUESS THERE'S ONLY ONE SOLU-TION.

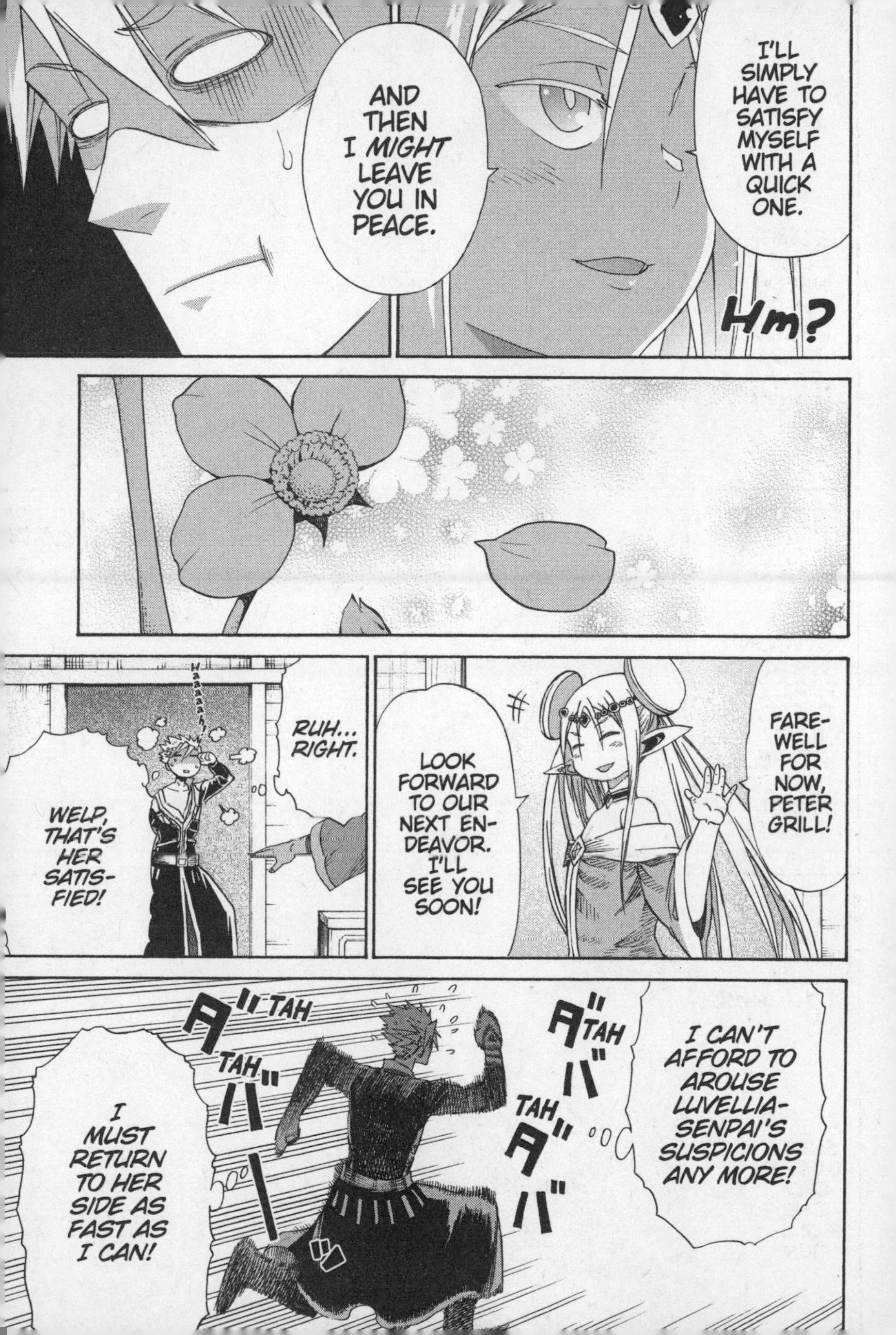
I'LL SIMPLY HAVE TO SATISFY MYSELF WITH A QUICK ONE.
AND THEN I *MIGHT* LEAVE YOU IN PEACE.
Hm?
FARE-WELL FOR NOW, PETER GRILL!
LOOK FORWARD TO OUR NEXT EN-DEAVOR. I'LL SEE YOU SOON!
RUH... RIGHT.
Haaaaah!
WELP, THAT'S HER SATIS-FIED!
I CAN'T AFFORD TO AROUSE LUVELLIA-SENPAI'S SUSPICIONS ANY MORE!
TAH
TAH
TAH
TAH
TAH
I MUST RETURN TO HER SIDE AS FAST AS I CAN!

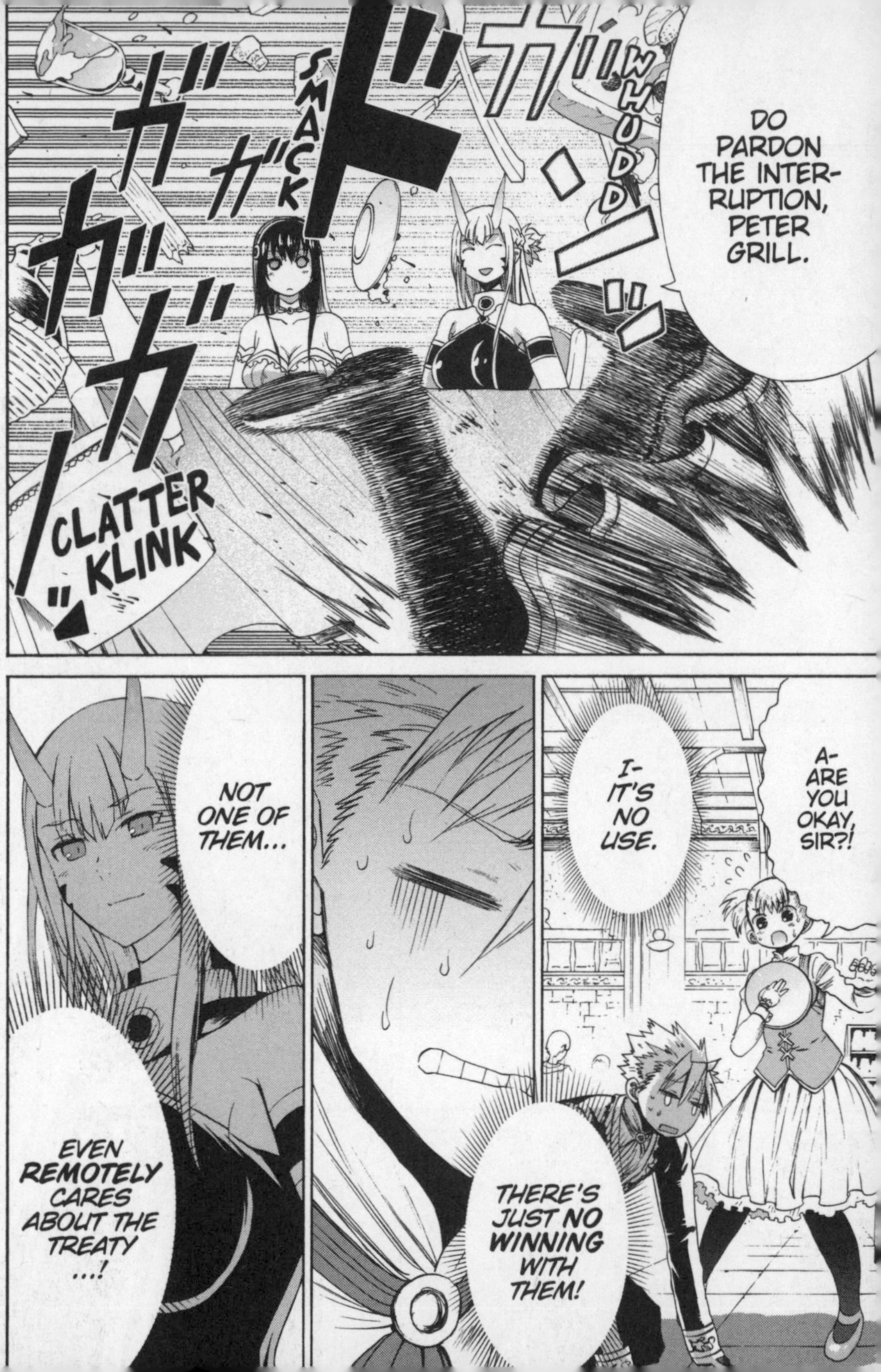

DO PARDON THE INTER-RUPTION, PETER GRILL.
WHUDD
SMACK
CLATTER
KLINK
A- ARE YOU OKAY, SIR?!
I- IT'S NO USE.
THERE'S JUST NO WINNING WITH THEM!
NOT ONE OF THEM...
EVEN REMOTELY CARES ABOUT THE TREATY ...!

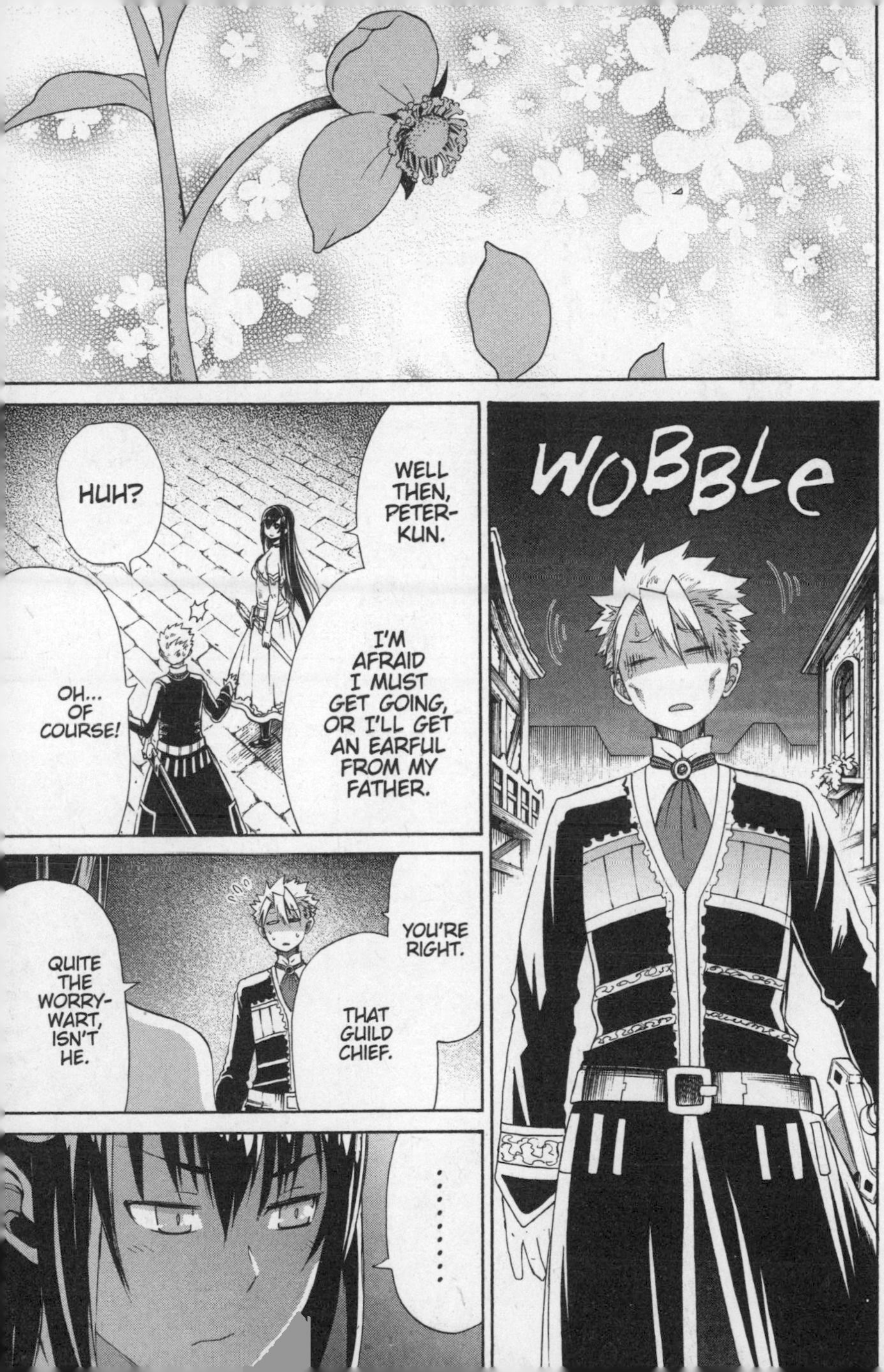
WOBBLE
WELL THEN, PETER-KUN.
HUH?
I'M AFRAID I MUST GET GOING, OR I'LL GET AN EARFUL FROM MY FATHER.
OH... OF COURSE!
YOU'RE RIGHT.
THAT GUILD CHIEF.
QUITE THE WORRY-WART, ISN'T HE.
......

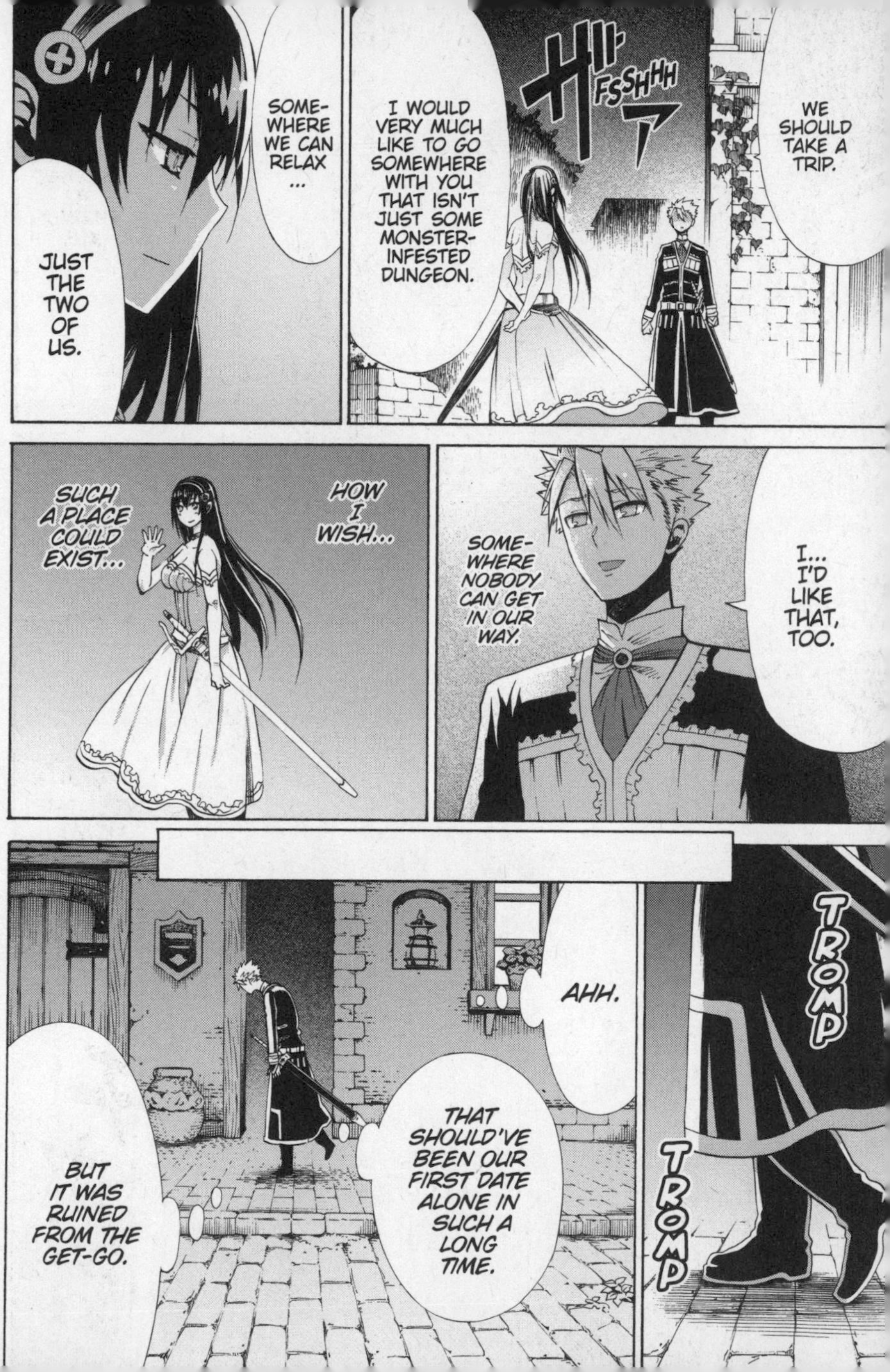
WE SHOULD TAKE A TRIP.
FS-SHHH
I WOULD VERY MUCH LIKE TO GO SOMEWHERE WITH YOU THAT ISN'T JUST SOME MONSTER-INFESTED DUNGEON.
SOME-WHERE WE CAN RELAX ...
JUST THE TWO OF US.
I... I'D LIKE THAT, TOO.
SOME-WHERE NOBODY CAN GET IN OUR WAY.
HOW I WISH...
SUCH A PLACE COULD EXIST...
TROMP
TROMP
AHH.
THAT SHOULD'VE BEEN OUR FIRST DATE ALONE IN SUCH A LONG TIME.
BUT IT WAS RUINED FROM THE GET-GO.

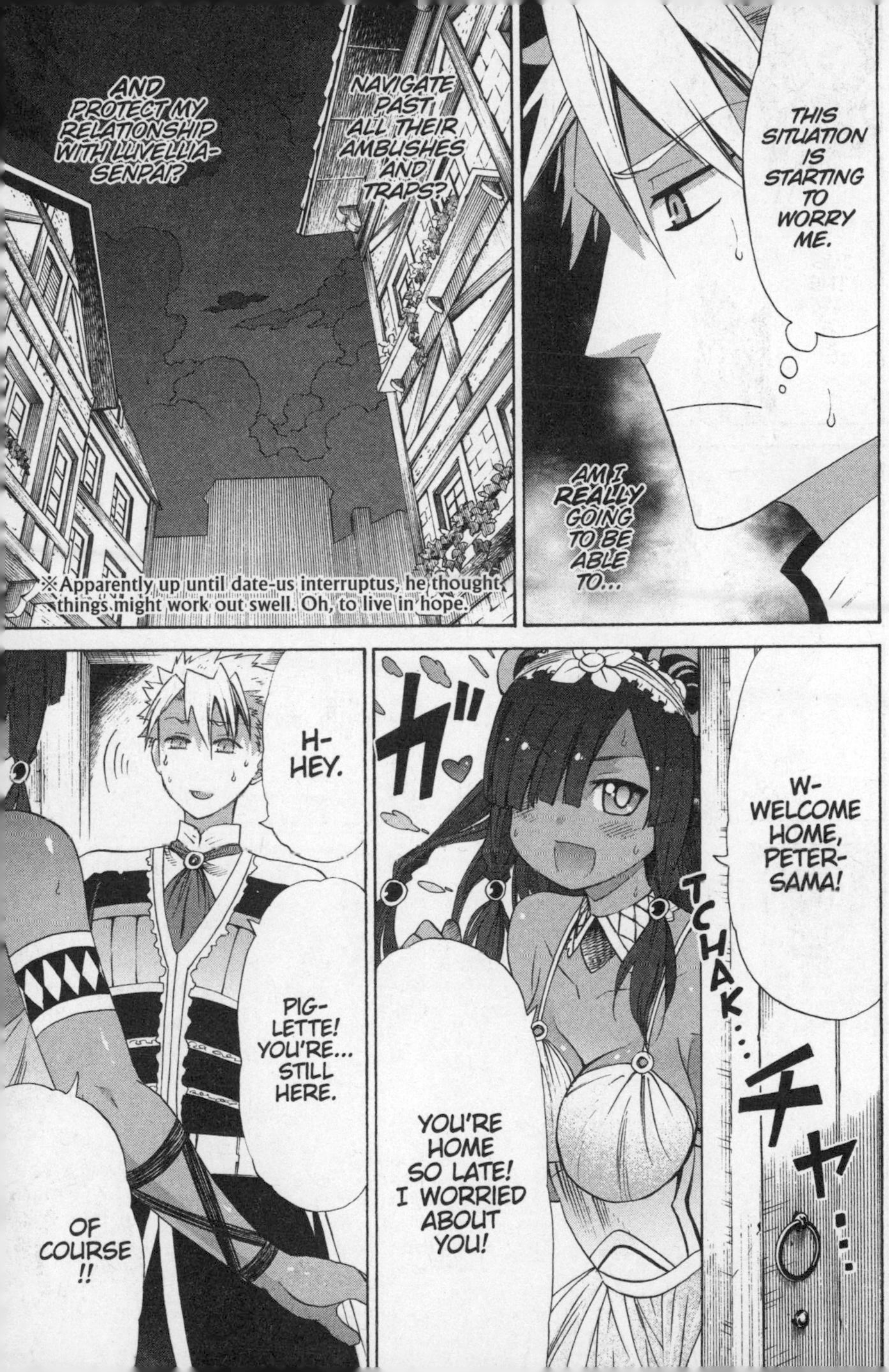
THIS SITUATION IS STARTING TO WORRY ME.
AM I REALLY GOING TO BE ABLE TO...
NAVIGATE PAST ALL THEIR AMBUSHES AND TRAPS?
AND PROTECT MY RELATIONSHIP WITH LUVELLIA-SENPAI?
※Apparently up until date-us interruptus, he thought things might work out swell. Oh, to live in hope.
W-WELCOME HOME, PETER-SAMA!
TCHAK...
チャ
ガ
YOU'RE HOME SO LATE! I WORRIED ABOUT YOU!
H-HEY.
PIG-LETTE! YOU'RE... STILL HERE.
OF COURSE!!

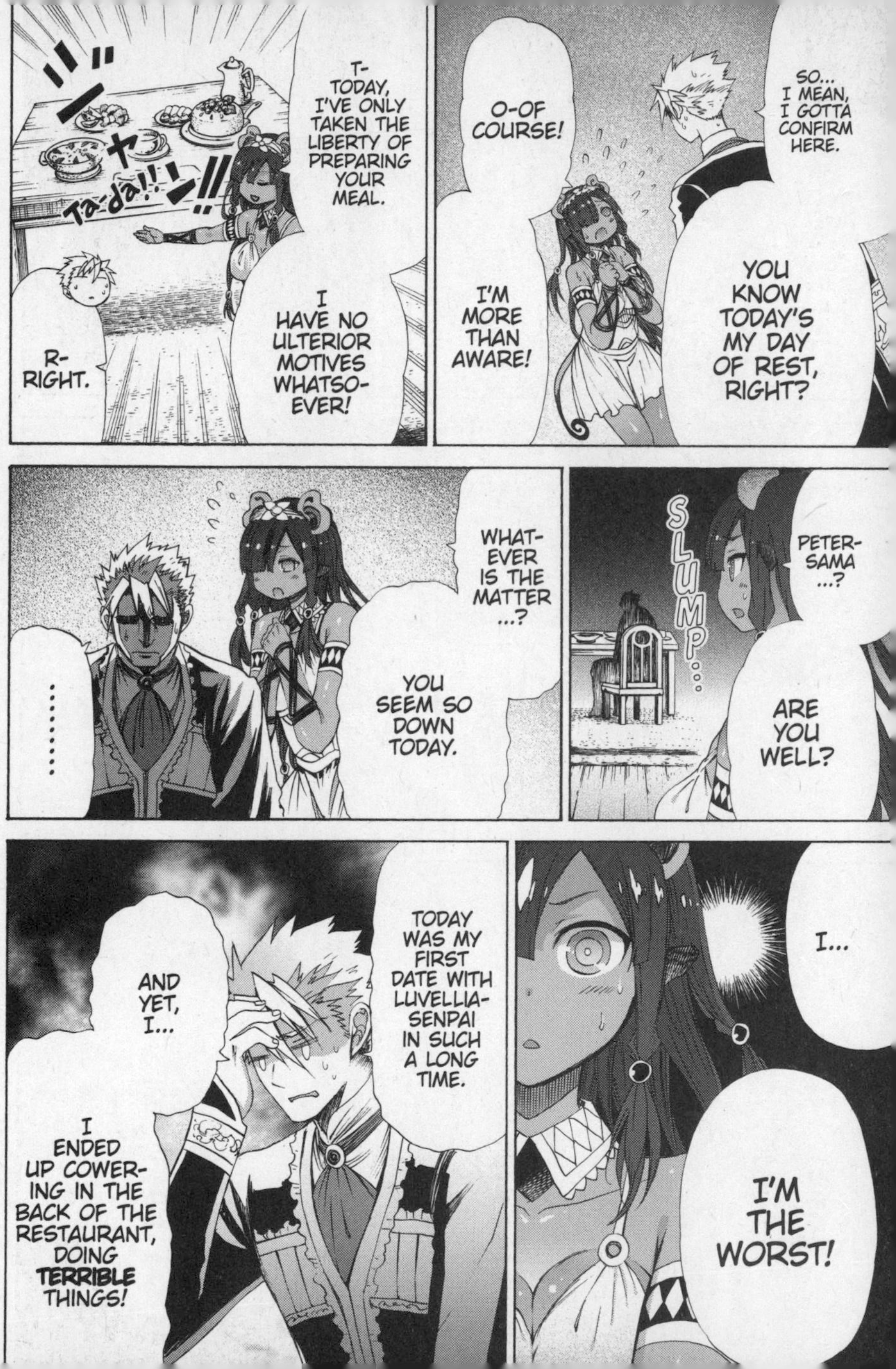
SO... I MEAN, I GOTTA CONFIRM HERE.
YOU KNOW TODAY'S MY DAY OF REST, RIGHT?
O-OF COURSE!
I'M MORE THAN AWARE!
T-TODAY, I'VE ONLY TAKEN THE LIBERTY OF PREPARING YOUR MEAL.
Ta-da!!
I HAVE NO ULTERIOR MOTIVES WHATSOEVER!
R-RIGHT.
PETER-SAMA ...?
SLUMP...
ARE YOU WELL?
WHATEVER IS THE MATTER ...?
YOU SEEM SO DOWN TODAY.
......
I...
I'M THE WORST!
TODAY WAS MY FIRST DATE WITH LUVELLIA-SENPAI IN SUCH A LONG TIME.
AND YET, I...
I ENDED UP COWERING IN THE BACK OF THE RESTAURANT, DOING TERRIBLE THINGS!

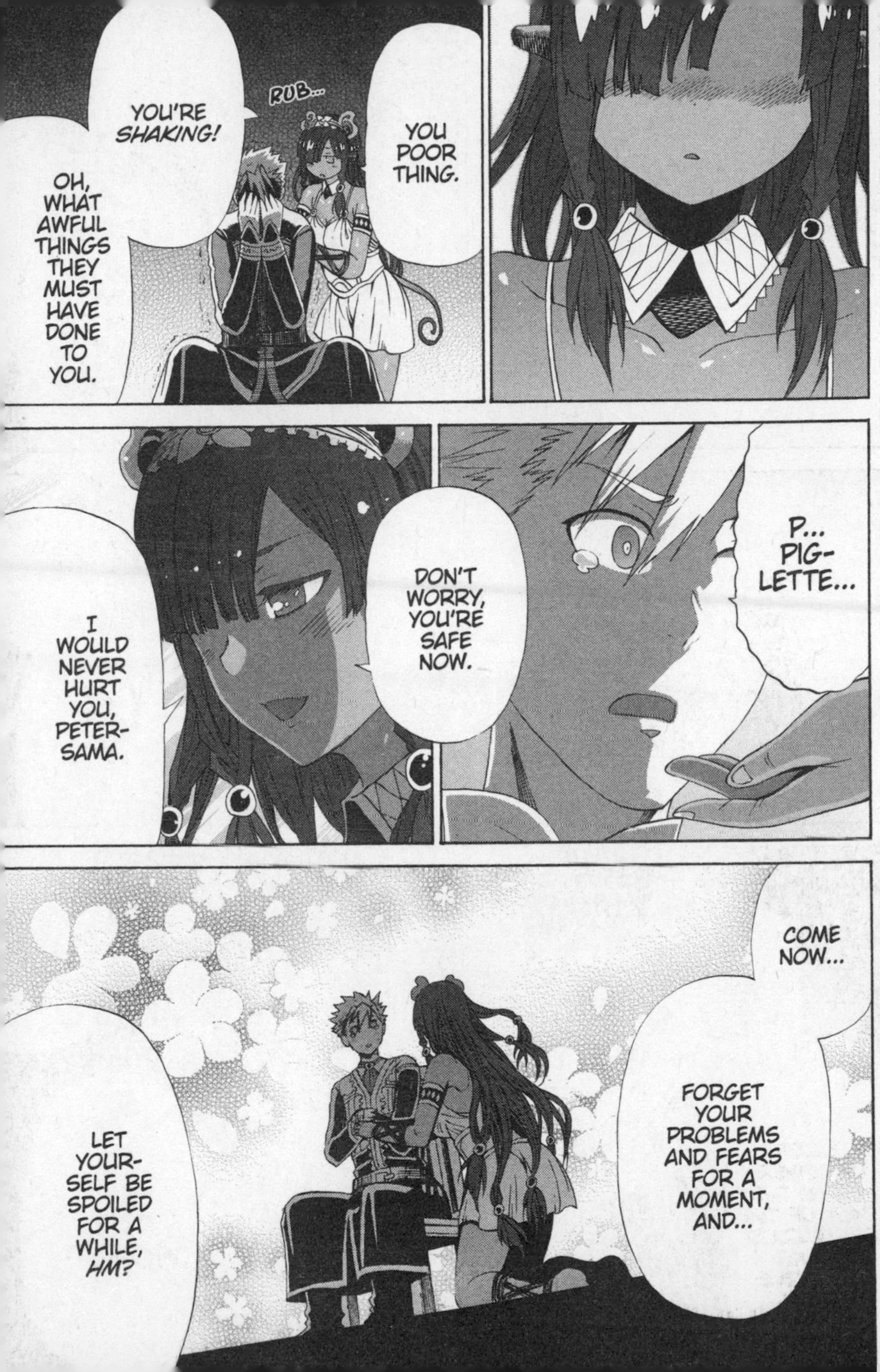

RUB...
YOU POOR THING.
YOU'RE *SHAKING!*
OH, WHAT AWFUL THINGS THEY MUST HAVE DONE TO YOU.
P... PIG-LETTE...
DON'T WORRY, YOU'RE SAFE NOW.
I WOULD NEVER HURT YOU, PETER-SAMA.
COME NOW...
FORGET YOUR PROBLEMS AND FEARS FOR A MOMENT, AND...
LET YOUR-SELF BE SPOILED FOR A WHILE, *HM?*

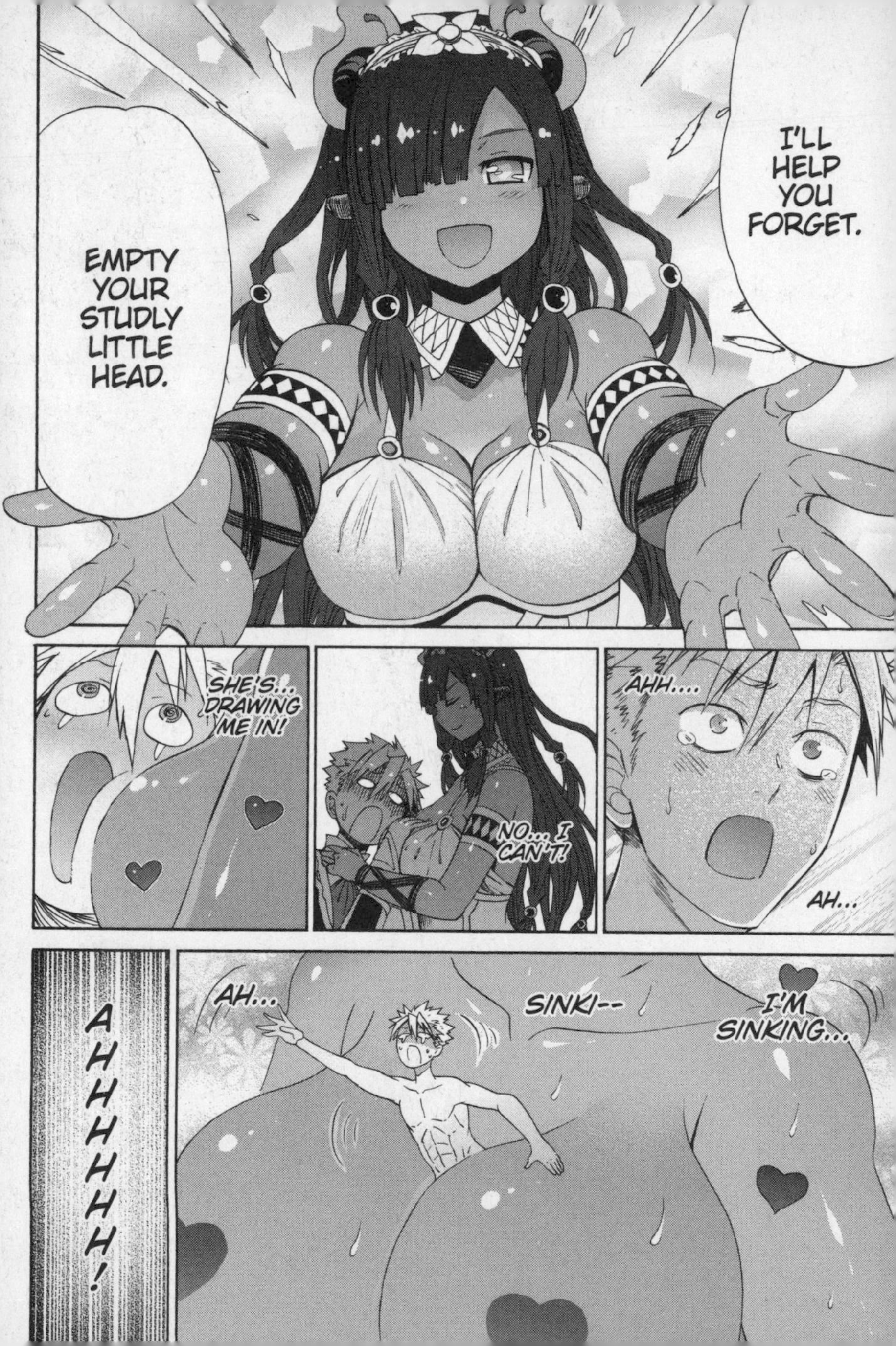
I'LL HELP YOU FORGET.
EMPTY YOUR STUDLY LITTLE HEAD.
AHH....
AH...
NO... I CAN'T!
SHE'S... DRAWING ME IN!
I'M SINKING...
SINKI--
AH...
AHHHHHH!

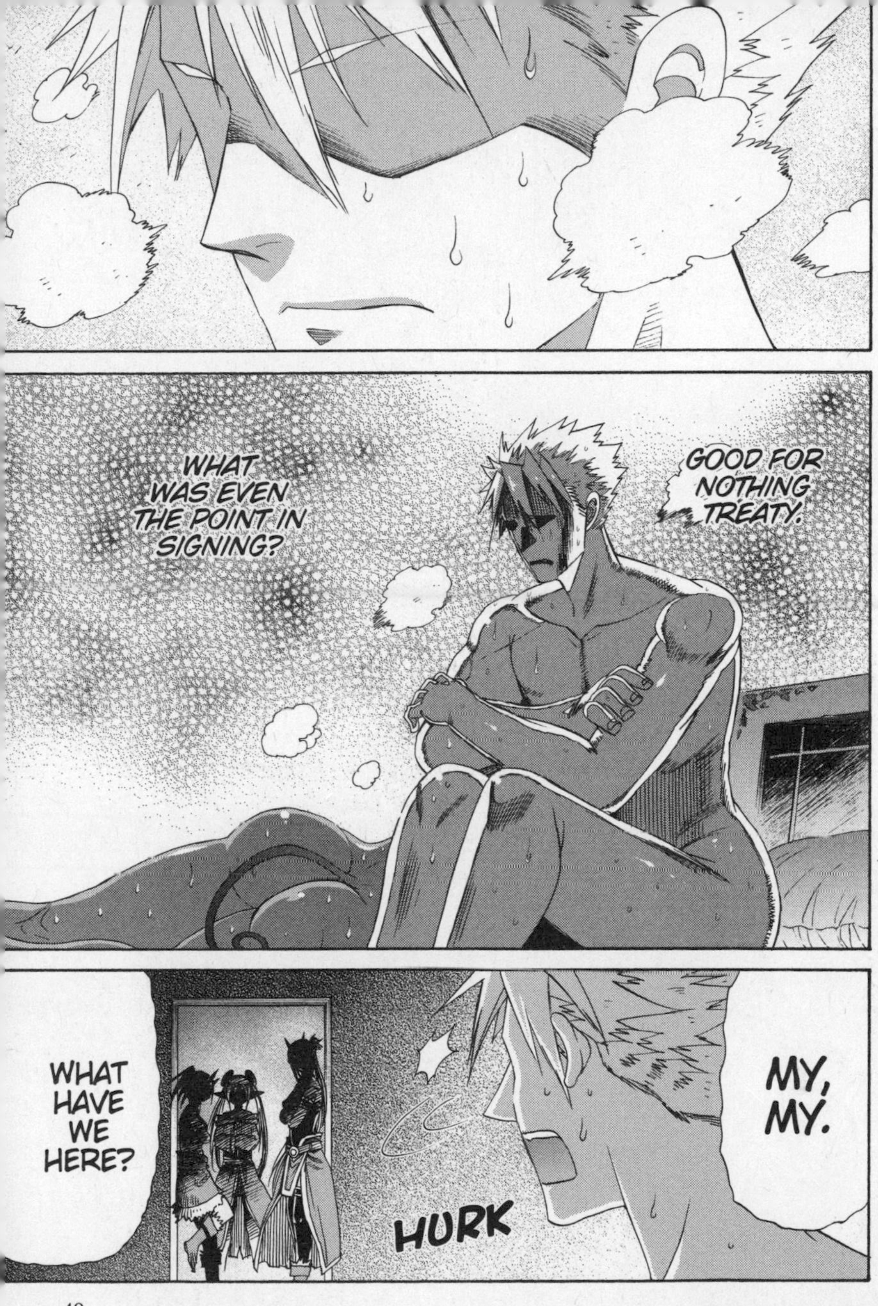
GOOD FOR NOTHING TREATY.
WHAT WAS EVEN THE POINT IN SIGNING?
MY, MY.
WHAT HAVE WE HERE?
HURK

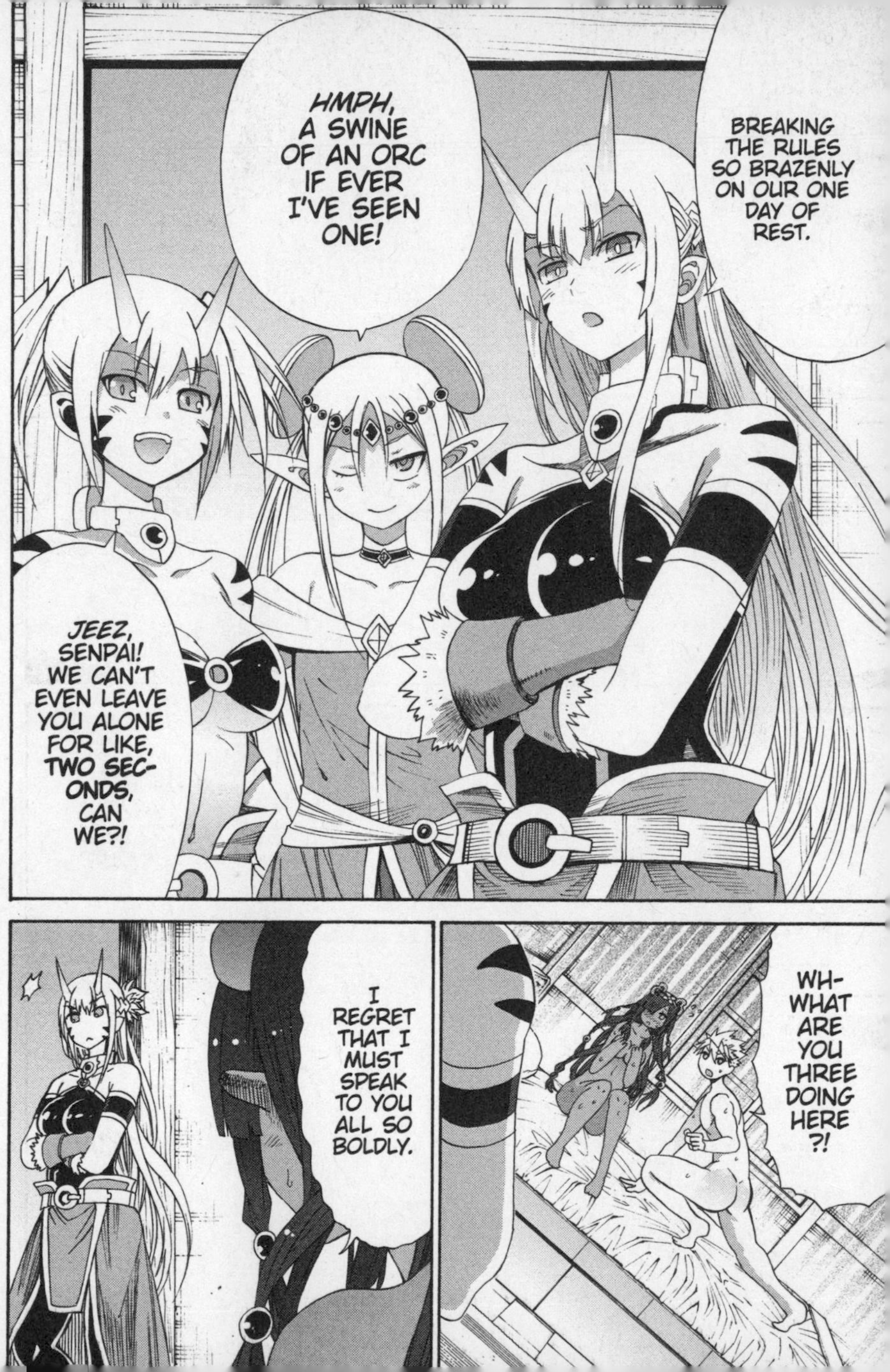
BREAKING THE RULES SO BRAZENLY ON OUR ONE DAY OF REST.
HMPH, A SWINE OF AN ORC IF EVER I'VE SEEN ONE!
JEEZ, SENPAI! WE CAN'T EVEN LEAVE YOU ALONE FOR LIKE, TWO SEC-ONDS, CAN WE?!
WH-WHAT ARE YOU THREE DOING HERE?!
I REGRET THAT I MUST SPEAK TO YOU ALL SO BOLDLY.

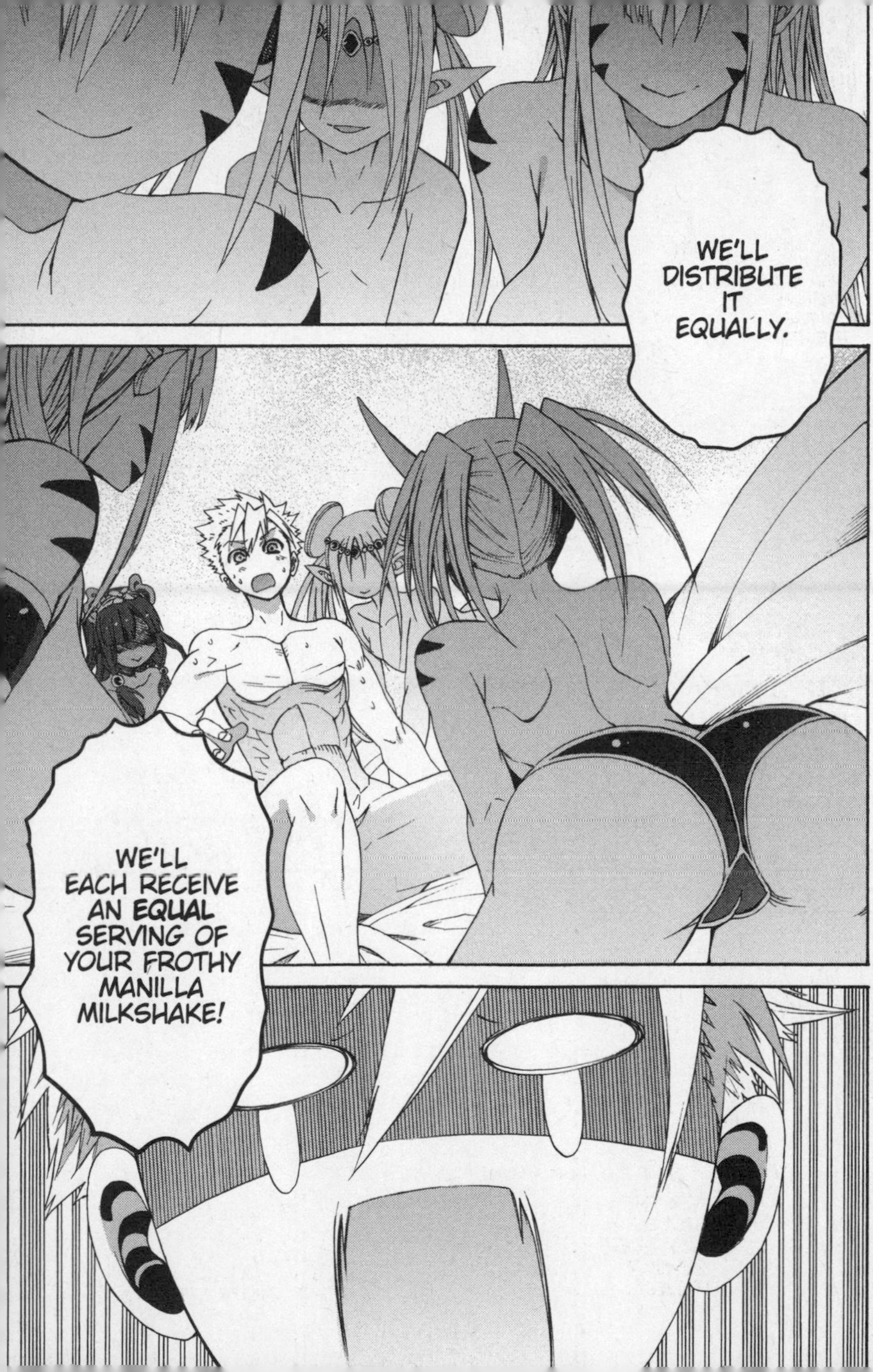
WE'LL DISTRIBUTE IT EQUALLY.
WE'LL EACH RECEIVE AN **EQUAL** SERVING OF YOUR FROTHY MANILLA MILKSHAKE!

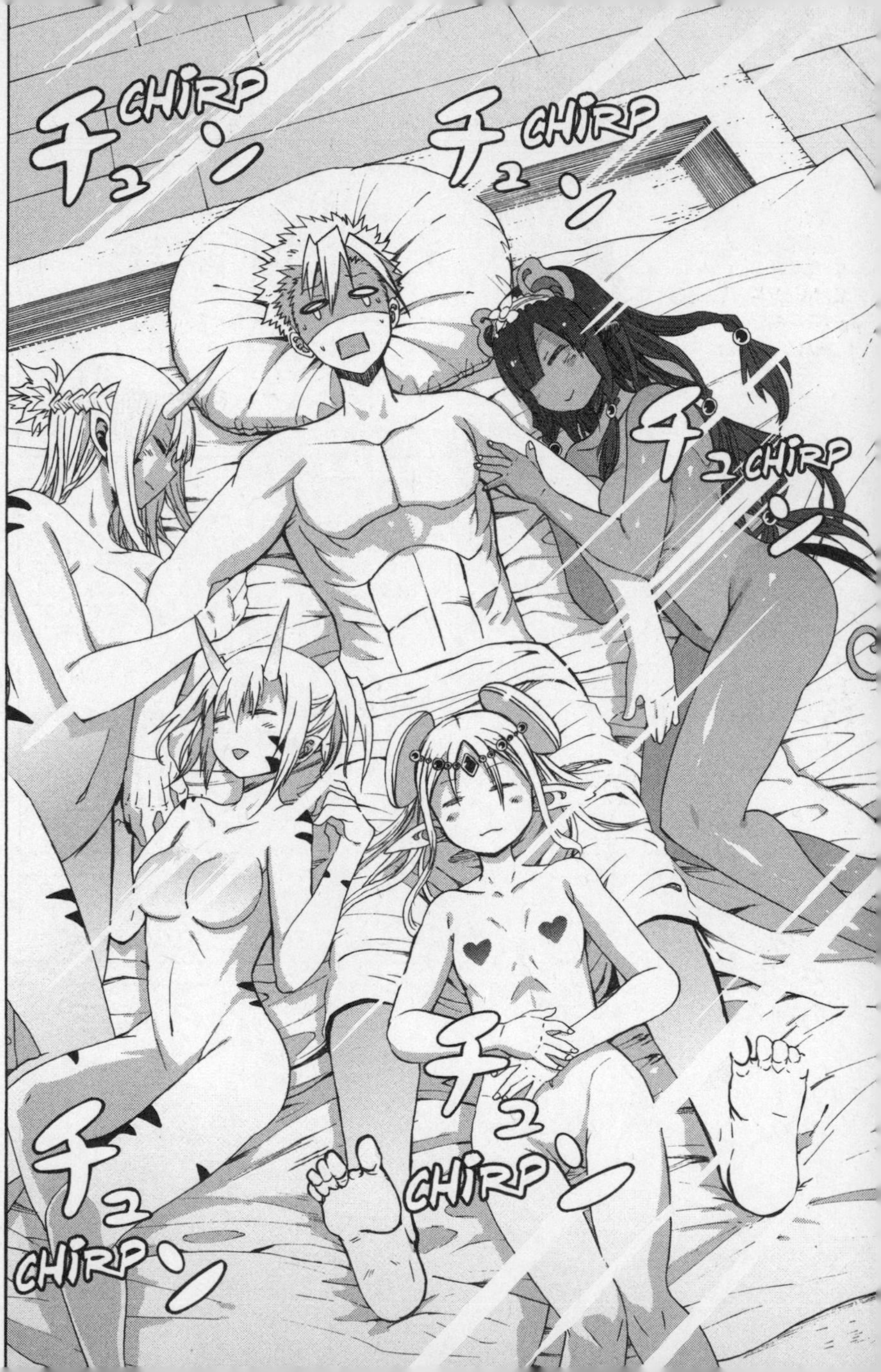
チュ CHIRP
チュ CHIRP
チュ CHIRP
チュ CHIRP
チュ CHIRP

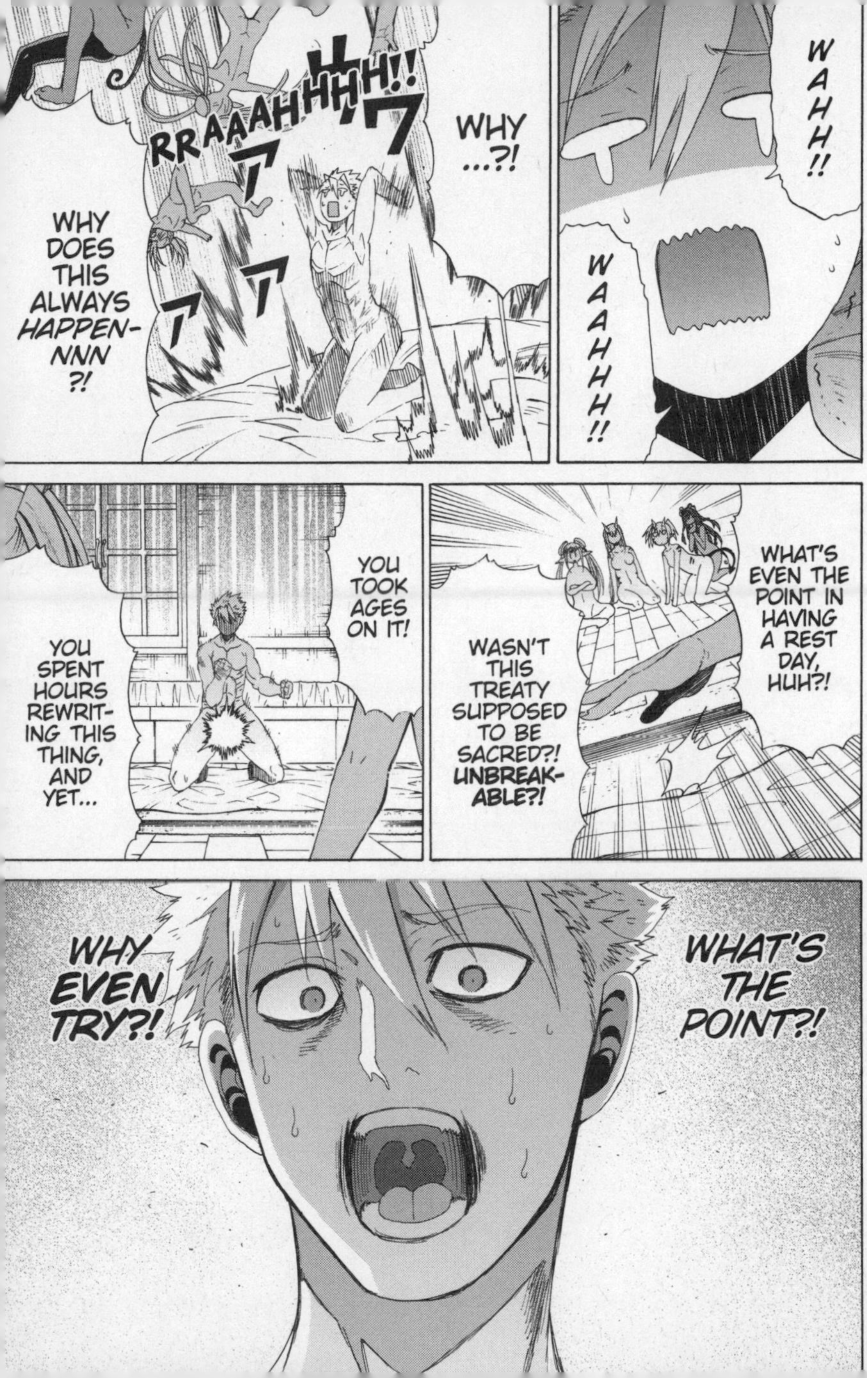
WAHH!!
WAAHHHH!!
WHY ...?!
RRAAAHHHH!!
WHY DOES THIS ALWAYS HAPPEN-NNN?!
WHAT'S EVEN THE POINT IN HAVING A REST DAY, HUH?!
WASN'T THIS TREATY SUPPOSED TO BE SACRED?! UNBREAKABLE?!
YOU TOOK AGES ON IT!
YOU SPENT HOURS REWRITING THIS THING, AND YET...
WHAT'S THE POINT?!
WHY EVEN TRY?!

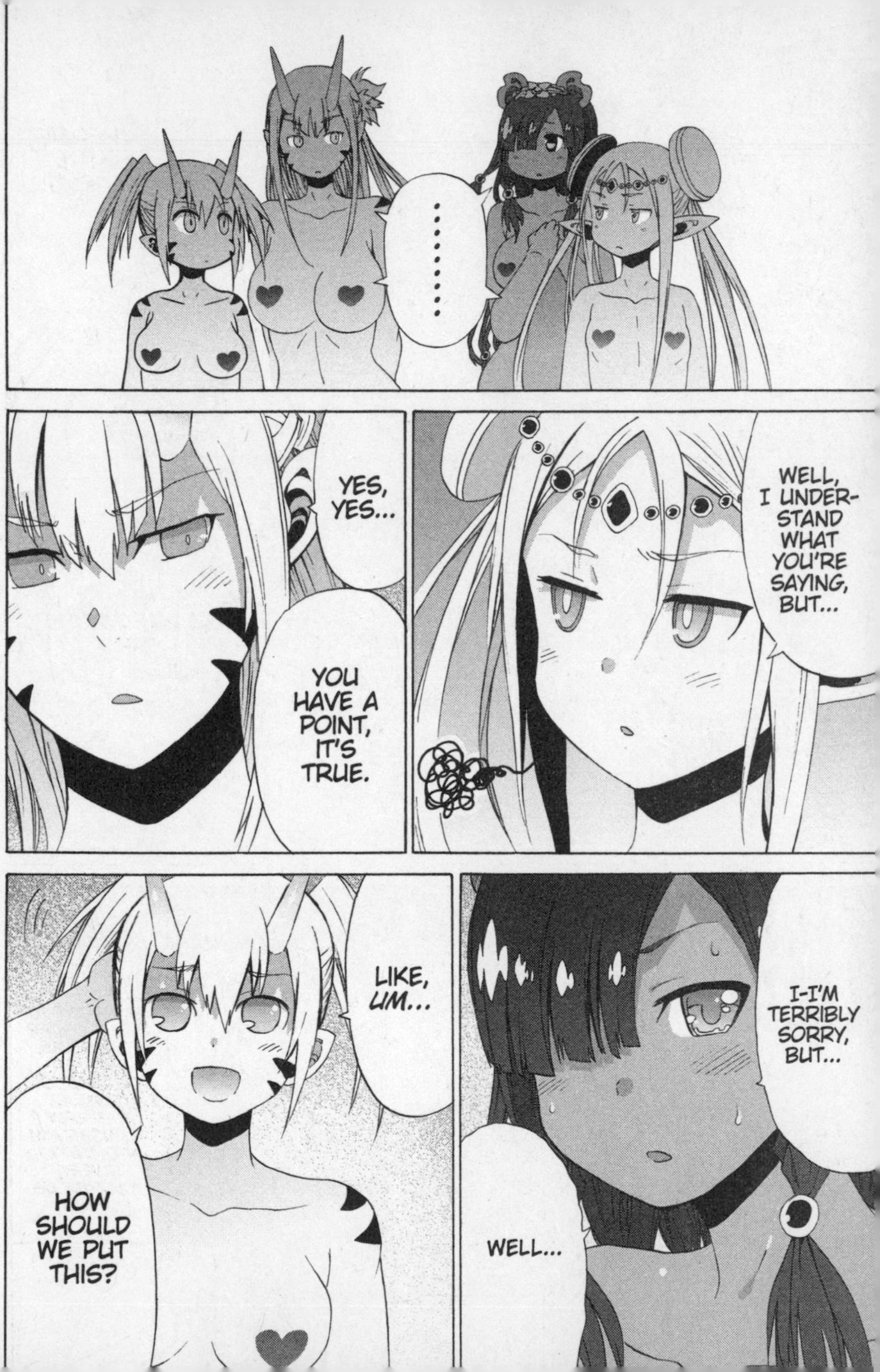
......
WELL, I UNDERSTAND WHAT YOU'RE SAYING, BUT...
YES, YES...
YOU HAVE A POINT, IT'S TRUE.
I-I'M TERRIBLY SORRY, BUT...
WELL...
LIKE, UM...
HOW SHOULD WE PUT THIS?

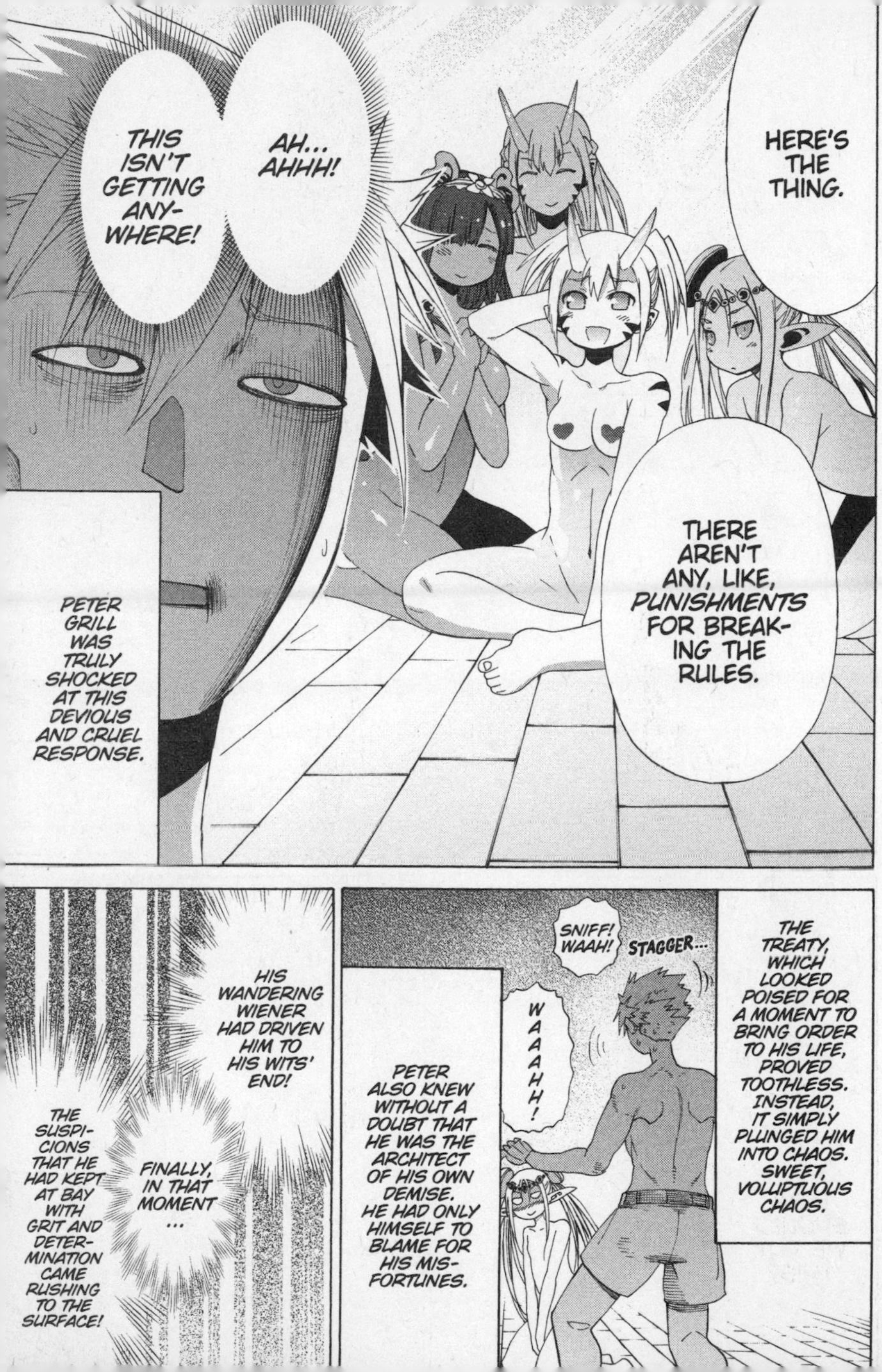
HERE'S THE THING.
THERE AREN'T ANY, LIKE, PUNISHMENTS FOR BREAK-ING THE RULES.
AH... AHHH!
THIS ISN'T GETTING ANY-WHERE!
PETER GRILL WAS TRULY SHOCKED AT THIS DEVIOUS AND CRUEL RESPONSE.
THE TREATY, WHICH LOOKED POISED FOR A MOMENT TO BRING ORDER TO HIS LIFE, PROVED TOOTHLESS. INSTEAD, IT SIMPLY PLUNGED HIM INTO CHAOS. SWEET, VOLUPTUOUS CHAOS.
SNIFF! WAAH!
STAGGER...
WAAAAHH!
PETER ALSO KNEW WITHOUT A DOUBT THAT HE WAS THE ARCHITECT OF HIS OWN DEMISE. HE HAD ONLY HIMSELF TO BLAME FOR HIS MIS-FORTUNES.
HIS WANDERING WIENER HAD DRIVEN HIM TO HIS WITS' END!
FINALLY, IN THAT MOMENT ...
THE SUSPI-CIONS THAT HE HAD KEPT AT BAY WITH GRIT AND DETER-MINATION CAME RUSHING TO THE SURFACE!

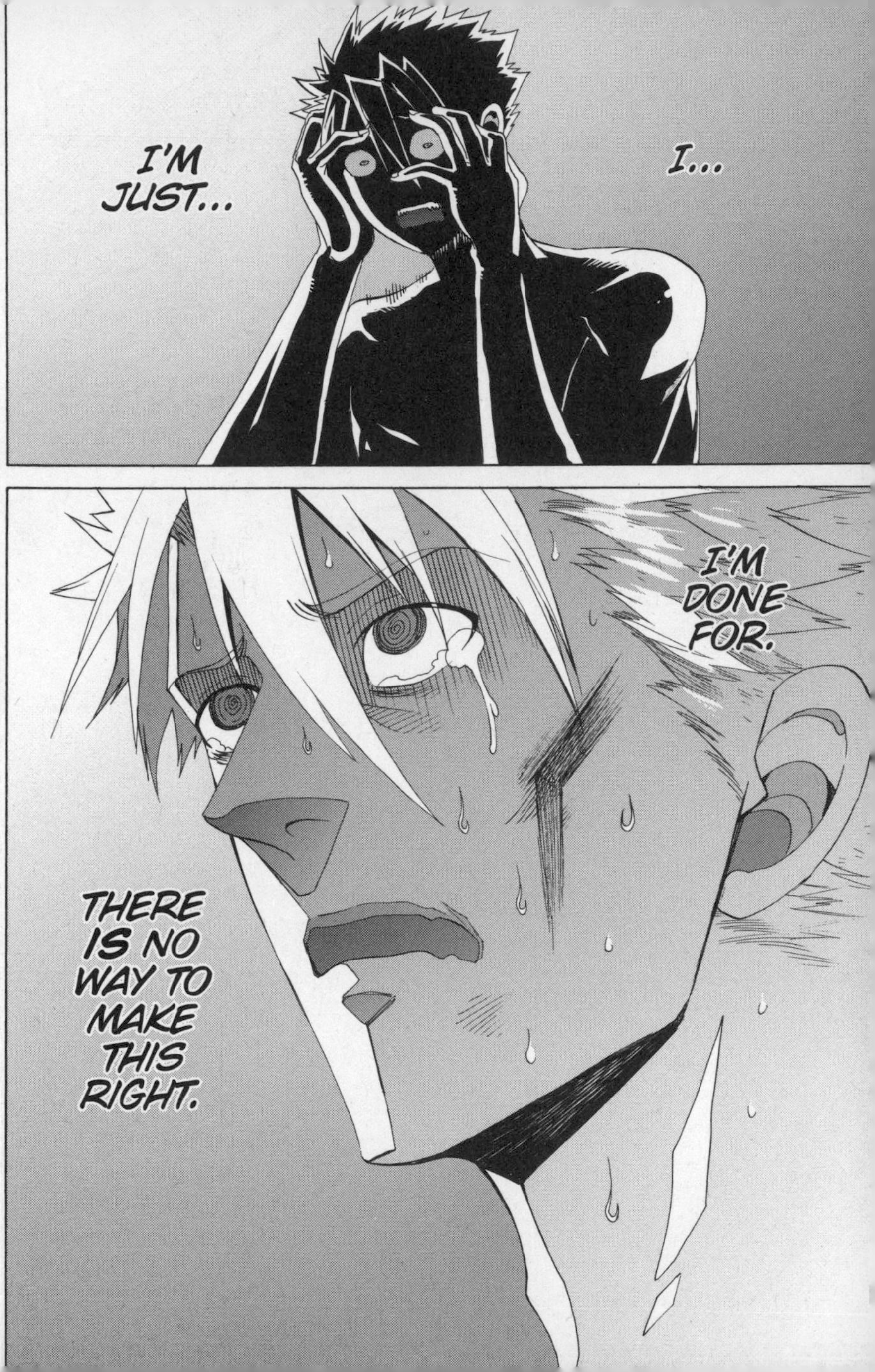
I...
I'M JUST...
I'M DONE FOR.
THERE IS NO WAY TO MAKE THIS RIGHT.

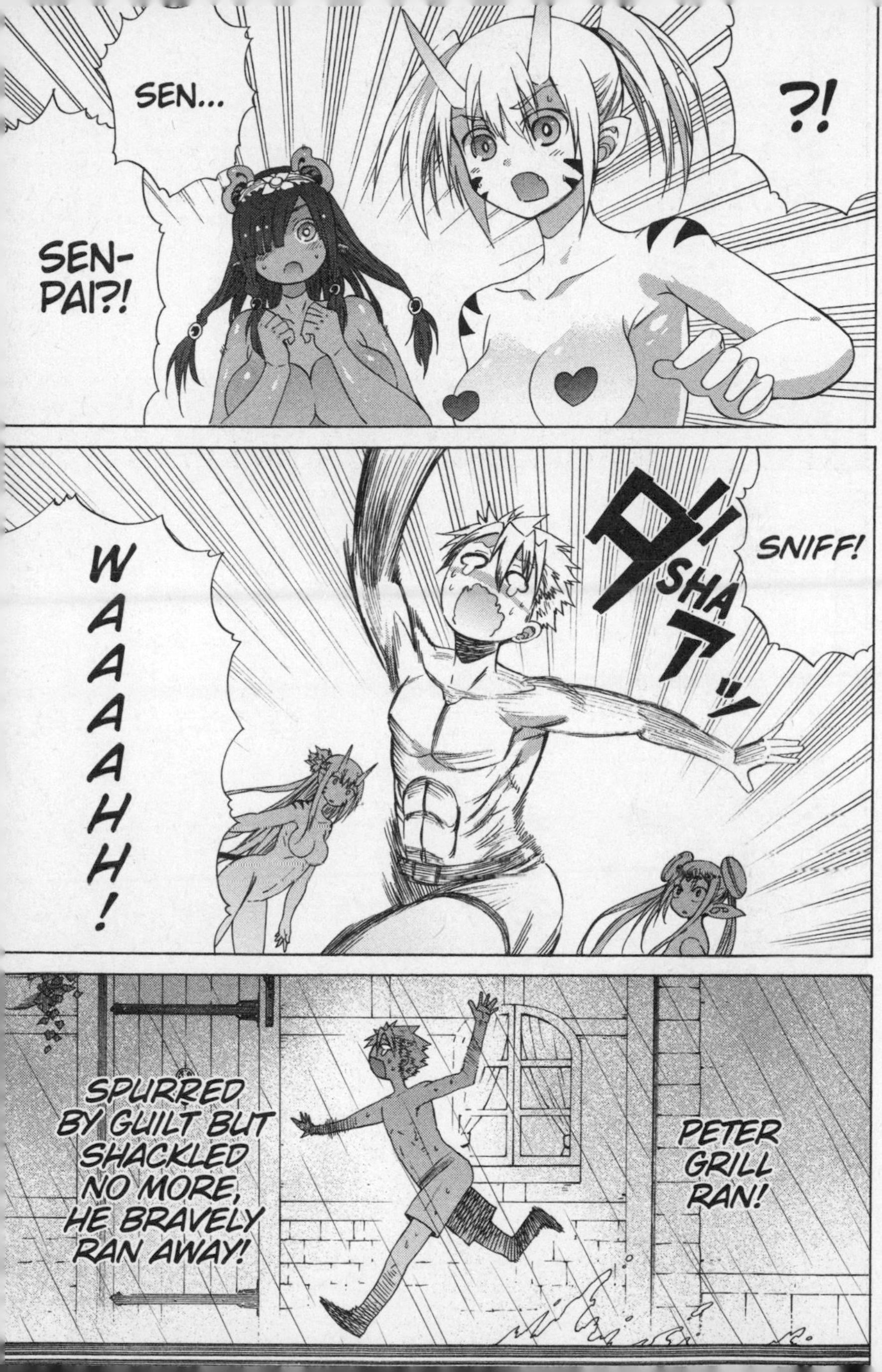
?!
SEN...
SEN-PAI?!
SNIFF!
ダ SHA アッ
WAAAAAHH!
PETER GRILL RAN!
SPURRED BY GUILT BUT SHACKLED NO MORE, HE BRAVELY RAN AWAY!

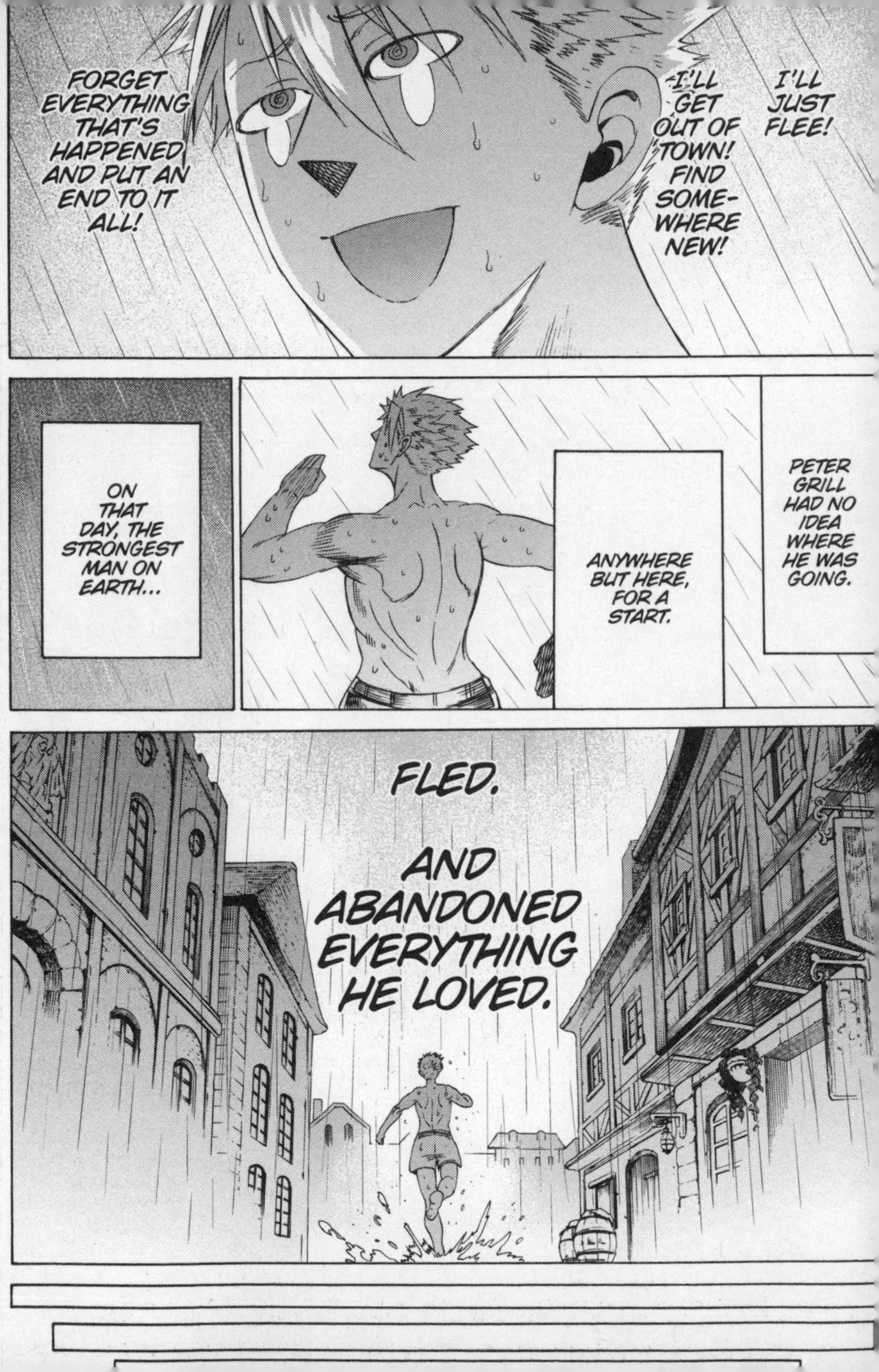
I'LL JUST FLEE!
I'LL GET OUT OF TOWN! FIND SOMEWHERE NEW!
FORGET EVERYTHING THAT'S HAPPENED AND PUT AN END TO IT ALL!
PETER GRILL HAD NO IDEA WHERE HE WAS GOING.
ANYWHERE BUT HERE, FOR A START.
ON THAT DAY, THE STRONGEST MAN ON EARTH...
FLED.
AND ABANDONED EVERYTHING HE LOVED.

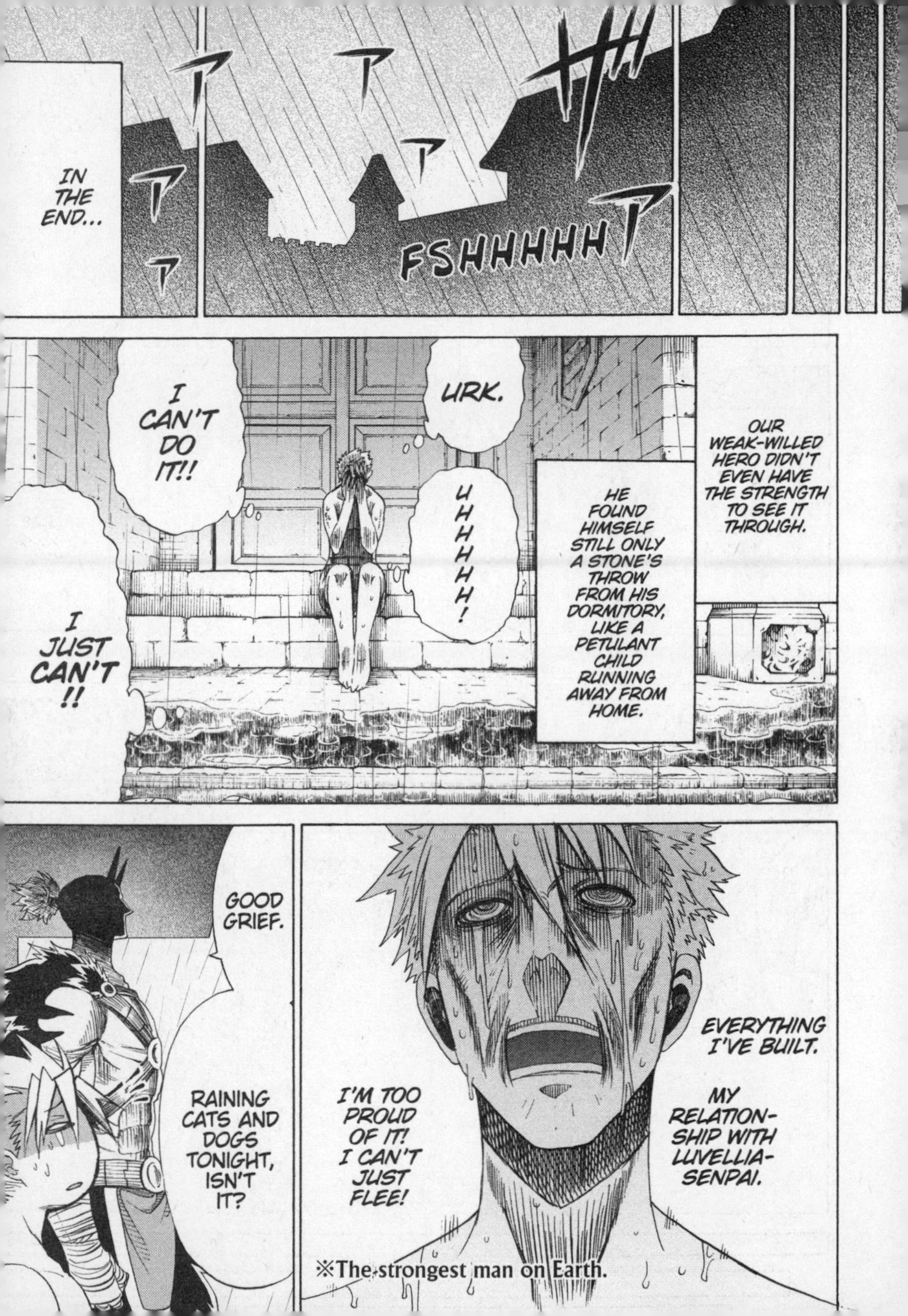
FSHHHHHH
IN THE END...
OUR WEAK-WILLED HERO DIDN'T EVEN HAVE THE STRENGTH TO SEE IT THROUGH.
HE FOUND HIMSELF STILL ONLY A STONE'S THROW FROM HIS DORMITORY, LIKE A PETULANT CHILD RUNNING AWAY FROM HOME.
URK.
UHHHHHH!
I CAN'T DO IT!!
I JUST CAN'T!!
EVERYTHING I'VE BUILT.
MY RELATIONSHIP WITH LUVELLIA-SENPAI.
I'M TOO PROUD OF IT! I CAN'T JUST FLEE!
※The strongest man on Earth.
GOOD GRIEF.
RAINING CATS AND DOGS TONIGHT, ISN'T IT?

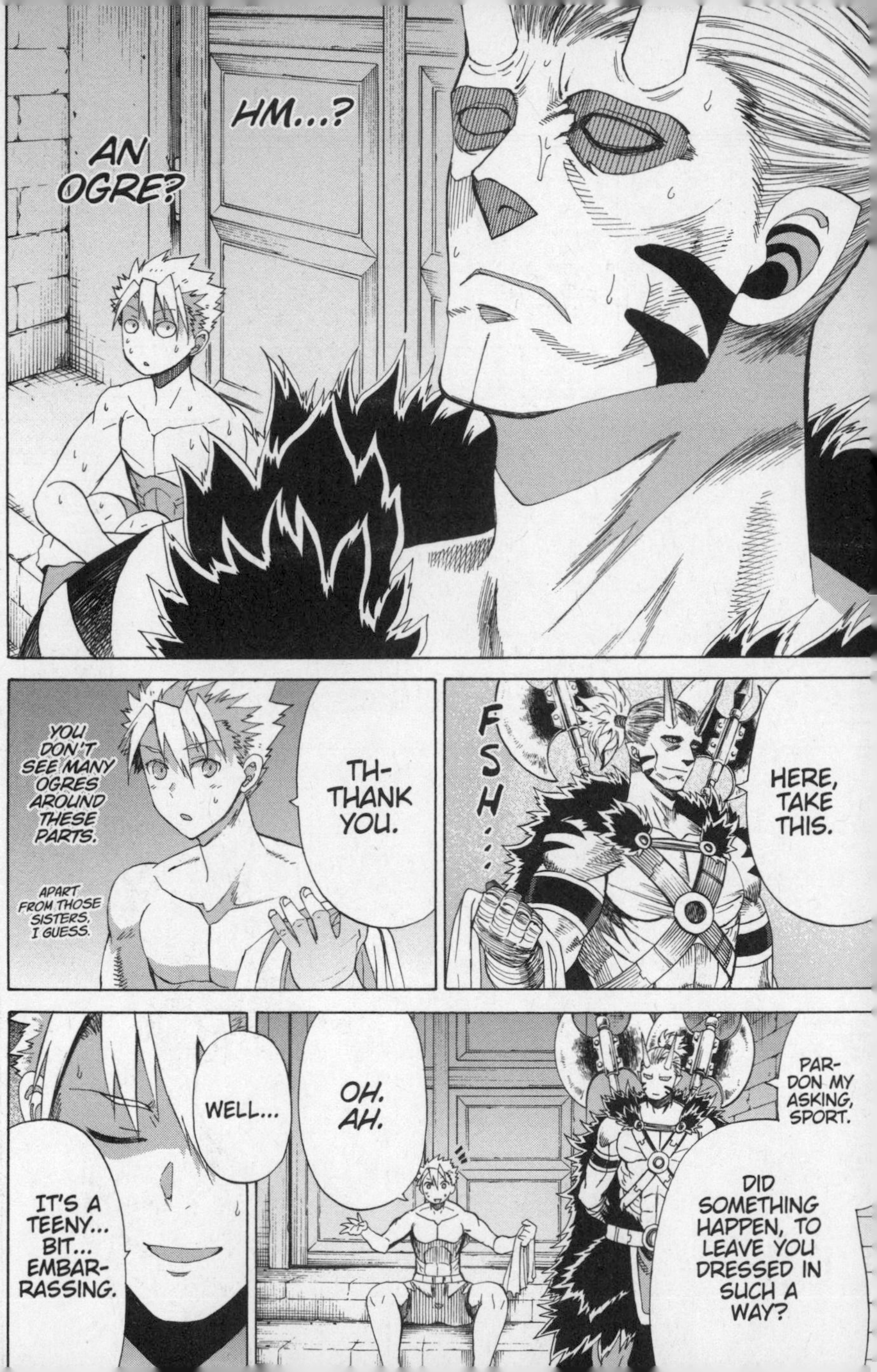
HM...?
AN OGRE?
HERE, TAKE THIS.
FSH...
TH-THANK YOU.
YOU DON'T SEE MANY OGRES AROUND THESE PARTS.
APART FROM THOSE SISTERS, I GUESS.
PARDON MY ASKING, SPORT.
DID SOMETHING HAPPEN, TO LEAVE YOU DRESSED IN SUCH A WAY?
OH. AH.
WELL...
IT'S A TEENY... BIT... EMBARRASSING.

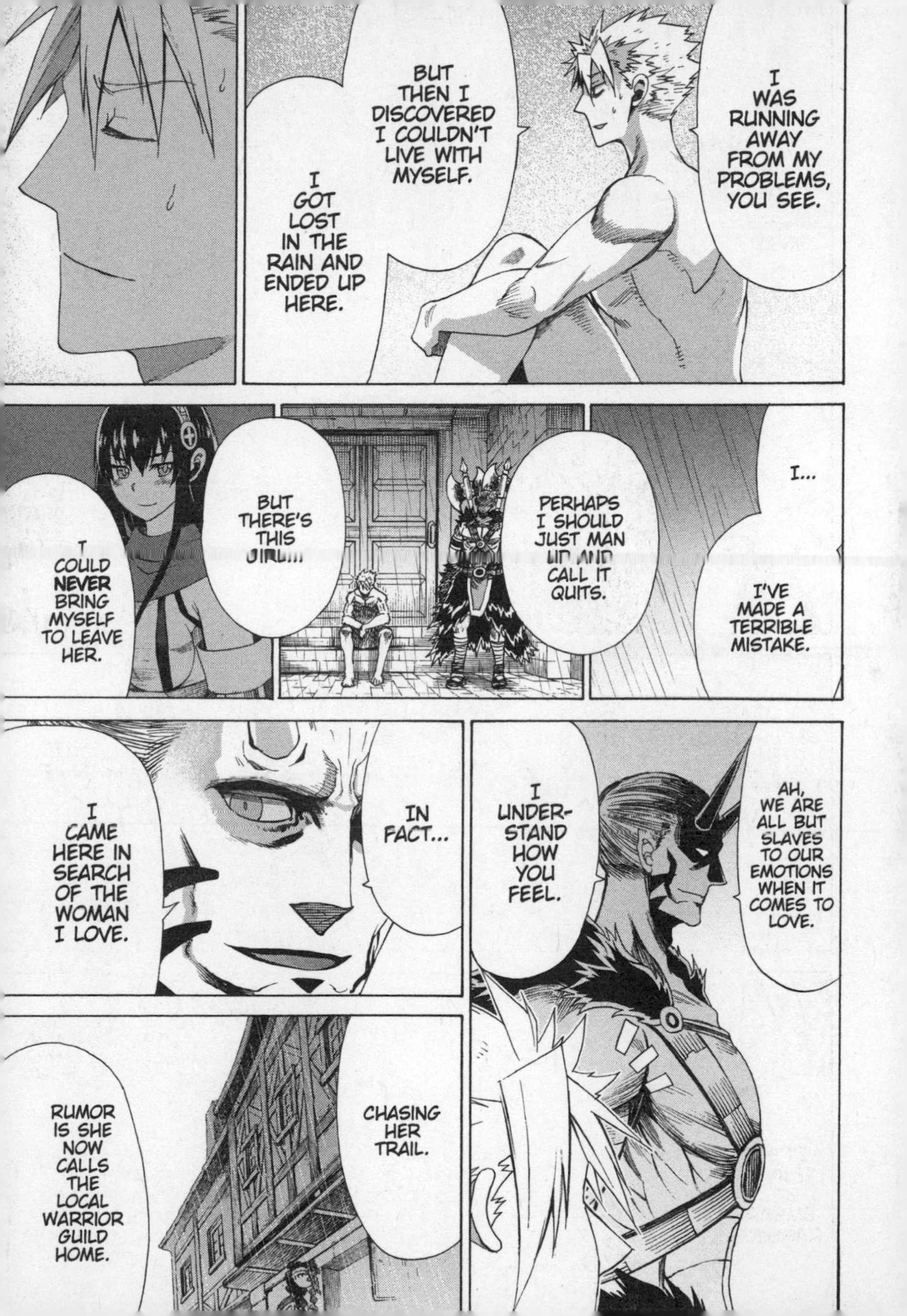
I WAS RUNNING AWAY FROM MY PROBLEMS, YOU SEE.
BUT THEN I DISCOVERED I COULDN'T LIVE WITH MYSELF.
I GOT LOST IN THE RAIN AND ENDED UP HERE.
I...
I'VE MADE A TERRIBLE MISTAKE.
PERHAPS I SHOULD JUST MAN UP AND CALL IT QUITS.
BUT THERE'S THIS GIRL...
I COULD **NEVER** BRING MYSELF TO LEAVE HER.
AH, WE ARE ALL BUT SLAVES TO OUR EMOTIONS WHEN IT COMES TO LOVE.
I UNDERSTAND HOW YOU FEEL.
IN FACT...
I CAME HERE IN SEARCH OF THE WOMAN I LOVE.
CHASING HER TRAIL.
RUMOR IS SHE NOW CALLS THE LOCAL WARRIOR GUILD HOME.

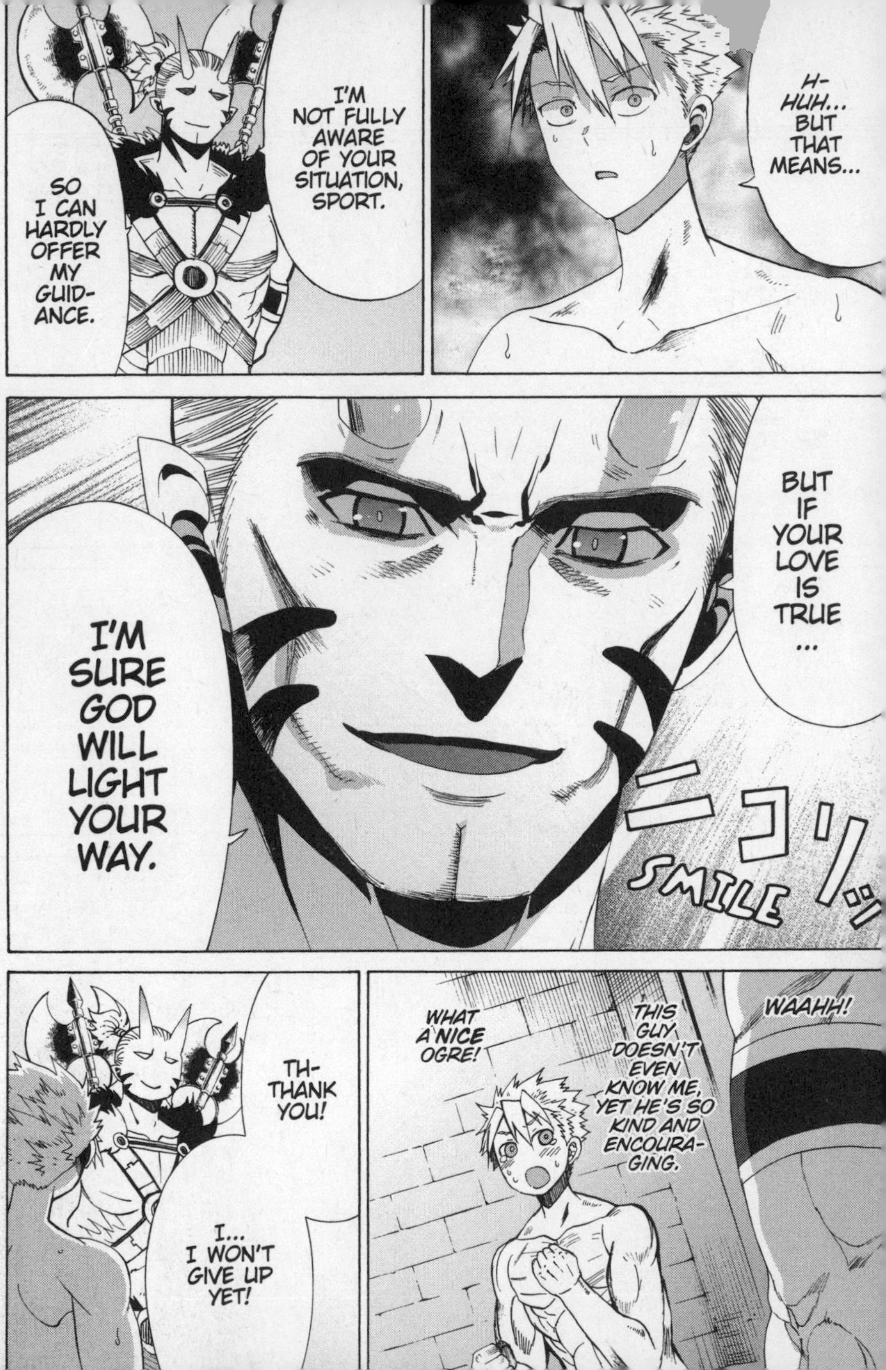
H-HUH... BUT THAT MEANS...
I'M NOT FULLY AWARE OF YOUR SITUATION, SPORT.
SO I CAN HARDLY OFFER MY GUIDANCE.
BUT IF YOUR LOVE IS TRUE...
I'M SURE GOD WILL LIGHT YOUR WAY.
ニコッ
SMILE
WAAHH!
THIS GUY DOESN'T EVEN KNOW ME, YET HE'S SO KIND AND ENCOURAGING.
WHAT A NICE OGRE!
TH-THANK YOU!
I... I WON'T GIVE UP YET!

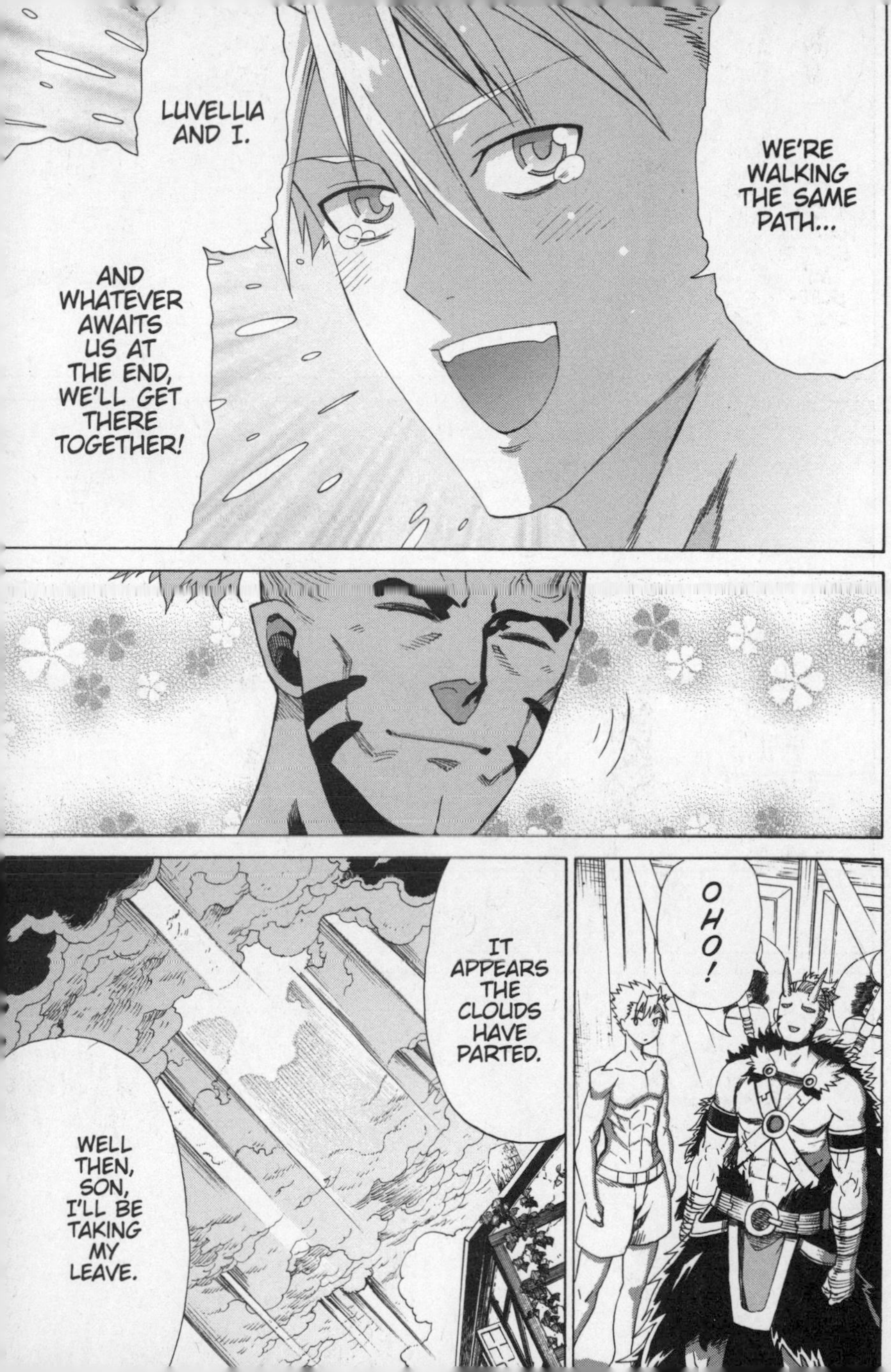
WE'RE WALKING THE SAME PATH...
LUVELLIA AND I.
AND WHATEVER AWAITS US AT THE END, WE'LL GET THERE TOGETHER!
OHO!
IT APPEARS THE CLOUDS HAVE PARTED.
WELL THEN, SON, I'LL BE TAKING MY LEAVE.

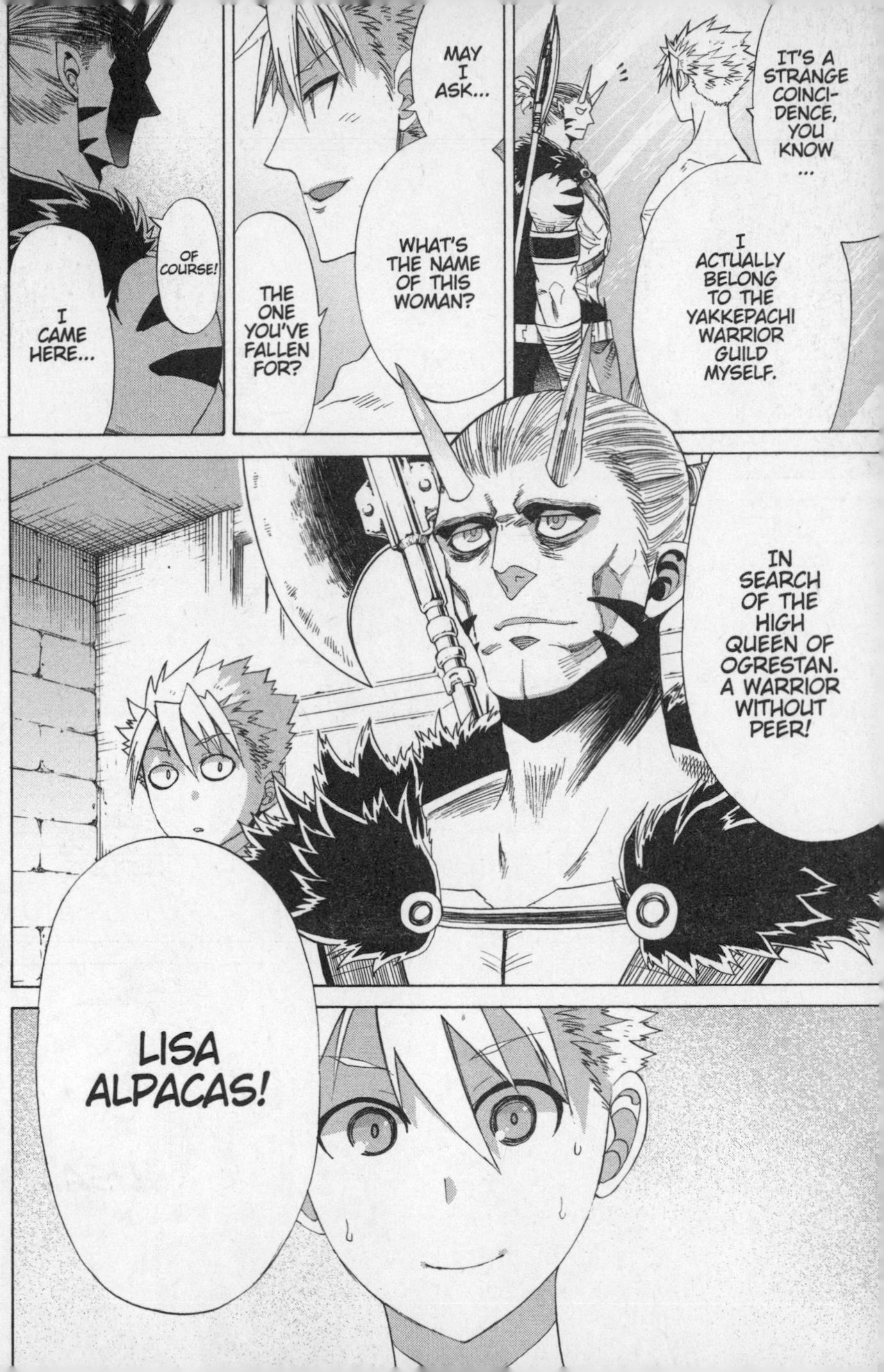
IT'S A STRANGE COINCI-DENCE, YOU KNOW ...
I ACTUALLY BELONG TO THE YAKKEPACHI WARRIOR GUILD MYSELF.
MAY I ASK...
WHAT'S THE NAME OF THIS WOMAN?
THE ONE YOU'VE FALLEN FOR?
OF COURSE!
I CAME HERE...
IN SEARCH OF THE HIGH QUEEN OF OGRESTAN. A WARRIOR WITHOUT PEER!
LISA ALPACAS!

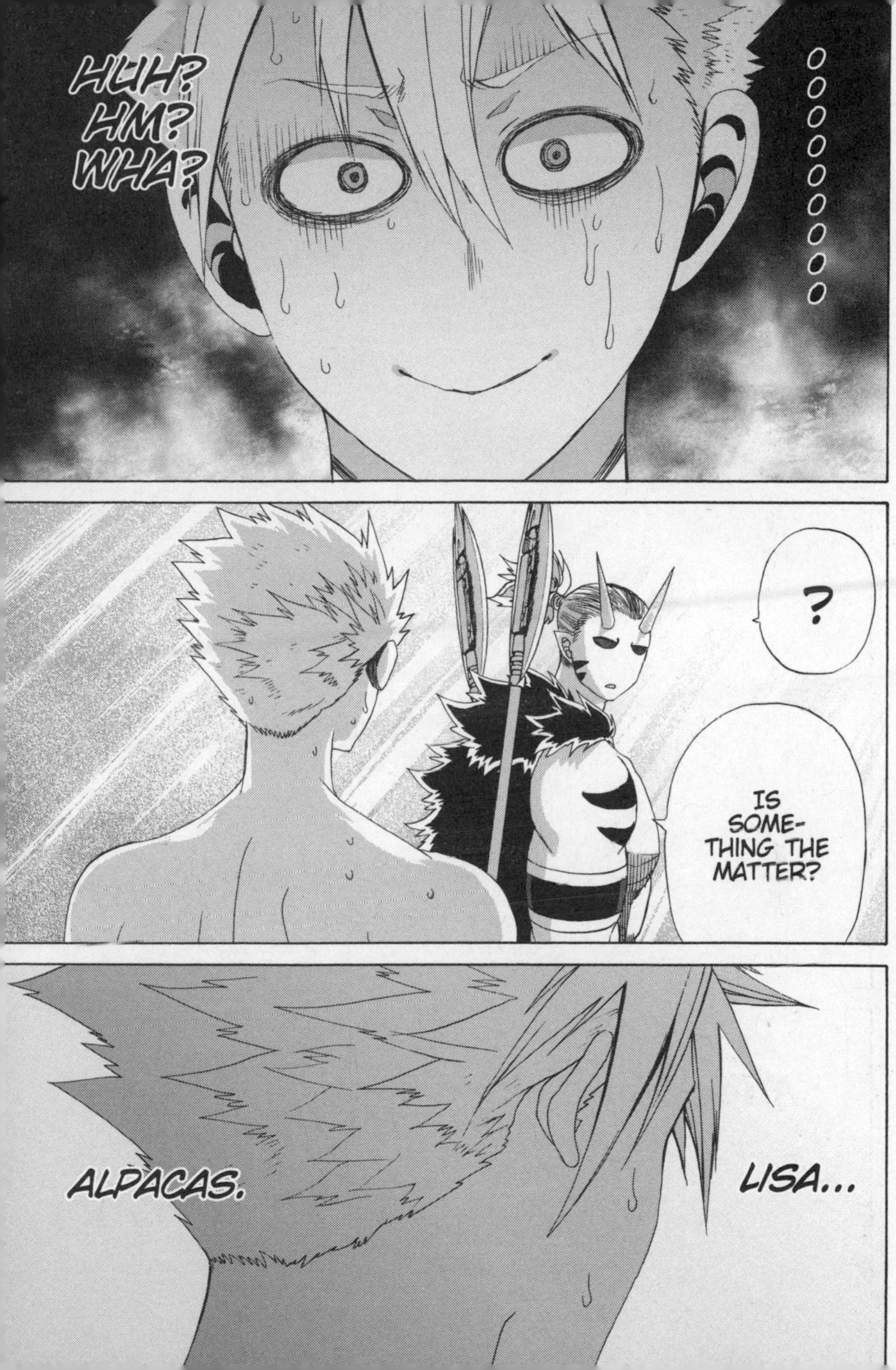

OOOOOOOOOOOOO
HUH? HM? WHA?
?
IS SOME-THING THE MATTER?
LISA...
ALPACAS.

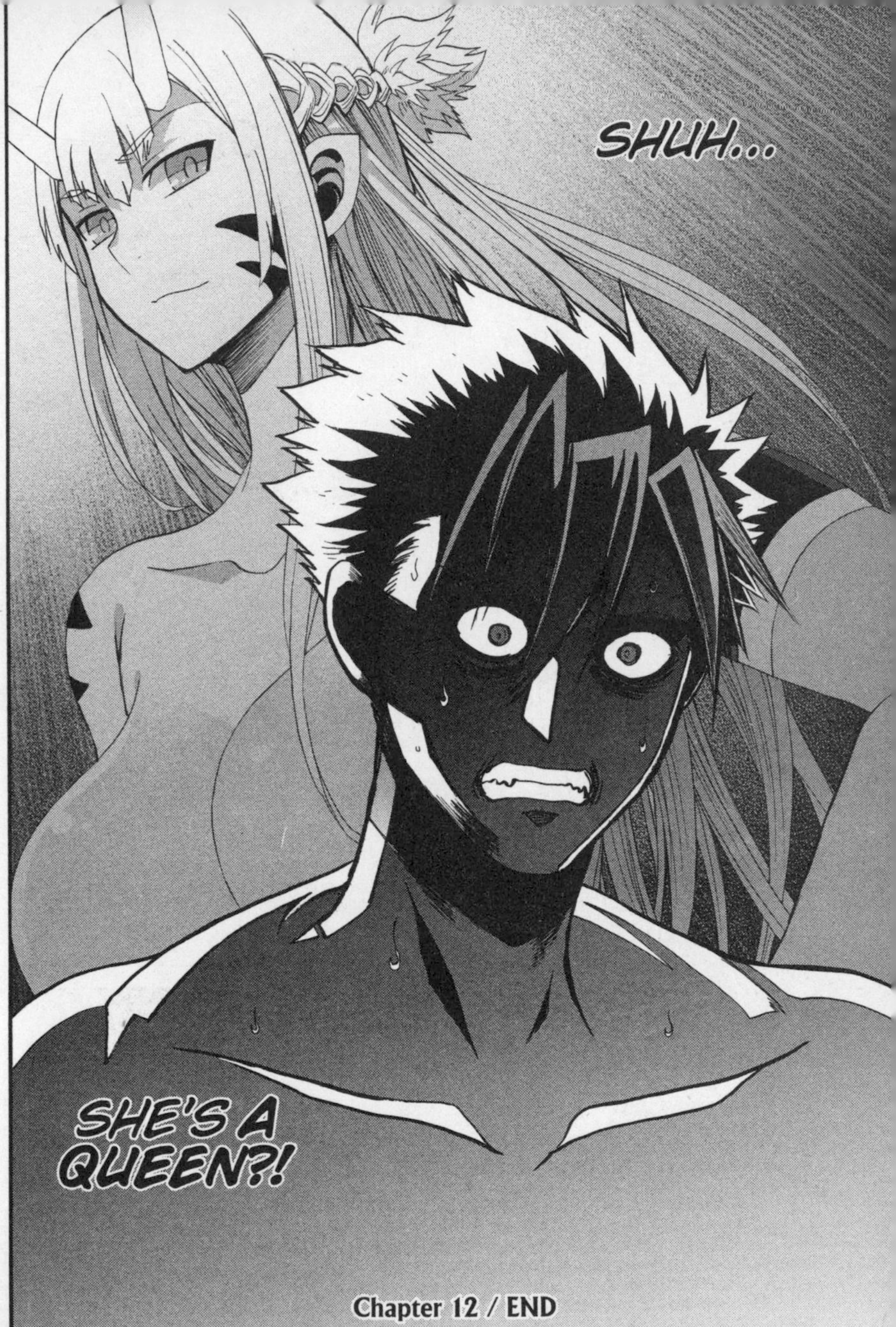
SHUH...
SHE'S A QUEEN?!

Chapter 12 / END

Previously, on *Peter Grill*...

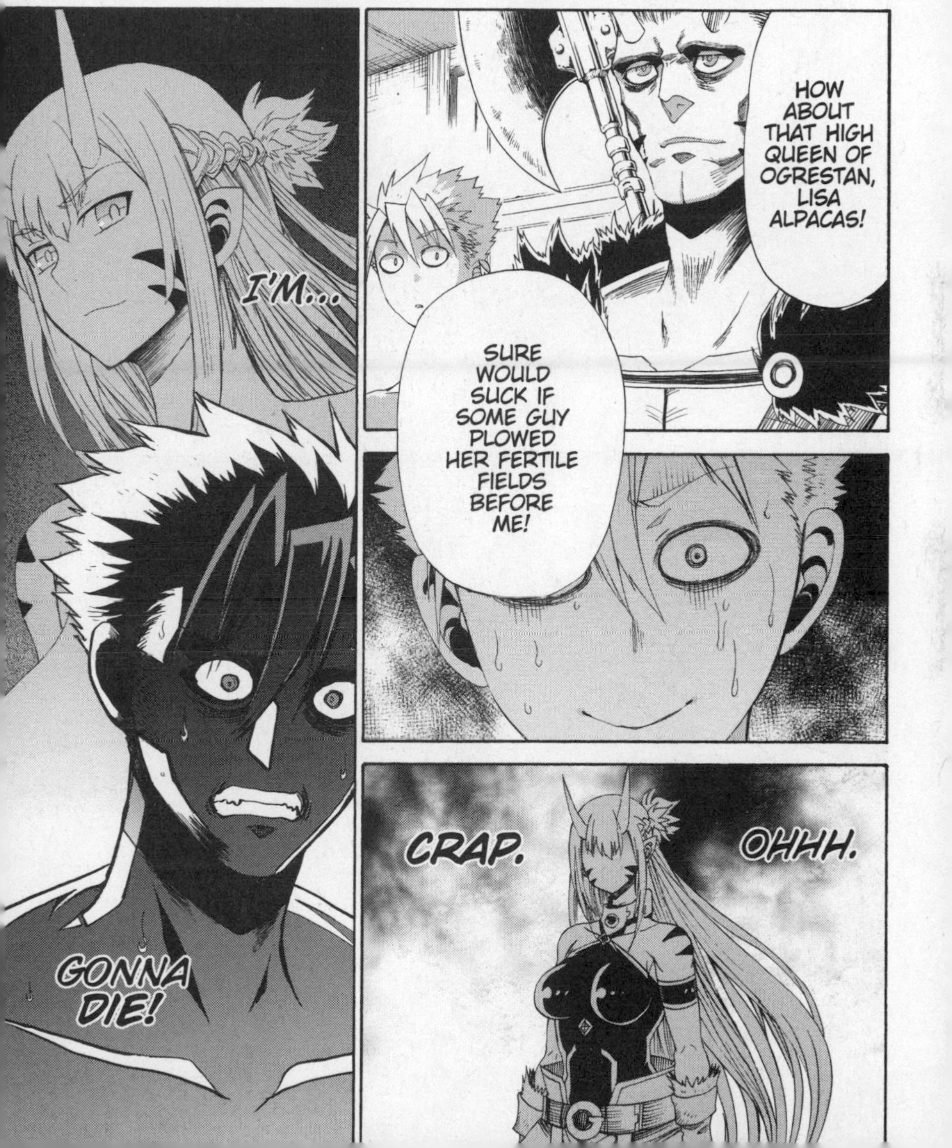
HOW ABOUT THAT HIGH QUEEN OF OGRESTAN, LISA ALPACAS!
SURE WOULD SUCK IF SOME GUY PLOWED HER FERTILE FIELDS BEFORE ME!
OHHH.
CRAP.
I'M...
GONNA DIE!

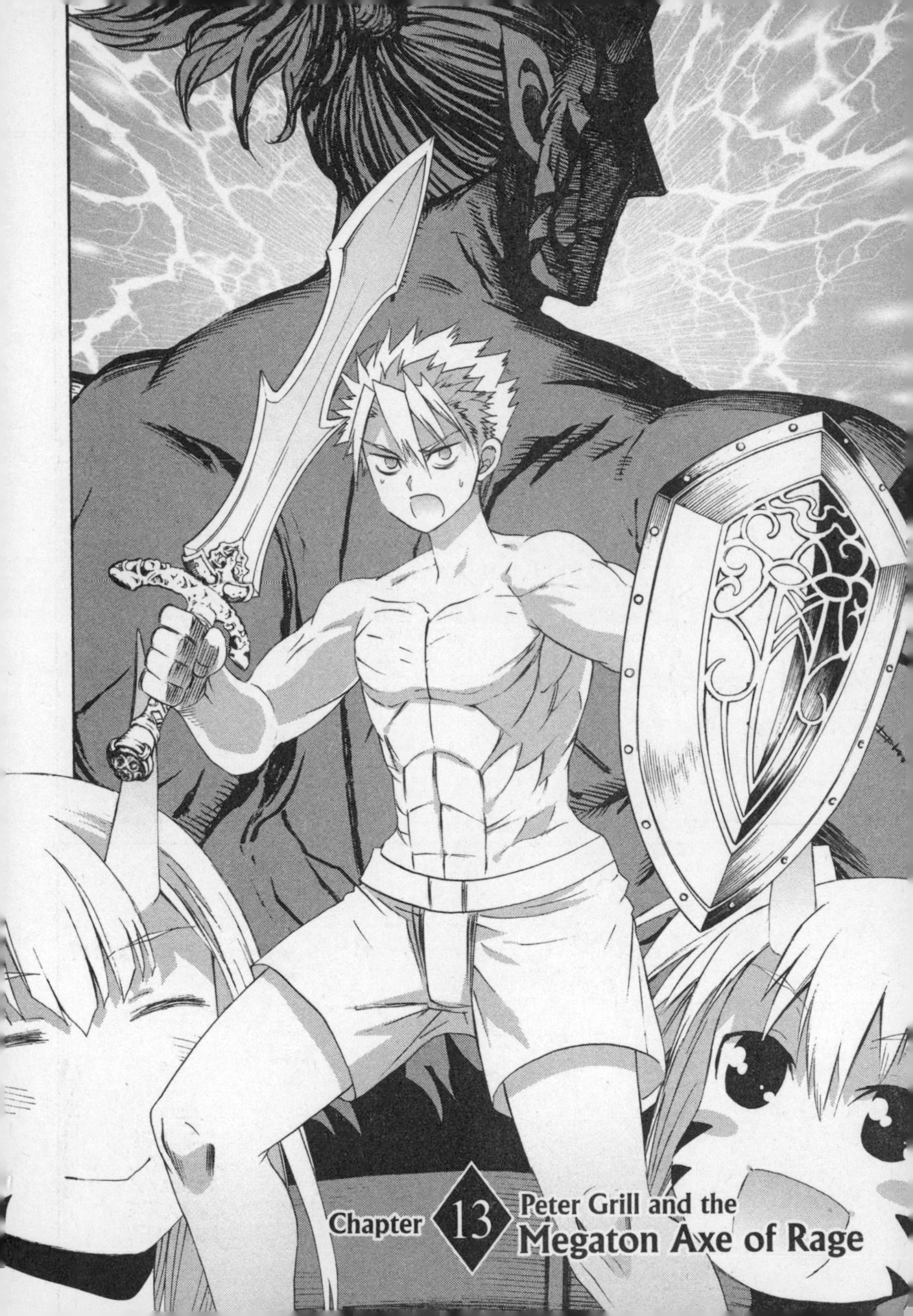
Chapter 13 Peter Grill and the
Megaton Axe of Rage

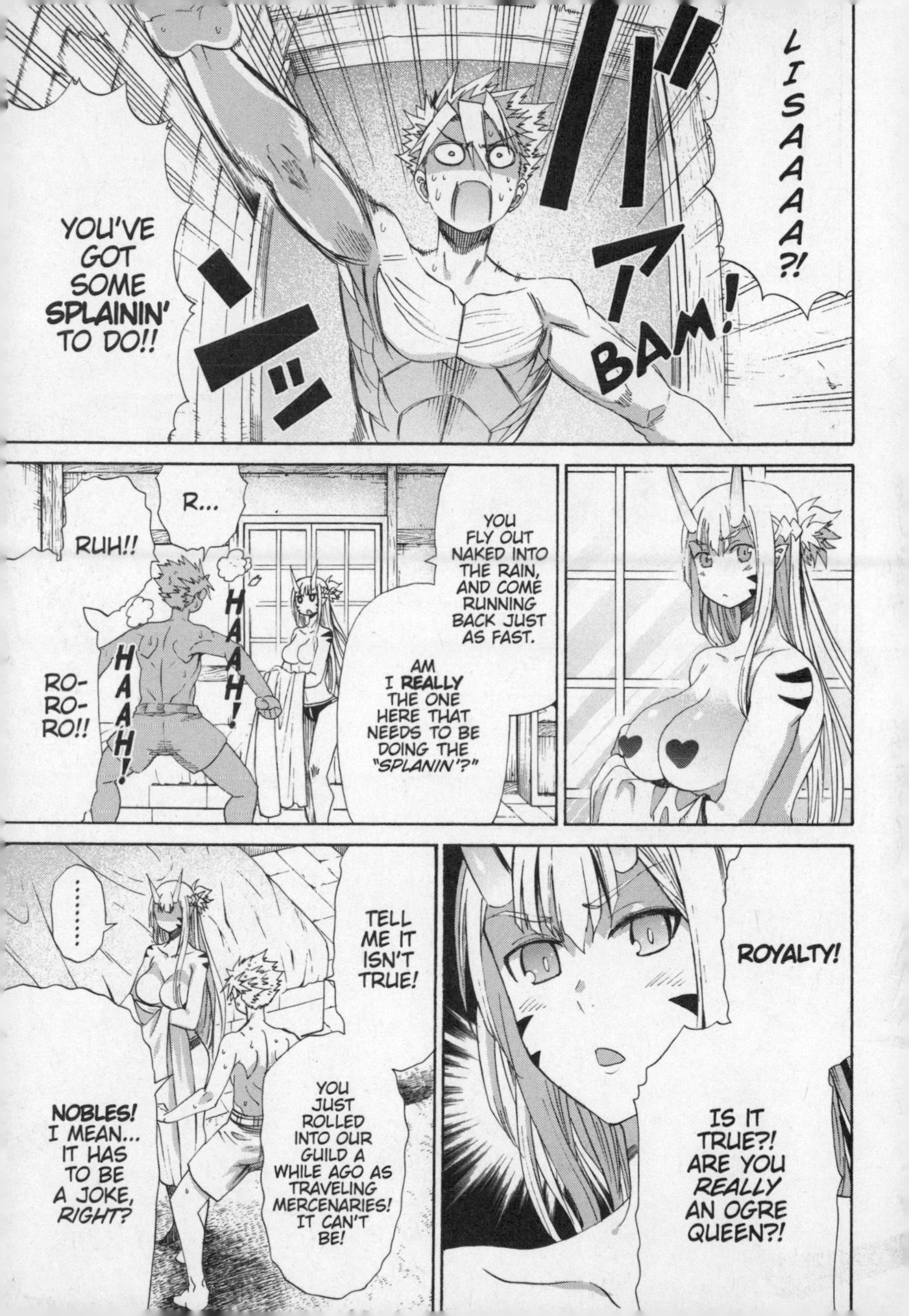
LISAAAAA?!
BAM!
YOU'VE GOT SOME SPLAININ' TO DO!!
YOU FLY OUT NAKED INTO THE RAIN, AND COME RUNNING BACK JUST AS FAST.
AM I REALLY THE ONE HERE THAT NEEDS TO BE DOING THE "SPLANIN'?"
R...
RUH!!
HAAH!
HAAH!
RO-RO-RO!!
ROYALTY!
IS IT TRUE?! ARE YOU REALLY AN OGRE QUEEN?!
TELL ME IT ISN'T TRUE!
YOU JUST ROLLED INTO OUR GUILD A WHILE AGO AS TRAVELING MERCENARIES! IT CAN'T BE!
NOBLES! I MEAN... IT HAS TO BE A JOKE, RIGHT?
......

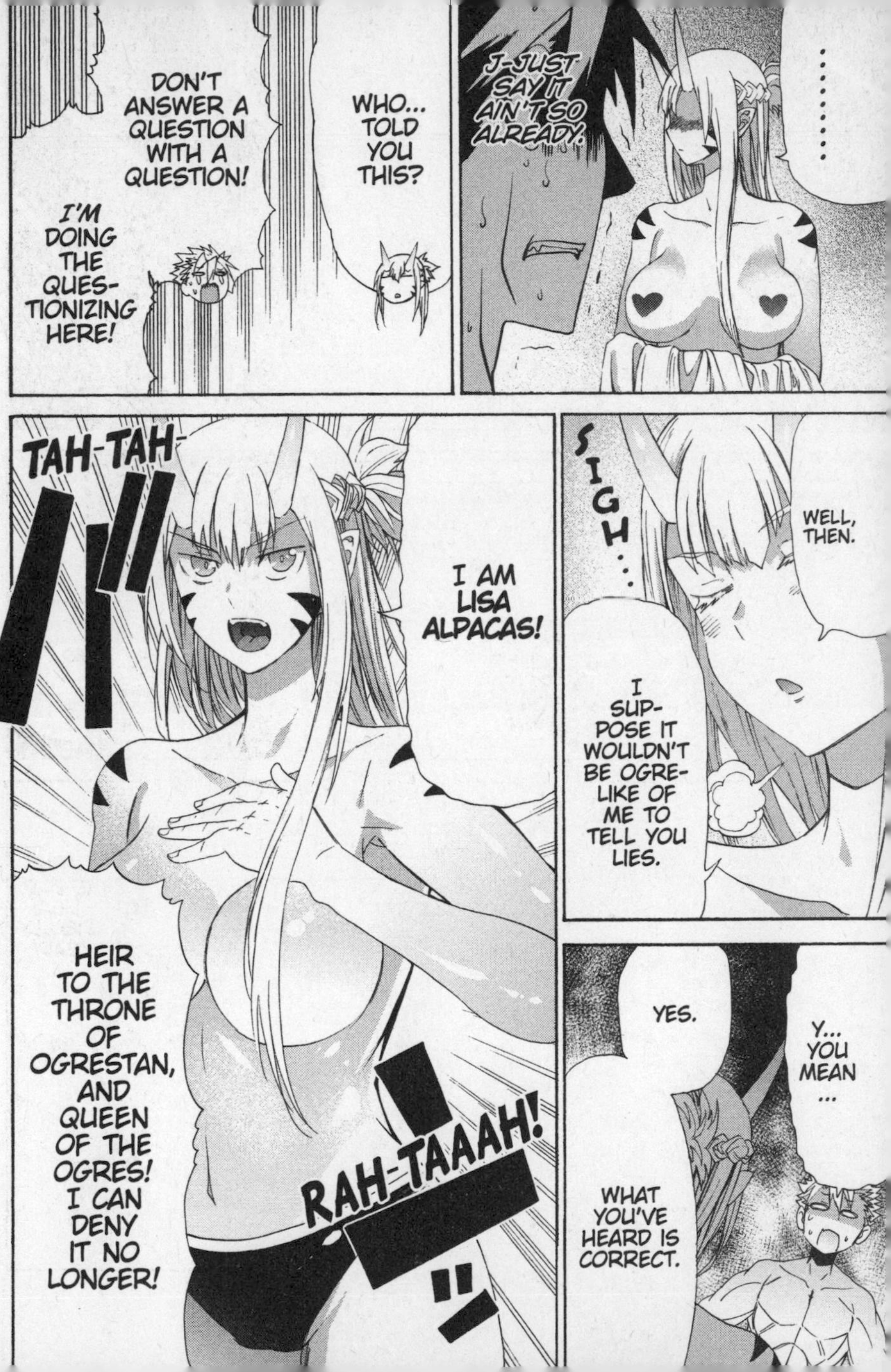

......
J-JUST SAY IT AIN'T SO ALREADY.
WHO... TOLD YOU THIS?
DON'T ANSWER A QUESTION WITH A QUESTION!
I'M DOING THE QUES-TIONIZING HERE!
SIGH...
WELL, THEN.
I SUP-POSE IT WOULDN'T BE OGRE-LIKE OF ME TO TELL YOU LIES.
Y... YOU MEAN ...
YES.
WHAT YOU'VE HEARD IS CORRECT.
TAH-TAH-
I AM LISA ALPACAS!
HEIR TO THE THRONE OF OGRESTAN, AND QUEEN OF THE OGRES! I CAN DENY IT NO LONGER!
RAH-TAAAH!

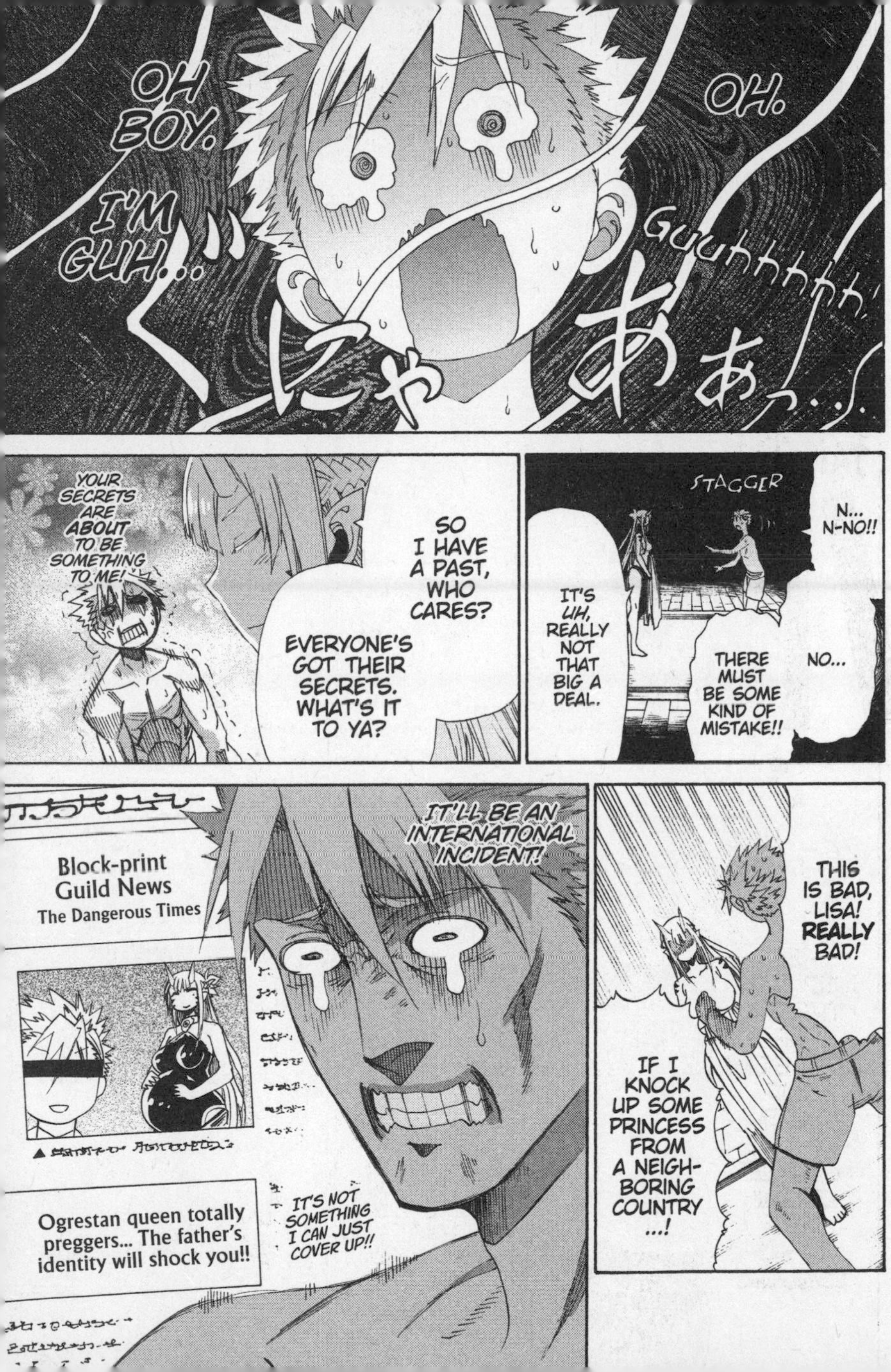
OH.
Guuhhhhhh
OH BOY.
I'M GUH...
にゃあっ…
N... N-NO!!
STAGGER
NO...
THERE MUST BE SOME KIND OF MISTAKE!!
IT'S UH, REALLY NOT THAT BIG A DEAL.
SO I HAVE A PAST, WHO CARES?
EVERYONE'S GOT THEIR SECRETS. WHAT'S IT TO YA?
YOUR SECRETS ARE ABOUT TO BE SOMETHING TO ME!
THIS IS BAD, LISA! REALLY BAD!
IF I KNOCK UP SOME PRINCESS FROM A NEIGH-BORING COUNTRY ...!
IT'LL BE AN INTERNATIONAL INCIDENT!
Block-print Guild News
The Dangerous Times
IT'S NOT SOMETHING I CAN JUST COVER UP!!
Ogrestan queen totally preggers... The father's identity will shock you!!

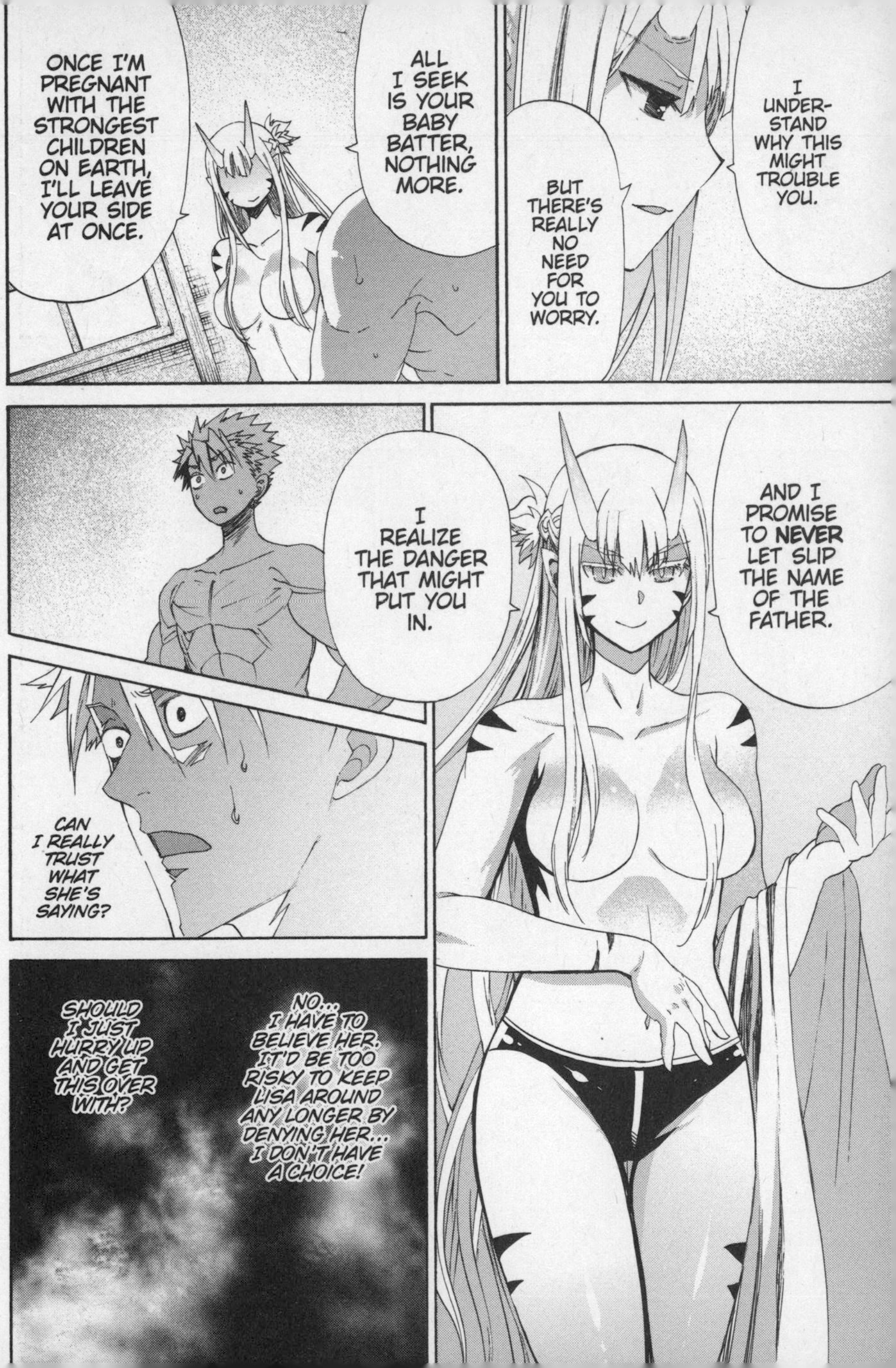
I UNDERSTAND WHY THIS MIGHT TROUBLE YOU.
BUT THERE'S REALLY NO NEED FOR YOU TO WORRY.
ALL I SEEK IS YOUR BABY BATTER, NOTHING MORE.
ONCE I'M PREGNANT WITH THE STRONGEST CHILDREN ON EARTH, I'LL LEAVE YOUR SIDE AT ONCE.
I REALIZE THE DANGER THAT MIGHT PUT YOU IN.
AND I PROMISE TO NEVER LET SLIP THE NAME OF THE FATHER.
CAN I REALLY TRUST WHAT SHE'S SAYING?
SHOULD I JUST HURRY UP AND GET THIS OVER WITH?
NO... I HAVE TO BELIEVE HER. IT'D BE TOO RISKY TO KEEP LISA AROUND ANY LONGER BY DENYING HER... I DON'T HAVE A CHOICE!

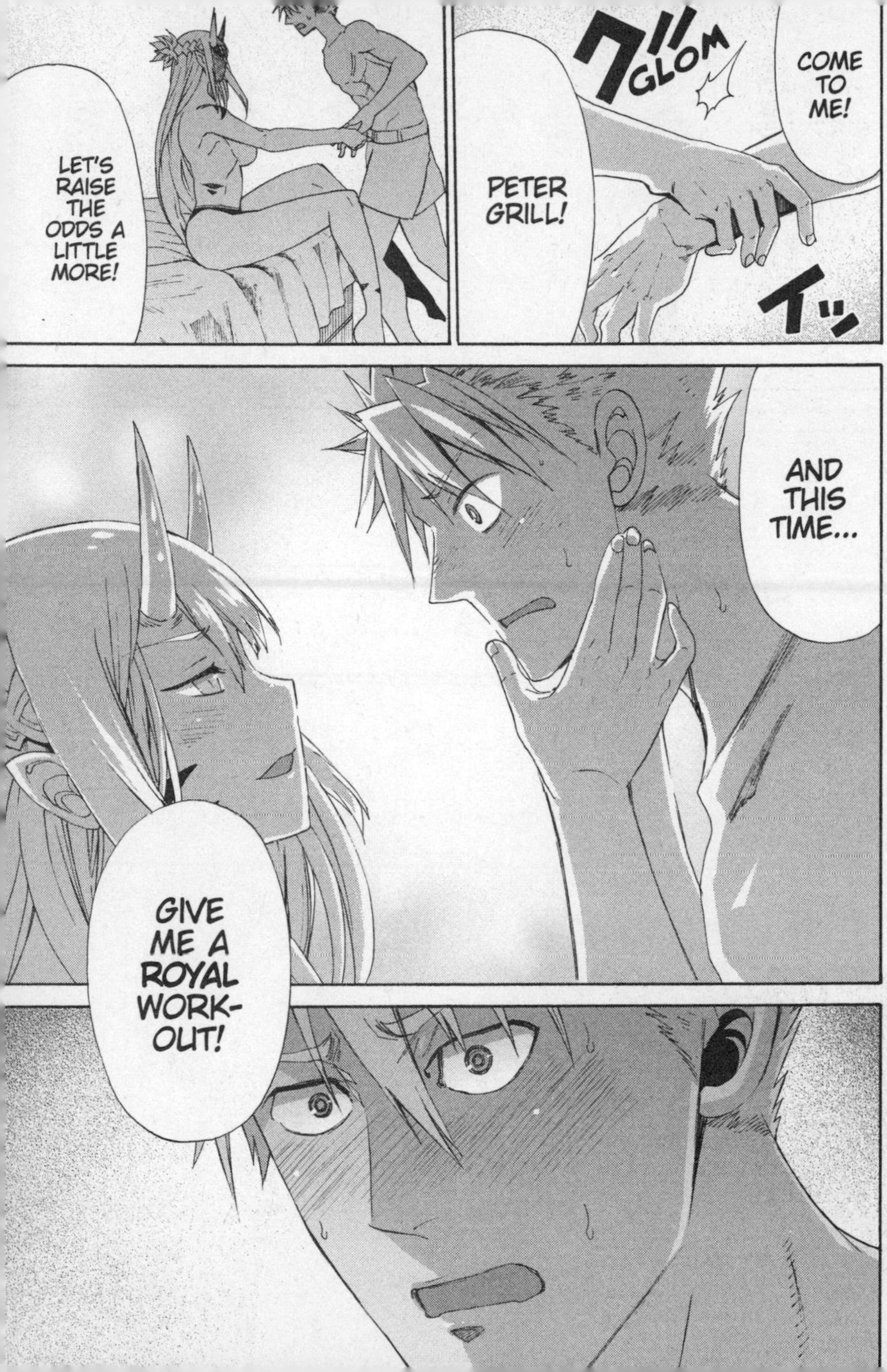
COME TO ME!
PETER GRILL!
クッ GLOM
イッ
LET'S RAISE THE ODDS A LITTLE MORE!
AND THIS TIME...
GIVE ME A ROYAL WORK-OUT!

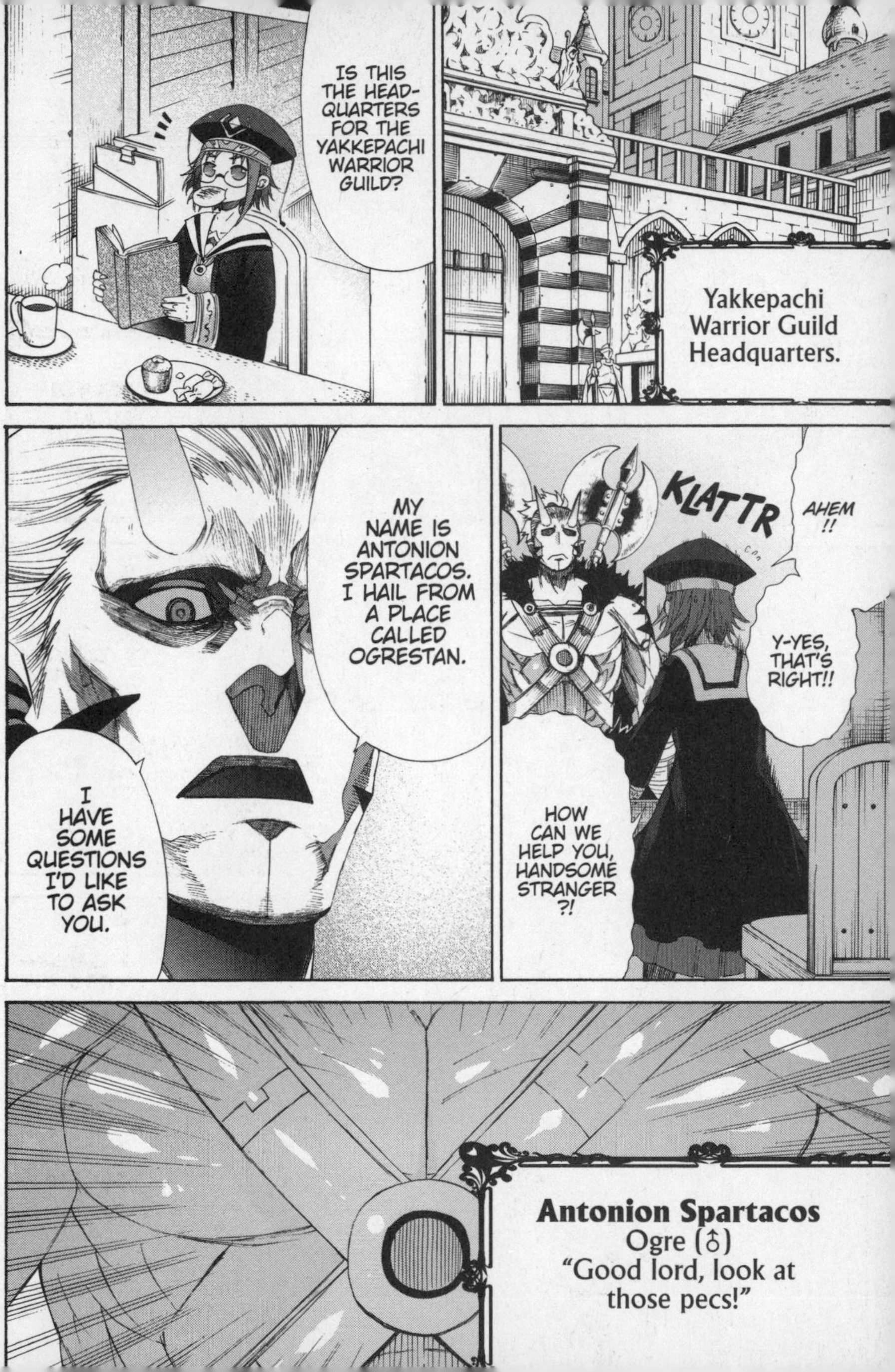
Yakkepachi Warrior Guild Headquarters.
IS THIS THE HEAD-QUARTERS FOR THE YAKKEPACHI WARRIOR GUILD?
KLATTR
AHEM!!
Y-YES, THAT'S RIGHT!!
HOW CAN WE HELP YOU, HANDSOME STRANGER?!
MY NAME IS ANTONION SPARTACOS. I HAIL FROM A PLACE CALLED OGRESTAN.
I HAVE SOME QUESTIONS I'D LIKE TO ASK YOU.
Antonion Spartacos
Ogre (♂)
“Good lord, look at those pecs!”

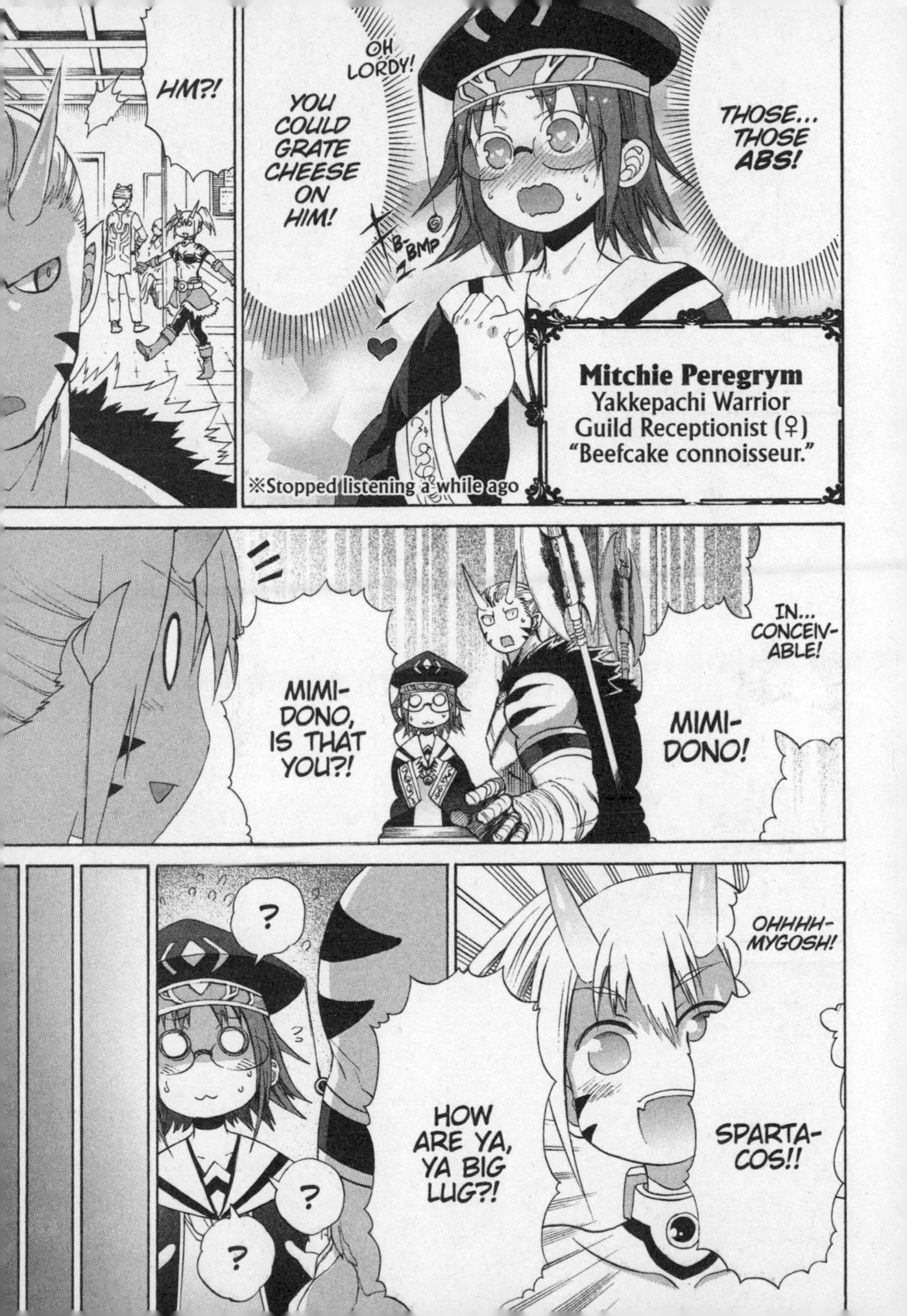
THOSE... THOSE ABS!
OH LORDY!
YOU COULD GRATE CHEESE ON HIM!
B-BMP
Mitchie Peregrym
Yakkepachi Warrior Guild Receptionist (♀)
"Beefcake connoisseur."
※Stopped listening a while ago
HM?!
IN... CONCEIV-ABLE!
MIMI-DONO!
MIMI-DONO, IS THAT YOU?!
OHHHH-MYGOSH!
SPARTA-COS!!
HOW ARE YA, YA BIG LUG?!
?
?
?

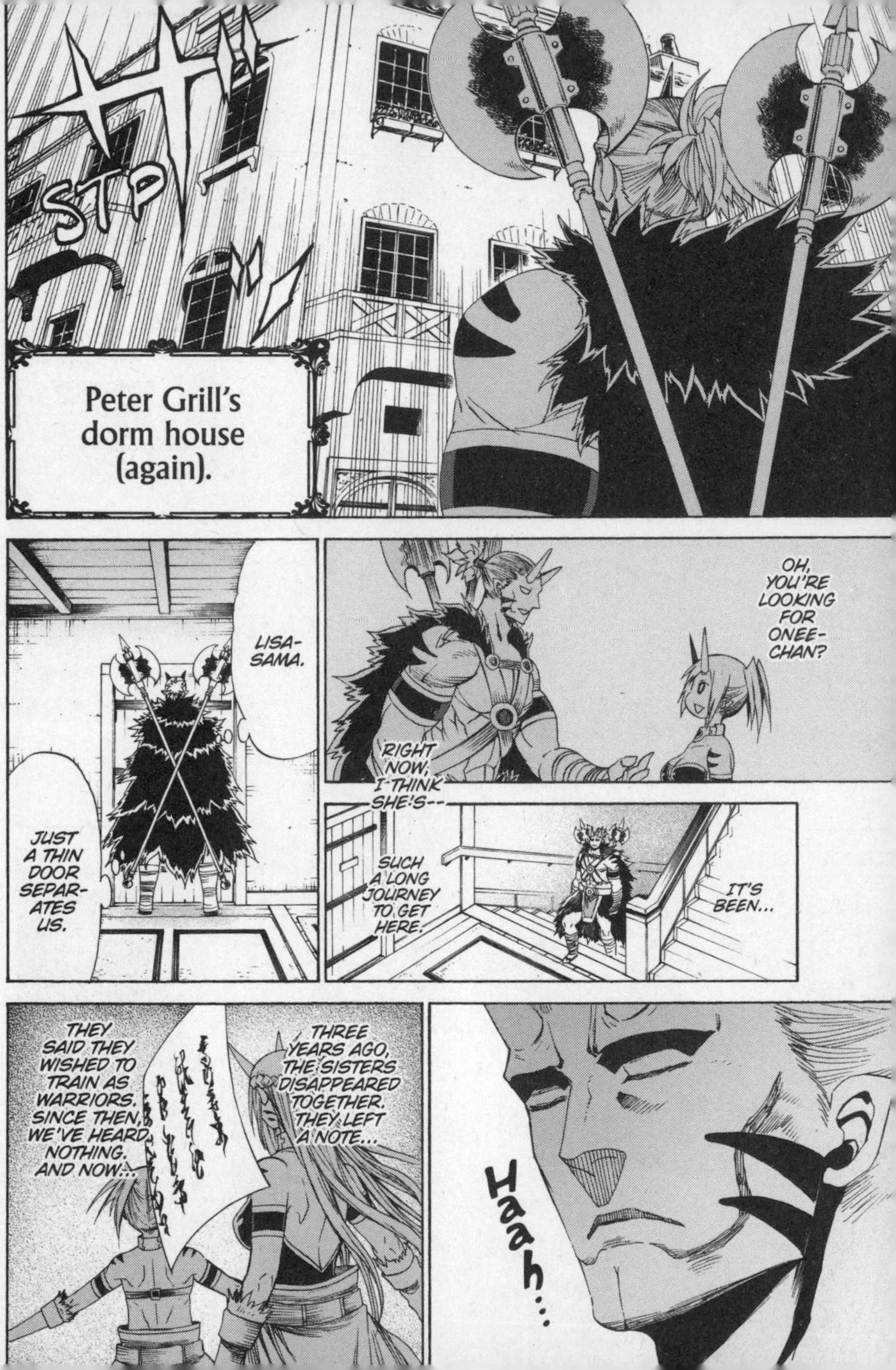
STP
Peter Grill's dorm house (again).
OH, YOU'RE LOOKING FOR ONEE-CHAN?
RIGHT NOW, I THINK SHE'S--
IT'S BEEN...
SUCH A LONG JOURNEY TO GET HERE.
LISA-SAMA.
JUST A THIN DOOR SEPARATES US.
Haah...
THREE YEARS AGO, THE SISTERS DISAPPEARED TOGETHER. THEY LEFT A NOTE...
THEY SAID THEY WISHED TO TRAIN AS WARRIORS. SINCE THEN, WE'VE HEARD NOTHING. AND NOW...

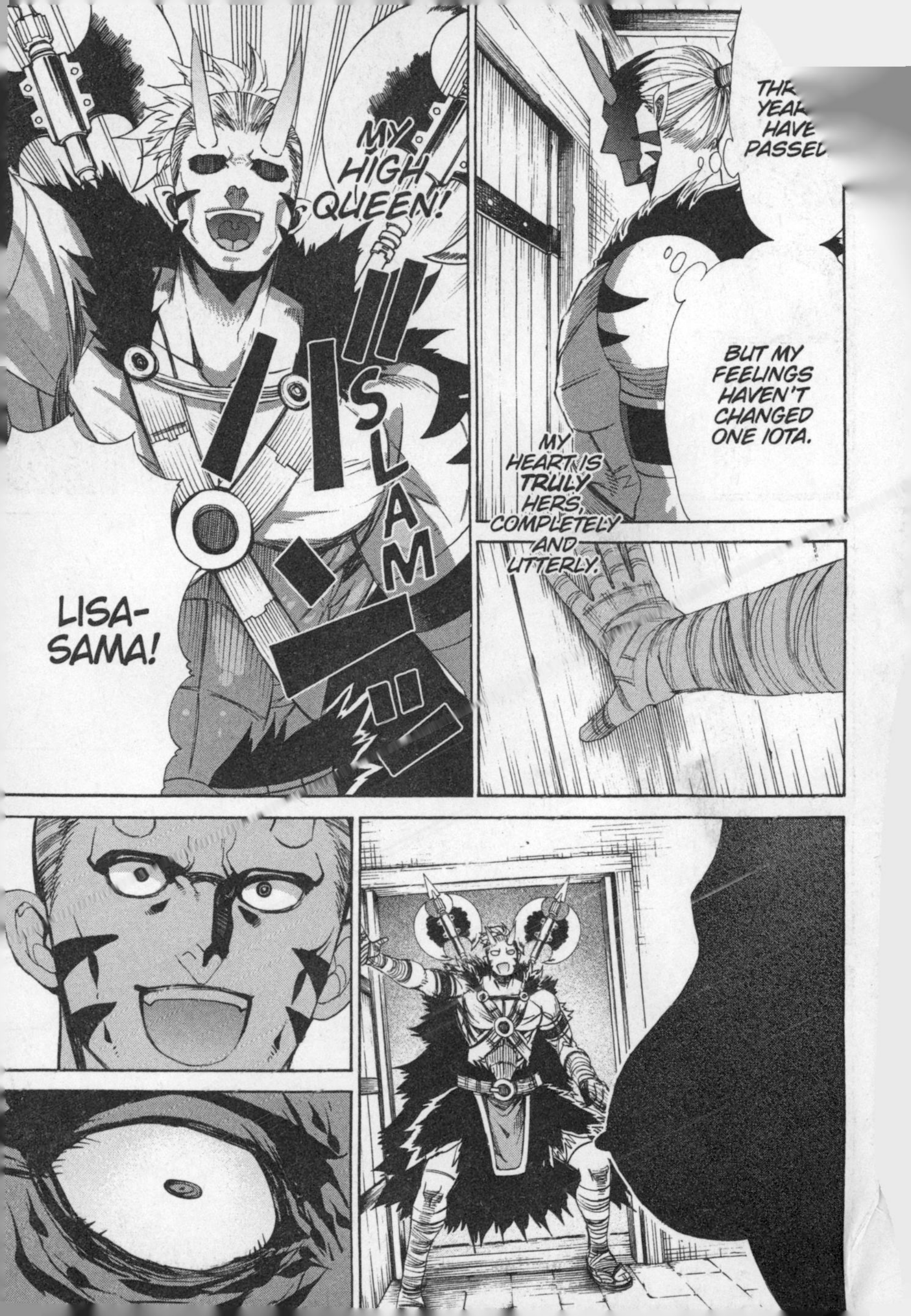
THR
YEAR
HAVE
PASSED
BUT MY FEELINGS HAVEN'T CHANGED ONE IOTA.
MY HEART IS TRULY HERS, COMPLETELY AND UTTERLY.
SLAM
MY HIGH QUEEN!
LISA-SAMA!

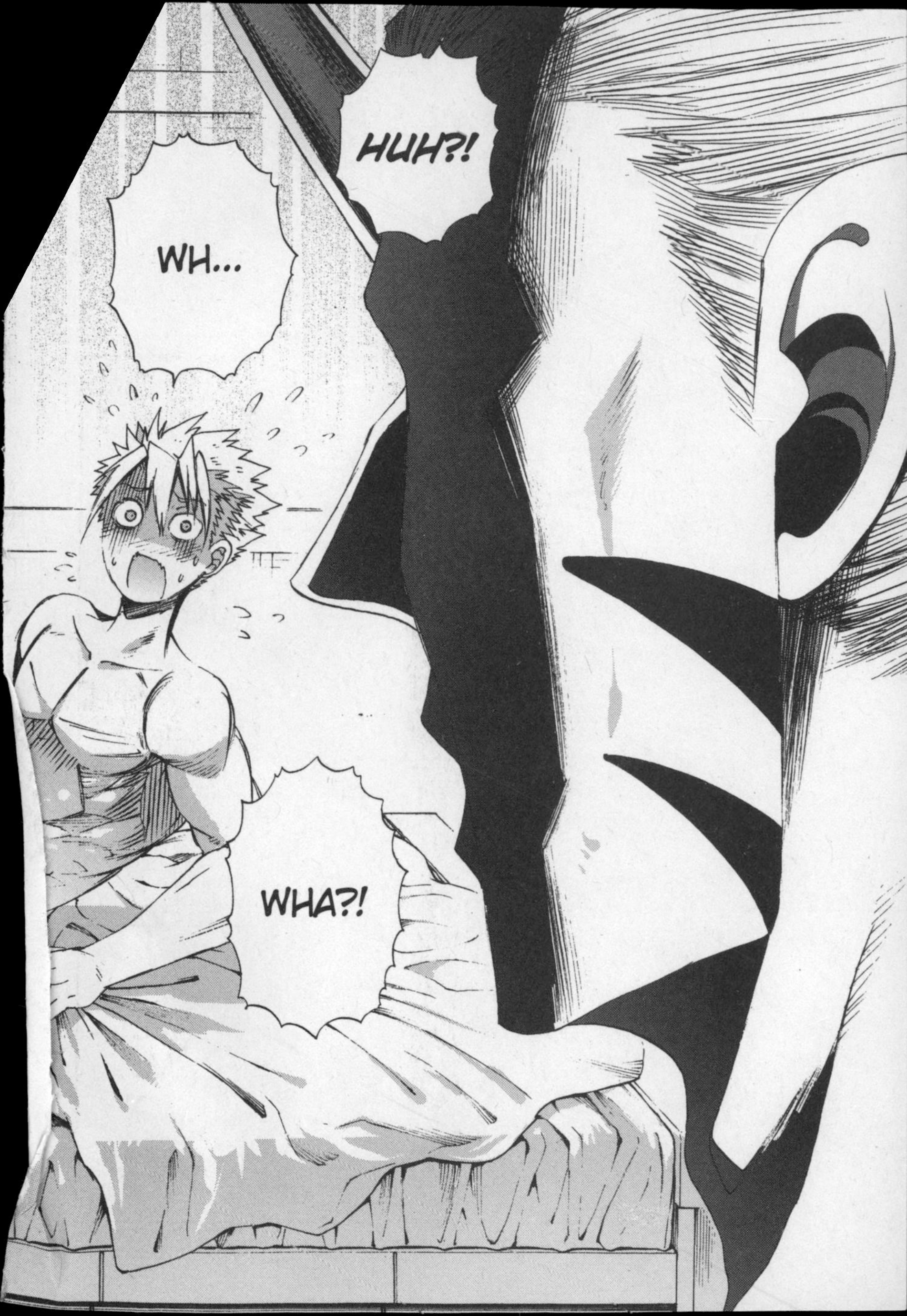
HUH?!
WH...
WHA?!

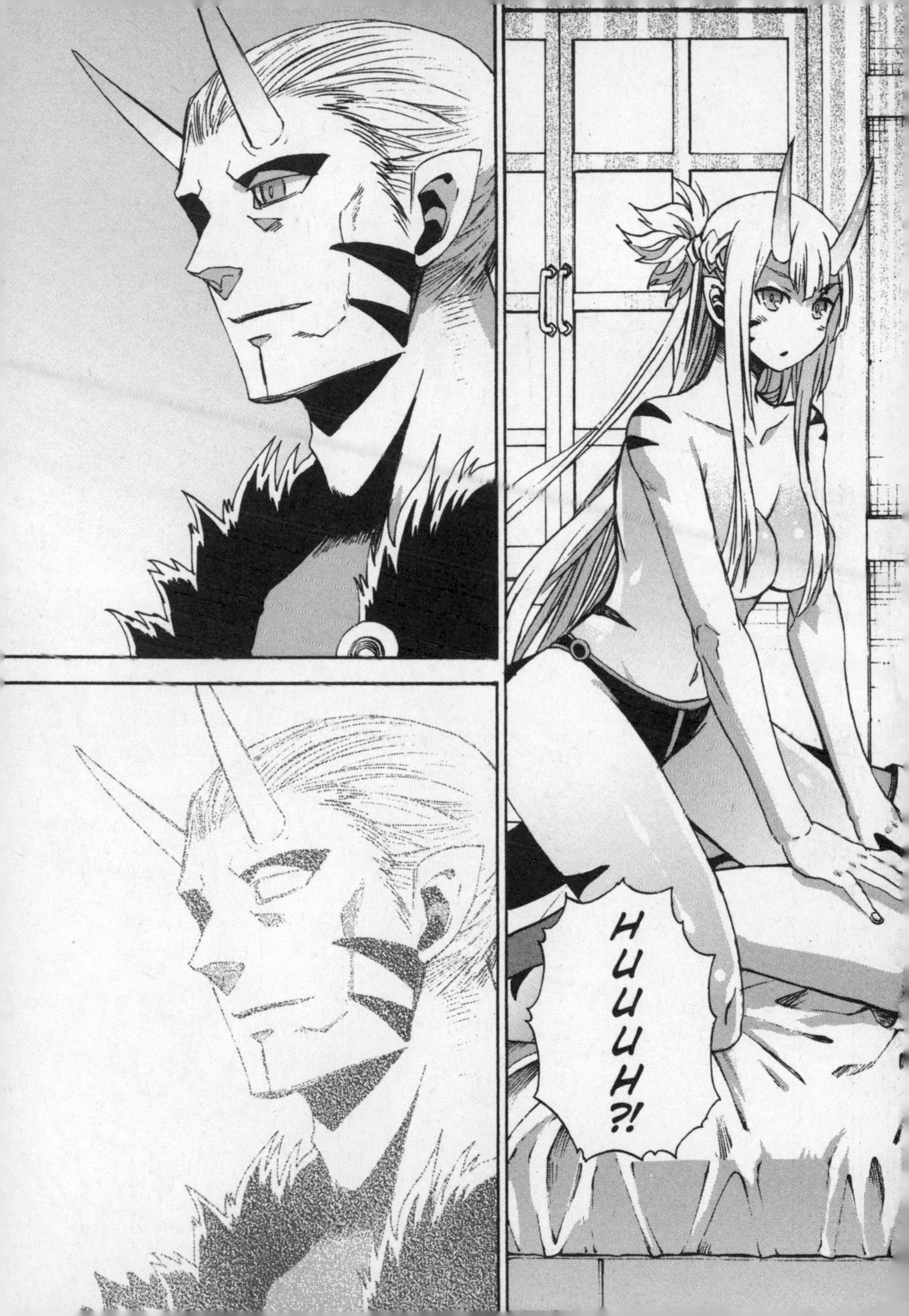
HUUUUH?!

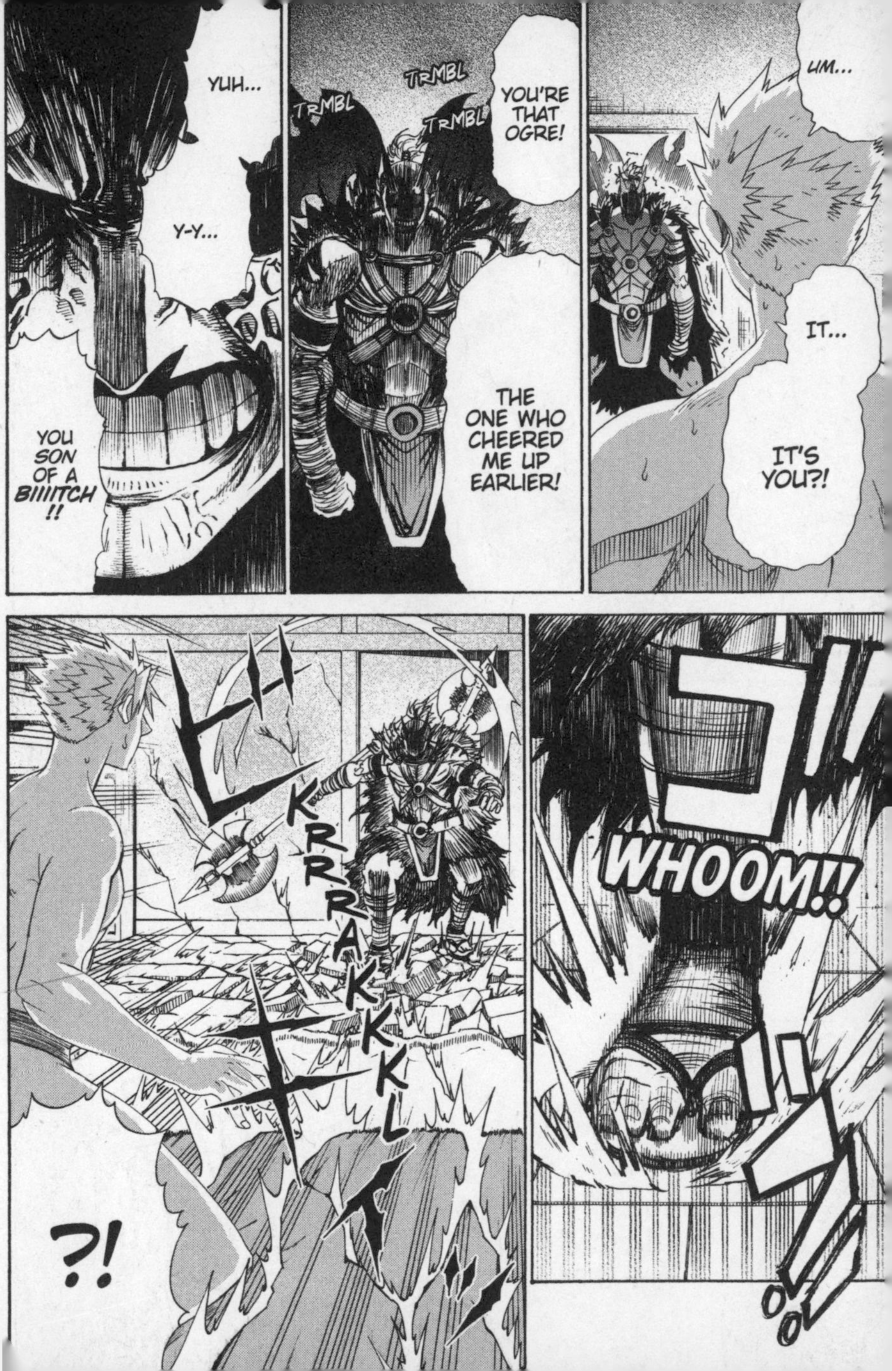
UM...
IT...
IT'S YOU?!
TRMBL
TRMBL
TRMBL
YOU'RE THAT OGRE!
THE ONE WHO CHEERED ME UP EARLIER!
YUH...
Y-Y...
YOU SON OF A BIIIITCH !!
WHOOM!!
KRRRAKKKL
?!

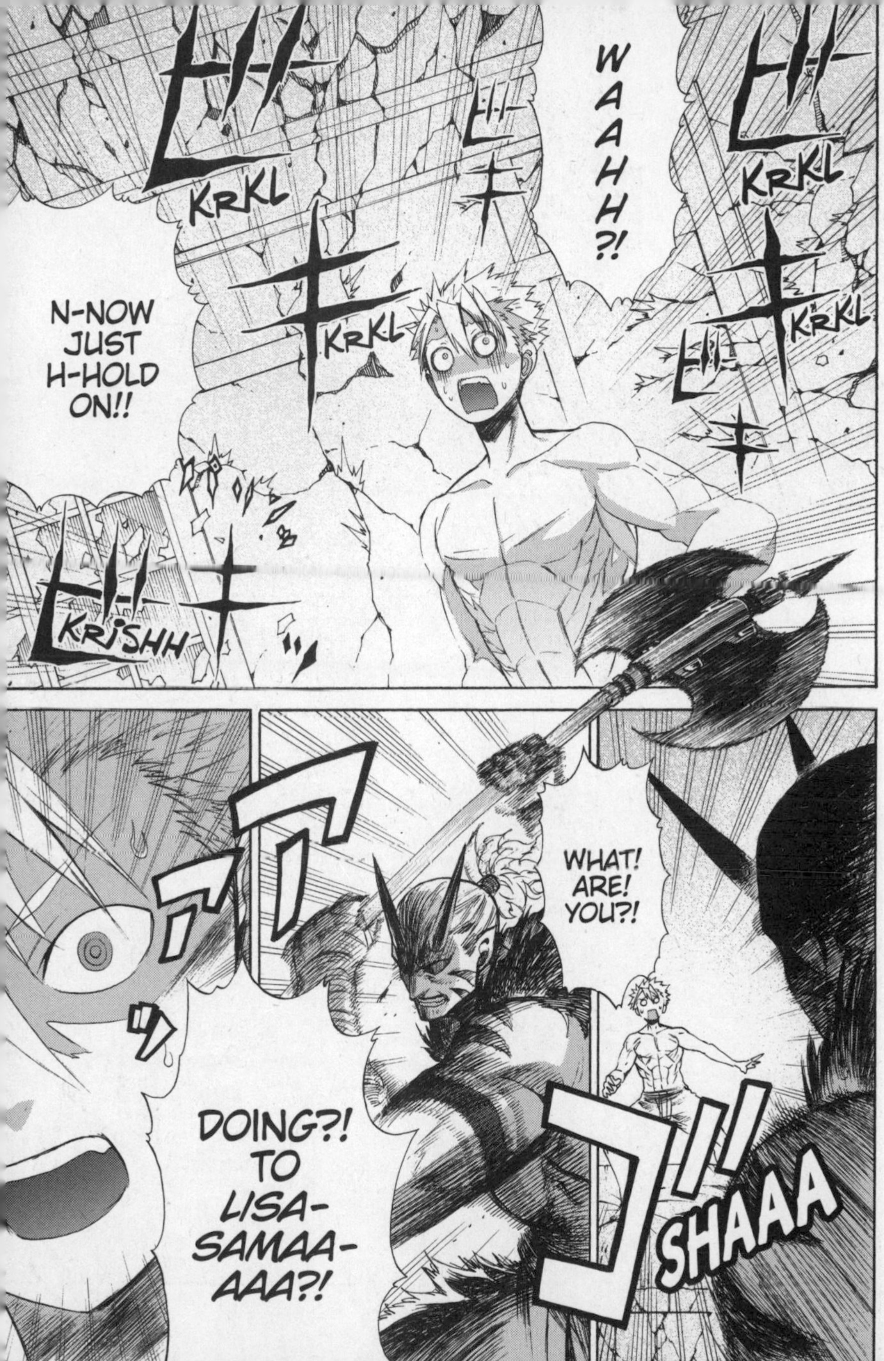
WAAAHH?!
KRKL
KRKL
KRKL
KRKL
N-NOW JUST H-HOLD ON!!
KRISHH
WHAT! ARE! YOU?!
SHAAA
DOING?! TO LISA-SAMAAA-AAA?!

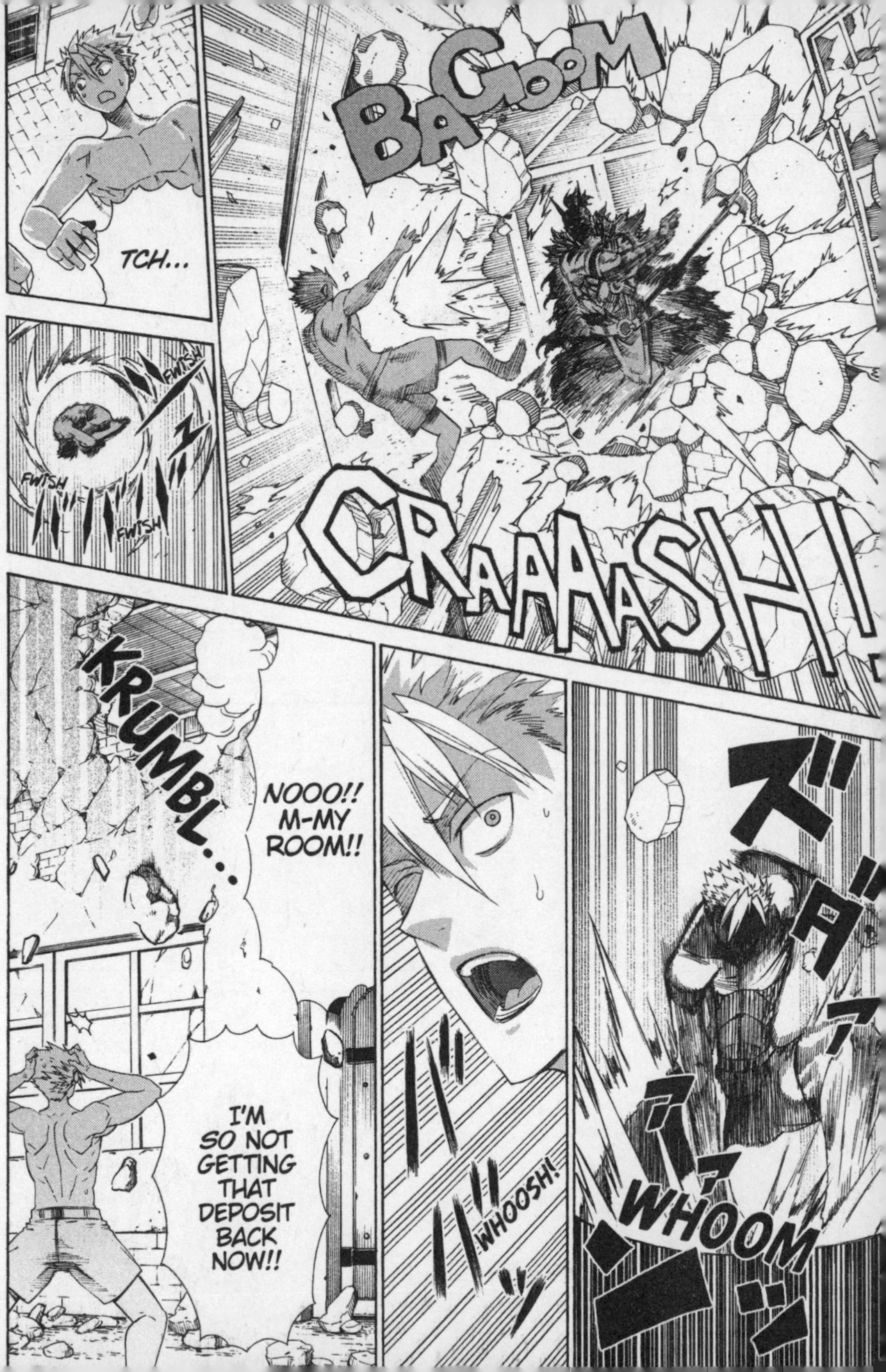
BAGOOM
CRAAASH!!
TCH...
FWISH
FWISH
FWISH
ズダ
WHOOM
WHOOSH!
KRUMBL...
NOOO!! M-MY ROOM!!
I'M SO NOT GETTING THAT DEPOSIT BACK NOW!!

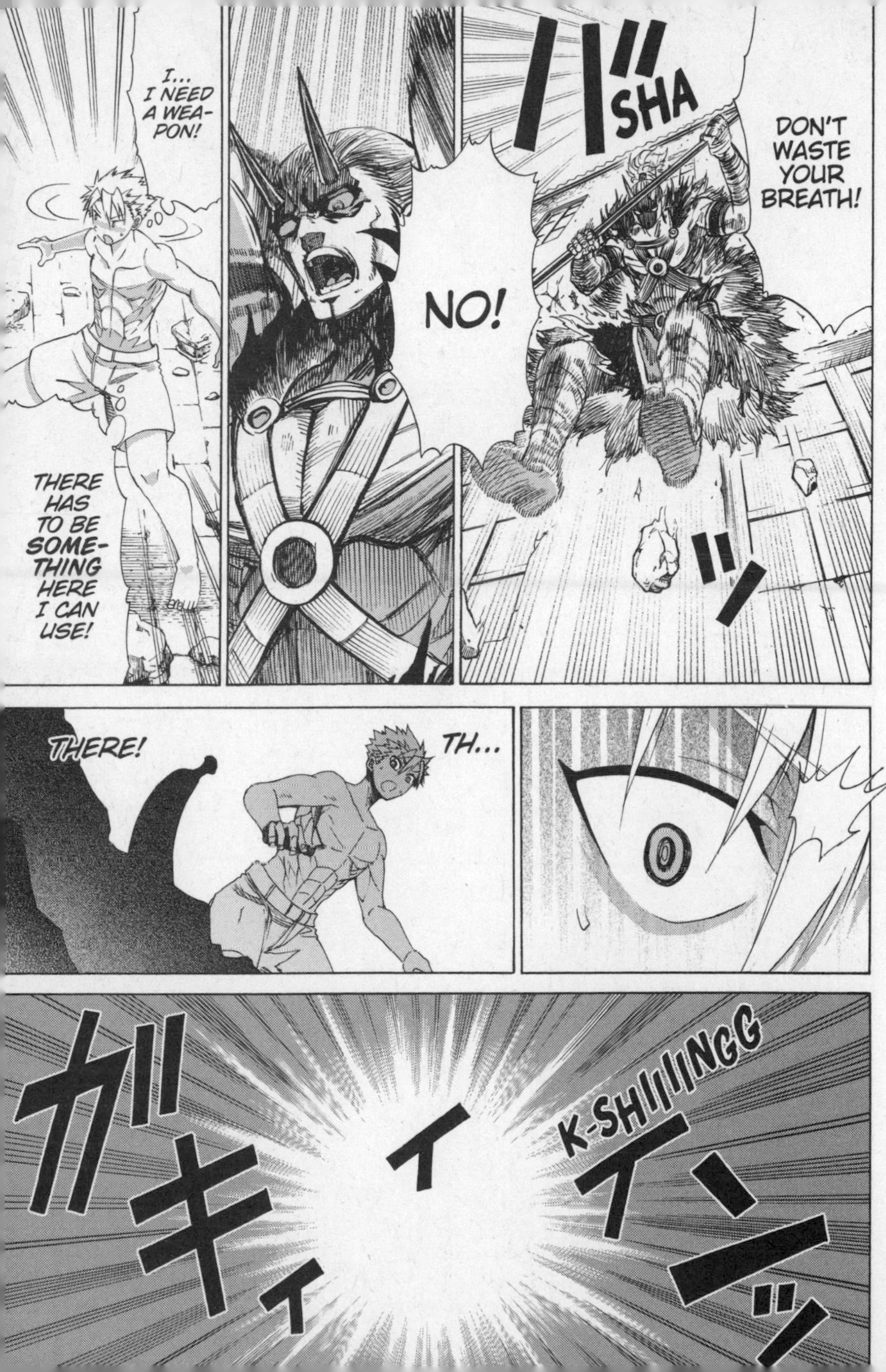
バッ
SHA
DON'T WASTE YOUR BREATH!
NO!
I... I NEED A WEAPON!
THERE HAS TO BE SOMETHING HERE I CAN USE!
TH...
THERE!
K-SHIIIINGG
ガキィイインッ

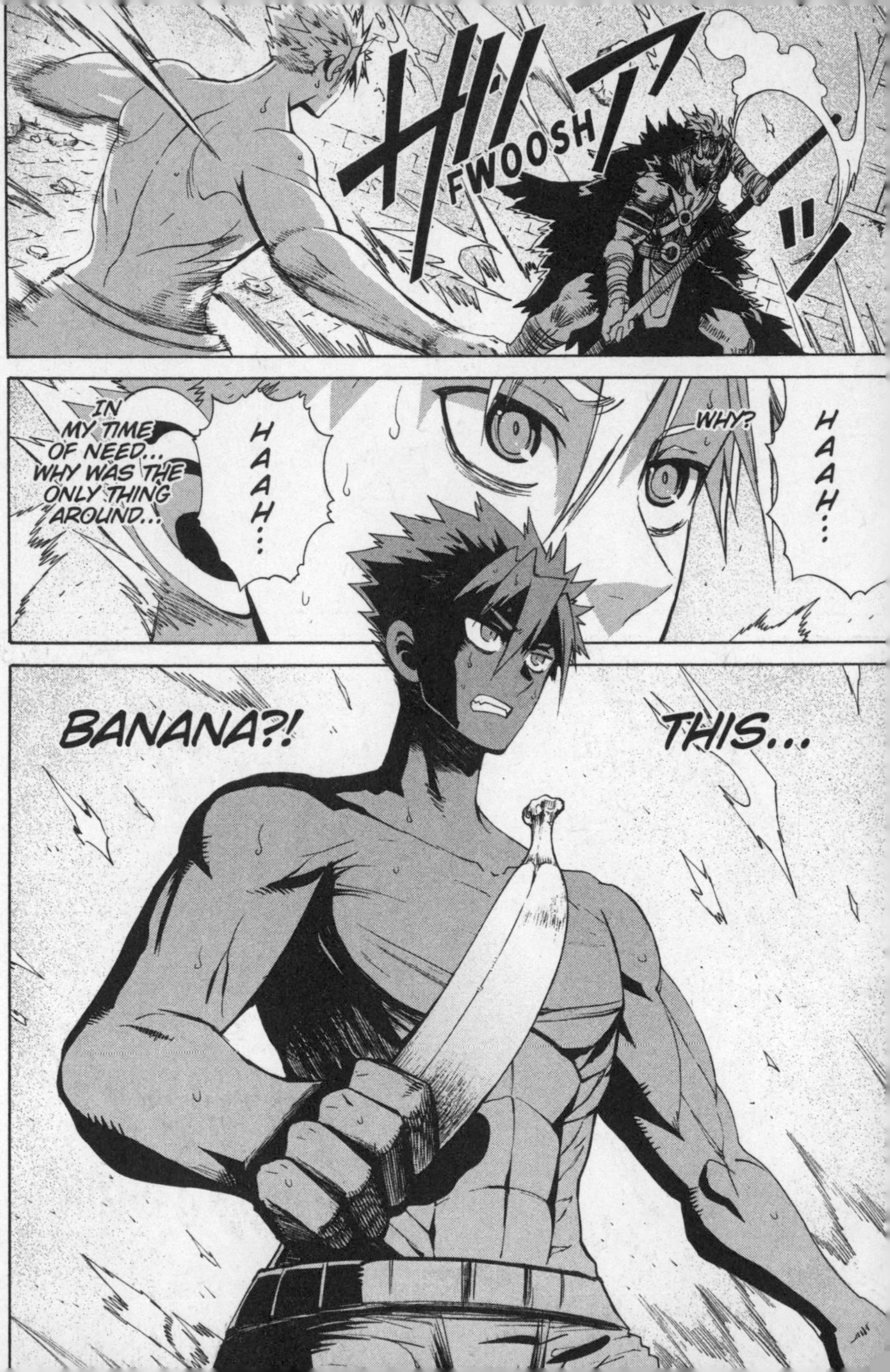
FWOOSH
HAAAH...
WHY?
HAAAH...
IN MY TIME OF NEED... WHY WAS THE ONLY THING AROUND...
THIS...
BANANA?!

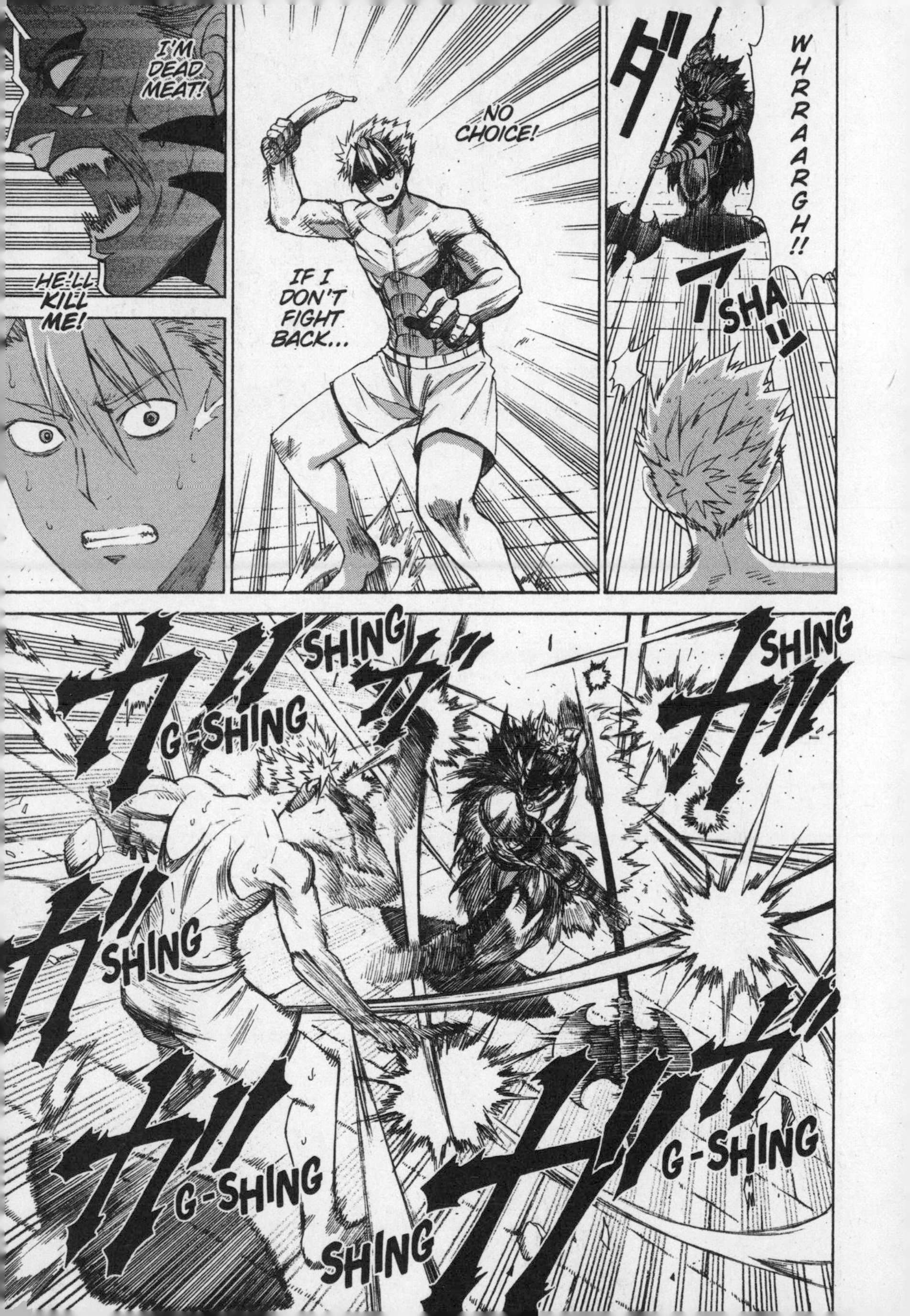
WHRRAARGH!!
SHA
NO CHOICE!
IF I DON'T FIGHT BACK...
I'M DEAD MEAT!
HE'LL KILL ME!
SHING
SHING
G-SHING
SHING
G-SHING
G-SHING
SHING

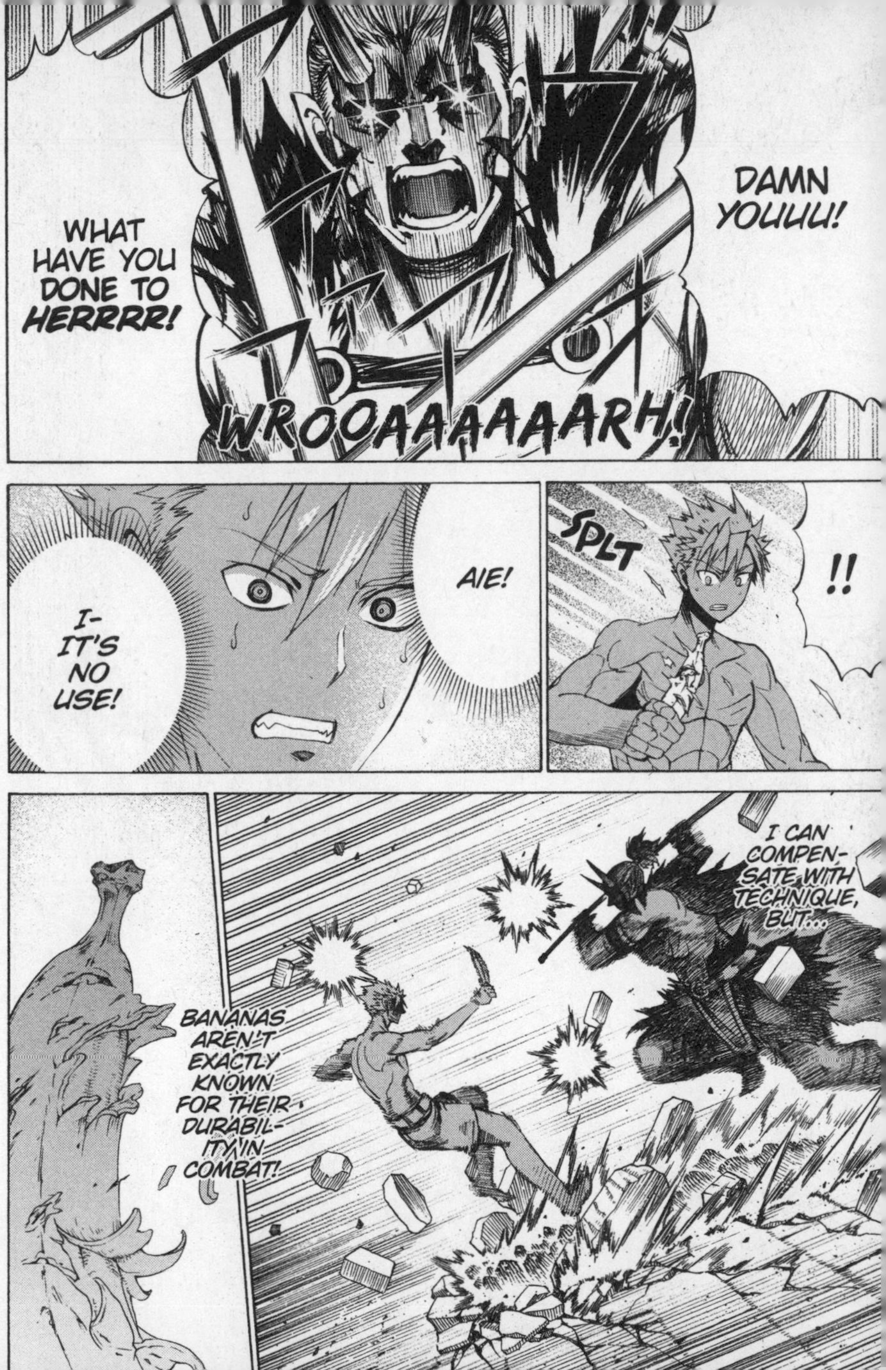
DAMN YOUUUU!
WHAT HAVE YOU DONE TO HERRRR!
WROOAAAAAAARH!
!!
SPLT
AIE!
I- IT'S NO USE!
I CAN COMPEN-SATE WITH TECHNIQUE, BUT...
BANANAS AREN'T EXACTLY KNOWN FOR THEIR DURABIL-ITY IN COMBAT!

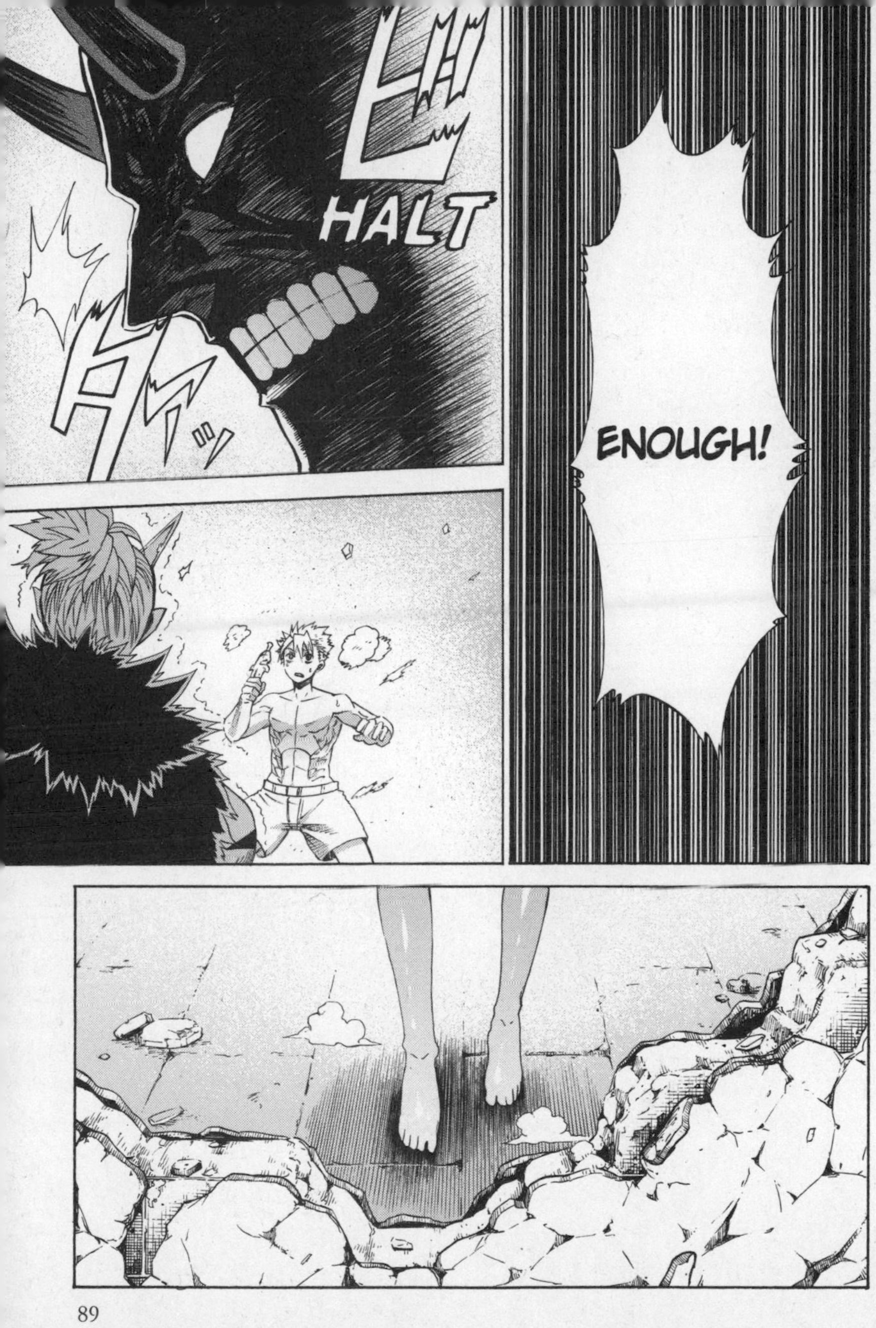
ENOUGH!
HALT

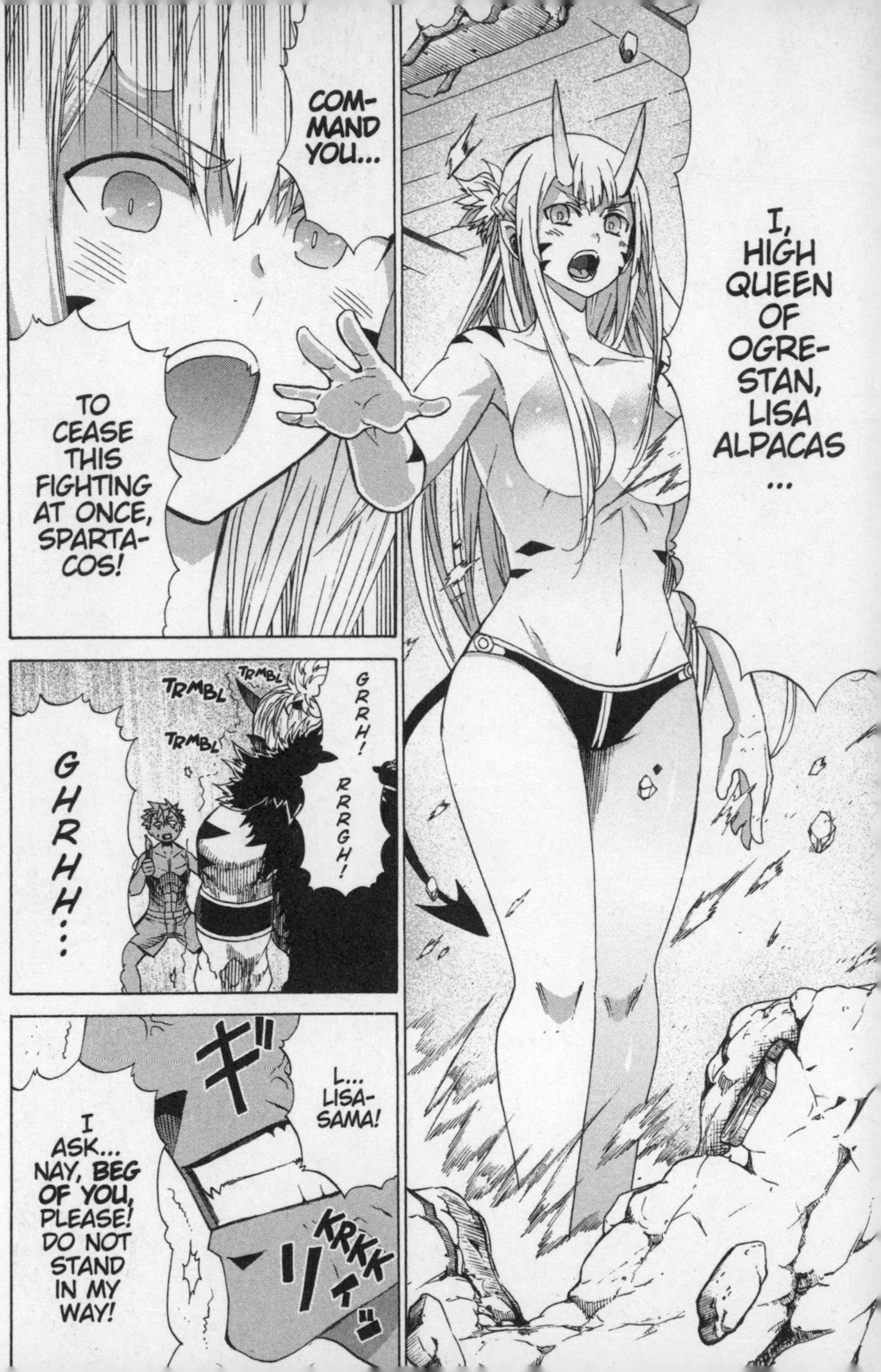

I, HIGH QUEEN OF OGRE-STAN, LISA ALPACAS ...
COM-MAND YOU...
TO CEASE THIS FIGHTING AT ONCE, SPARTA-COS!
TRMBL
TRMBL
GRRH!
RRRGH!
TRMBL
GHRHH...
L... LISA-SAMA!
ギ
I ASK... NAY, BEG OF YOU, PLEASE! DO NOT STAND IN MY WAY!
KRKK
リィ

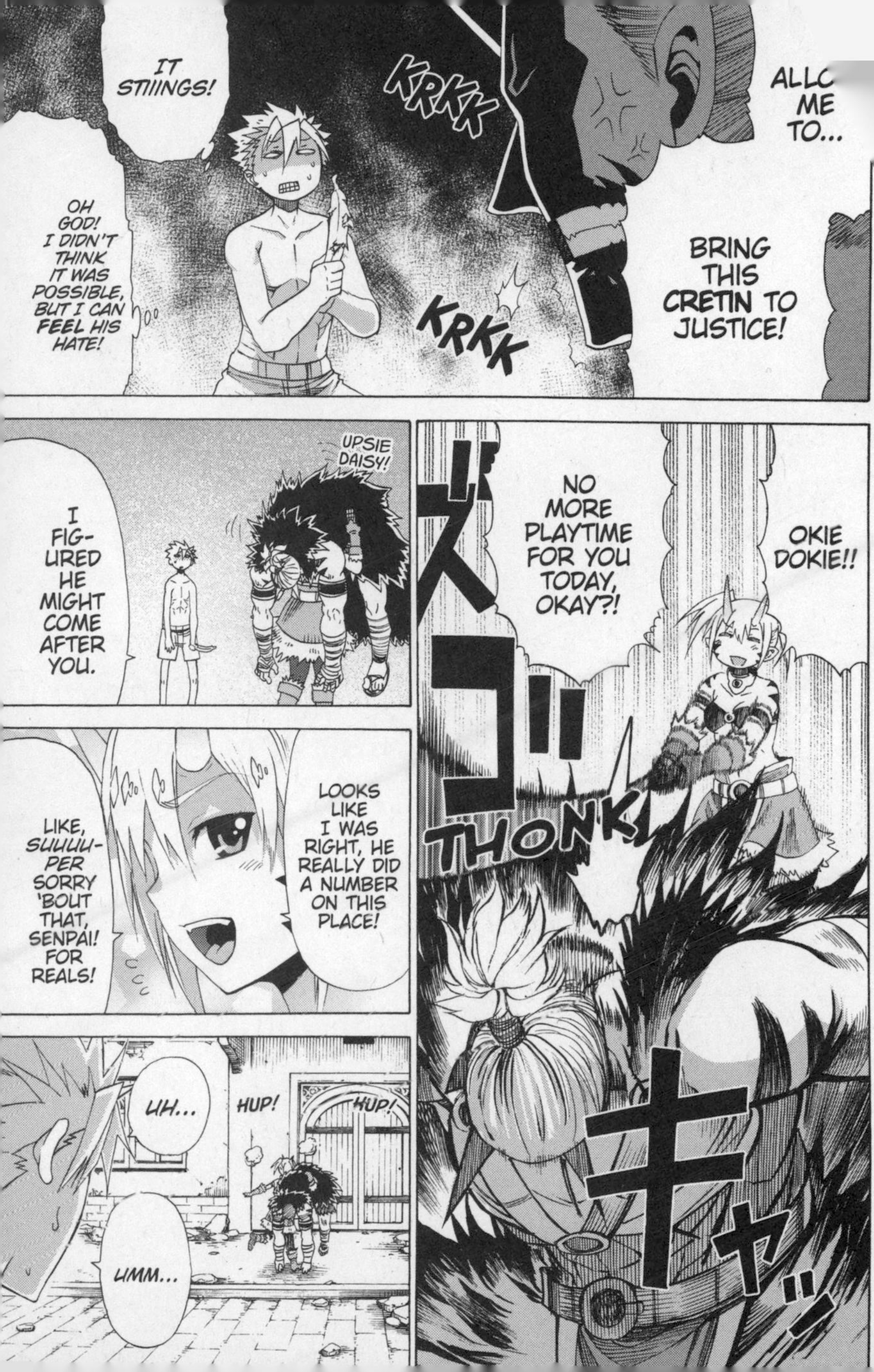
ALLOW ME TO...
BRING THIS CRETIN TO JUSTICE!
KRKK
KRKK
IT STIIINGS!
OH GOD! I DIDN'T THINK IT WAS POSSIBLE, BUT I CAN FEEL HIS HATE!
NO MORE PLAYTIME FOR YOU TODAY, OKAY?!
OKIE DOKIE!!
ズゴ
THONK
キャ
UPSIE DAISY!
I FIG-URED HE MIGHT COME AFTER YOU.
LOOKS LIKE I WAS RIGHT, HE REALLY DID A NUMBER ON THIS PLACE!
LIKE, SUUUU-PER SORRY 'BOUT THAT, SENPAI! FOR REALS!
HUP!
HUP!
UH...
UMM...

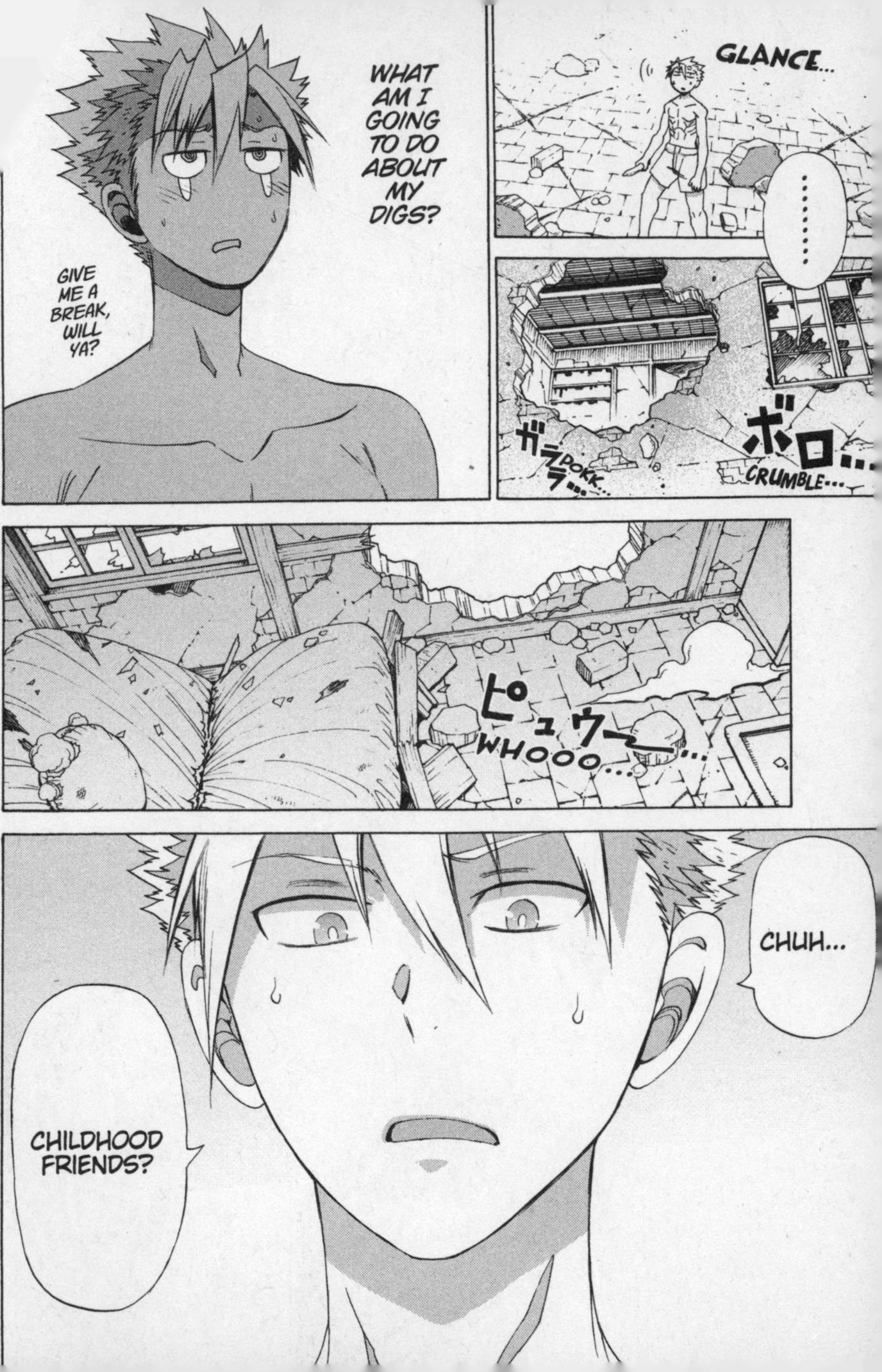
GLANCE...
....
ボロ...
CRUMBLE...
ガラガラ...
POKK...
WHAT AM I GOING TO DO ABOUT MY DIGS?
GIVE ME A BREAK, WILL YA?
ピュウ～…
WHOOO...
CHUH...
CHILDHOOD FRIENDS?

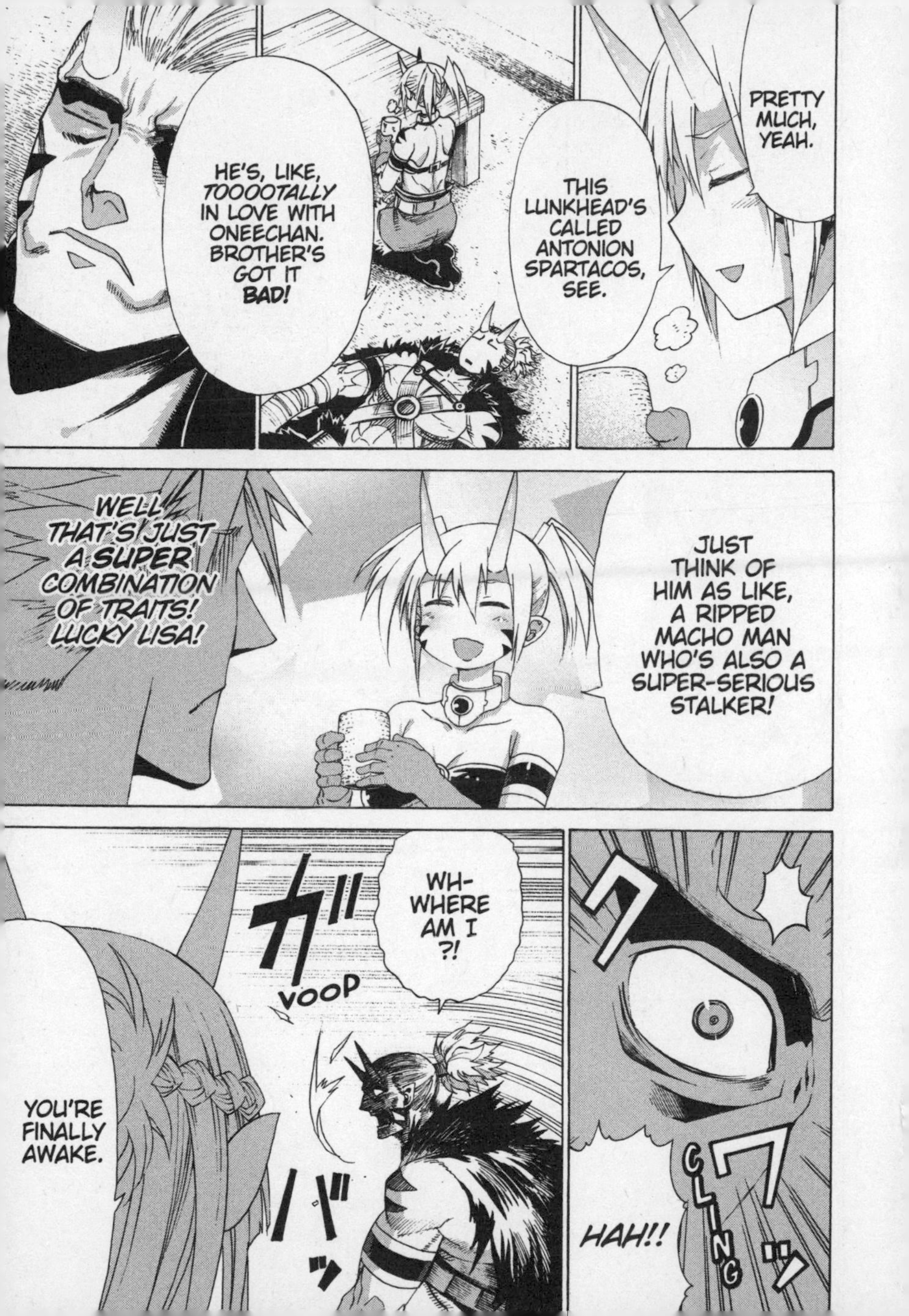
PRETTY MUCH, YEAH.
THIS LUNKHEAD'S CALLED ANTONION SPARTACOS, SEE.
HE'S, LIKE, *TOOOOTALLY* IN LOVE WITH ONEECHAN. BROTHER'S GOT IT BAD!
JUST THINK OF HIM AS LIKE, A RIPPED MACHO MAN WHO'S ALSO A SUPER-SERIOUS STALKER!
WELL THAT'S JUST A SUPER COMBINATION OF TRAITS! LUCKY LISA!
HAH!!
CLING
WH-WHERE AM I ?!
VOOP
YOU'RE FINALLY AWAKE.

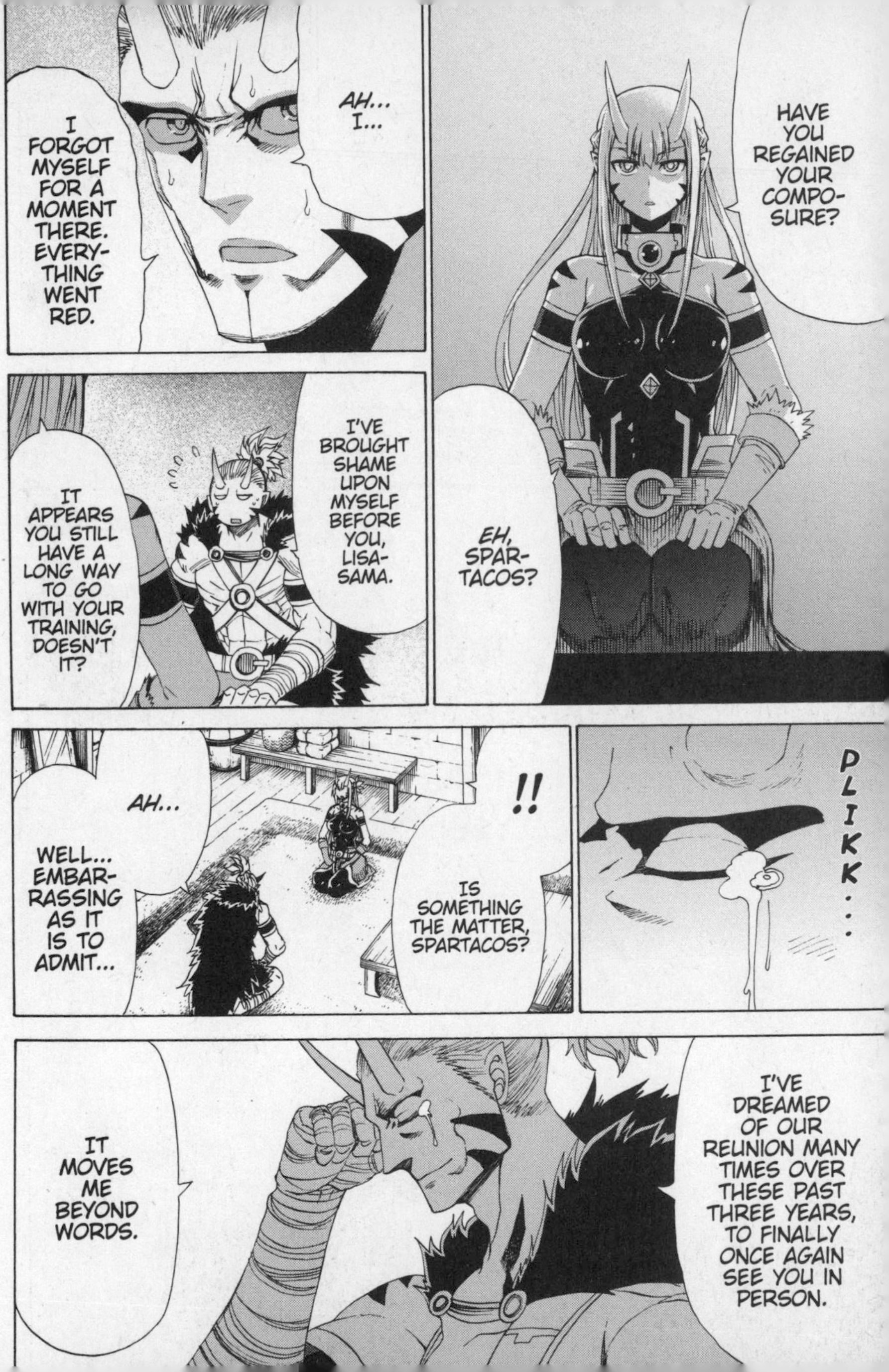
HAVE YOU REGAINED YOUR COMPO-SURE?
EH, SPAR-TACOS?
AH... I...
I FORGOT MYSELF FOR A MOMENT THERE. EVERY-THING WENT RED.
I'VE BROUGHT SHAME UPON MYSELF BEFORE YOU, LISA-SAMA.
IT APPEARS YOU STILL HAVE A LONG WAY TO GO WITH YOUR TRAINING, DOESN'T IT?
PLIKK...
!!
IS SOMETHING THE MATTER, SPARTACOS?
AH...
WELL... EMBAR-RASSING AS IT IS TO ADMIT...
I'VE DREAMED OF OUR REUNION MANY TIMES OVER THESE PAST THREE YEARS, TO FINALLY ONCE AGAIN SEE YOU IN PERSON.
IT MOVES ME BEYOND WORDS.

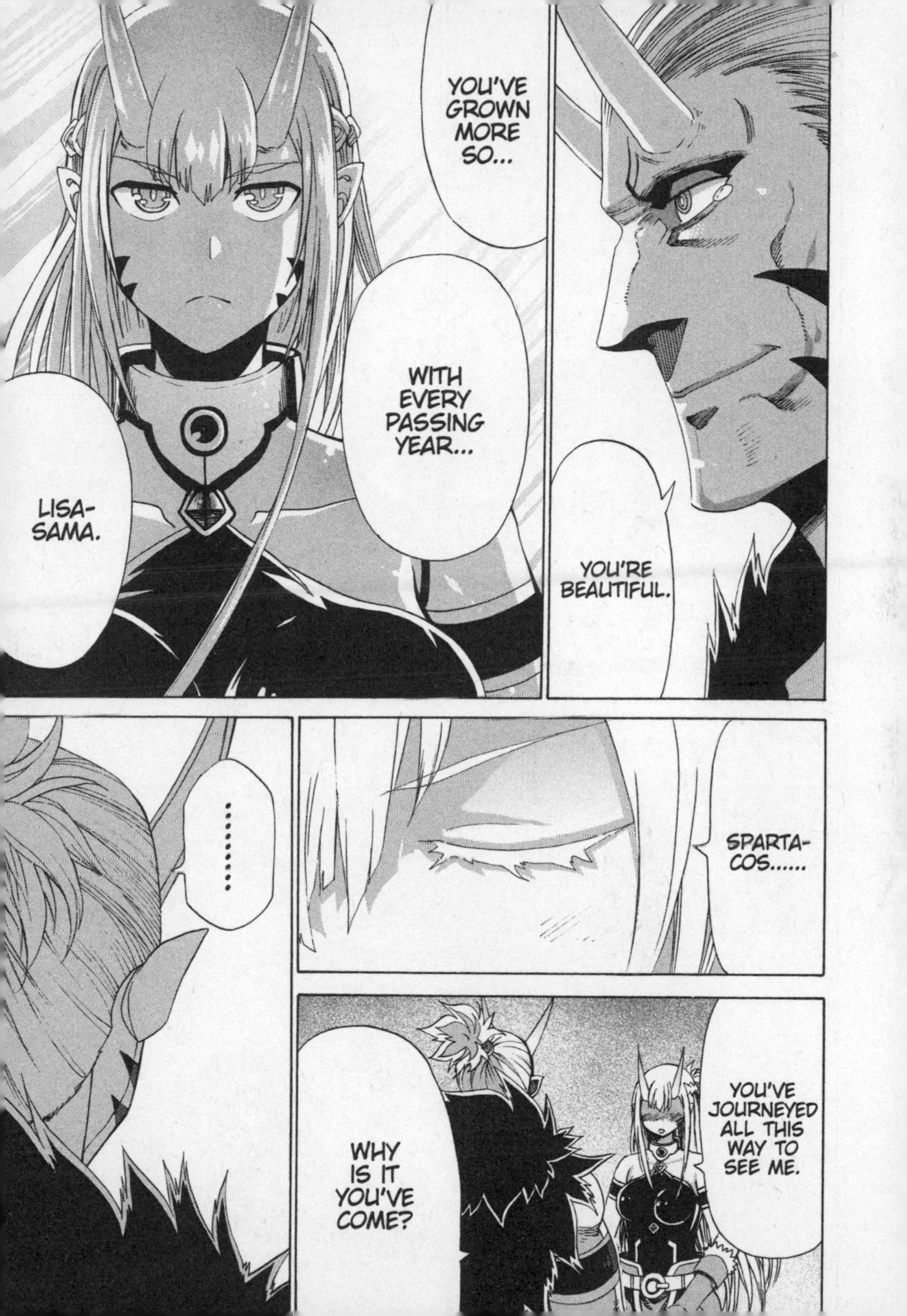
YOU'RE BEAUTIFUL.
YOU'VE GROWN MORE SO...
WITH EVERY PASSING YEAR...
LISA-SAMA.
SPARTA-COS......
YOU'VE JOURNEYED ALL THIS WAY TO SEE ME.
WHY IS IT YOU'VE COME?
......

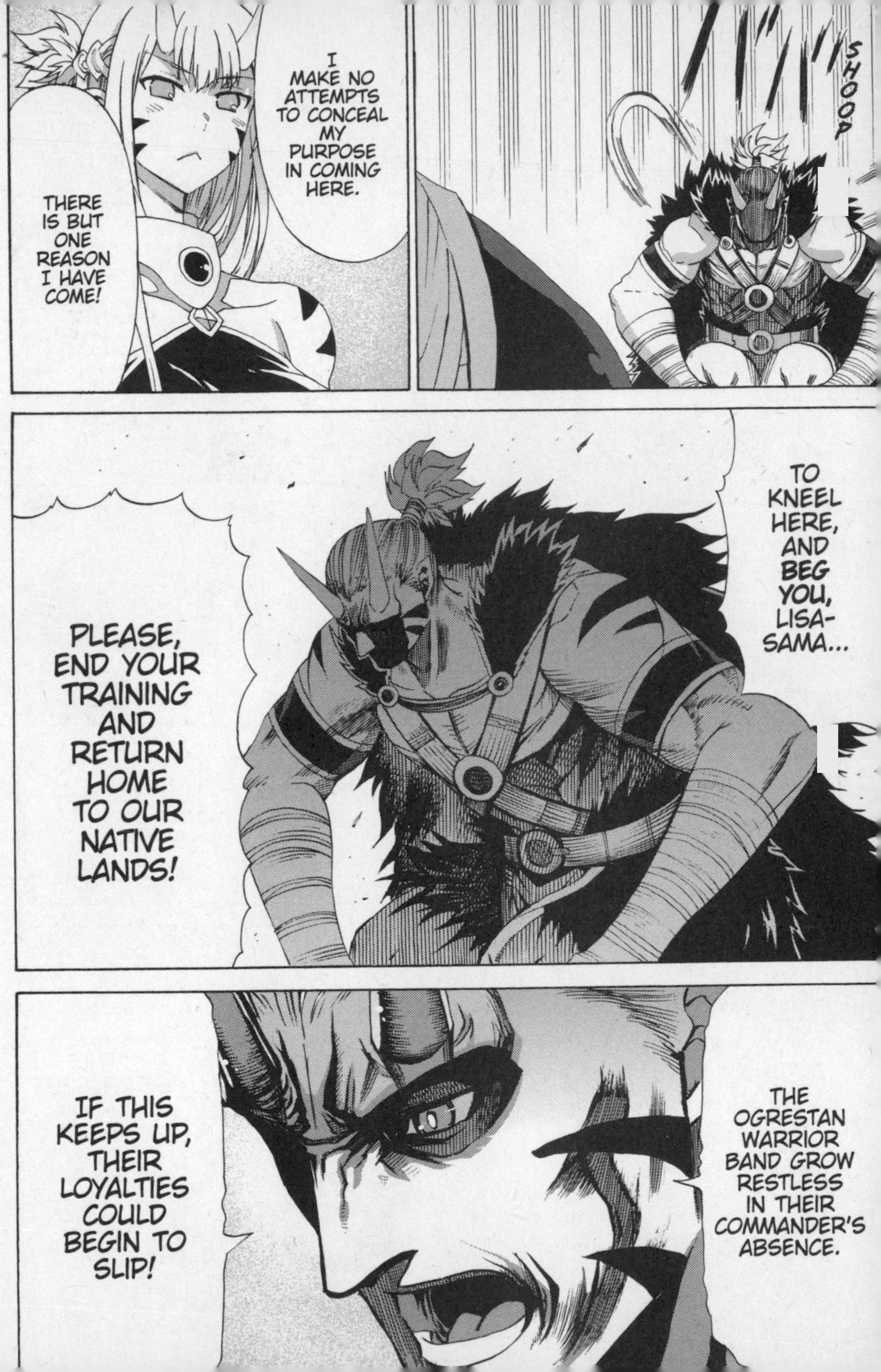
SHOOP
I MAKE NO ATTEMPTS TO CONCEAL MY PURPOSE IN COMING HERE.
THERE IS BUT ONE REASON I HAVE COME!
TO KNEEL HERE, AND BEG YOU, LISA-SAMA...
PLEASE, END YOUR TRAINING AND RETURN HOME TO OUR NATIVE LANDS!
THE OGRESTAN WARRIOR BAND GROW RESTLESS IN THEIR COMMANDER'S ABSENCE.
IF THIS KEEPS UP, THEIR LOYALTIES COULD BEGIN TO SLIP!

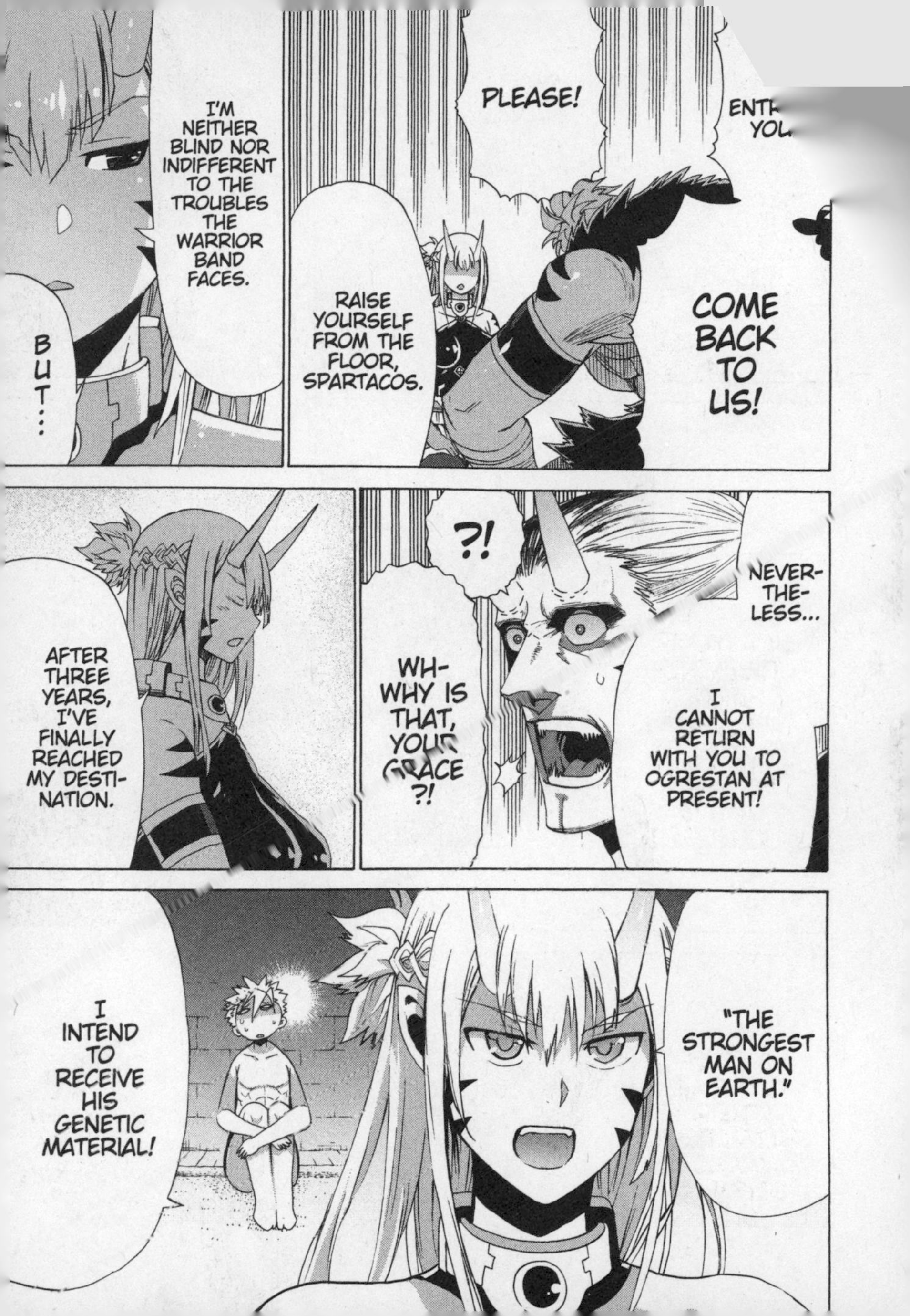
ENTR
YOU
COME BACK TO US!
PLEASE!
RAISE YOURSELF FROM THE FLOOR, SPARTACOS.
I'M NEITHER BLIND NOR INDIFFERENT TO THE TROUBLES THE WARRIOR BAND FACES.
BUT...
NEVER-THE-LESS...
I CANNOT RETURN WITH YOU TO OGRESTAN AT PRESENT!
?!
WH-WHY IS THAT, YOUR GRACE?!
AFTER THREE YEARS, I'VE FINALLY REACHED MY DESTI-NATION.
"THE STRONGEST MAN ON EARTH."
I INTEND TO RECEIVE HIS GENETIC MATERIAL!

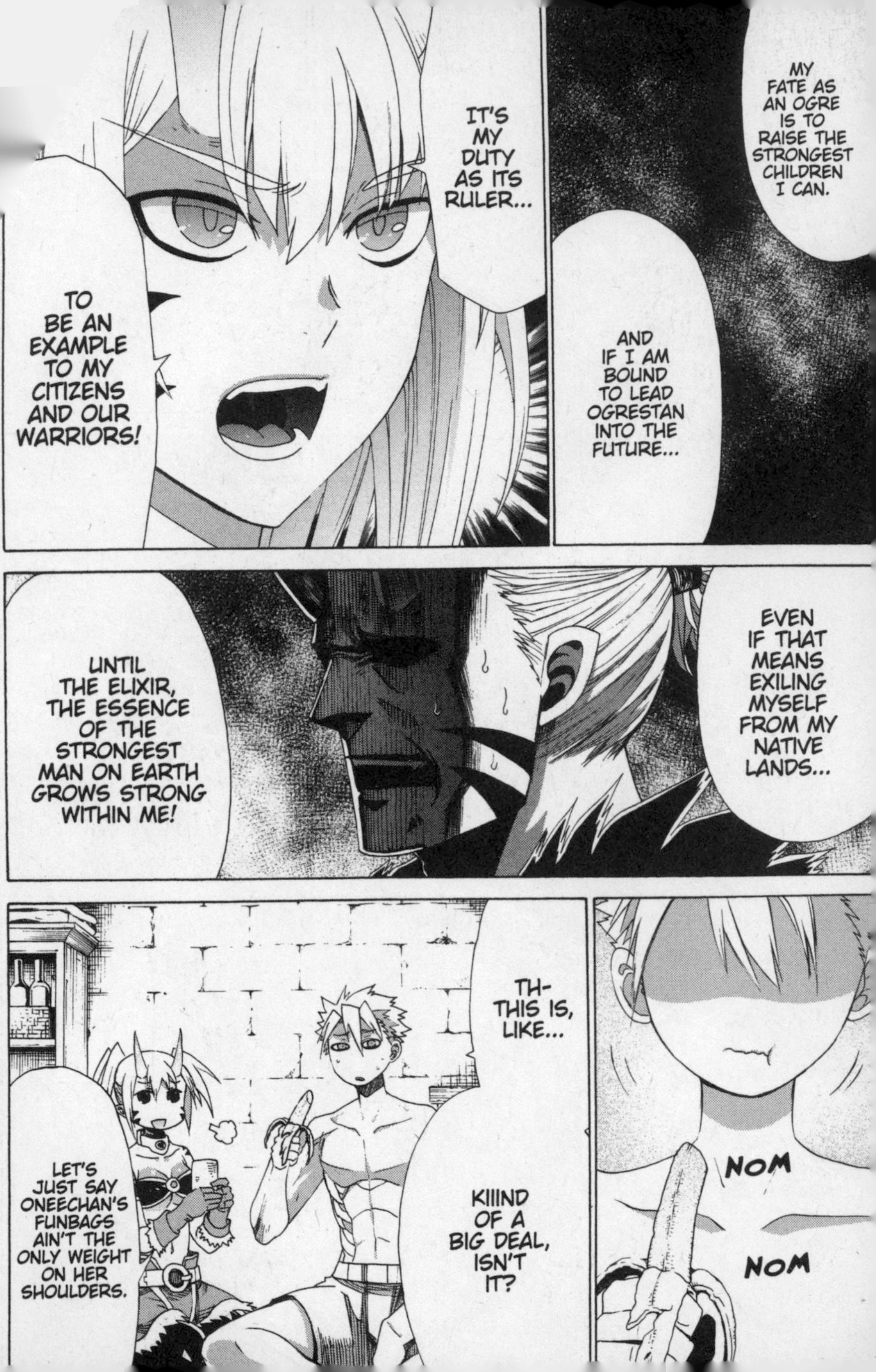
MY FATE AS AN OGRE IS TO RAISE THE STRONGEST CHILDREN I CAN.
AND IF I AM BOUND TO LEAD OGRESTAN INTO THE FUTURE...
IT'S MY DUTY AS ITS RULER...
TO BE AN EXAMPLE TO MY CITIZENS AND OUR WARRIORS!
EVEN IF THAT MEANS EXILING MYSELF FROM MY NATIVE LANDS...
UNTIL THE ELIXIR, THE ESSENCE OF THE STRONGEST MAN ON EARTH GROWS STRONG WITHIN ME!
NOM
NOM
TH- THIS IS, LIKE...
KIIIND OF A BIG DEAL, ISN'T IT?
LET'S JUST SAY ONEECHAN'S FUNBAGS AIN'T THE ONLY WEIGHT ON HER SHOULDERS.

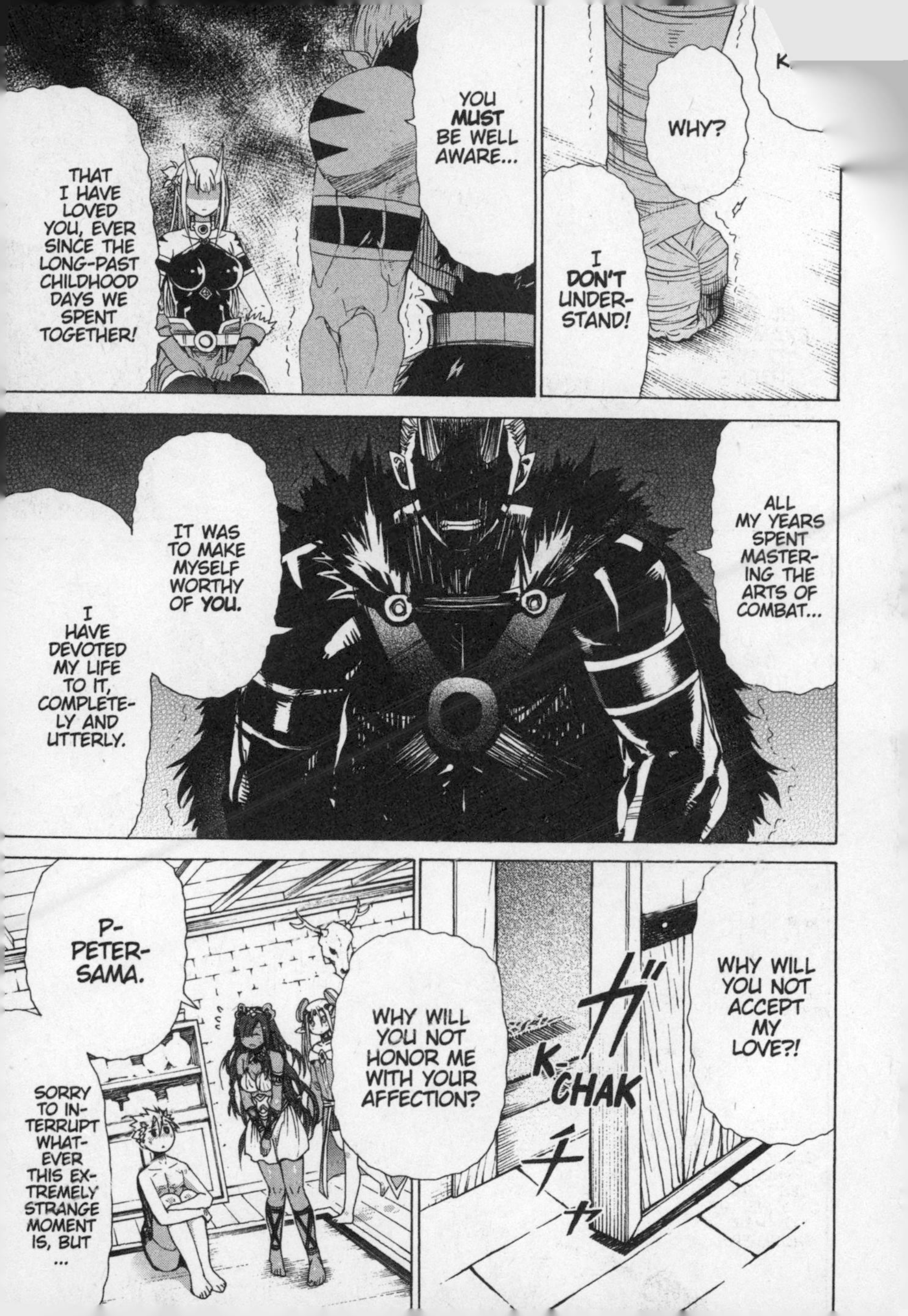

WHY?
I DON'T UNDERSTAND!
YOU MUST BE WELL AWARE...
THAT I HAVE LOVED YOU, EVER SINCE THE LONG-PAST CHILDHOOD DAYS WE SPENT TOGETHER!
ALL MY YEARS SPENT MASTERING THE ARTS OF COMBAT...
IT WAS TO MAKE MYSELF WORTHY OF YOU.
I HAVE DEVOTED MY LIFE TO IT, COMPLETELY AND UTTERLY.
WHY WILL YOU NOT ACCEPT MY LOVE?!
ガチャ
K-CHAK
WHY WILL YOU NOT HONOR ME WITH YOUR AFFECTION?
P-PETER-SAMA.
SORRY TO INTERRUPT WHATEVER THIS EXTREMELY STRANGE MOMENT IS, BUT ...

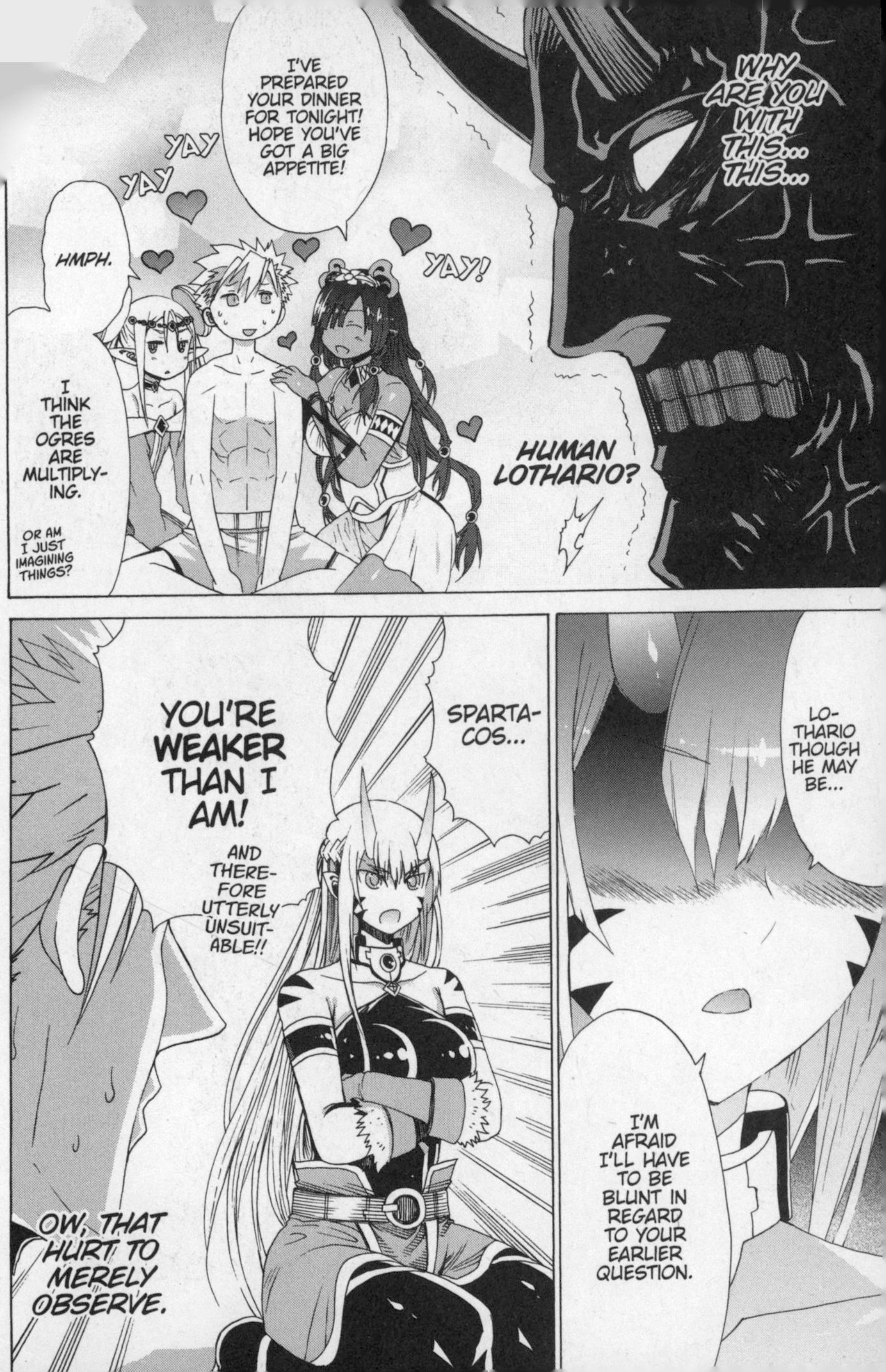
WHY ARE YOU WITH THIS... THIS...
HUMAN LOTHARIO?
I'VE PREPARED YOUR DINNER FOR TONIGHT! HOPE YOU'VE GOT A BIG APPETITE!
YAY
YAY
YAY!
HMPH.
I THINK THE OGRES ARE MULTIPLY-ING.
OR AM I JUST IMAGINING THINGS?
LO-THARIO THOUGH HE MAY BE...
I'M AFRAID I'LL HAVE TO BE BLUNT IN REGARD TO YOUR EARLIER QUESTION.
SPARTA-COS...
YOU'RE WEAKER THAN I AM!
AND THERE-FORE UTTERLY UNSUIT-ABLE!!
OW, THAT HURT TO MERELY OBSERVE.

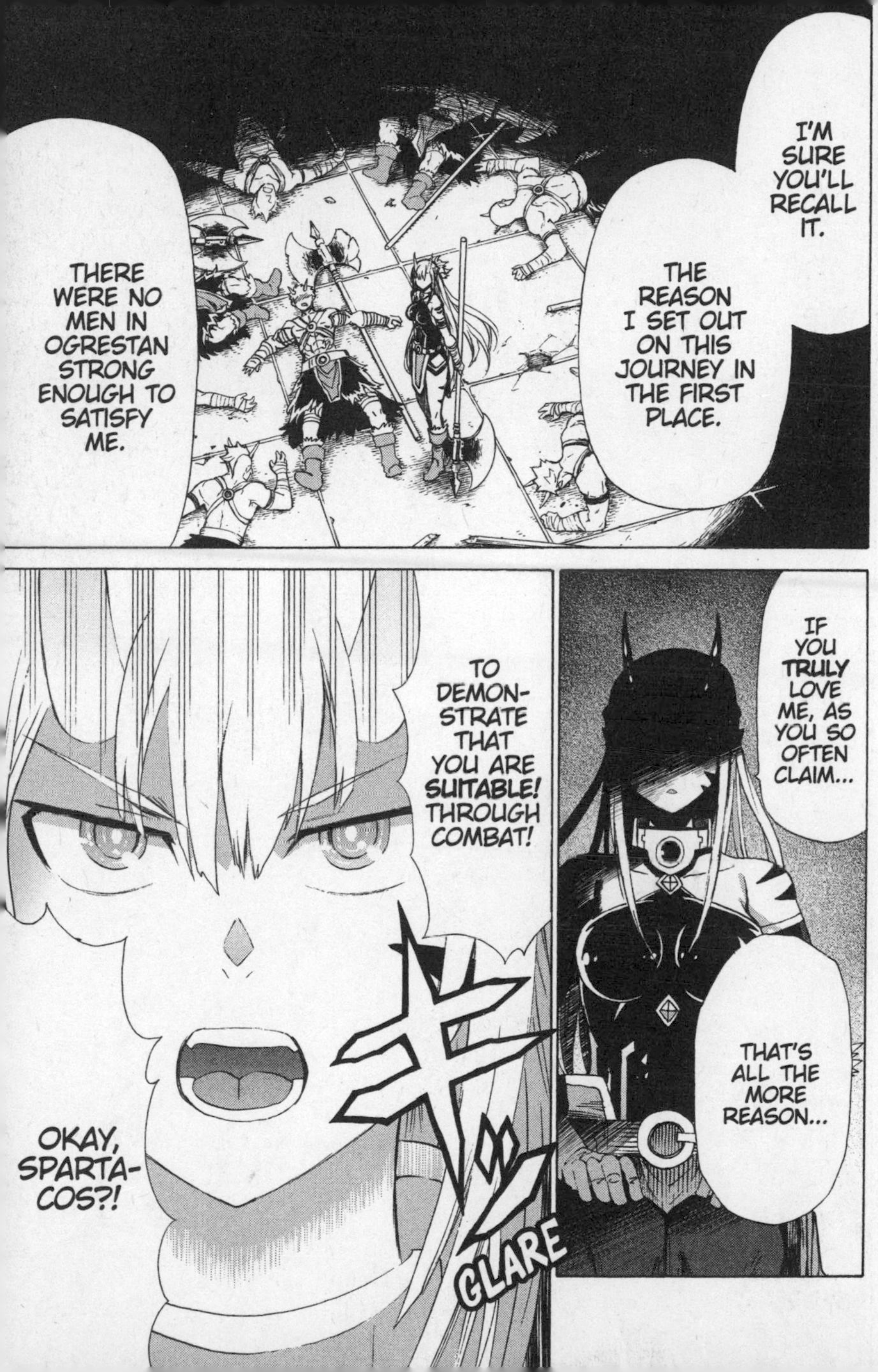

I'M SURE YOU'LL RECALL IT.
THE REASON I SET OUT ON THIS JOURNEY IN THE FIRST PLACE.
THERE WERE NO MEN IN OGRESTAN STRONG ENOUGH TO SATISFY ME.
IF YOU **TRULY** LOVE ME, AS YOU SO OFTEN CLAIM...
THAT'S ALL THE MORE REASON...
TO DEMON-STRATE THAT YOU ARE **SUITABLE!** THROUGH COMBAT!
OKAY, SPARTA-COS?!
GLARE

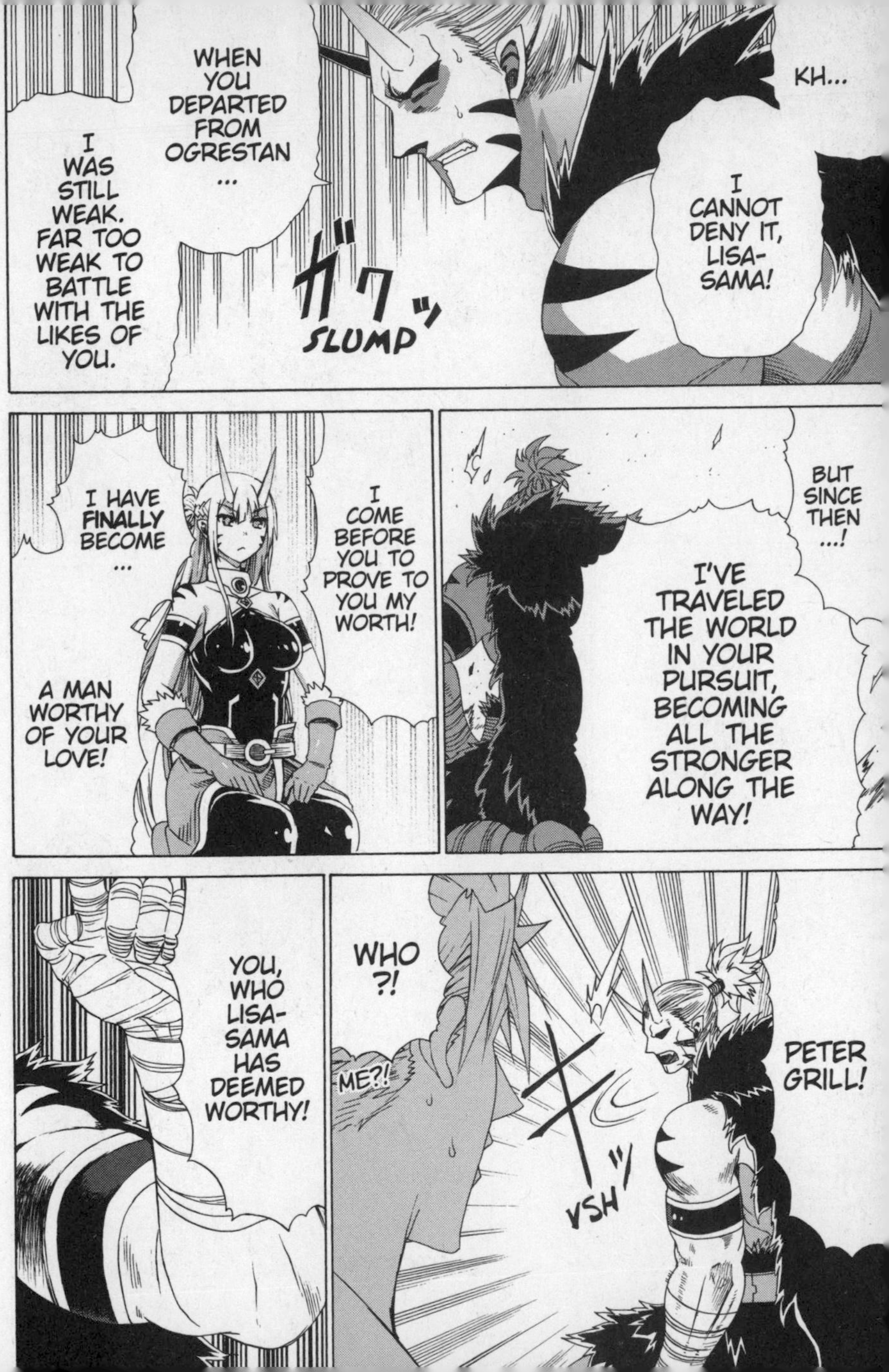
KH...
I CANNOT DENY IT, LISA-SAMA!
ガクッ
SLUMP
WHEN YOU DEPARTED FROM OGRESTAN ...
I WAS STILL WEAK. FAR TOO WEAK TO BATTLE WITH THE LIKES OF YOU.
BUT SINCE THEN ...!
I'VE TRAVELED THE WORLD IN YOUR PURSUIT, BECOMING ALL THE STRONGER ALONG THE WAY!
I COME BEFORE YOU TO PROVE TO YOU MY WORTH!
I HAVE FINALLY BECOME ...
A MAN WORTHY OF YOUR LOVE!
PETER GRILL!
ツ
VSH
WHO ?!
ME?!
YOU, WHO LISA-SAMA HAS DEEMED WORTHY!

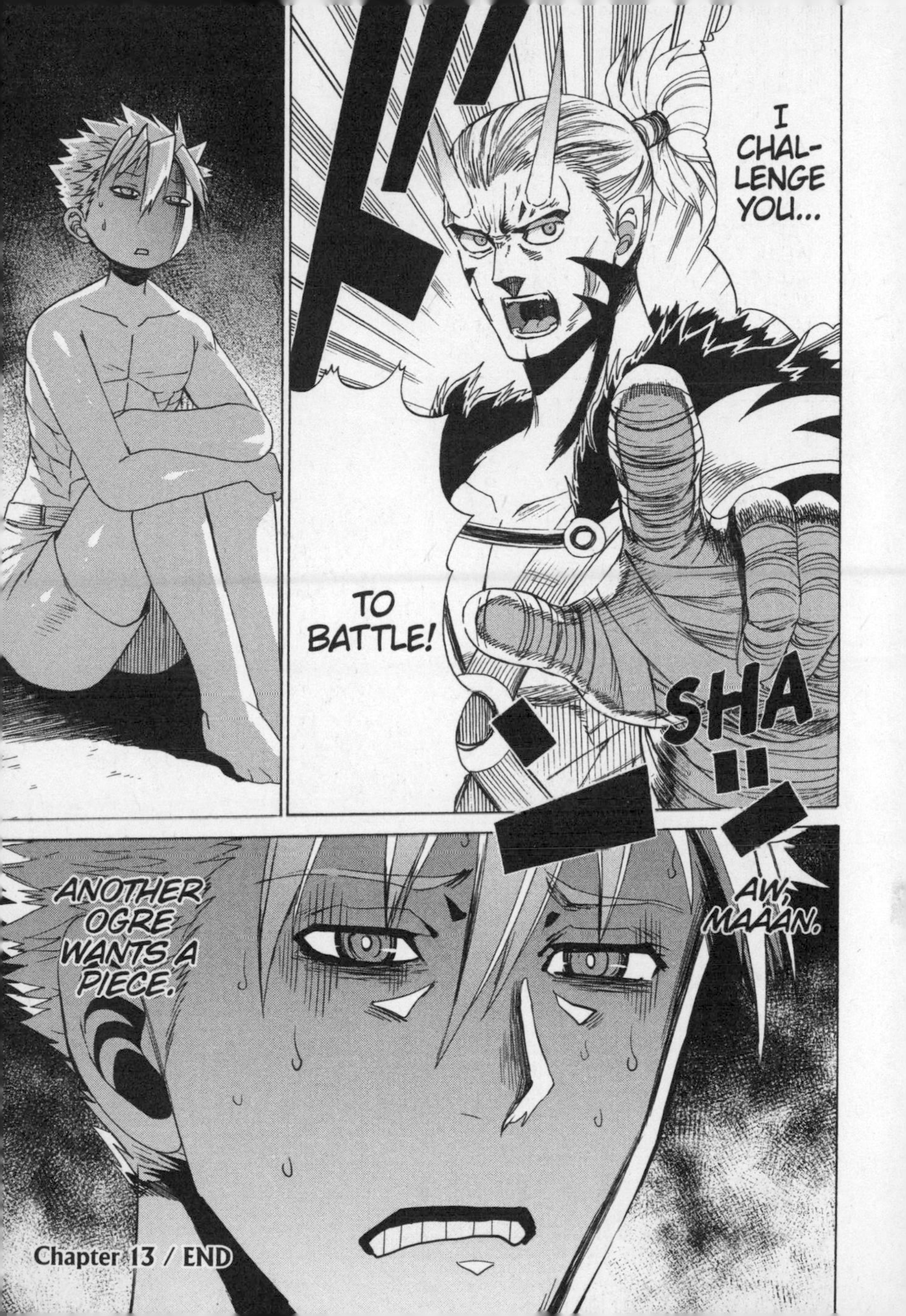
I CHAL-LENGE YOU...
TO BATTLE!
SHA!!
AW, MAAAN.
ANOTHER OGRE WANTS A PIECE.
Chapter 13 / END

PETER GRILL
AND THE PHILOSOPHER'S TIME

Previously, on *Peter Grill*...

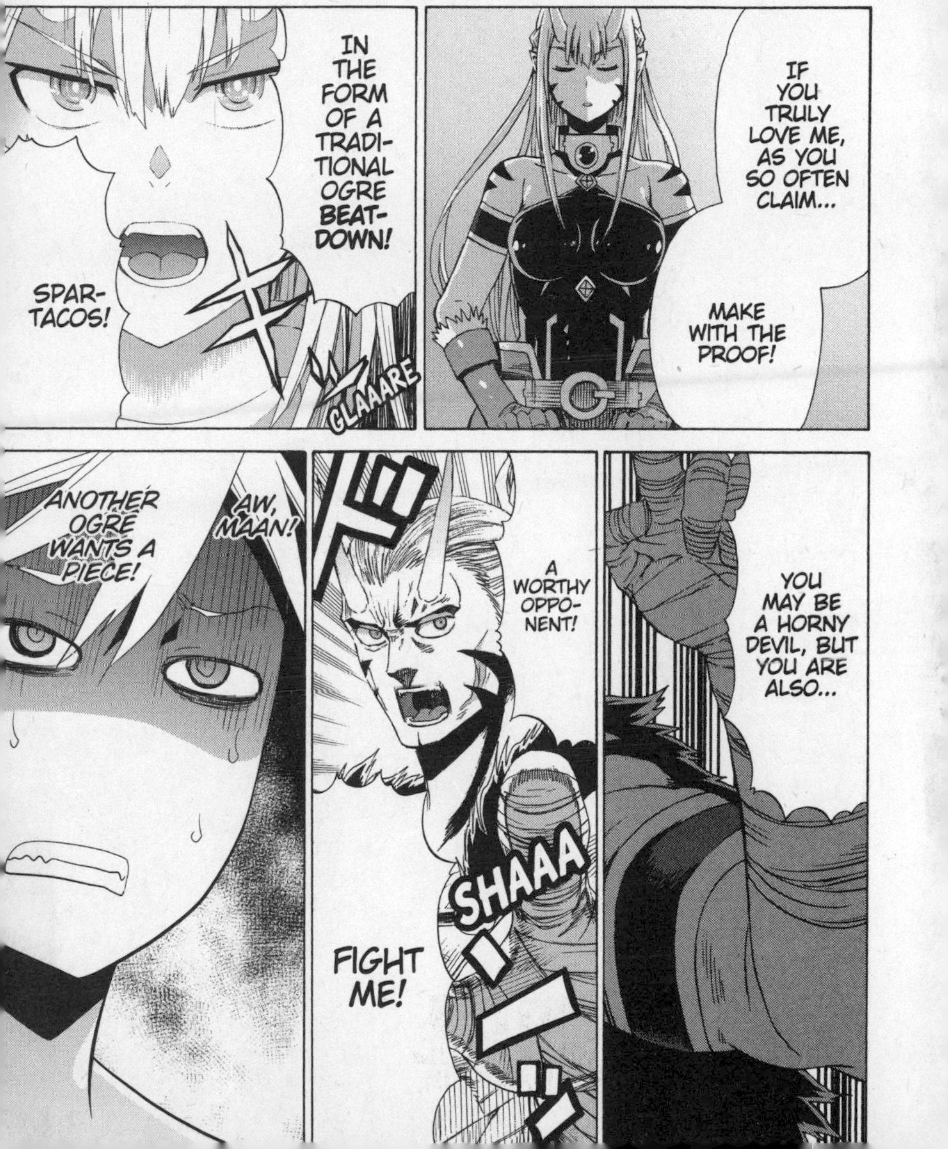

IF YOU TRULY LOVE ME, AS YOU SO OFTEN CLAIM...
MAKE WITH THE PROOF!
IN THE FORM OF A TRADITIONAL OGRE BEATDOWN!
SPARTACOS!
GLAAARE
YOU MAY BE A HORNY DEVIL, BUT YOU ARE ALSO...
A WORTHY OPPONENT!
SHAAA
FIGHT ME!
AW, MAAN!
ANOTHER OGRE WANTS A PIECE!

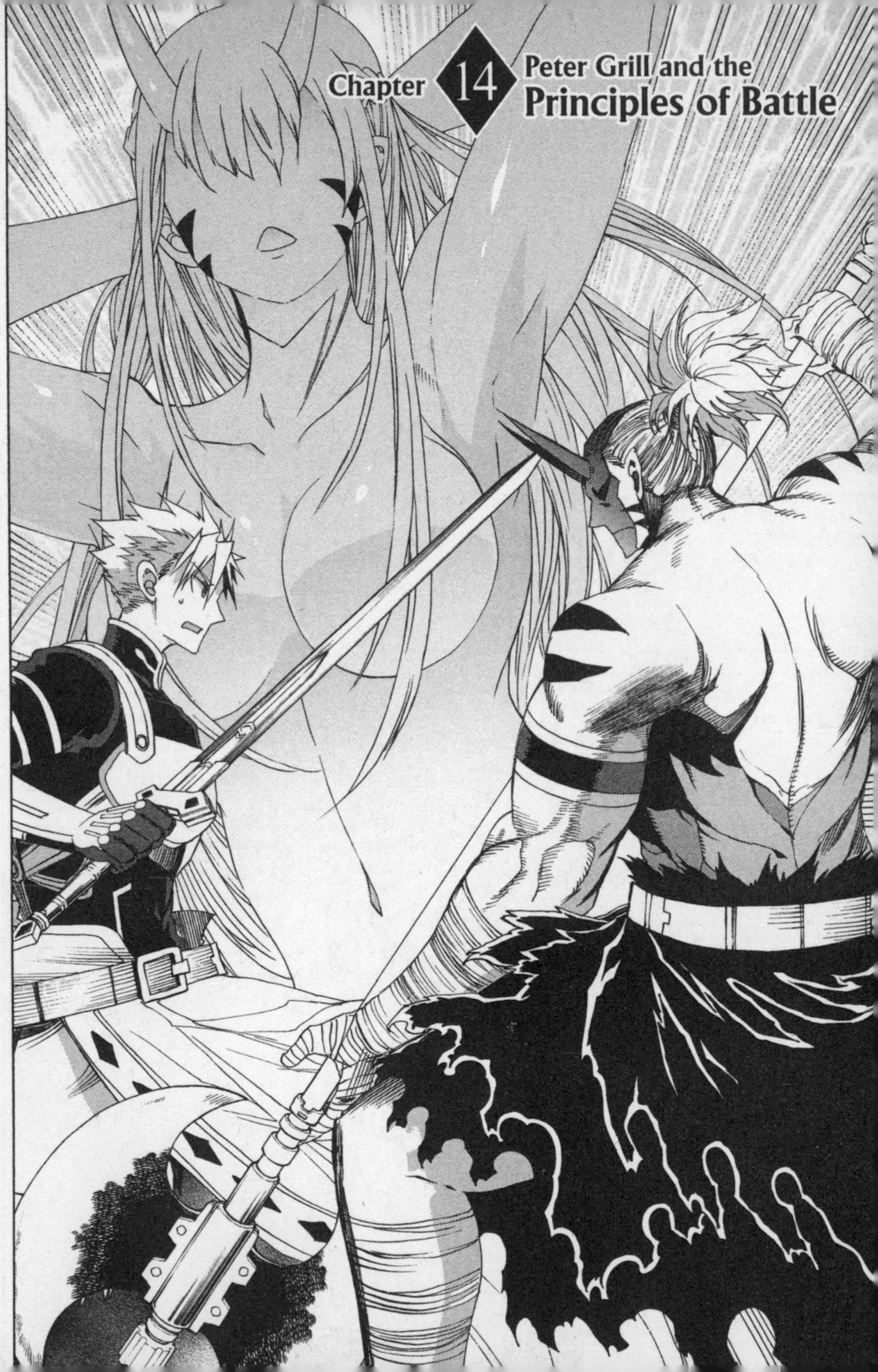
Chapter 14 Peter Grill and the Principles of Battle

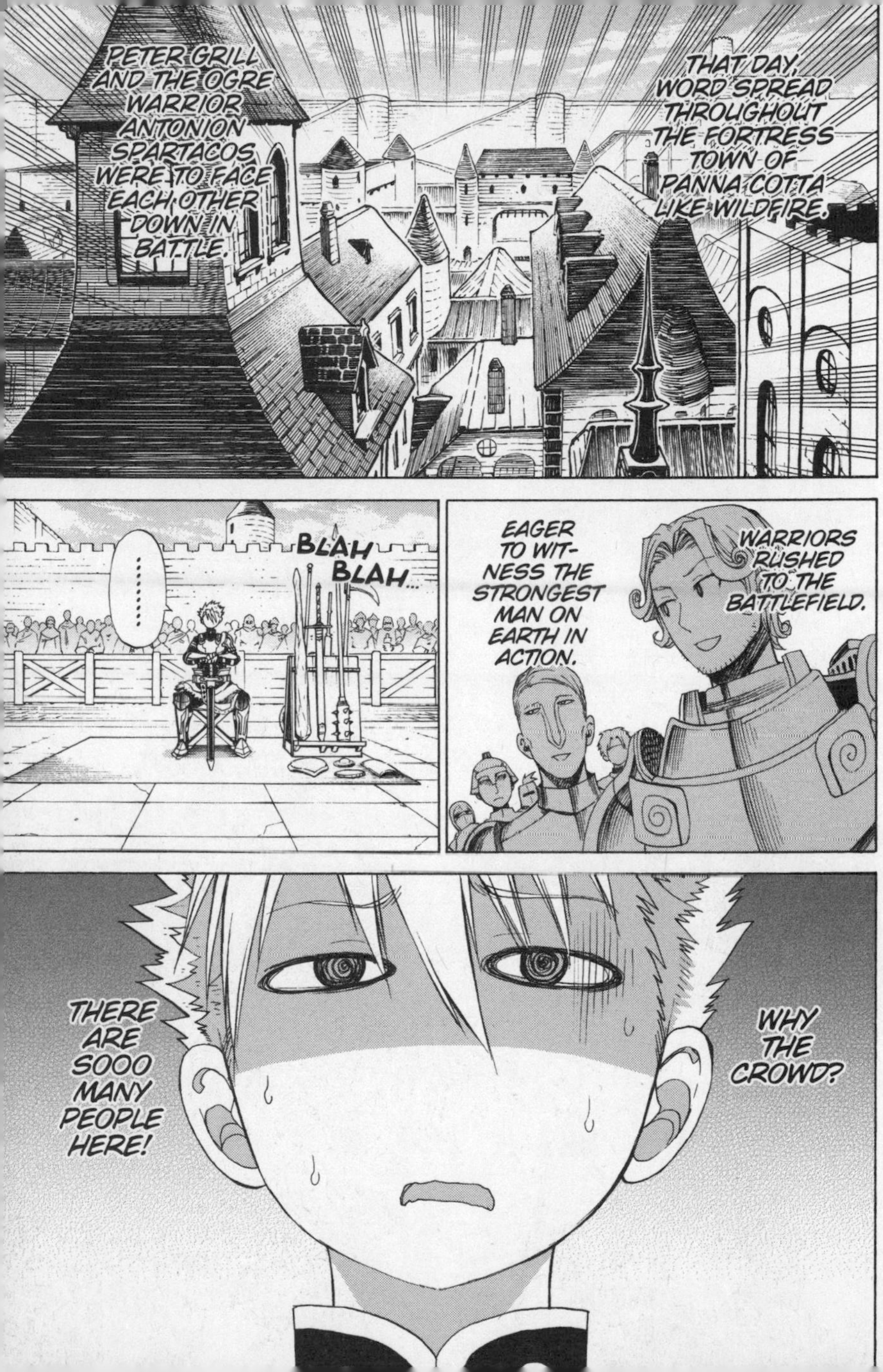
THAT DAY, WORD SPREAD THROUGHOUT THE FORTRESS TOWN OF PANNA COTTA LIKE WILDFIRE.
PETER GRILL AND THE OGRE WARRIOR ANTONION SPARTACOS WERE TO FACE EACH OTHER DOWN IN BATTLE.
WARRIORS RUSHED TO THE BATTLEFIELD.
EAGER TO WITNESS THE STRONGEST MAN ON EARTH IN ACTION.
BLAH BLAH...
......
WHY THE CROWD?
THERE ARE SOOO MANY PEOPLE HERE!

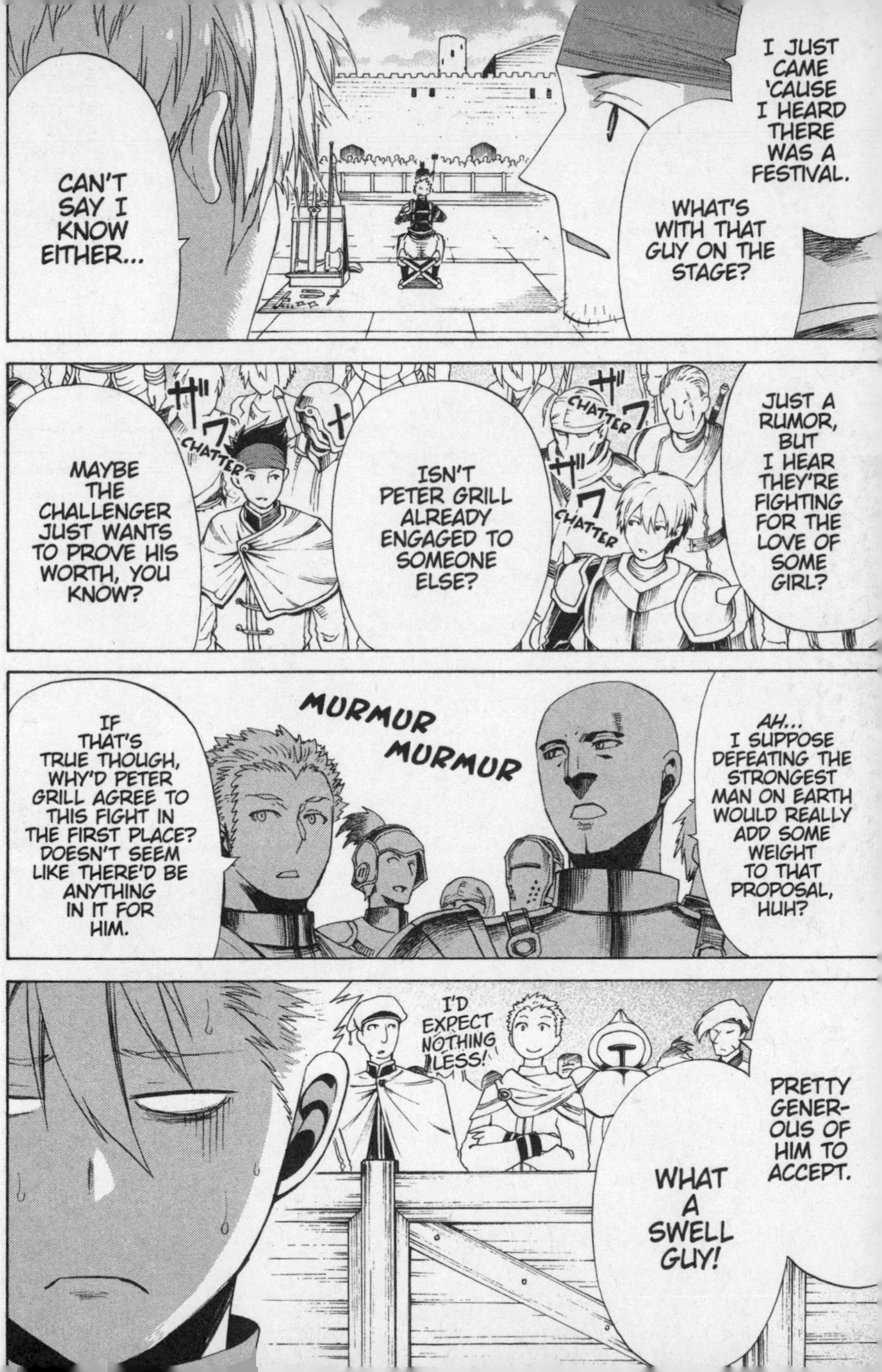
I JUST CAME 'CAUSE I HEARD THERE WAS A FESTIVAL.
WHAT'S WITH THAT GUY ON THE STAGE?
CAN'T SAY I KNOW EITHER...
JUST A RUMOR, BUT I HEAR THEY'RE FIGHTING FOR THE LOVE OF SOME GIRL?
ザワ CHATTER
ザワ CHATTER
ISN'T PETER GRILL ALREADY ENGAGED TO SOMEONE ELSE?
ザワ CHATTER
MAYBE THE CHALLENGER JUST WANTS TO PROVE HIS WORTH, YOU KNOW?
AH... I SUPPOSE DEFEATING THE STRONGEST MAN ON EARTH WOULD REALLY ADD SOME WEIGHT TO THAT PROPOSAL, HUH?
MURMUR MURMUR
IF THAT'S TRUE THOUGH, WHY'D PETER GRILL AGREE TO THIS FIGHT IN THE FIRST PLACE? DOESN'T SEEM LIKE THERE'D BE ANYTHING IN IT FOR HIM.
PRETTY GENER-OUS OF HIM TO ACCEPT.
WHAT A SWELL GUY!
I'D EXPECT NOTHING LESS!

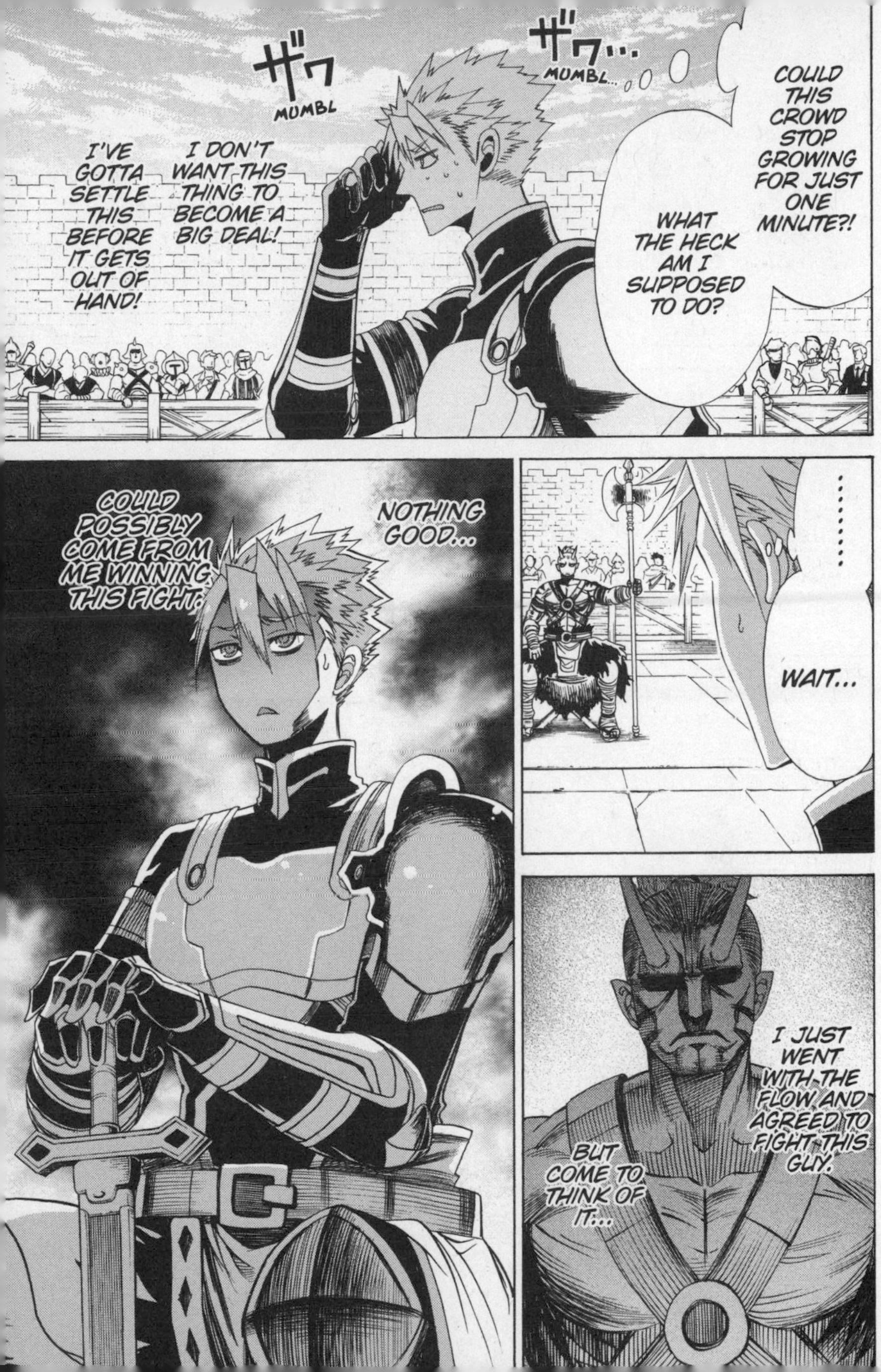
COULD THIS CROWD STOP GROWING FOR JUST ONE MINUTE?!
WHAT THE HECK AM I SUPPOSED TO DO?
ザワ…
MUMBL…
I DON'T WANT THIS THING TO BECOME A BIG DEAL!
ザワ
MUMBL
I'VE GOTTA SETTLE THIS BEFORE IT GETS OUT OF HAND!
......
WAIT...
I JUST WENT WITH THE FLOW AND AGREED TO FIGHT THIS GUY.
BUT COME TO THINK OF IT...
NOTHING GOOD...
COULD POSSIBLY COME FROM ME WINNING THIS FIGHT.

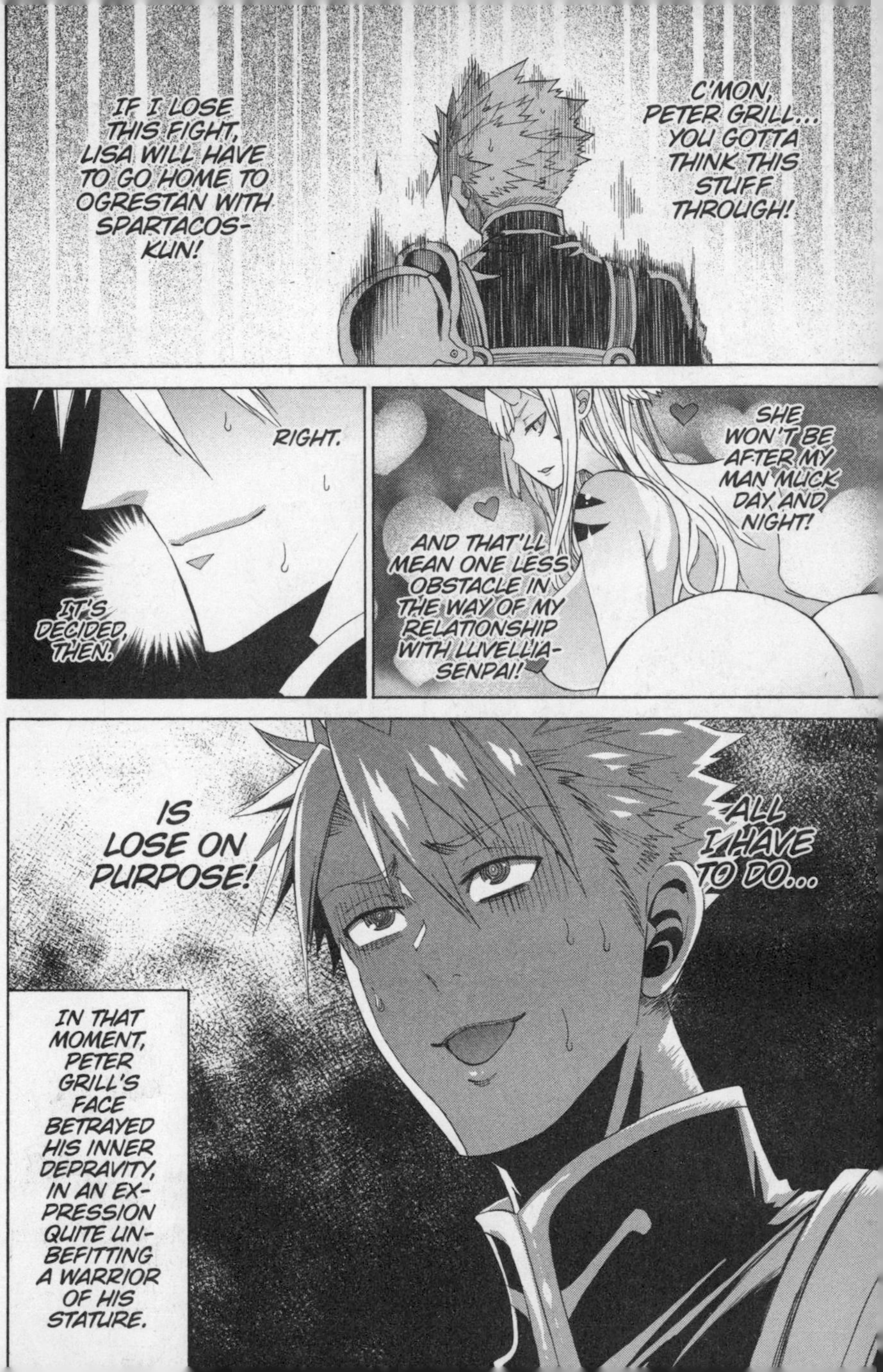
C'MON, PETER GRILL... YOU GOTTA THINK THIS STUFF THROUGH!
IF I LOSE THIS FIGHT, LISA WILL HAVE TO GO HOME TO OGRESTAN WITH SPARTACOS-KUN!
SHE WON'T BE AFTER MY MAN MUCK DAY AND NIGHT!
AND THAT'LL MEAN ONE LESS OBSTACLE IN THE WAY OF MY RELATIONSHIP WITH LUVELLIA-SENPAI!
RIGHT.
IT'S DECIDED, THEN.
ALL I HAVE TO DO...
IS LOSE ON PURPOSE!
IN THAT MOMENT, PETER GRILL'S FACE BETRAYED HIS INNER DEPRAVITY, IN AN EX-PRESSION QUITE UN-BEFITTING A WARRIOR OF HIS STATURE.

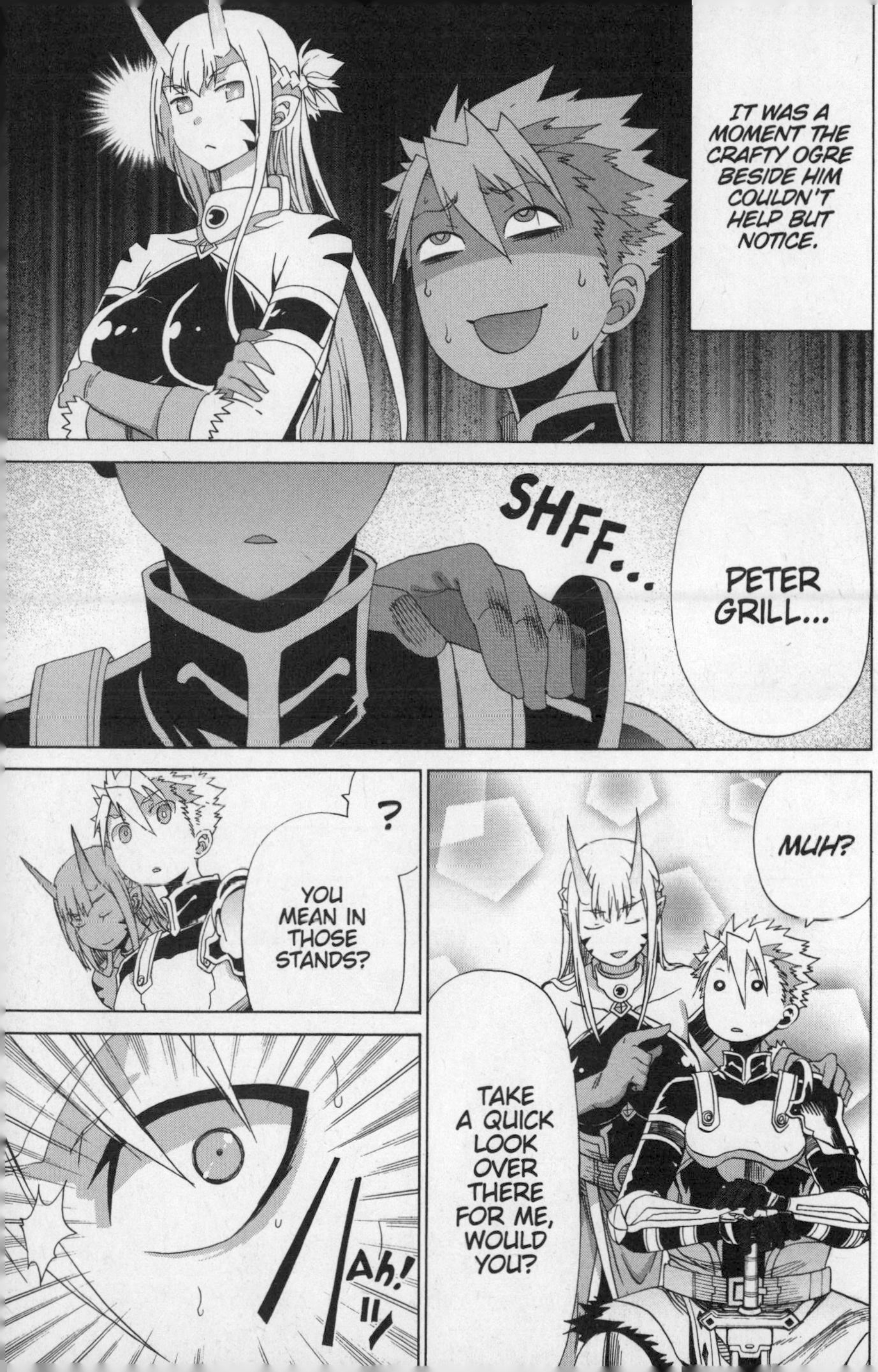
IT WAS A MOMENT THE CRAFTY OGRE BESIDE HIM COULDN'T HELP BUT NOTICE.
PETER GRILL...
SHFF...
MUH?
TAKE A QUICK LOOK OVER THERE FOR ME, WOULD YOU?
?
YOU MEAN IN THOSE STANDS?
Ah!

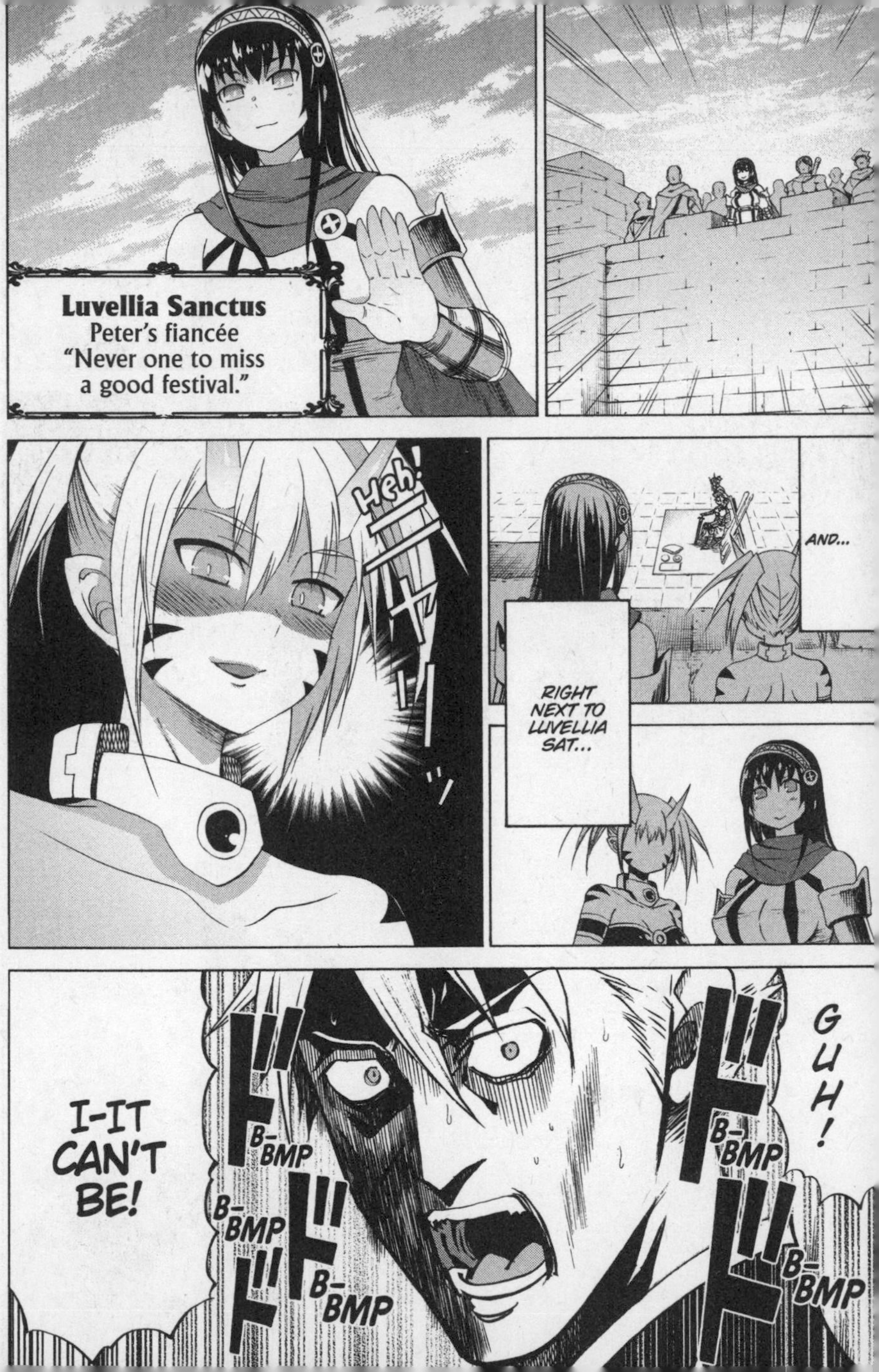
Luvellia Sanctus
Peter's fiancée
"Never one to miss a good festival."
AND...
RIGHT NEXT TO LUVELLIA SAT...
Heh!
GUH!
B-BMP
B-BMP
B-BMP
B-BMP
B-BMP
I-IT CAN'T BE!

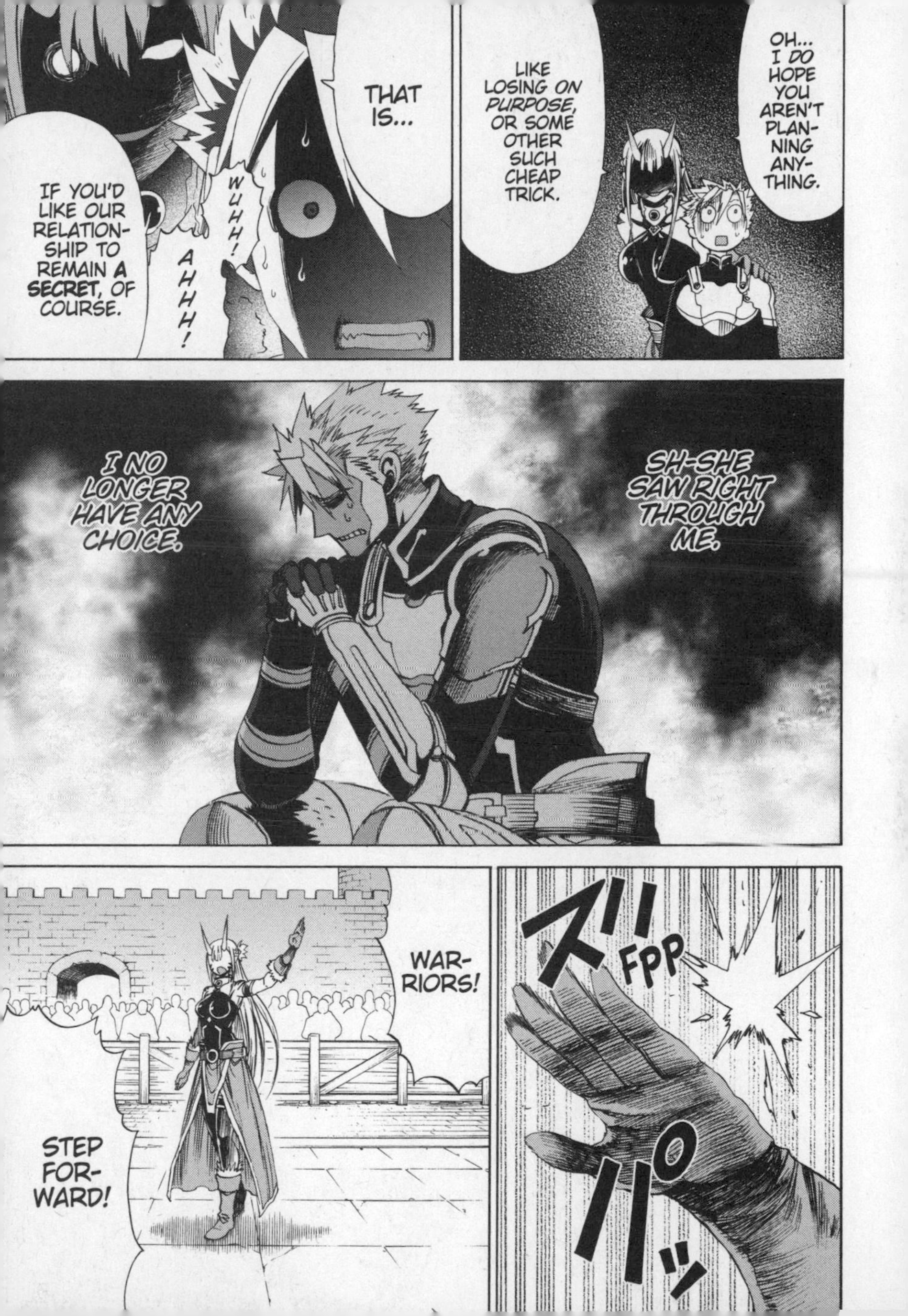
OH... I DO HOPE YOU AREN'T PLANNING ANYTHING.
LIKE LOSING ON PURPOSE, OR SOME OTHER SUCH CHEAP TRICK.
THAT IS...
WUHHH!
AHHHH!
IF YOU'D LIKE OUR RELATIONSHIP TO REMAIN A SECRET, OF COURSE.
SH-SHE SAW RIGHT THROUGH ME.
I NO LONGER HAVE ANY CHOICE.
ズパッ
FPP
WARRIORS!
STEP FORWARD!

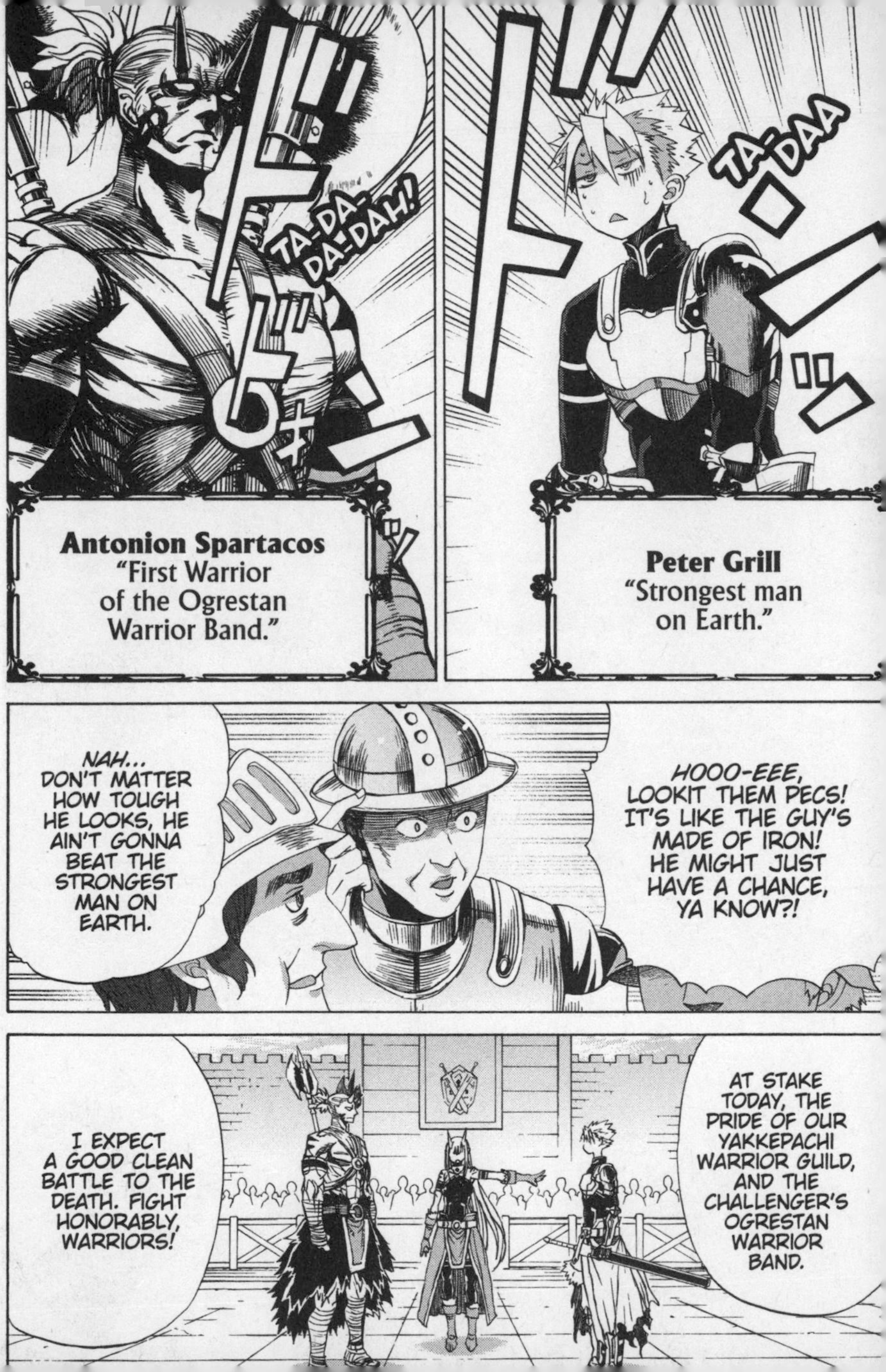

TA-DAA
Peter Grill
"Strongest man on Earth."
TA-DA-DA-DAH!
Antonion Spartacos
"First Warrior of the Ogrestan Warrior Band."
HOOO-EEE, LOOKIT THEM PECS! IT'S LIKE THE GUY'S MADE OF IRON! HE MIGHT JUST HAVE A CHANCE, YA KNOW?!
NAH... DON'T MATTER HOW TOUGH HE LOOKS, HE AIN'T GONNA BEAT THE STRONGEST MAN ON EARTH.
AT STAKE TODAY, THE PRIDE OF OUR YAKKEPACHI WARRIOR GUILD, AND THE CHALLENGER'S OGRESTAN WARRIOR BAND.
I EXPECT A GOOD CLEAN BATTLE TO THE DEATH. FIGHT HONORABLY, WARRIORS!

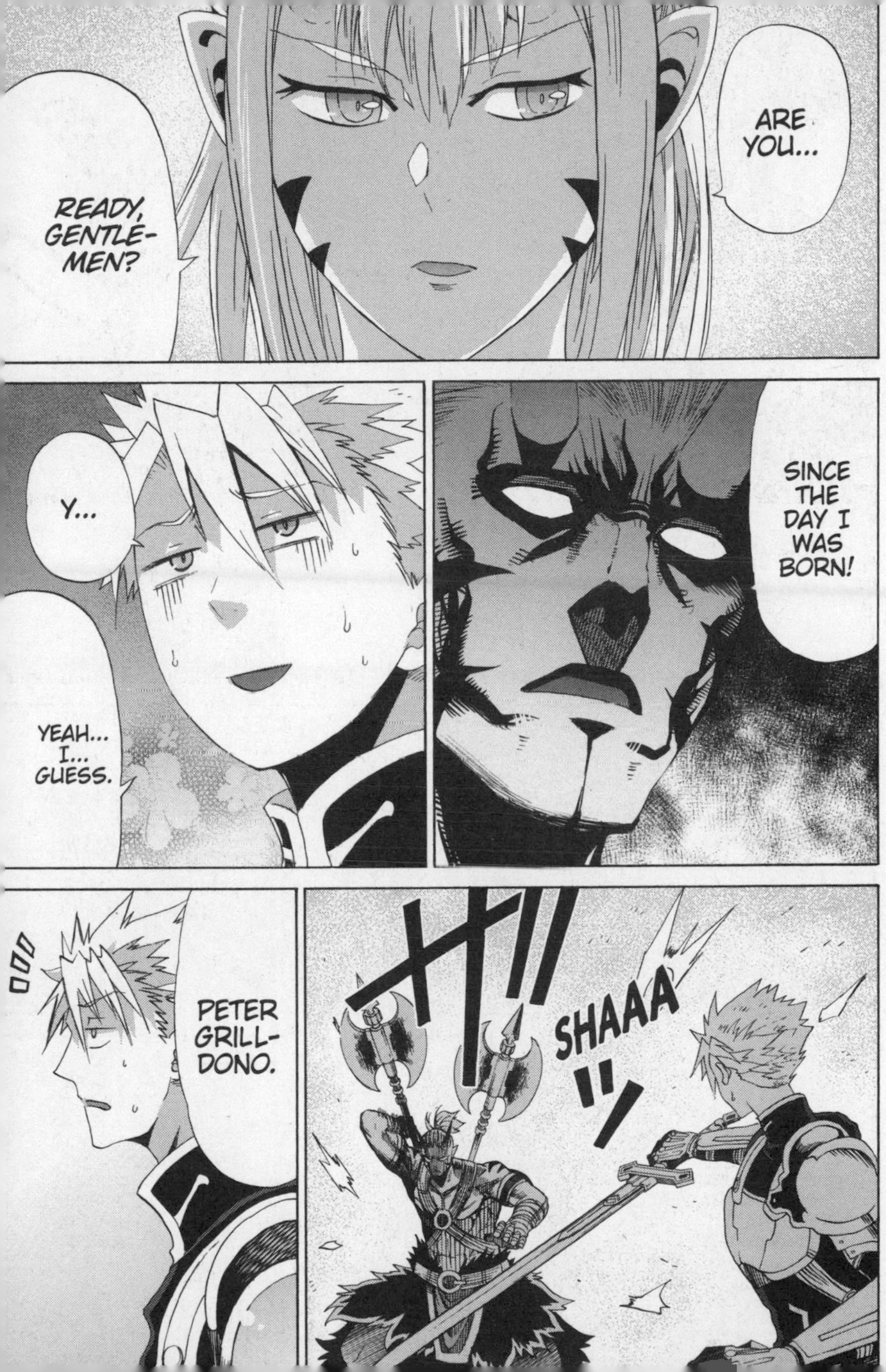
ARE YOU...
READY, GENTLEMEN?
SINCE THE DAY I WAS BORN!
Y...
YEAH... I... GUESS.
SHAAA
PETER GRILL-DONO.

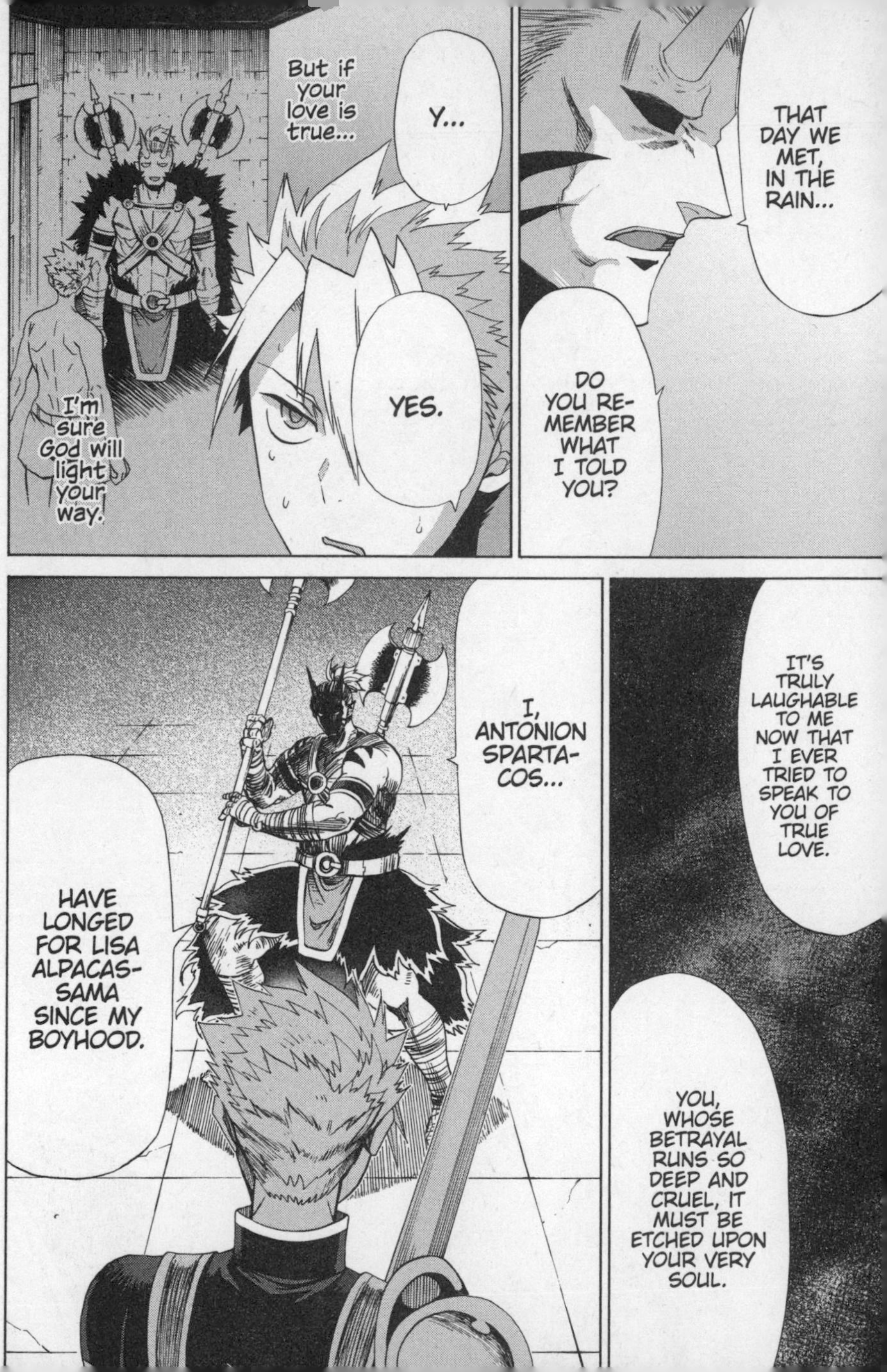
THAT DAY WE MET, IN THE RAIN...
DO YOU REMEMBER WHAT I TOLD YOU?
Y...
But if your love is true...
YES.
I'm sure God will light your way.
IT'S TRULY LAUGHABLE TO ME NOW THAT I EVER TRIED TO SPEAK TO YOU OF TRUE LOVE.
YOU, WHOSE BETRAYAL RUNS SO DEEP AND CRUEL, IT MUST BE ETCHED UPON YOUR VERY SOUL.
I, ANTONION SPARTACOS...
HAVE LONGED FOR LISA ALPACAS-SAMA SINCE MY BOYHOOD.

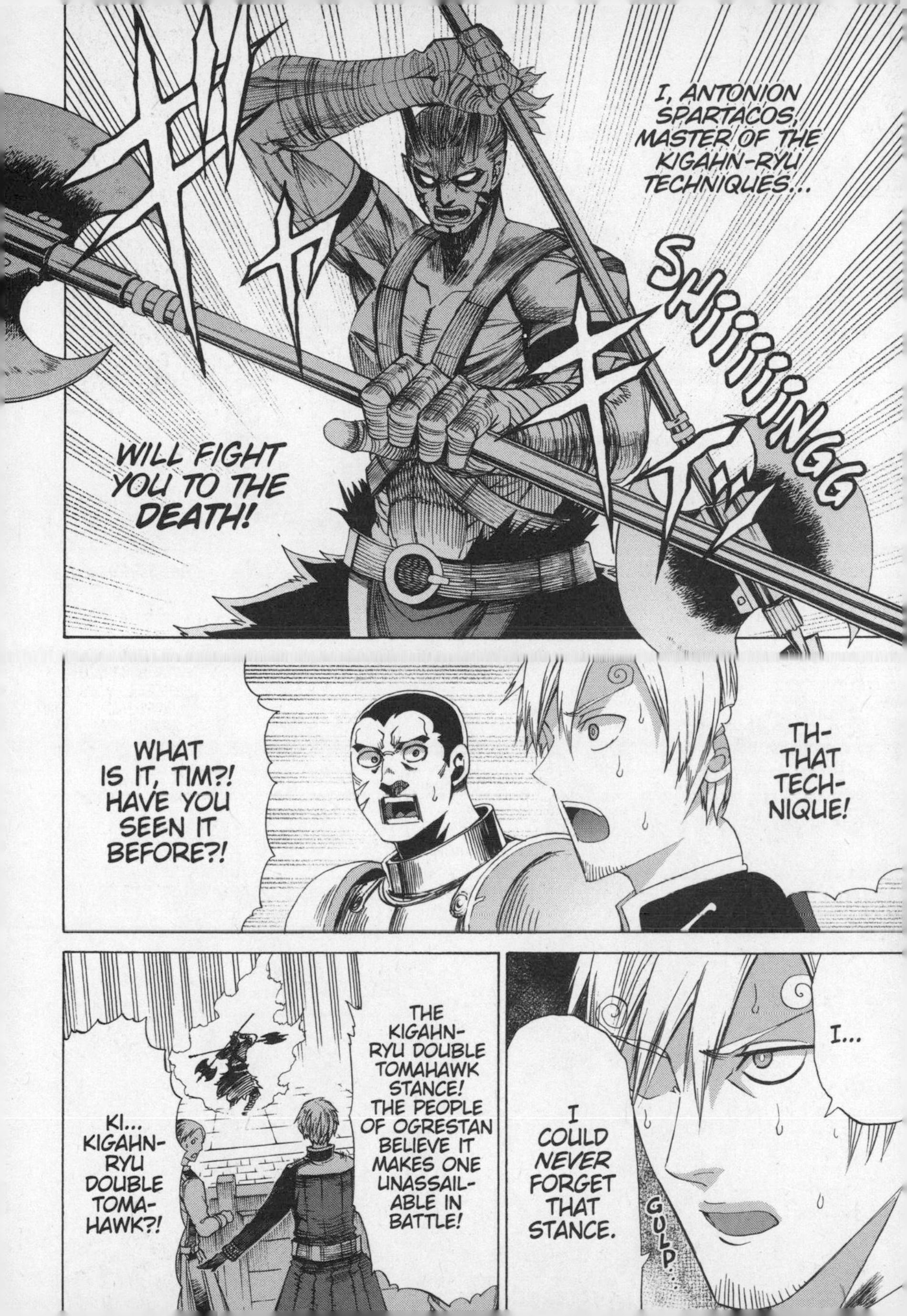
I, ANTONION SPARTACOS, MASTER OF THE KIGAHN-RYU TECHNIQUES...
SHIIIIINGG
WILL FIGHT YOU TO THE DEATH!
TH-THAT TECH-NIQUE!
WHAT IS IT, TIM?! HAVE YOU SEEN IT BEFORE?!
I...
I COULD NEVER FORGET THAT STANCE.
GULP...
THE KIGAHN-RYU DOUBLE TOMAHAWK STANCE! THE PEOPLE OF OGRESTAN BELIEVE IT MAKES ONE UNASSAIL-ABLE IN BATTLE!
KI... KIGAHN-RYU DOUBLE TOMA-HAWK?!

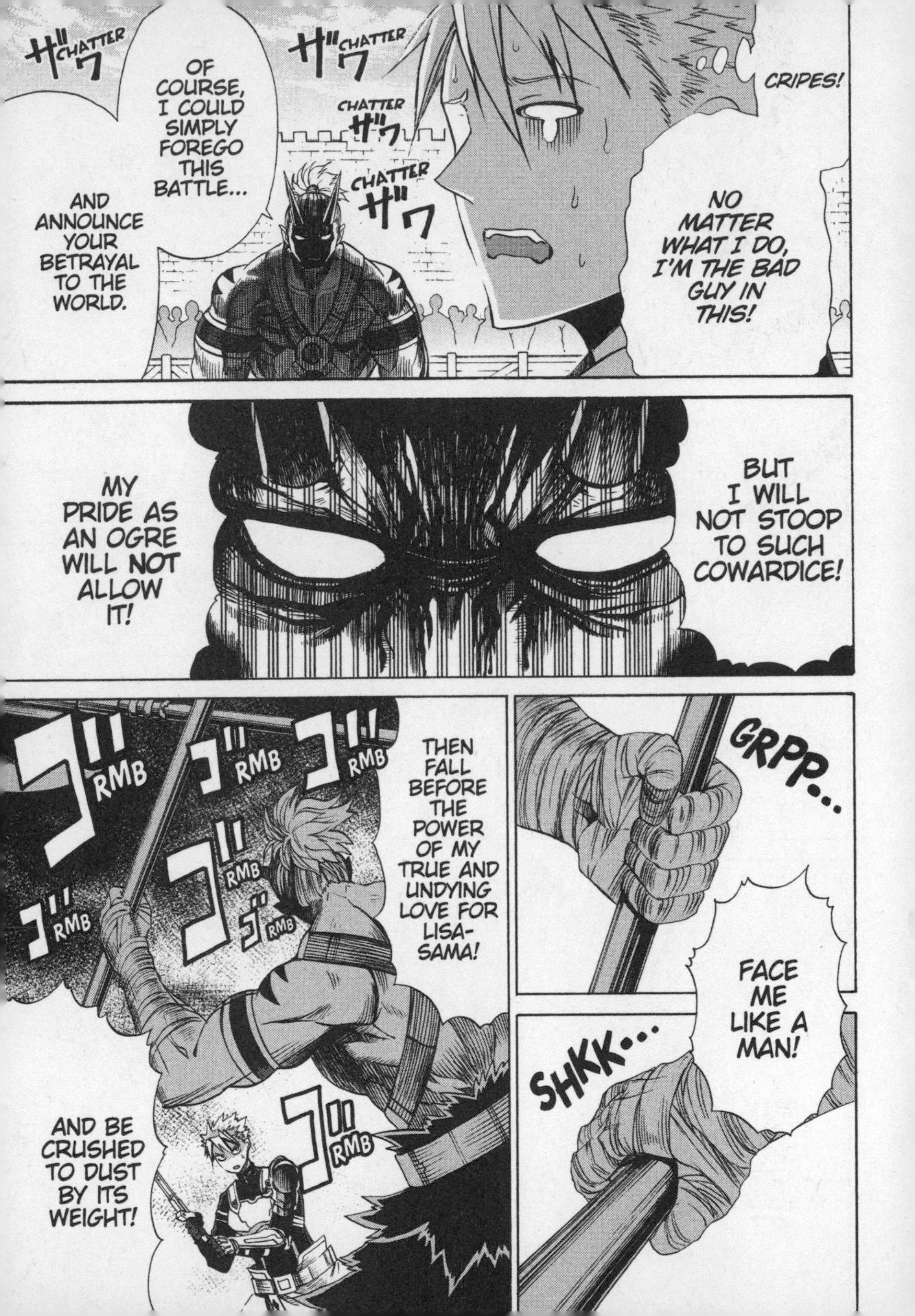
CRIPES!
NO MATTER WHAT I DO, I'M THE BAD GUY IN THIS!
ザワ CHATTER
ザワ CHATTER
ザワ CHATTER
OF COURSE, I COULD SIMPLY FOREGO THIS BATTLE...
ザワ CHATTER
AND ANNOUNCE YOUR BETRAYAL TO THE WORLD.
BUT I WILL NOT STOOP TO SUCH COWARDICE!
MY PRIDE AS AN OGRE WILL NOT ALLOW IT!
GRPP...
FACE ME LIKE A MAN!
SHKK...
THEN FALL BEFORE THE POWER OF MY TRUE AND UNDYING LOVE FOR LISA-SAMA!
ゴ RMB
ゴ RMB
ゴ RMB
ゴ RMB
ゴ RMB
ゴ RMB
ゴ RMB
AND BE CRUSHED TO DUST BY ITS WEIGHT!

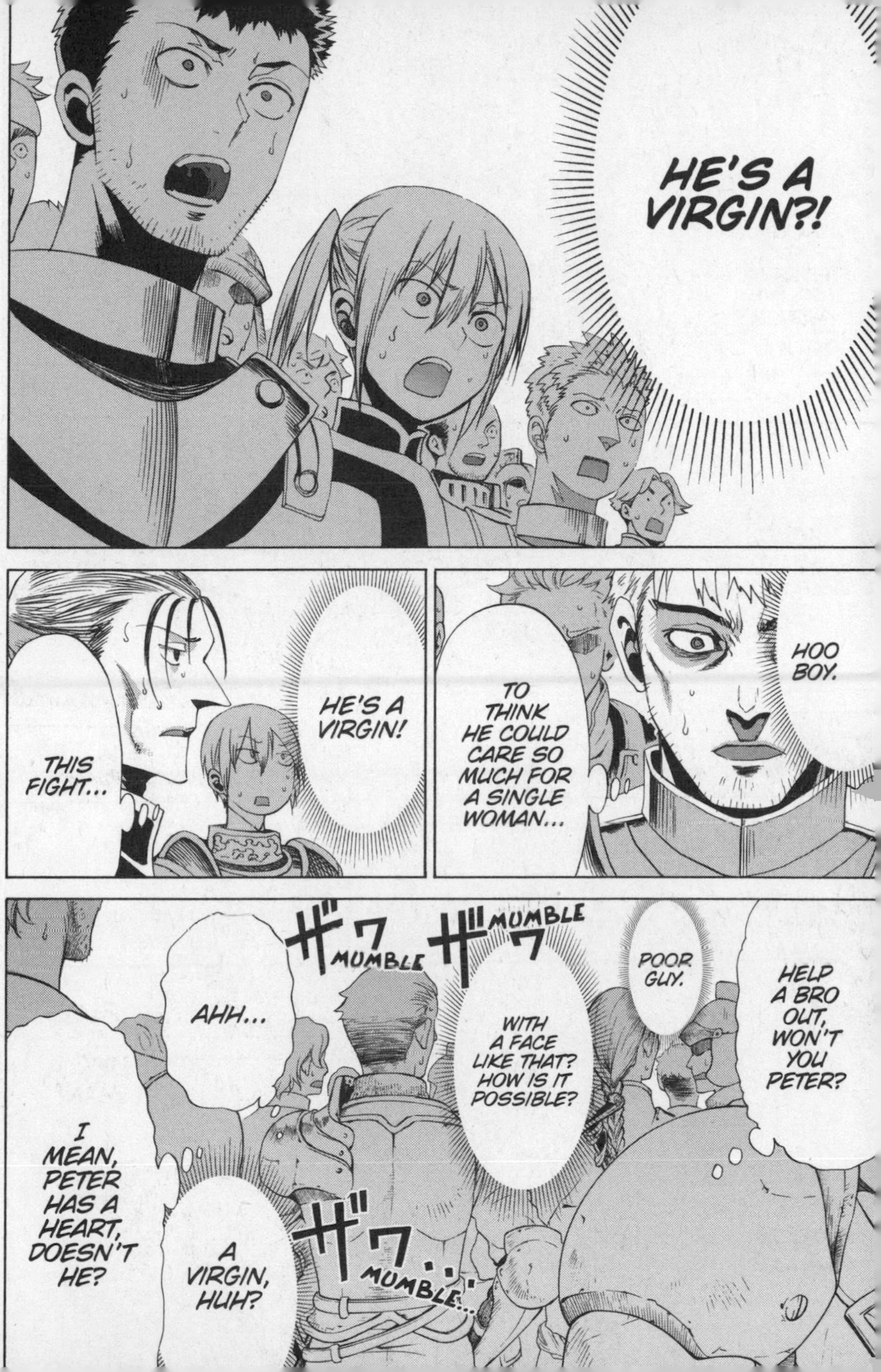
HE'S A VIRGIN?!
HOO BOY.
TO THINK HE COULD CARE SO MUCH FOR A SINGLE WOMAN...
HE'S A VIRGIN!
THIS FIGHT...
HELP A BRO OUT, WON'T YOU PETER?
POOR GUY.
ザワ MUMBLE
WITH A FACE LIKE THAT? HOW IS IT POSSIBLE?
ザワ MUMBLE
AHH...
I MEAN, PETER HAS A HEART, DOESN'T HE?
A VIRGIN, HUH?
ザワ MUMBLE...

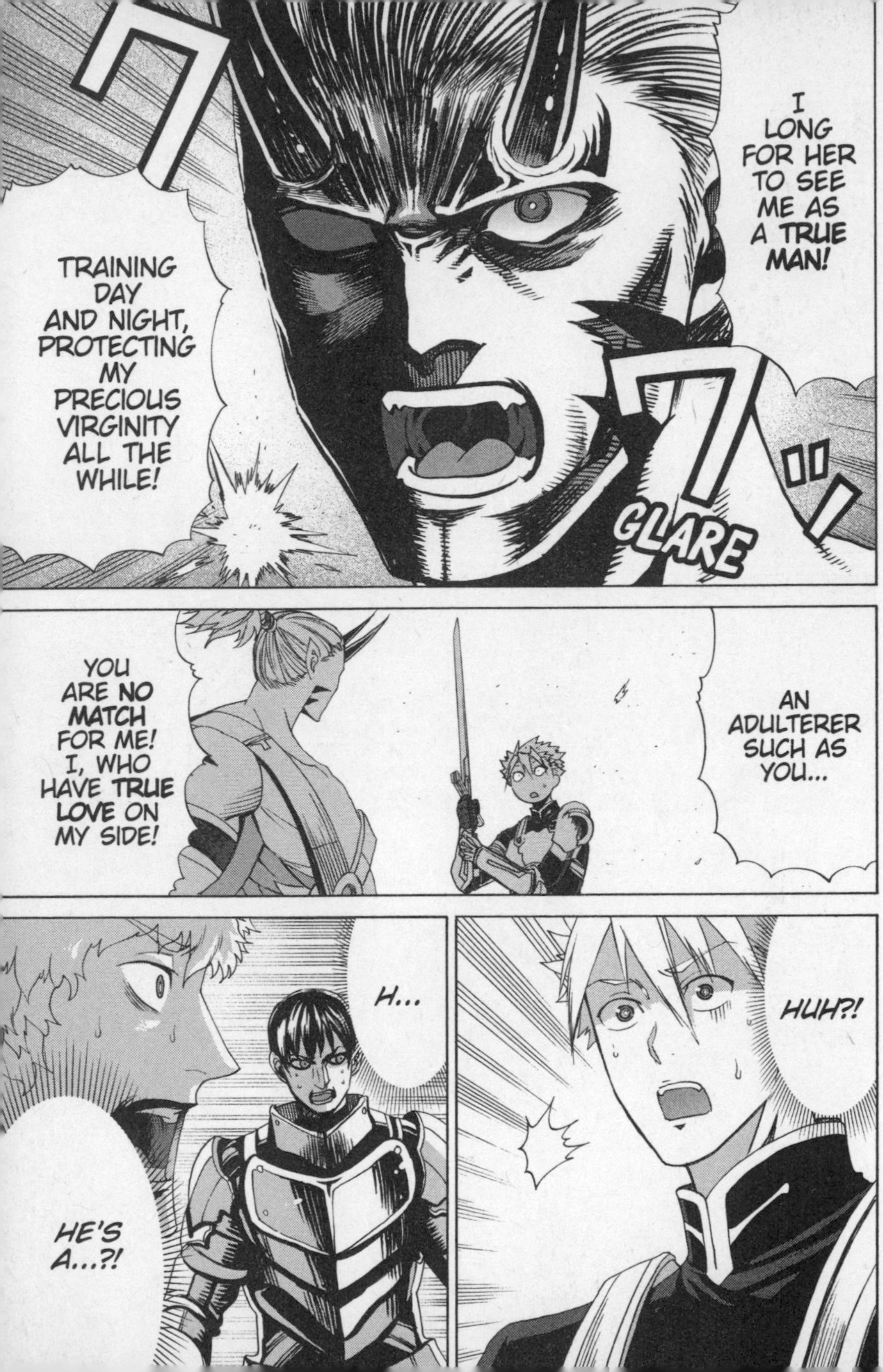
I LONG FOR HER TO SEE ME AS A TRUE MAN!
TRAINING DAY AND NIGHT, PROTECTING MY PRECIOUS VIRGINITY ALL THE WHILE!
GLARE
AN ADULTERER SUCH AS YOU...
YOU ARE NO MATCH FOR ME! I, WHO HAVE TRUE LOVE ON MY SIDE!
HUH?!
H...
HE'S A...?!

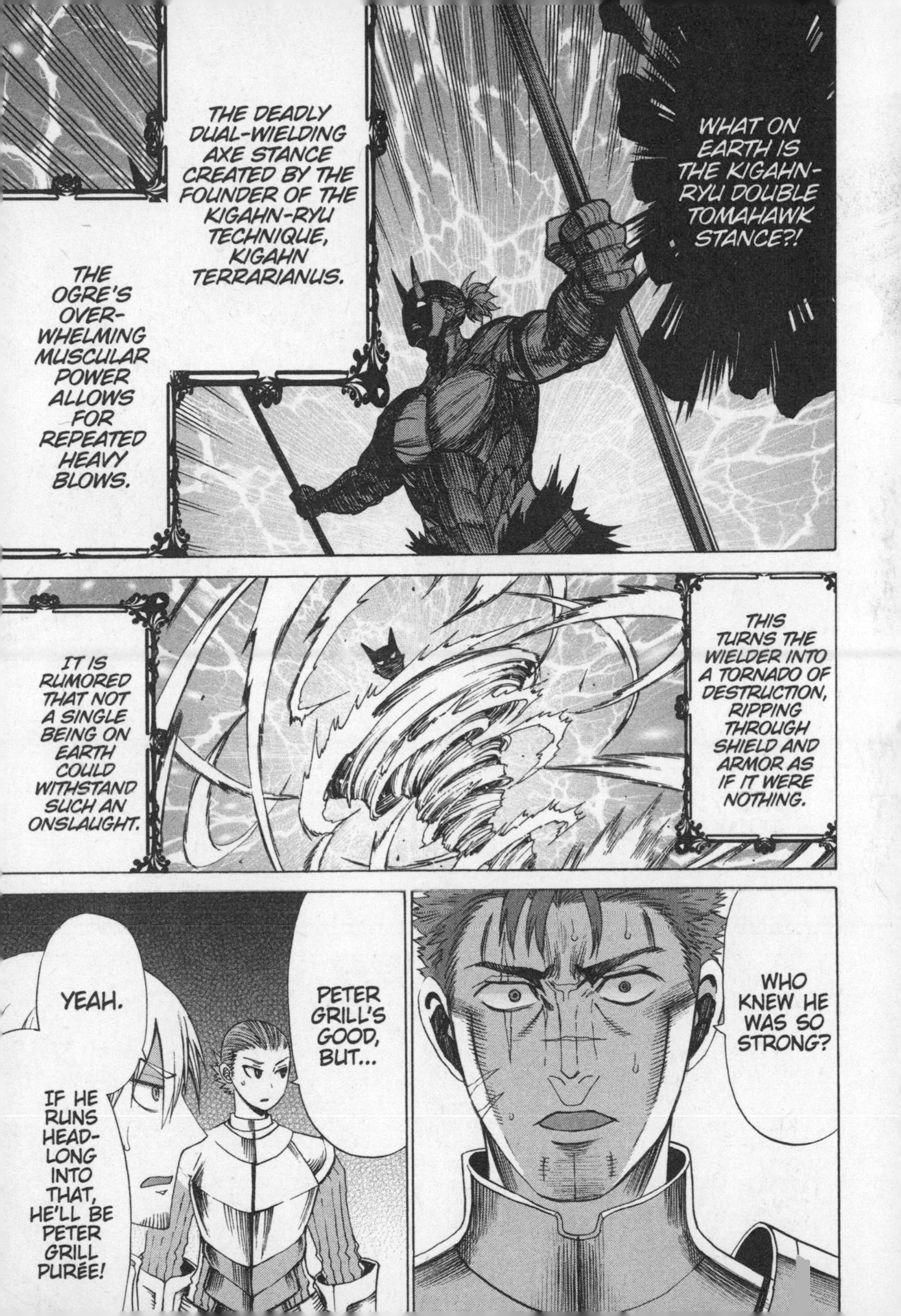
WHAT ON EARTH IS THE KIGAHN-RYU DOUBLE TOMAHAWK STANCE?!
THE DEADLY DUAL-WIELDING AXE STANCE CREATED BY THE FOUNDER OF THE KIGAHN-RYU TECHNIQUE, KIGAHN TERRARIANUS.
THE OGRE'S OVER-WHELMING MUSCULAR POWER ALLOWS FOR REPEATED HEAVY BLOWS.
THIS TURNS THE WIELDER INTO A TORNADO OF DESTRUCTION, RIPPING THROUGH SHIELD AND ARMOR AS IF IT WERE NOTHING.
IT IS RUMORED THAT NOT A SINGLE BEING ON EARTH COULD WITHSTAND SUCH AN ONSLAUGHT.
WHO KNEW HE WAS SO STRONG?
PETER GRILL'S GOOD, BUT...
YEAH.
IF HE RUNS HEAD-LONG INTO THAT, HE'LL BE PETER GRILL PURÉE!

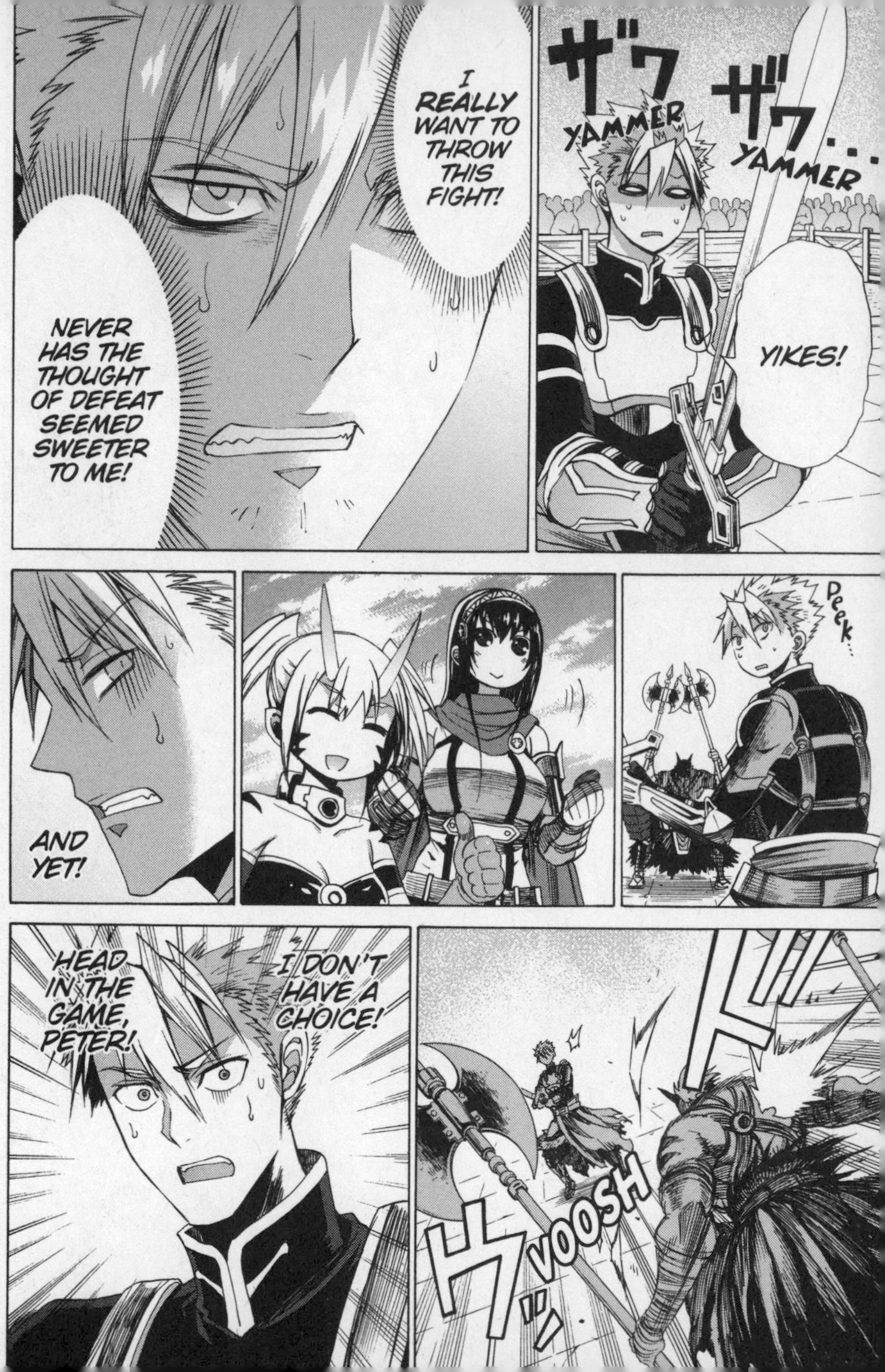
ザワ ザワ...
YAMMER YAMMER
YIKES!
I REALLY WANT TO THROW THIS FIGHT!
NEVER HAS THE THOUGHT OF DEFEAT SEEMED SWEETER TO ME!
Peek...
AND YET!
ドッ
VOOSH
I DON'T HAVE A CHOICE!
HEAD IN THE GAME, PETER!

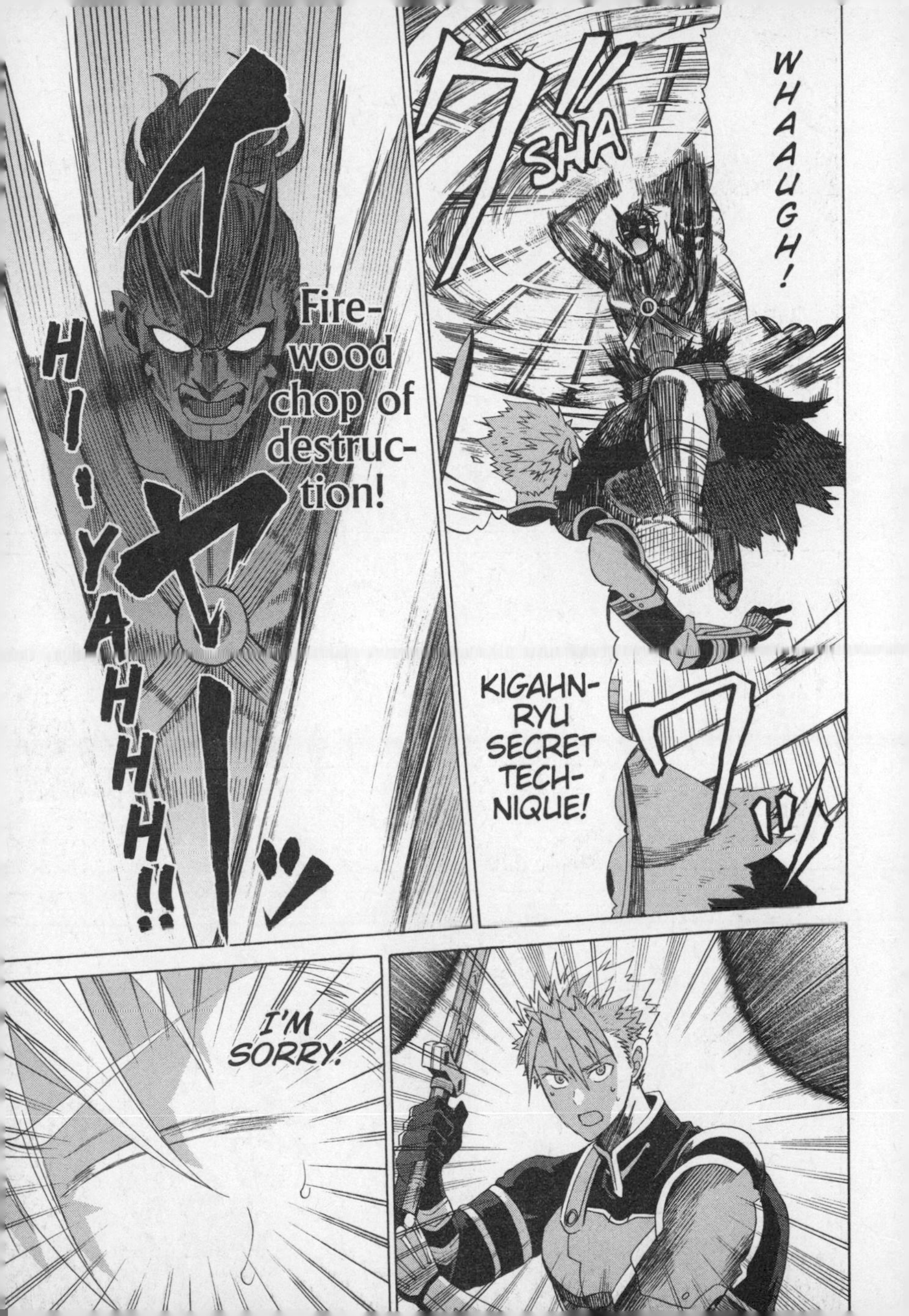
WHAAAUGH!
SHA
KIGAHN-RYU SECRET TECHNIQUE!
Firewood chop of destruction!
HI-YAHHHH!!
I'M SORRY.

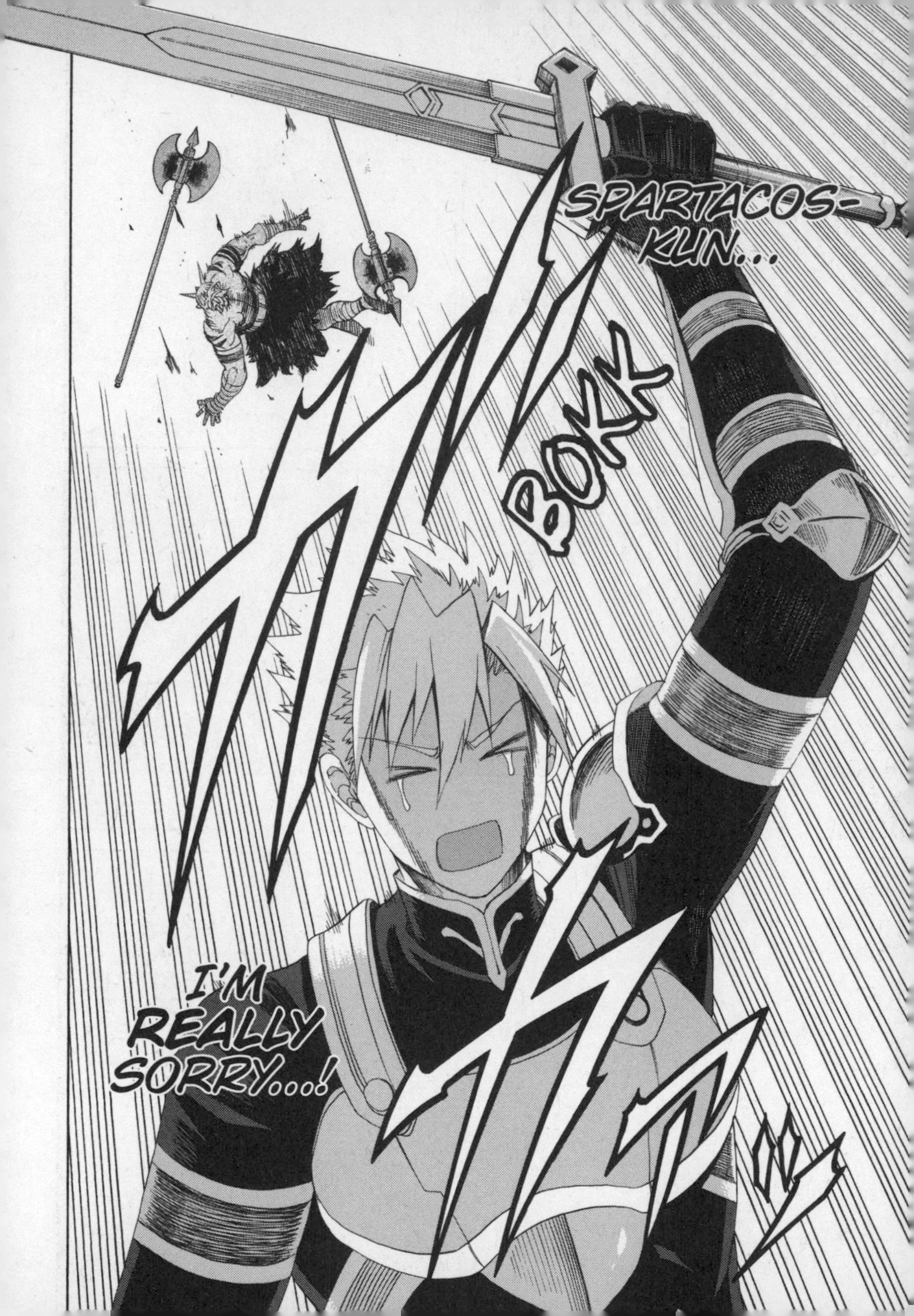
SPARTACOS-KUN...
BOKK
I'M REALLY SORRY...!

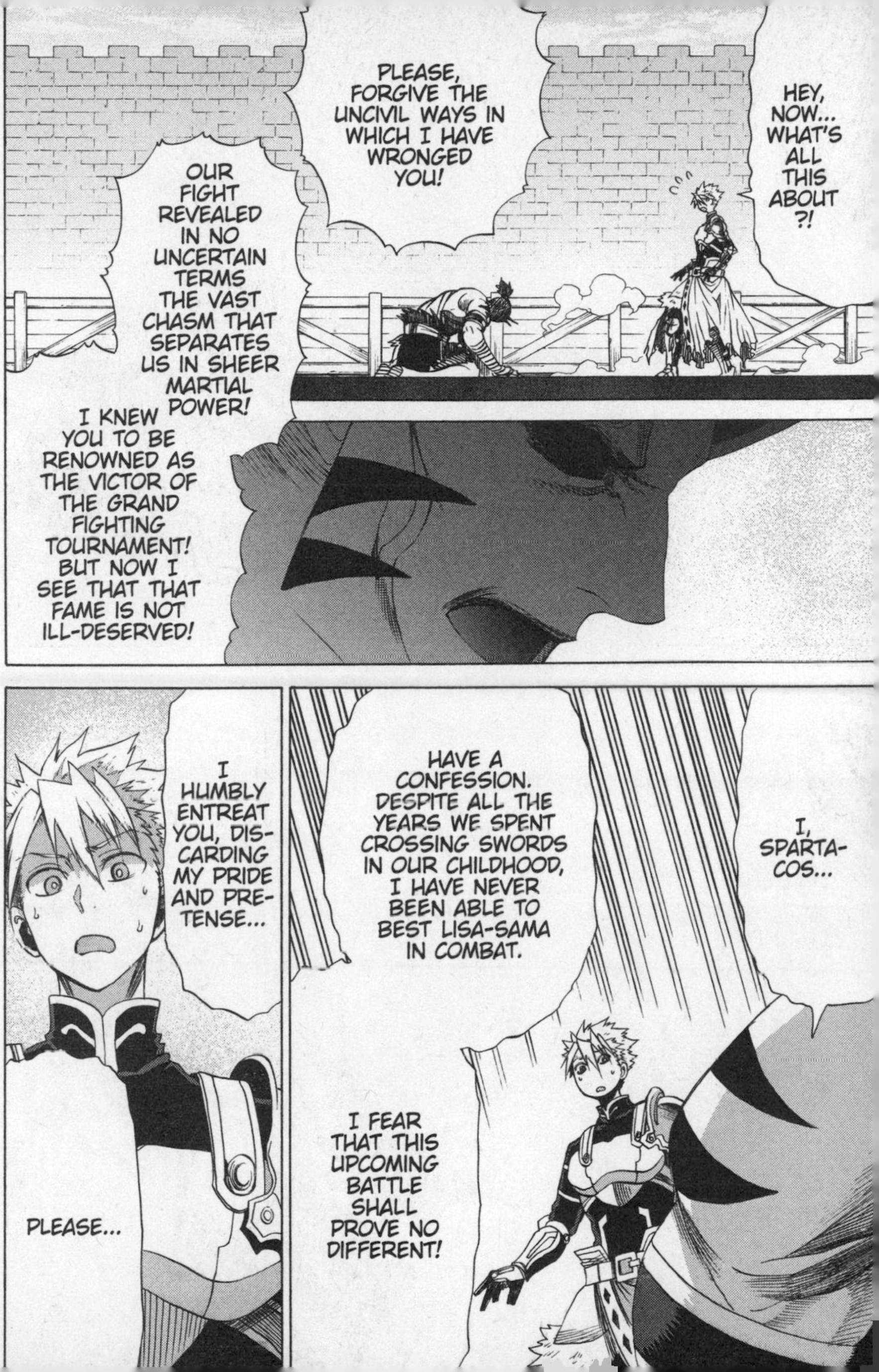
PLEASE, FORGIVE THE UNCIVIL WAYS IN WHICH I HAVE WRONGED YOU!
HEY, NOW... WHAT'S ALL THIS ABOUT?!
OUR FIGHT REVEALED IN NO UNCERTAIN TERMS THE VAST CHASM THAT SEPARATES US IN SHEER MARTIAL POWER!
I KNEW YOU TO BE RENOWNED AS THE VICTOR OF THE GRAND FIGHTING TOURNAMENT! BUT NOW I SEE THAT THAT FAME IS NOT ILL-DESERVED!
I, SPARTACOS...
HAVE A CONFESSION. DESPITE ALL THE YEARS WE SPENT CROSSING SWORDS IN OUR CHILDHOOD, I HAVE NEVER BEEN ABLE TO BEST LISA-SAMA IN COMBAT.
I FEAR THAT THIS UPCOMING BATTLE SHALL PROVE NO DIFFERENT!
I HUMBLY ENTREAT YOU, DISCARDING MY PRIDE AND PRETENSE...
PLEASE...

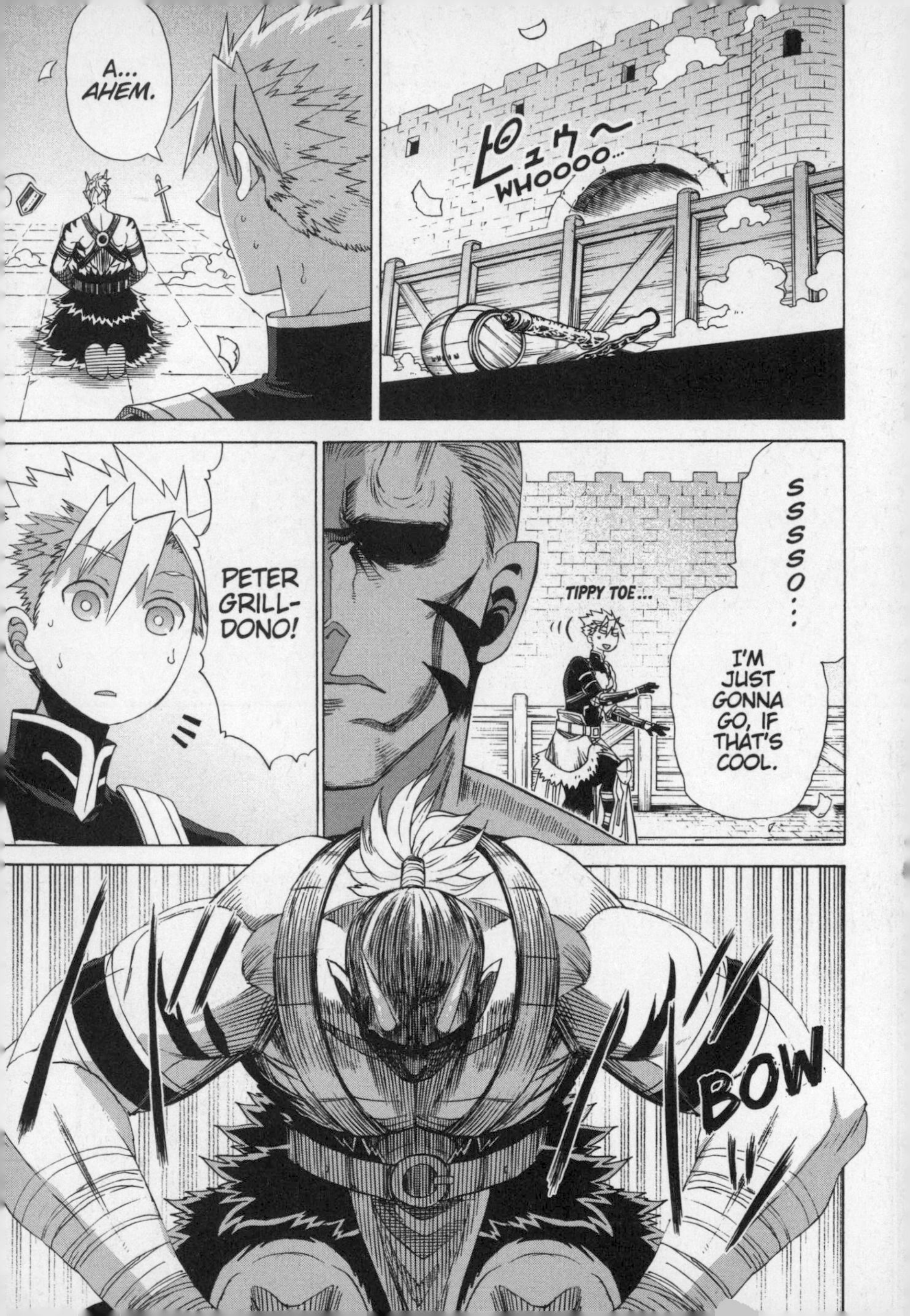
WHOOOO...
A... AHEM.
SSSSO...
TIPPY TOE...
I'M JUST GONNA GO, IF THAT'S COOL.
PETER GRILL-DONO!
BOW!!

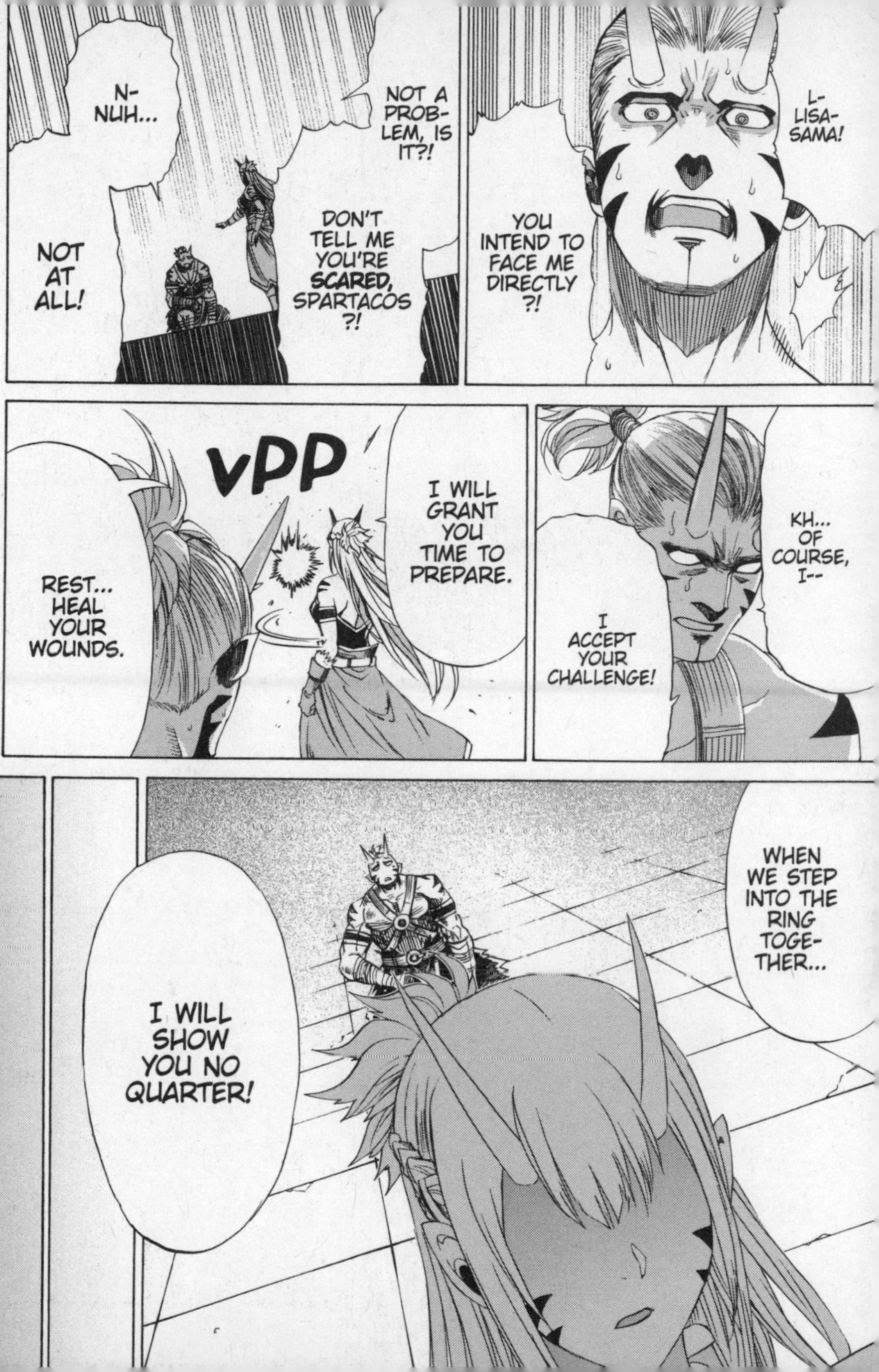
L-LISA-SAMA!
YOU INTEND TO FACE ME DIRECTLY?!
NOT A PROB-LEM, IS IT?!
DON'T TELL ME YOU'RE SCARED, SPARTACOS?!
N-NUH...
NOT AT ALL!
KH... OF COURSE, I--
I ACCEPT YOUR CHALLENGE!
I WILL GRANT YOU TIME TO PREPARE.
vPP
REST... HEAL YOUR WOUNDS.
WHEN WE STEP INTO THE RING TOGE-THER...
I WILL SHOW YOU NO QUARTER!

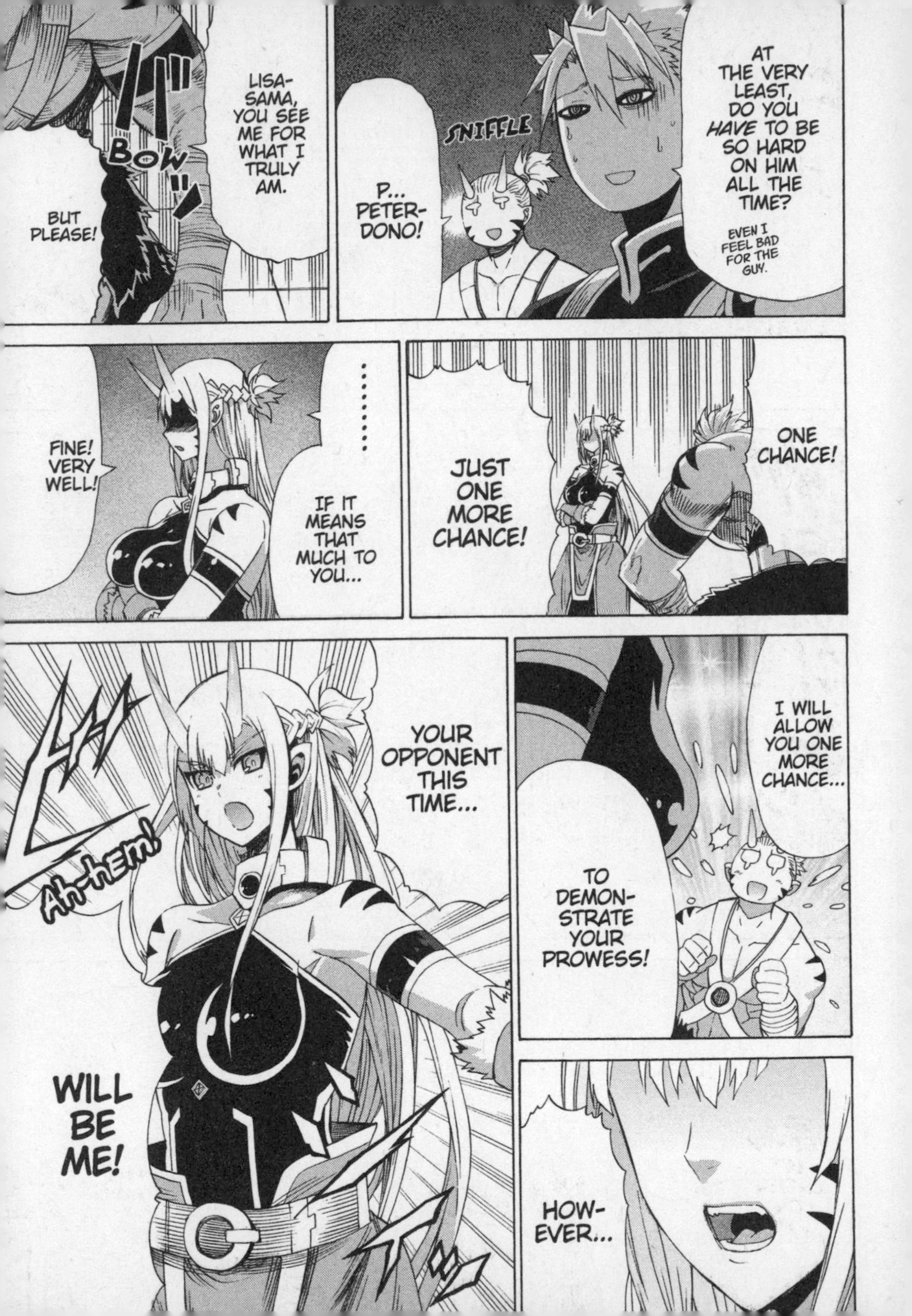
AT THE VERY LEAST, DO YOU HAVE TO BE SO HARD ON HIM ALL THE TIME?
EVEN I FEEL BAD FOR THE GUY.
SNIFFLE
P... PETER-DONO!
LISA-SAMA, YOU SEE ME FOR WHAT I TRULY AM.
BOW
BUT PLEASE!
ONE CHANCE!
JUST ONE MORE CHANCE!
......
IF IT MEANS THAT MUCH TO YOU...
FINE! VERY WELL!
I WILL ALLOW YOU ONE MORE CHANCE...
TO DEMONSTRATE YOUR PROWESS!
HOW-EVER...
Ah-hem!
YOUR OPPONENT THIS TIME...
WILL BE ME!

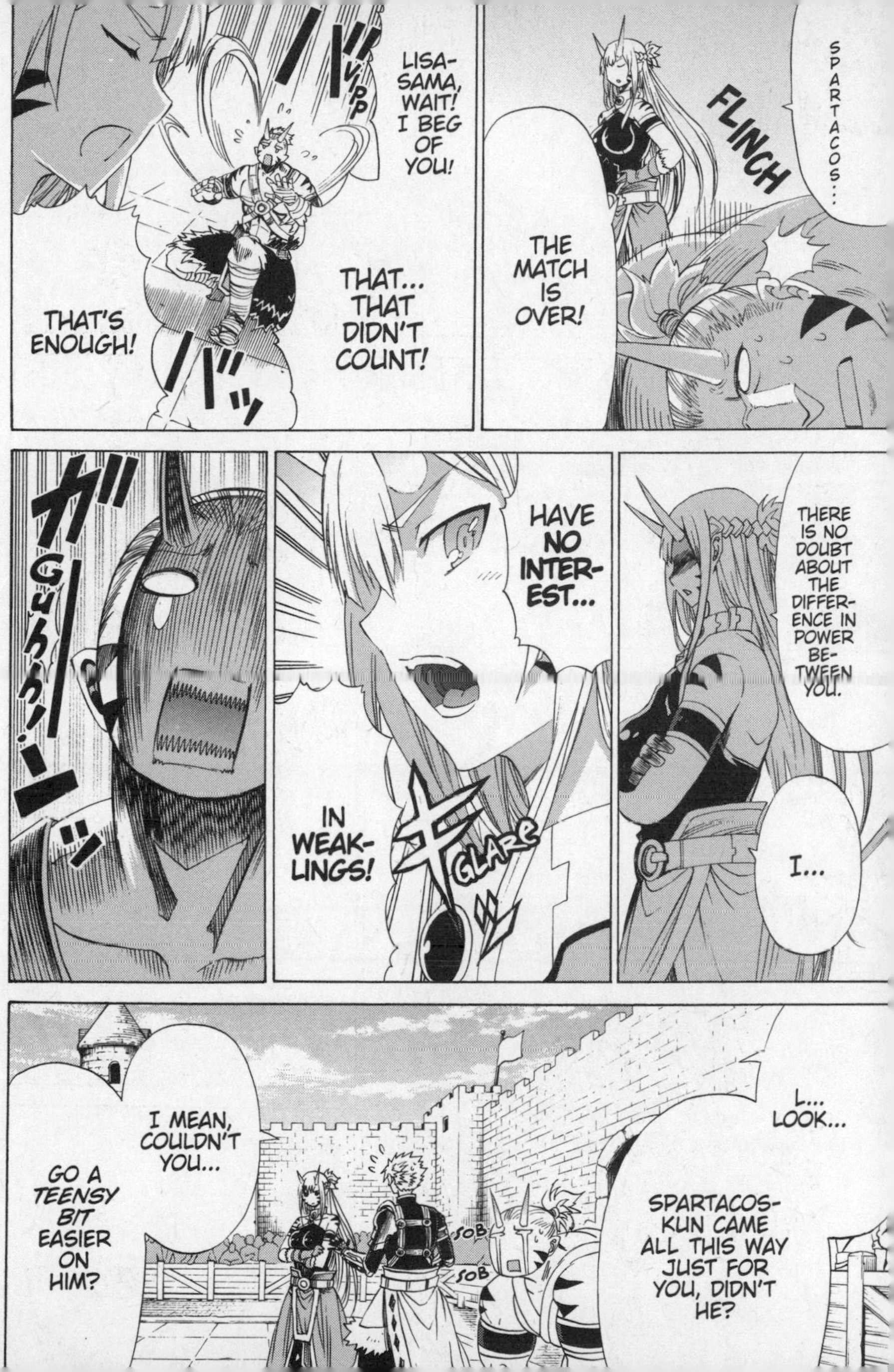
SPARTACOS...
FLINCH
THE MATCH IS OVER!
LISA-SAMA, WAIT! I BEG OF YOU!
VIPP
THAT... THAT DIDN'T COUNT!
THAT'S ENOUGH!
THERE IS NO DOUBT ABOUT THE DIFFER-ENCE IN POWER BE-TWEEN YOU.
I...
HAVE NO INTER-EST...
IN WEAK-LINGS!
GLARE
L... LOOK...
SPARTACOS-KUN CAME ALL THIS WAY JUST FOR YOU, DIDN'T HE?
SOB
SOB
I MEAN, COULDN'T YOU...
GO A TEENSY BIT EASIER ON HIM?

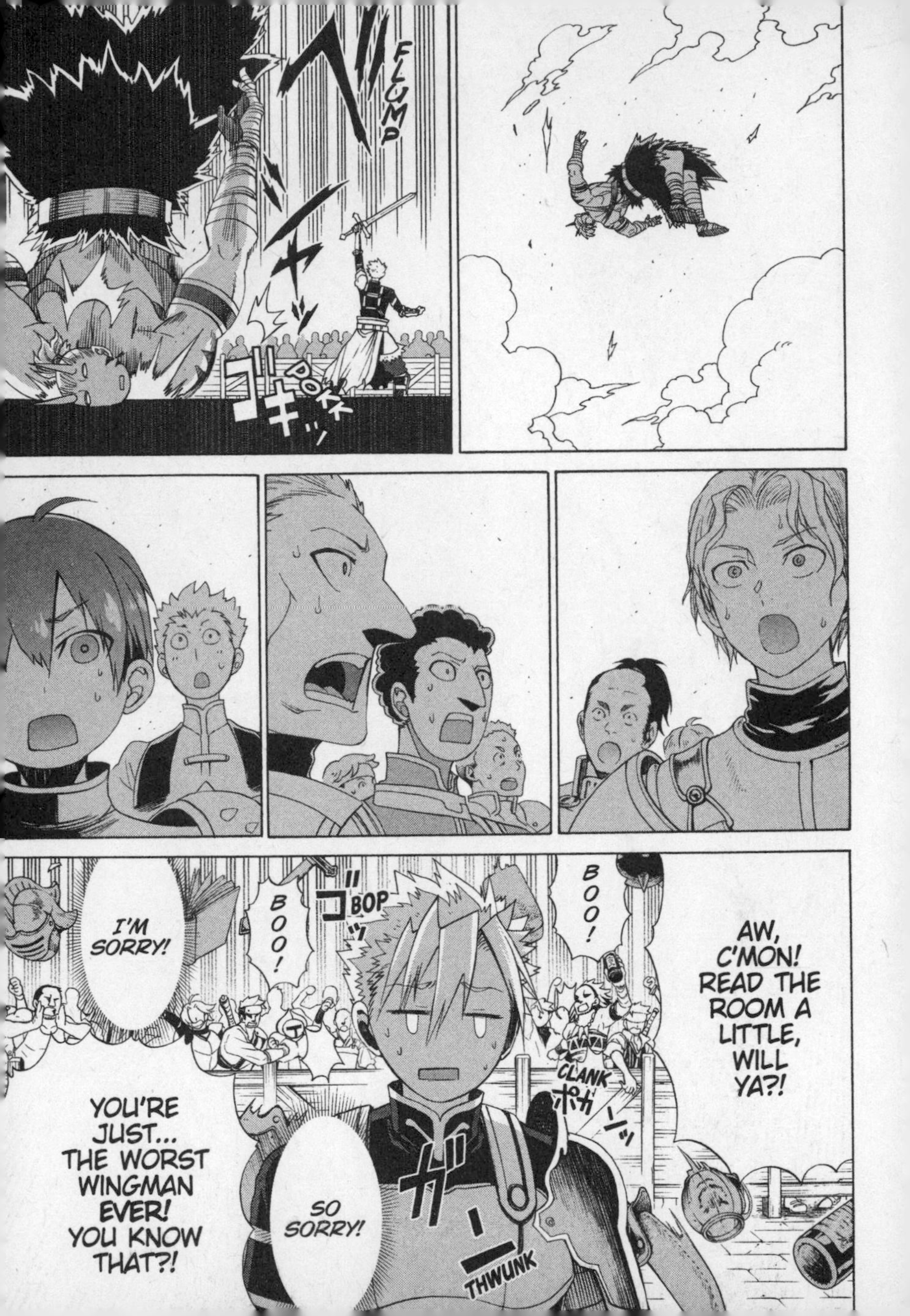
FLUMP
POKK
AW, C'MON! READ THE ROOM A LITTLE, WILL YA?!
BOO!
CLANK
BOP
BOO!
I'M SORRY!
THWUNK
SO SORRY!
YOU'RE JUST... THE WORST WINGMAN EVER! YOU KNOW THAT?!

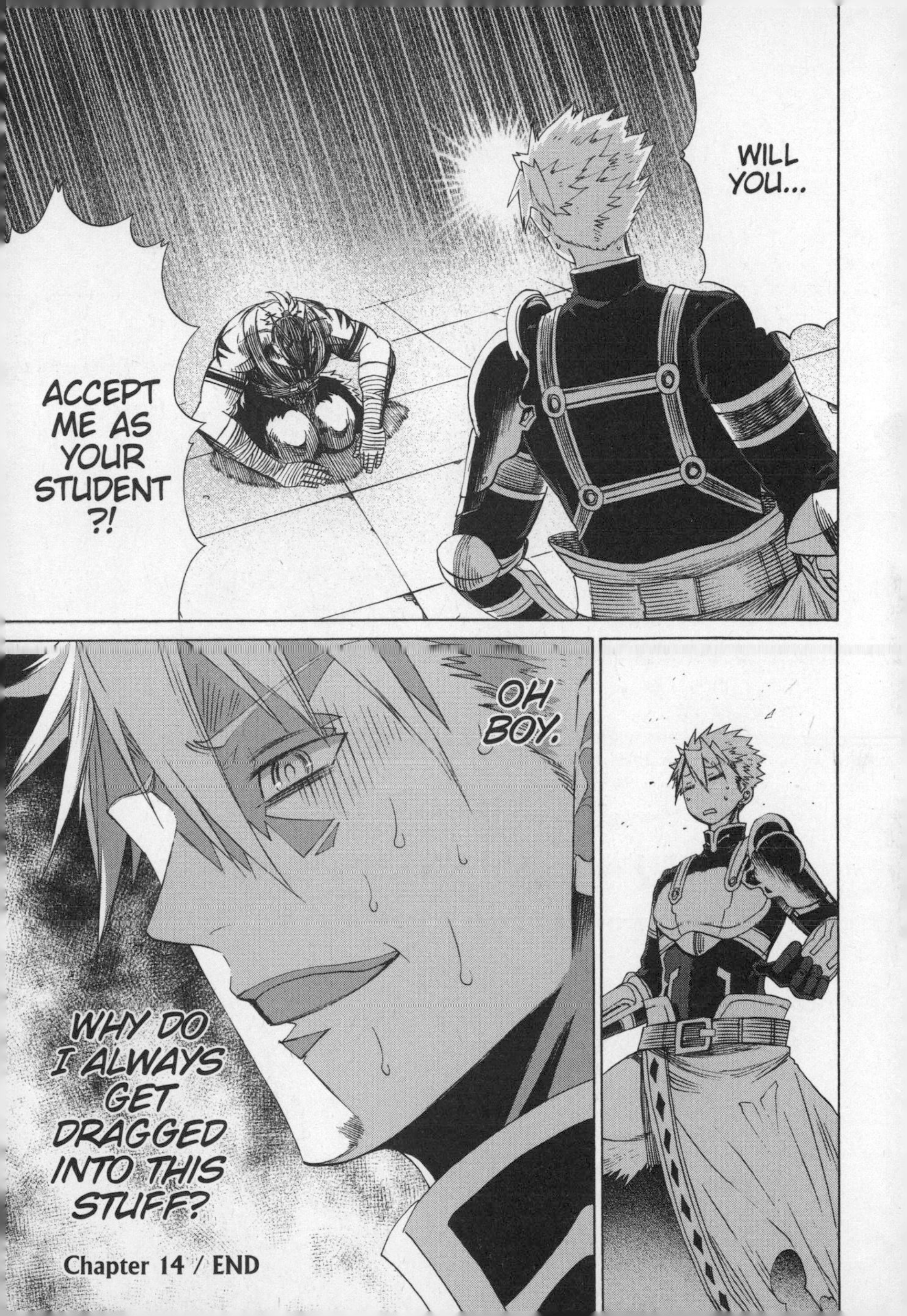
WILL YOU...
ACCEPT ME AS YOUR STUDENT ?!
OH BOY.
WHY DO I ALWAYS GET DRAGGED INTO THIS STUFF?
Chapter 14 / END

PETER GRILL
AND THE PHILOSOPHER'S TIME

Previously, on *Peter Grill*...

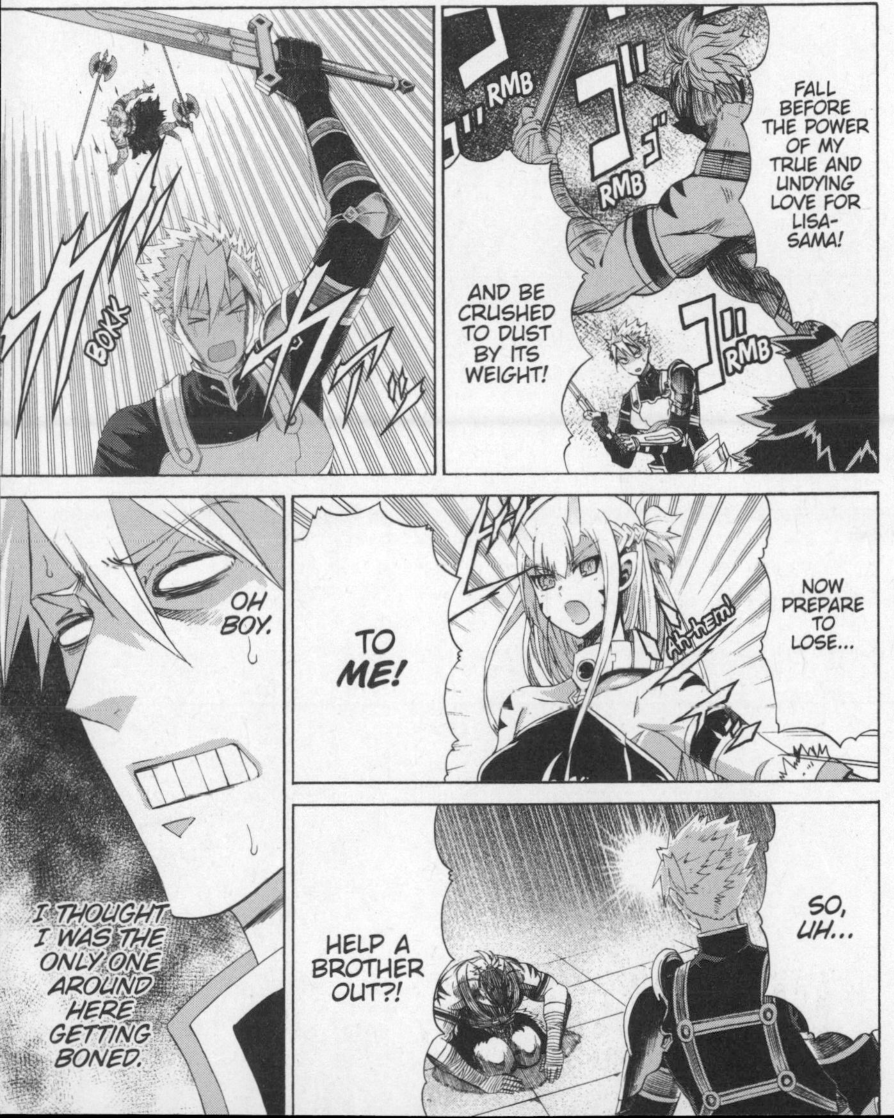
RMB
RMB
FALL BEFORE THE POWER OF MY TRUE AND UNDYING LOVE FOR LISA-SAMA!
AND BE CRUSHED TO DUST BY ITS WEIGHT!
RMB
BOKK
NOW PREPARE TO LOSE...
Ah-hem!
TO ME!
SO, UH...
HELP A BROTHER OUT?!
OH BOY.
I THOUGHT I WAS THE ONLY ONE AROUND HERE GETTING BONED.

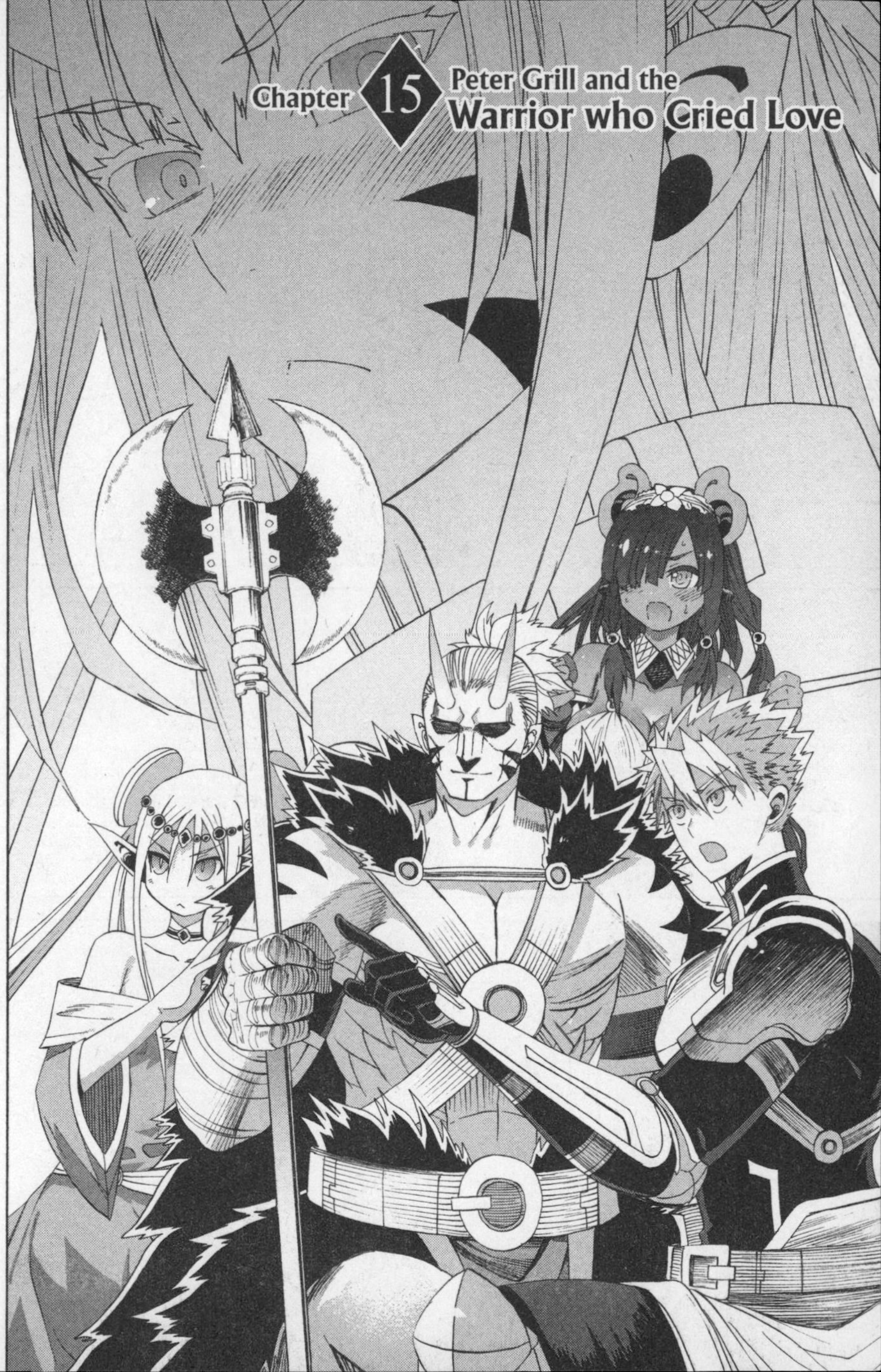
Chapter 15 Peter Grill and the Warrior who Cried Love

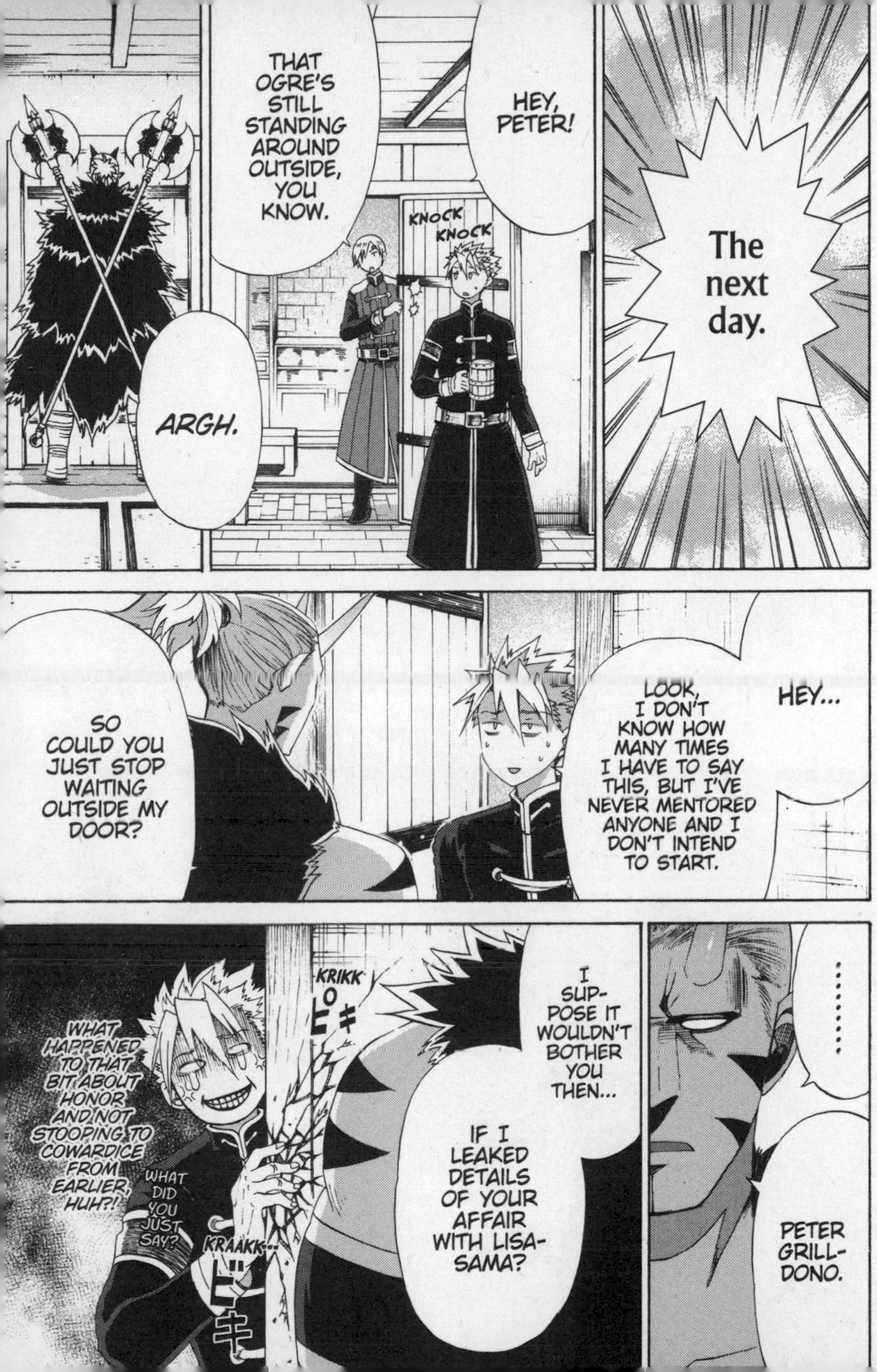
The next day.
HEY, PETER!
THAT OGRE'S STILL STANDING AROUND OUTSIDE, YOU KNOW.
KNOCK KNOCK
ARGH.
HEY...
LOOK, I DON'T KNOW HOW MANY TIMES I HAVE TO SAY THIS, BUT I'VE NEVER MENTORED ANYONE AND I DON'T INTEND TO START.
SO COULD YOU JUST STOP WAITING OUTSIDE MY DOOR?
......
PETER GRILL-DONO.
I SUP-POSE IT WOULDN'T BOTHER YOU THEN...
IF I LEAKED DETAILS OF YOUR AFFAIR WITH LISA-SAMA?
KRIKK
ピキ
WHAT DID YOU JUST SAY?
WHAT HAPPENED TO THAT BIT ABOUT HONOR AND NOT STOOPING TO COWARDICE FROM EARLIER, HUH?!
KRAAKK...
ビキ

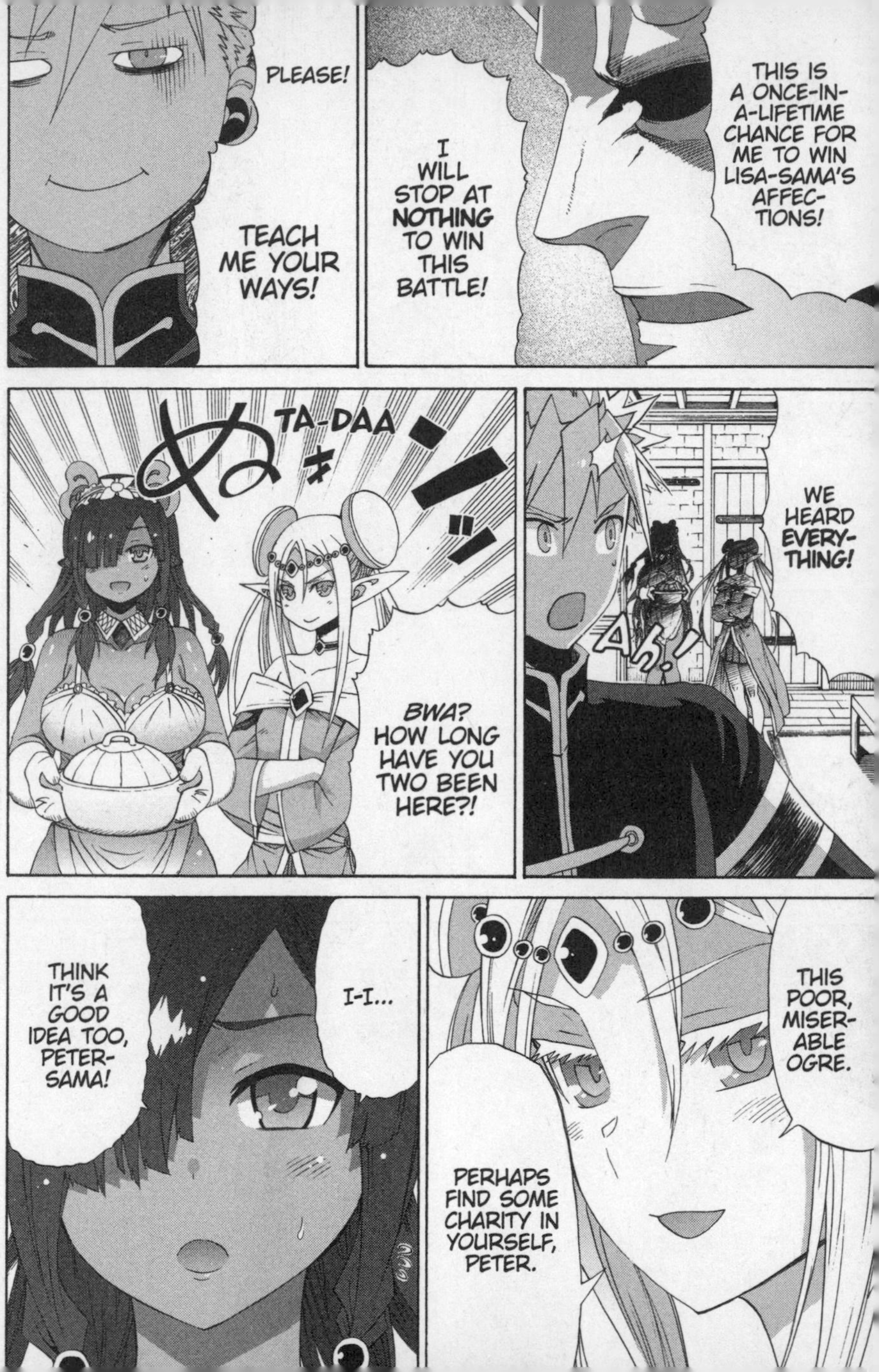
THIS IS A ONCE-IN-A-LIFETIME CHANCE FOR ME TO WIN LISA-SAMA'S AFFECTIONS!
I WILL STOP AT NOTHING TO WIN THIS BATTLE!
PLEASE!
TEACH ME YOUR WAYS!
WE HEARD EVERYTHING!
Ah!
TA-DAA
ぬ
BWA? HOW LONG HAVE YOU TWO BEEN HERE?!
THIS POOR, MISERABLE OGRE.
PERHAPS FIND SOME CHARITY IN YOURSELF, PETER.
I-I...
THINK IT'S A GOOD IDEA TOO, PETER-SAMA!

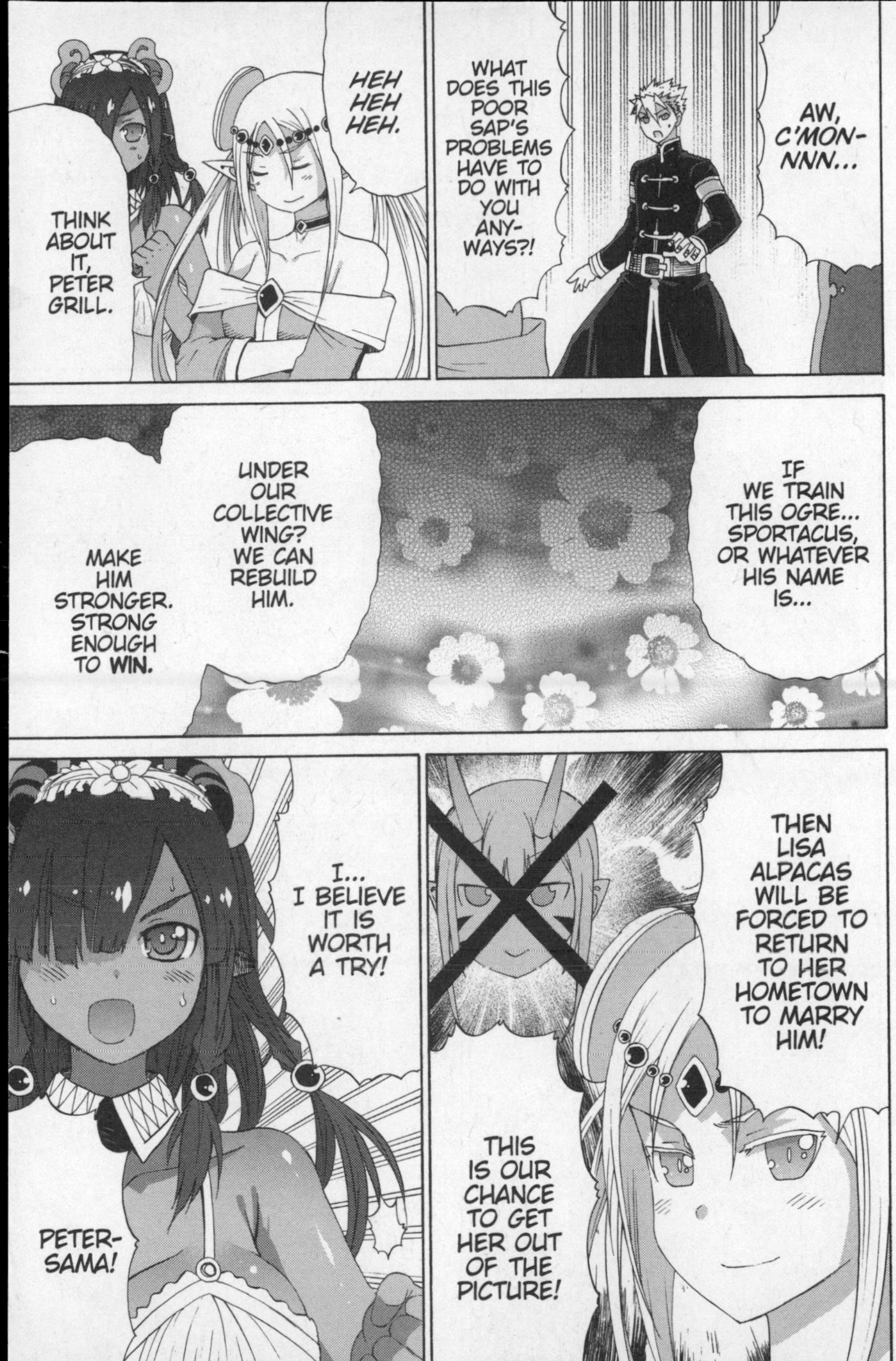
AW, C'MONNNN...
WHAT DOES THIS POOR SAP'S PROBLEMS HAVE TO DO WITH YOU ANYWAYS?!
HEH HEH HEH.
THINK ABOUT IT, PETER GRILL.
IF WE TRAIN THIS OGRE... SPORTACUS, OR WHATEVER HIS NAME IS...
UNDER OUR COLLECTIVE WING? WE CAN REBUILD HIM.
MAKE HIM STRONGER. STRONG ENOUGH TO WIN.
THEN LISA ALPACAS WILL BE FORCED TO RETURN TO HER HOMETOWN TO MARRY HIM!
THIS IS OUR CHANCE TO GET HER OUT OF THE PICTURE!
I... I BELIEVE IT IS WORTH A TRY!
PETER-SAMA!

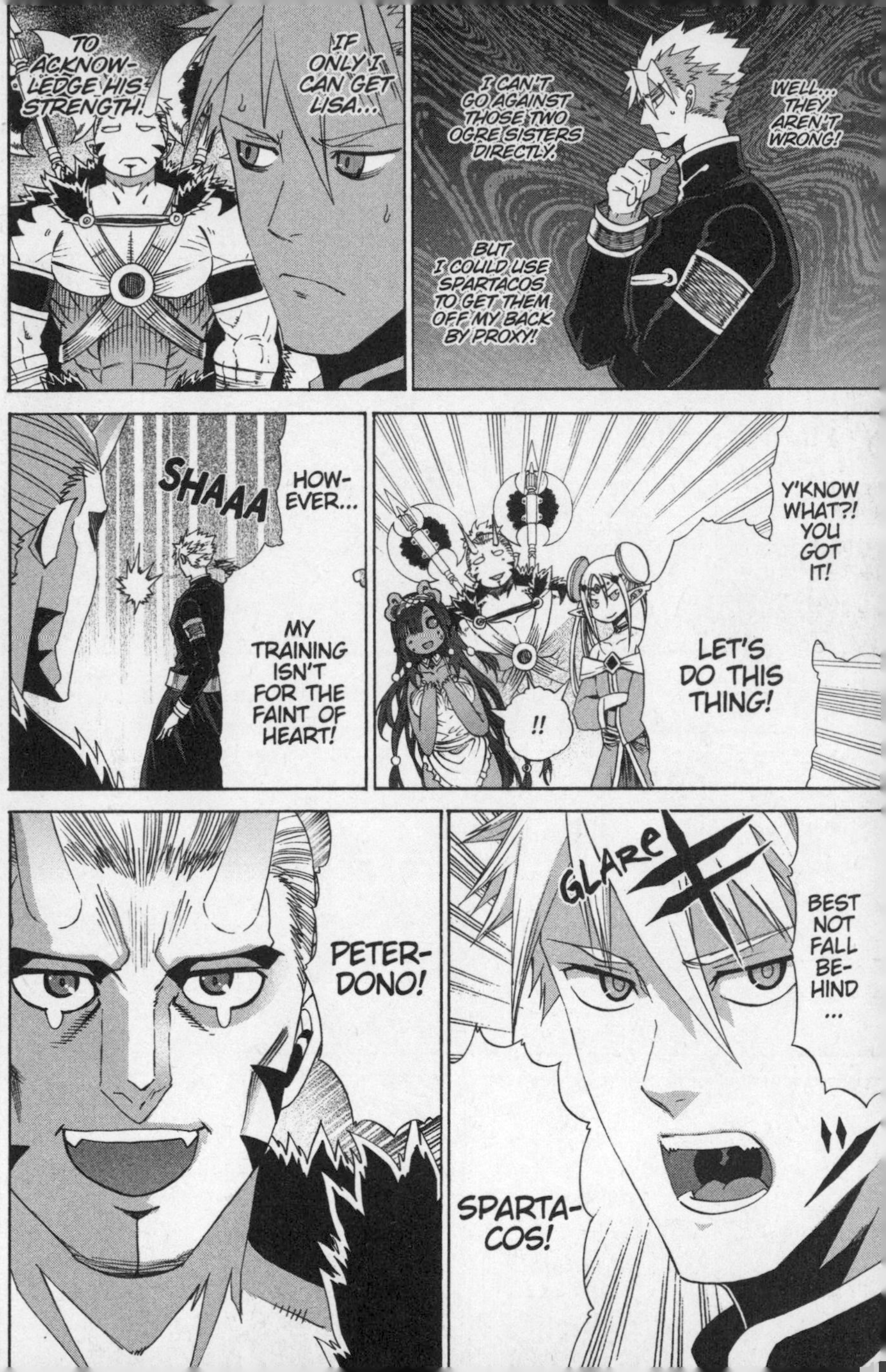
WELL... THEY AREN'T WRONG!
I CAN'T GO AGAINST THOSE TWO OGRE SISTERS DIRECTLY.
BUT I COULD USE SPARTACOS TO GET THEM OFF MY BACK BY PROXY!
IF ONLY I CAN GET LISA...
TO ACKNOW-LEDGE HIS STRENGTH!
Y'KNOW WHAT?! YOU GOT IT!
LET'S DO THIS THING!
!!
HOW-EVER...
SHAAA
MY TRAINING ISN'T FOR THE FAINT OF HEART!
GLARE
BEST NOT FALL BE-HIND ...
SPARTA-COS!
PETER-DONO!

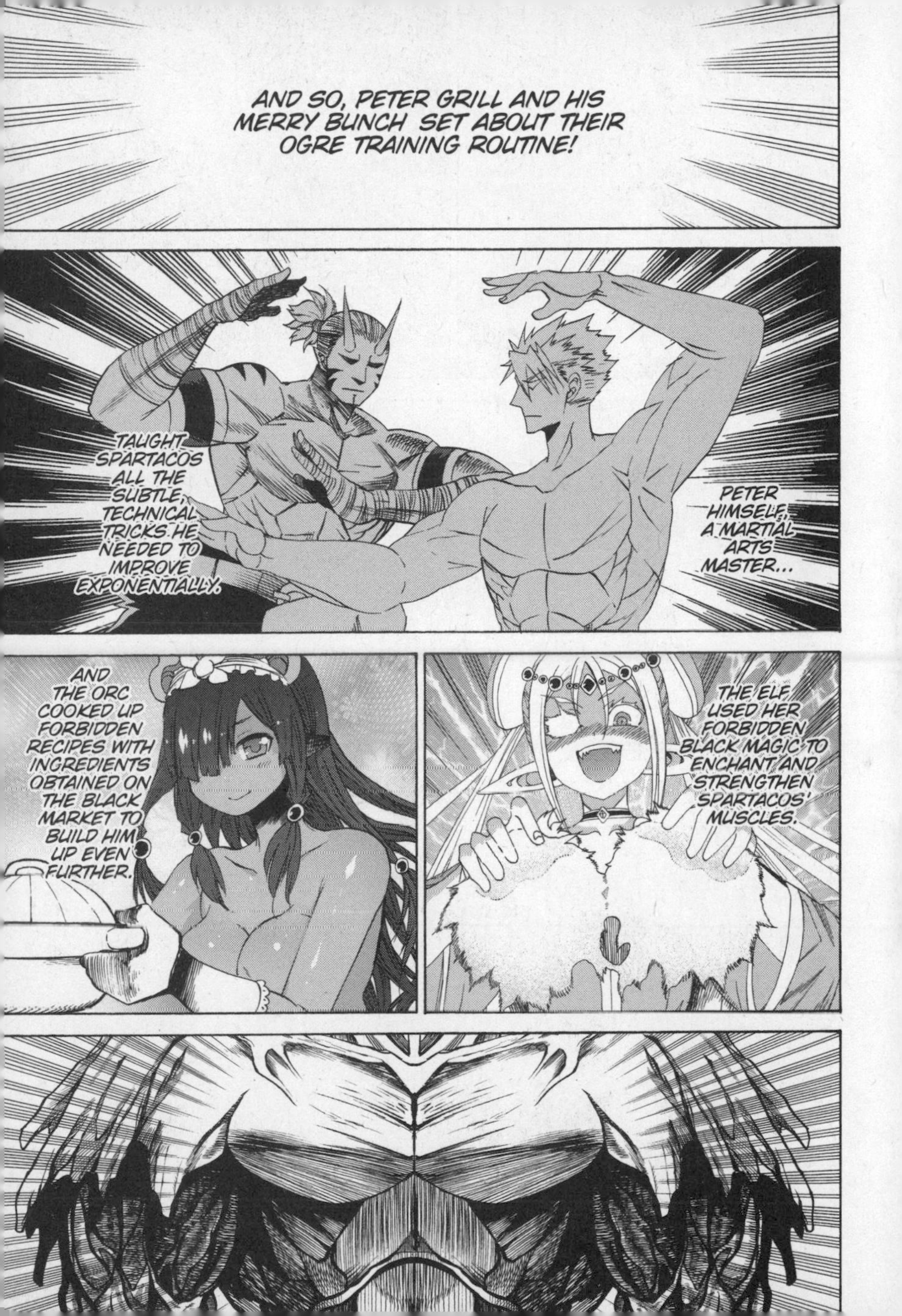
AND SO, PETER GRILL AND HIS MERRY BUNCH SET ABOUT THEIR OGRE TRAINING ROUTINE!
PETER HIMSELF, A MARTIAL ARTS MASTER...
TAUGHT SPARTACOS ALL THE SUBTLE, TECHNICAL TRICKS HE NEEDED TO IMPROVE EXPONENTIALLY.
THE ELF USED HER FORBIDDEN BLACK MAGIC TO ENCHANT AND STRENGTHEN SPARTACOS' MUSCLES.
AND THE ORC COOKED UP FORBIDDEN RECIPES WITH INGREDIENTS OBTAINED ON THE BLACK MARKET TO BUILD HIM UP EVEN FURTHER.

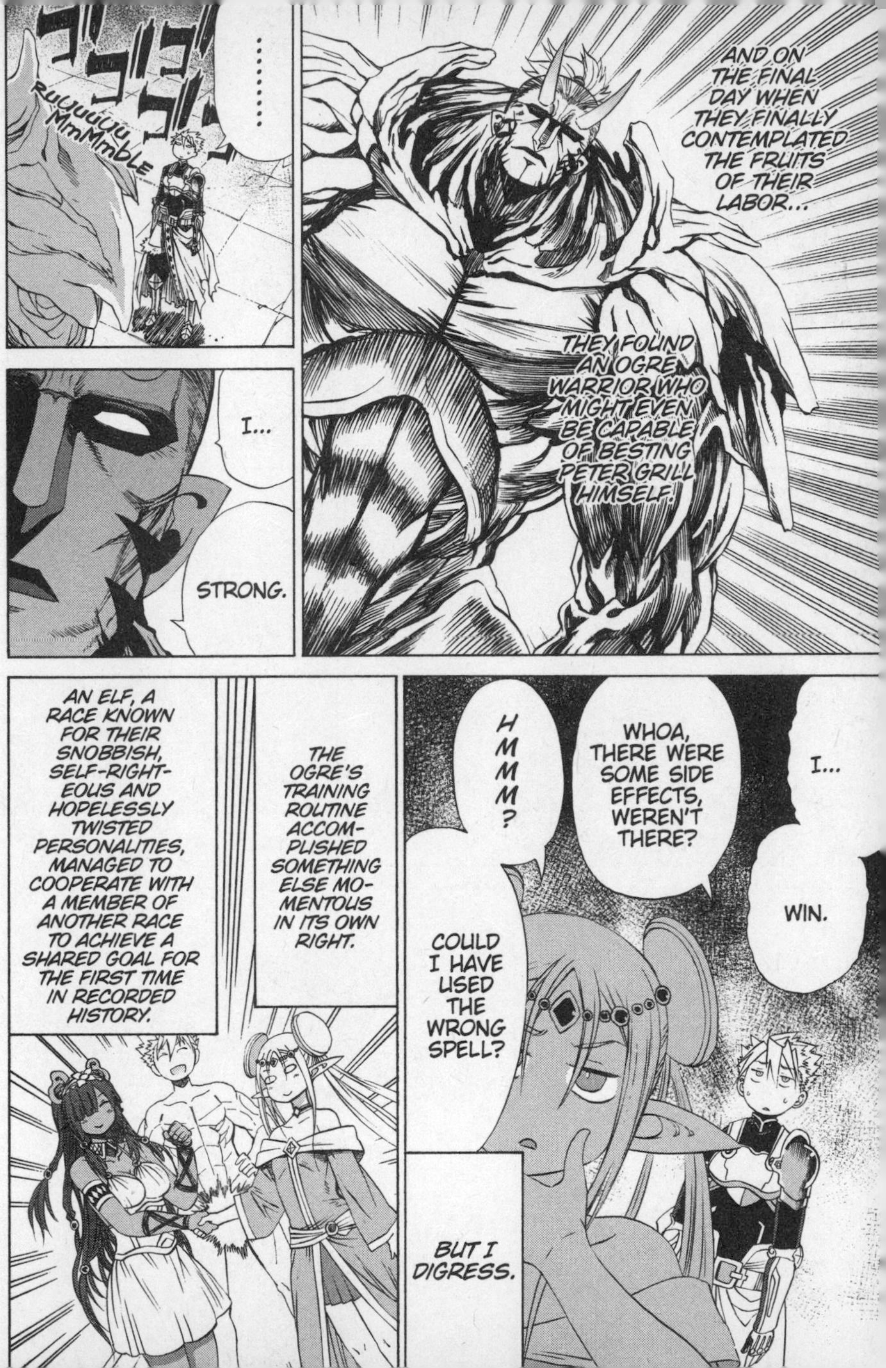
AND ON THE FINAL DAY WHEN THEY FINALLY CONTEMPLATED THE FRUITS OF THEIR LABOR...
THEY FOUND AN OGRE WARRIOR WHO MIGHT EVEN BE CAPABLE OF BESTING PETER GRILL HIMSELF.
RuuuuUu MmMmble
......
I...
STRONG.
I...
WIN.
WHOA, THERE WERE SOME SIDE EFFECTS, WEREN'T THERE?
HMMM?
COULD I HAVE USED THE WRONG SPELL?
BUT I DIGRESS.
THE OGRE'S TRAINING ROUTINE ACCOMPLISHED SOMETHING ELSE MOMENTOUS IN ITS OWN RIGHT.
AN ELF, A RACE KNOWN FOR THEIR SNOBBISH, SELF-RIGHTEOUS AND HOPELESSLY TWISTED PERSONALITIES, MANAGED TO COOPERATE WITH A MEMBER OF ANOTHER RACE TO ACHIEVE A SHARED GOAL FOR THE FIRST TIME IN RECORDED HISTORY.

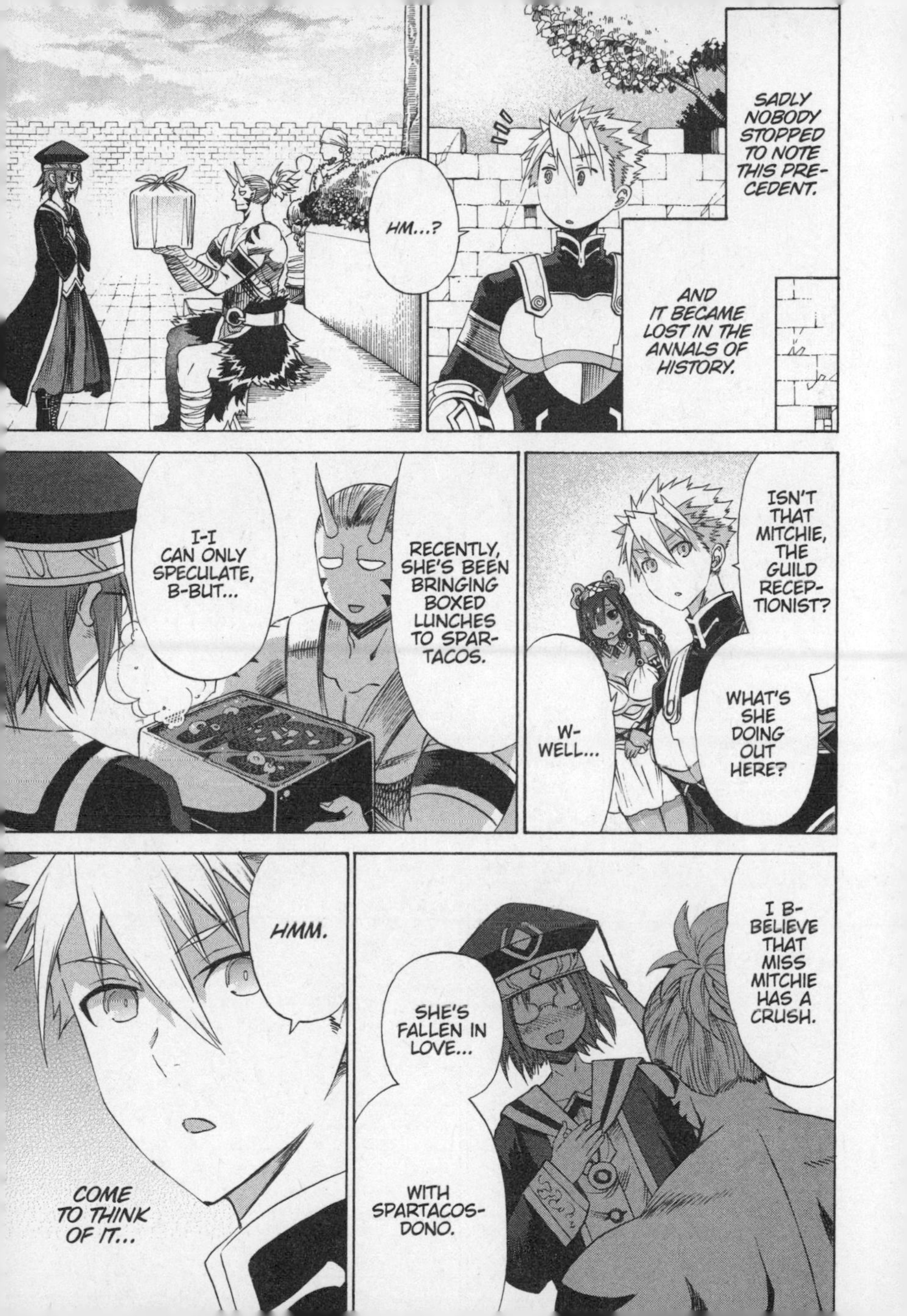
SADLY NOBODY STOPPED TO NOTE THIS PRE-CEDENT.
AND IT BECAME LOST IN THE ANNALS OF HISTORY.
HM...?
ISN'T THAT MITCHIE, THE GUILD RECEP-TIONIST?
WHAT'S SHE DOING OUT HERE?
W-WELL...
RECENTLY, SHE'S BEEN BRINGING BOXED LUNCHES TO SPAR-TACOS.
I-I CAN ONLY SPECULATE, B-BUT...
I B-BELIEVE THAT MISS MITCHIE HAS A CRUSH.
SHE'S FALLEN IN LOVE...
WITH SPARTACOS-DONO.
HMM.
COME TO THINK OF IT...

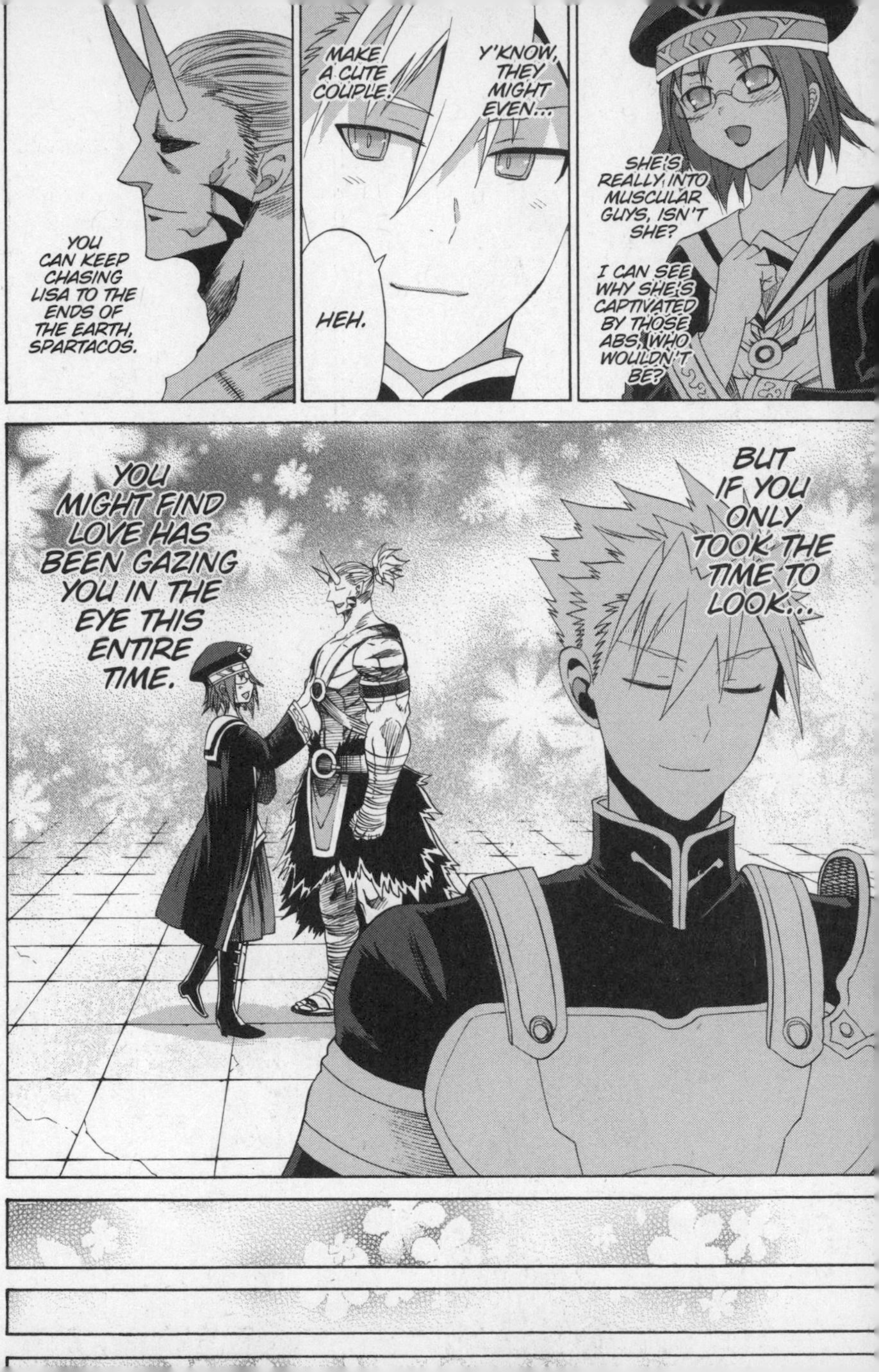
SHE'S REALLY INTO MUSCULAR GUYS, ISN'T SHE?
I CAN SEE WHY SHE'S CAPTIVATED BY THOSE ABS, WHO WOULDN'T BE?
Y'KNOW, THEY MIGHT EVEN...
MAKE A CUTE COUPLE.
HEH.
YOU CAN KEEP CHASING LISA TO THE ENDS OF THE EARTH, SPARTACOS.
BUT IF YOU ONLY TOOK THE TIME TO LOOK...
YOU MIGHT FIND LOVE HAS BEEN GAZING YOU IN THE EYE THIS ENTIRE TIME.

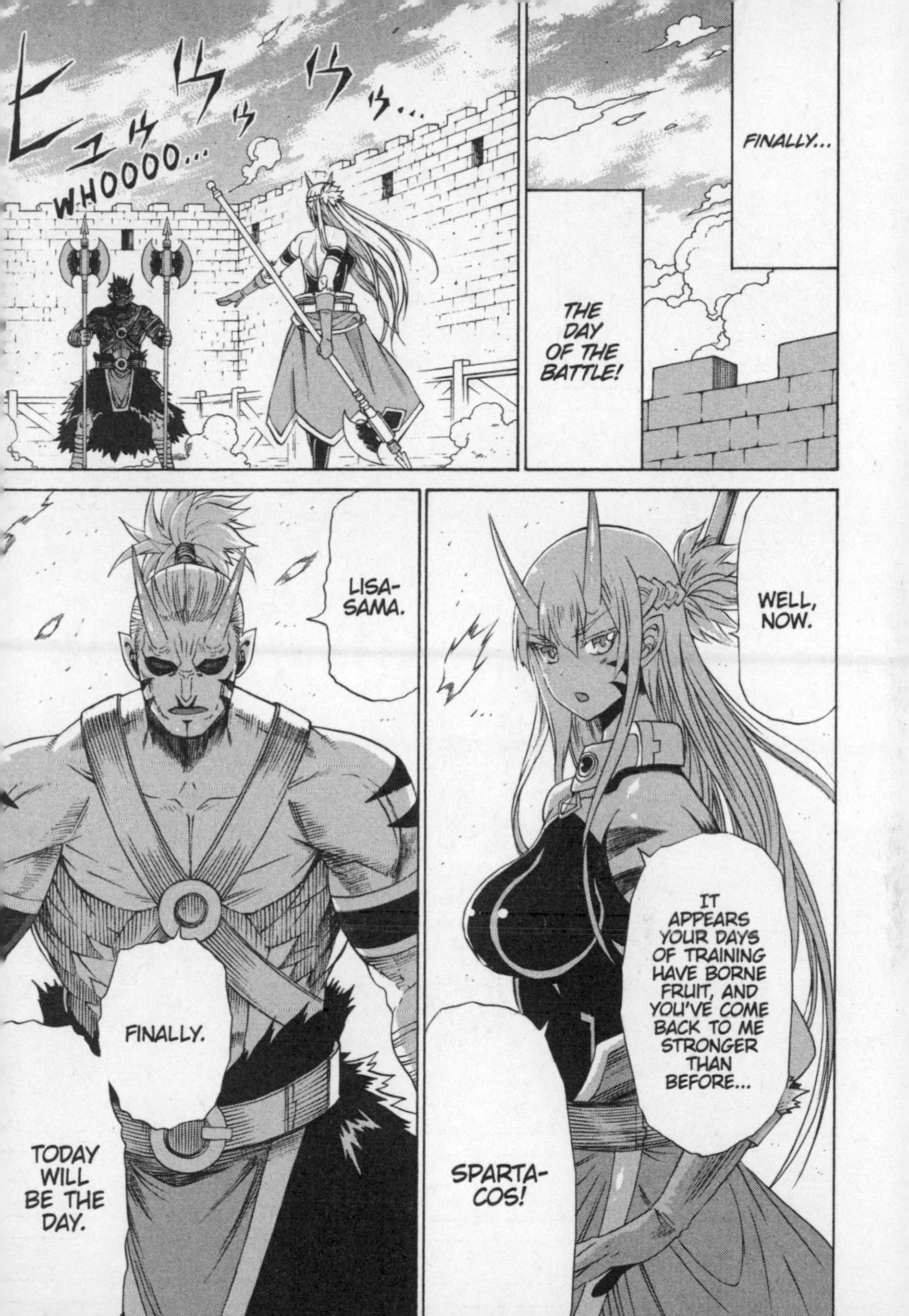
FINALLY...
THE DAY OF THE BATTLE!
WHOOOO...
WELL, NOW.
IT APPEARS YOUR DAYS OF TRAINING HAVE BORNE FRUIT, AND YOU'VE COME BACK TO ME STRONGER THAN BEFORE...
SPARTA-COS!
LISA-SAMA.
FINALLY.
TODAY WILL BE THE DAY.

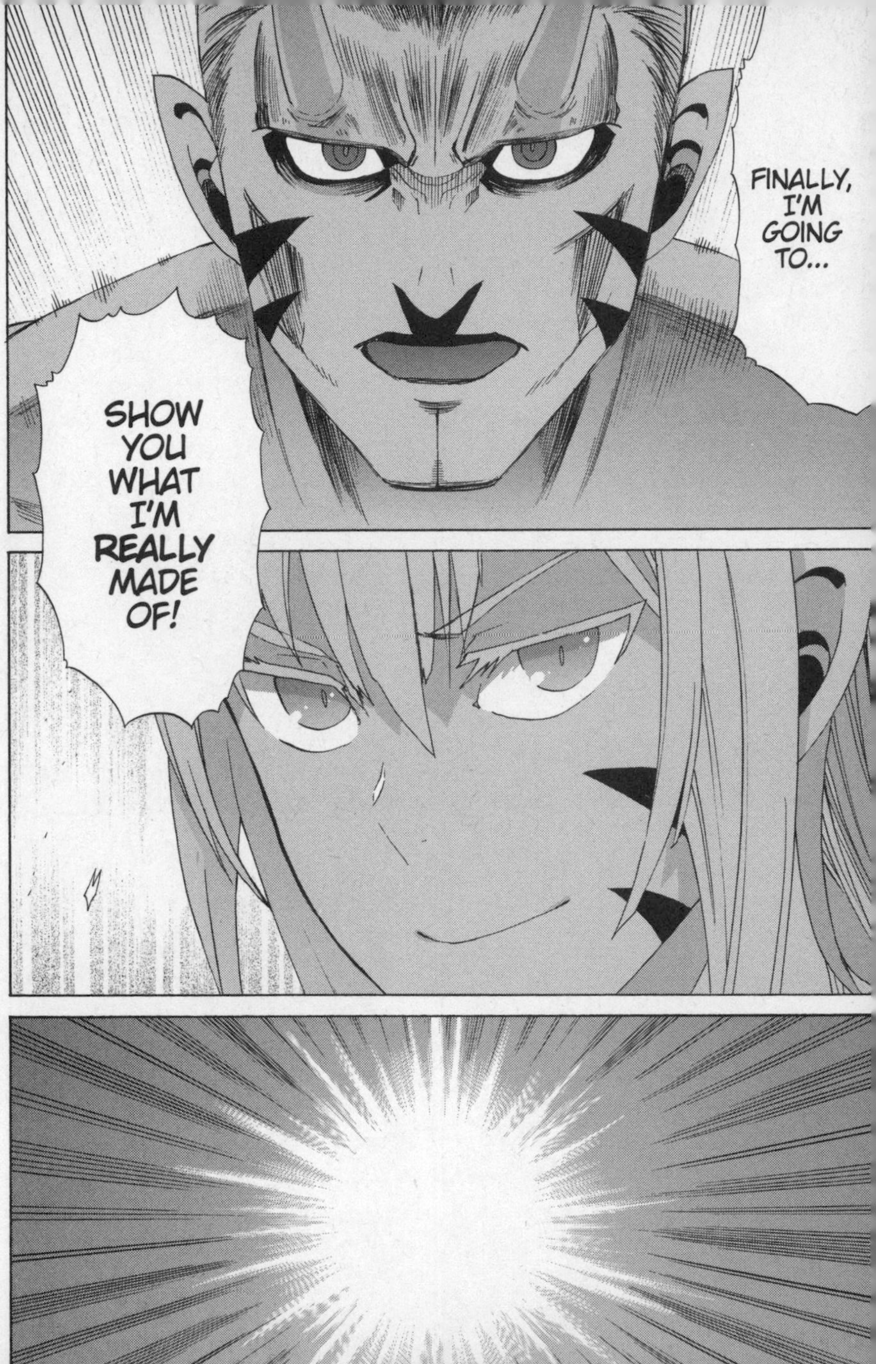
FINALLY, I'M GOING TO...
SHOW YOU WHAT I'M REALLY MADE OF!

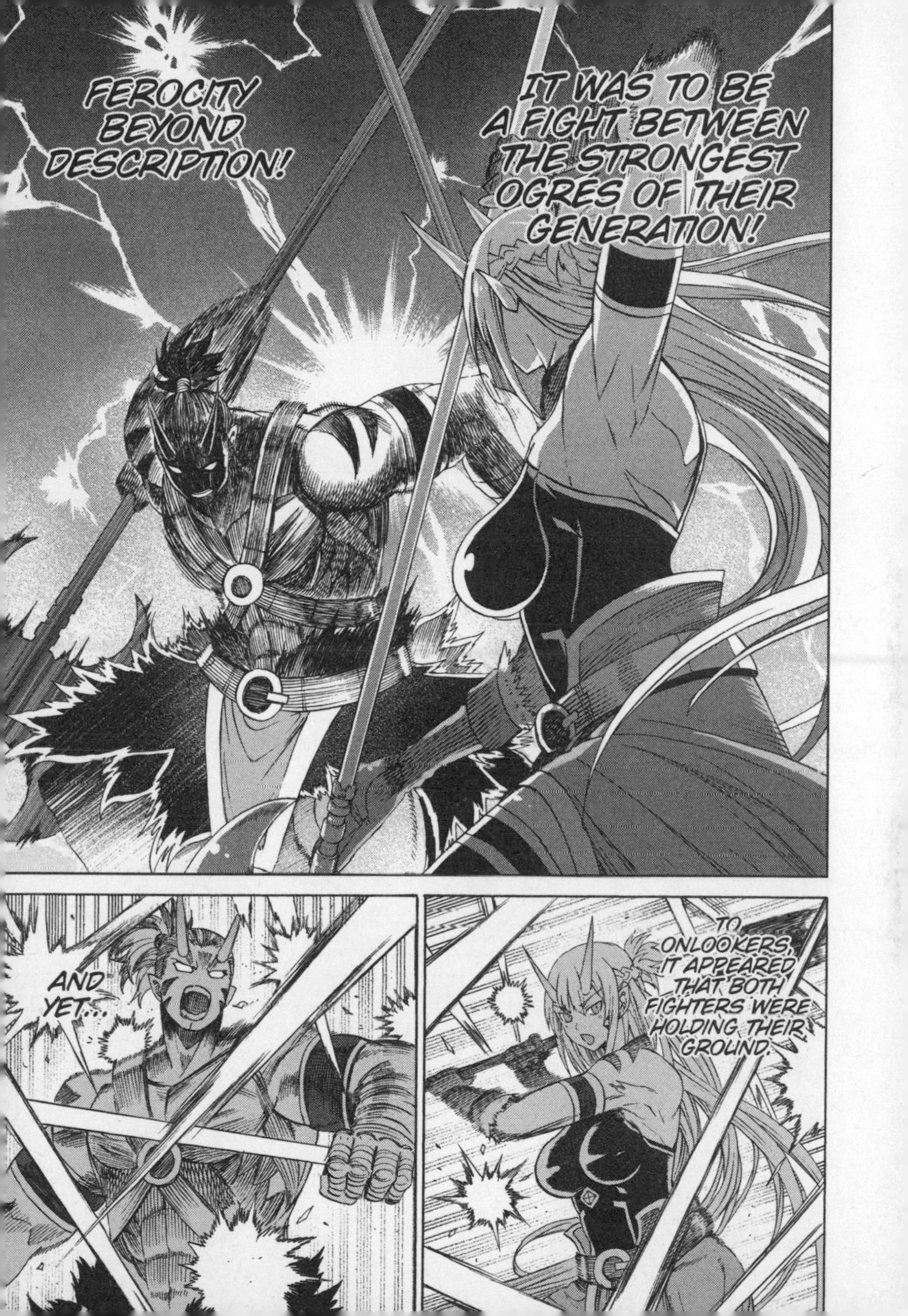
IT WAS TO BE A FIGHT BETWEEN THE STRONGEST OGRES OF THEIR GENERATION!
FEROCITY BEYOND DESCRIPTION!
TO ONLOOKERS, IT APPEARED THAT BOTH FIGHTERS WERE HOLDING THEIR GROUND.
AND YET...

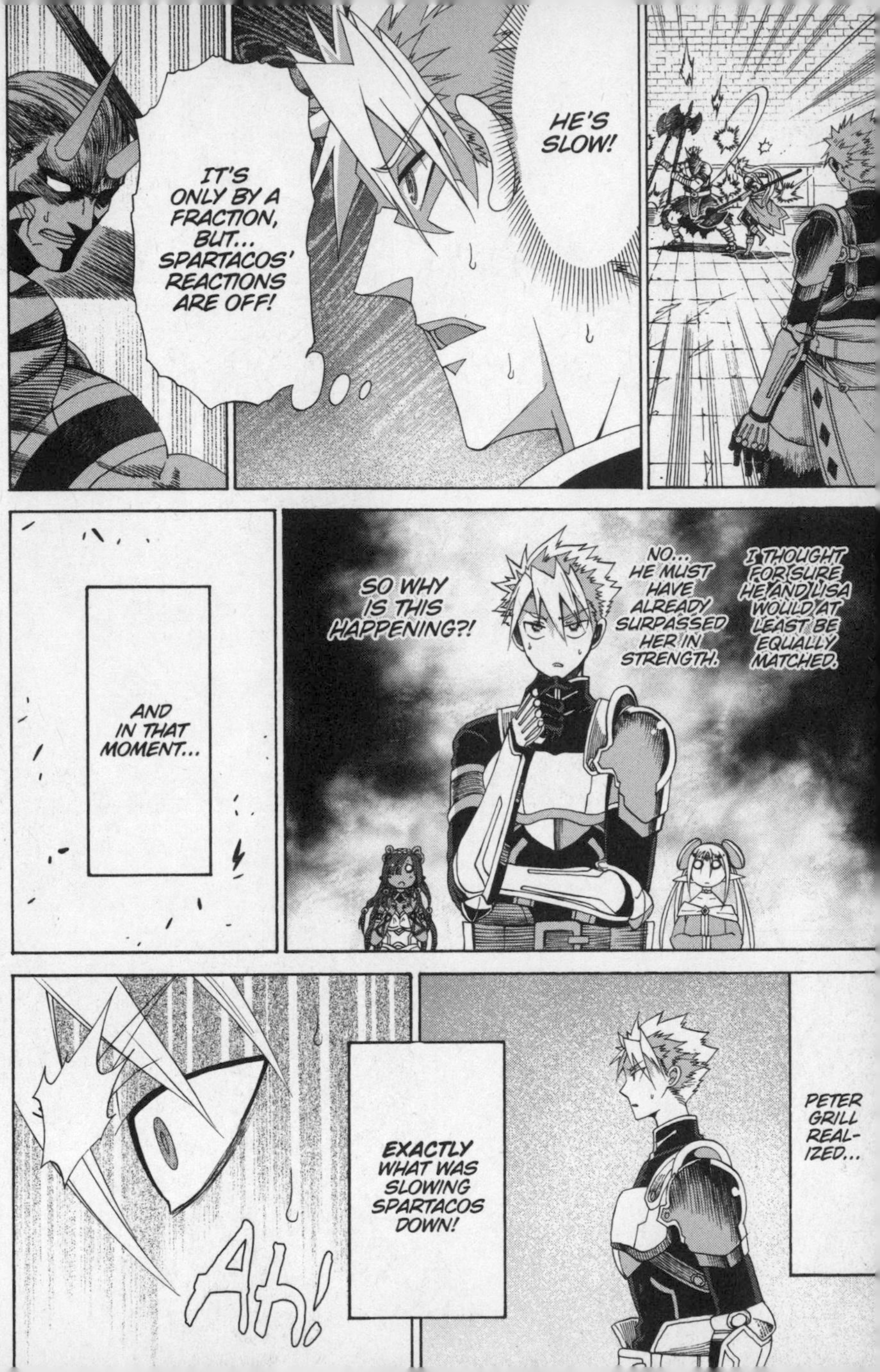
HE'S SLOW!
IT'S ONLY BY A FRACTION, BUT... SPARTACOS' REACTIONS ARE OFF!
I THOUGHT FOR SURE HE AND LISA WOULD AT LEAST BE EQUALLY MATCHED.
NO... HE MUST HAVE ALREADY SURPASSED HER IN STRENGTH.
SO WHY IS THIS HAPPENING?!
AND IN THAT MOMENT...
PETER GRILL REALIZED...
EXACTLY WHAT WAS SLOWING SPARTACOS DOWN!
Ah!

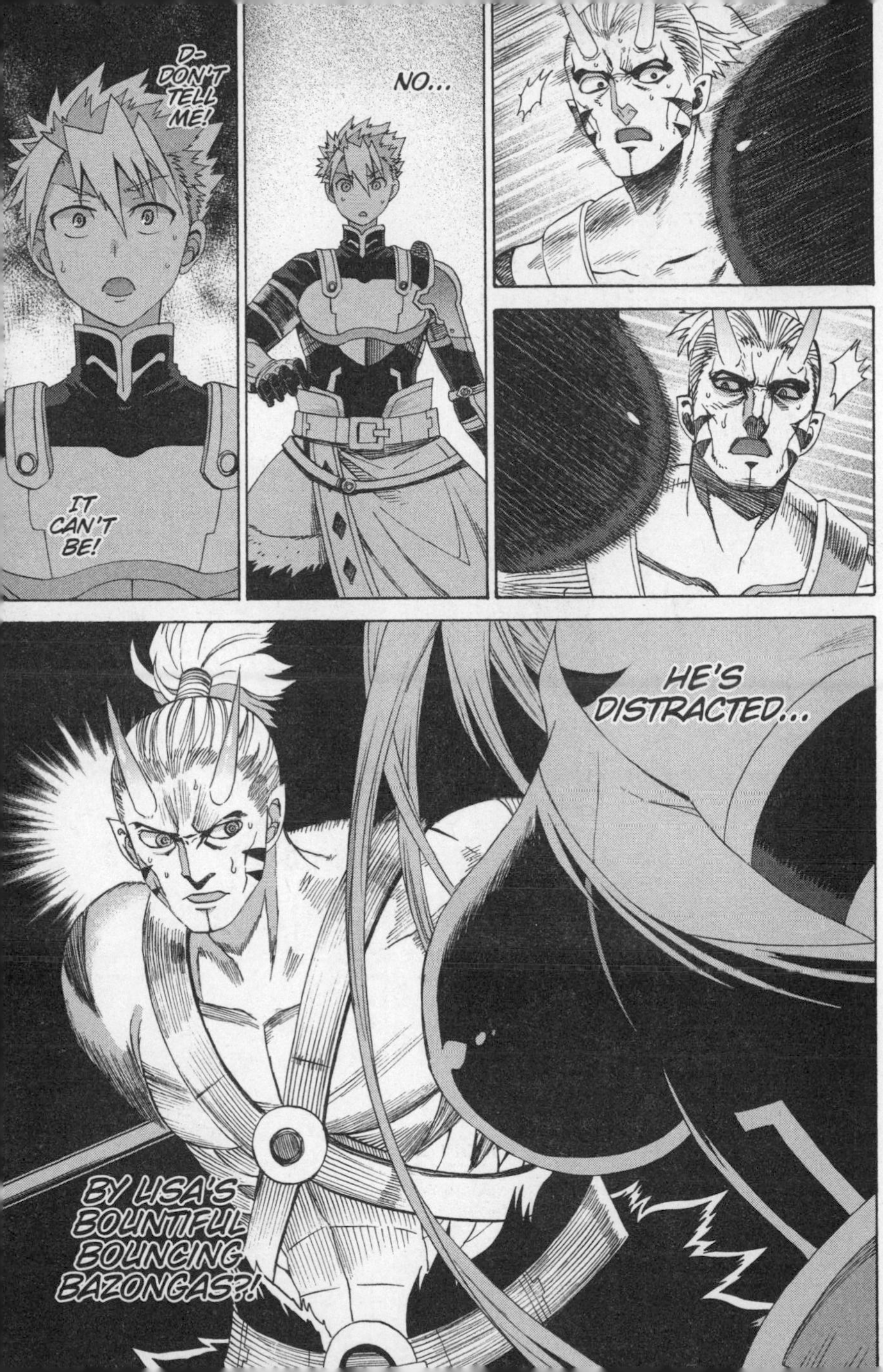
NO...
D-DON'T TELL ME!
IT CAN'T BE!
HE'S DISTRACTED...
BY LISA'S BOUNTIFUL BOUNCING BAZONGAS?!

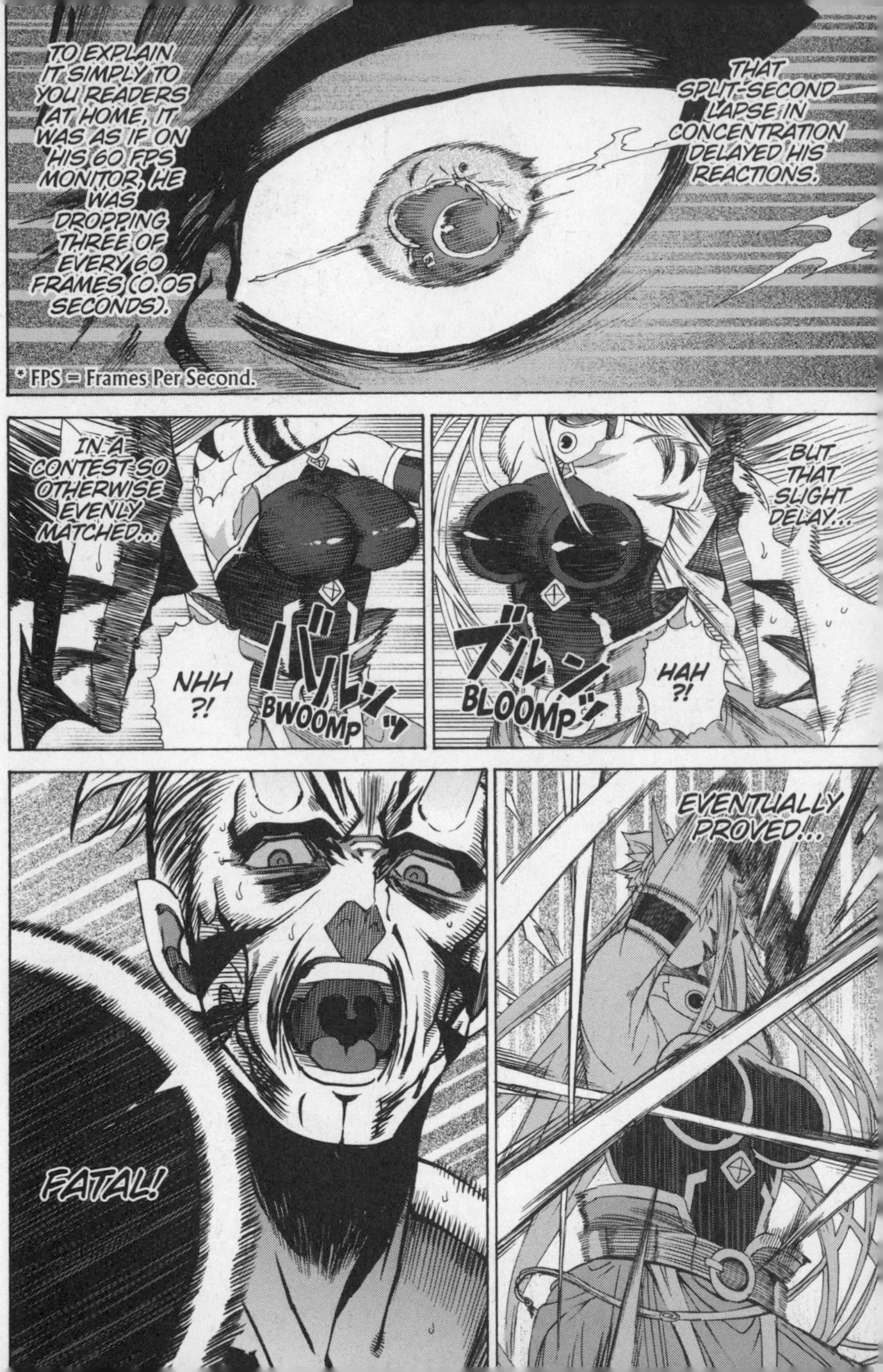
THAT SPLIT-SECOND LAPSE IN CONCENTRATION DELAYED HIS REACTIONS.
TO EXPLAIN IT SIMPLY TO YOU READERS AT HOME, IT WAS AS IF ON HIS 60 FPS MONITOR, HE WAS DROPPING THREE OF EVERY 60 FRAMES (0.05 SECONDS).
* FPS = Frames Per Second.
BUT THAT SLIGHT DELAY...
ブルンッ
BLOOMP
HAH ?!
IN A CONTEST SO OTHERWISE EVENLY MATCHED...
バルンッ
BWOOMP
NHH ?!
EVENTUALLY PROVED...
FATAL!

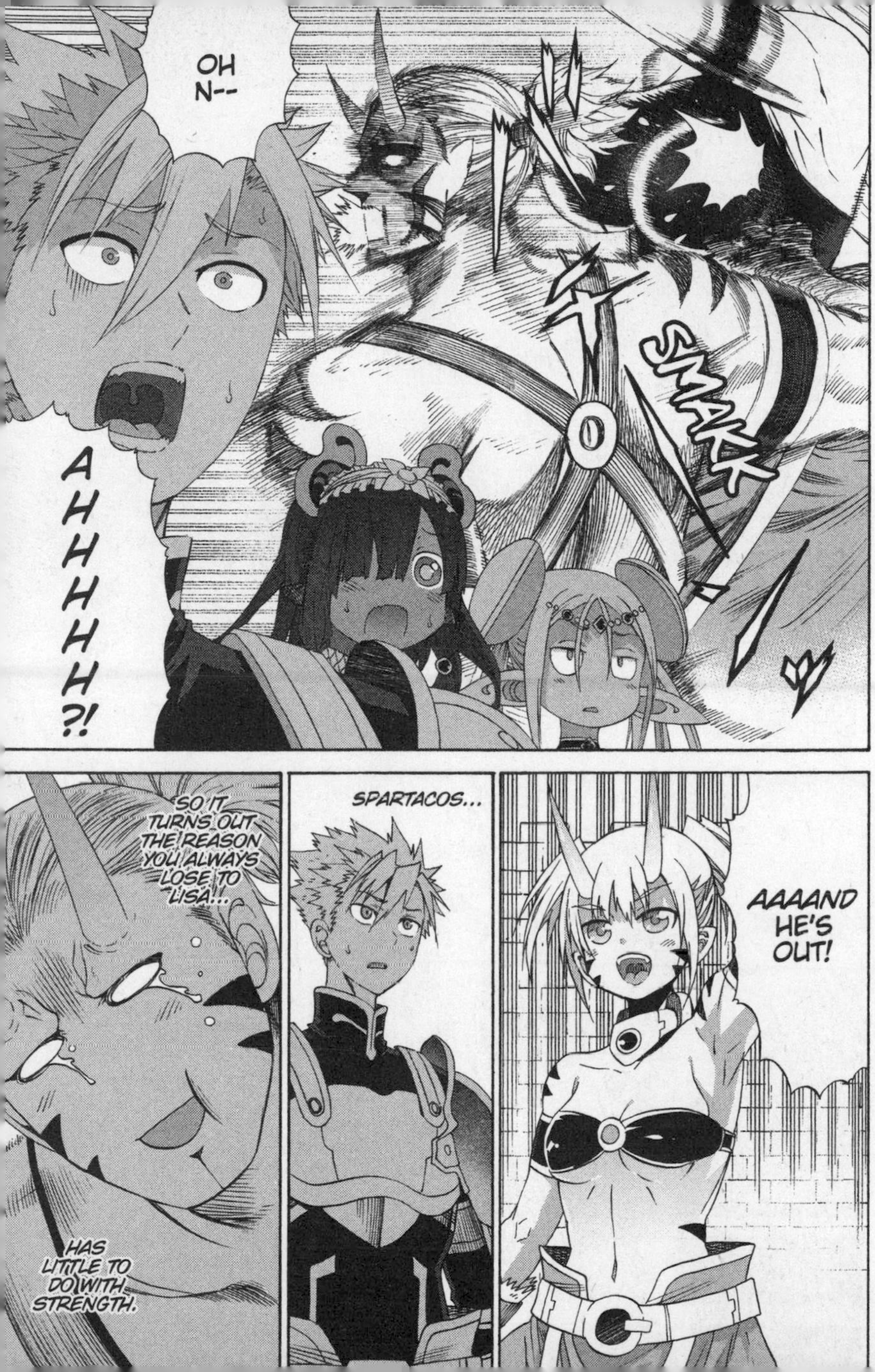
SMAKK
OH N--
AHHHHHH?!
AAAAND HE'S OUT!
SPARTACOS...
SO IT TURNS OUT THE REASON YOU ALWAYS LOSE TO LISA...
HAS LITTLE TO DO WITH STRENGTH.

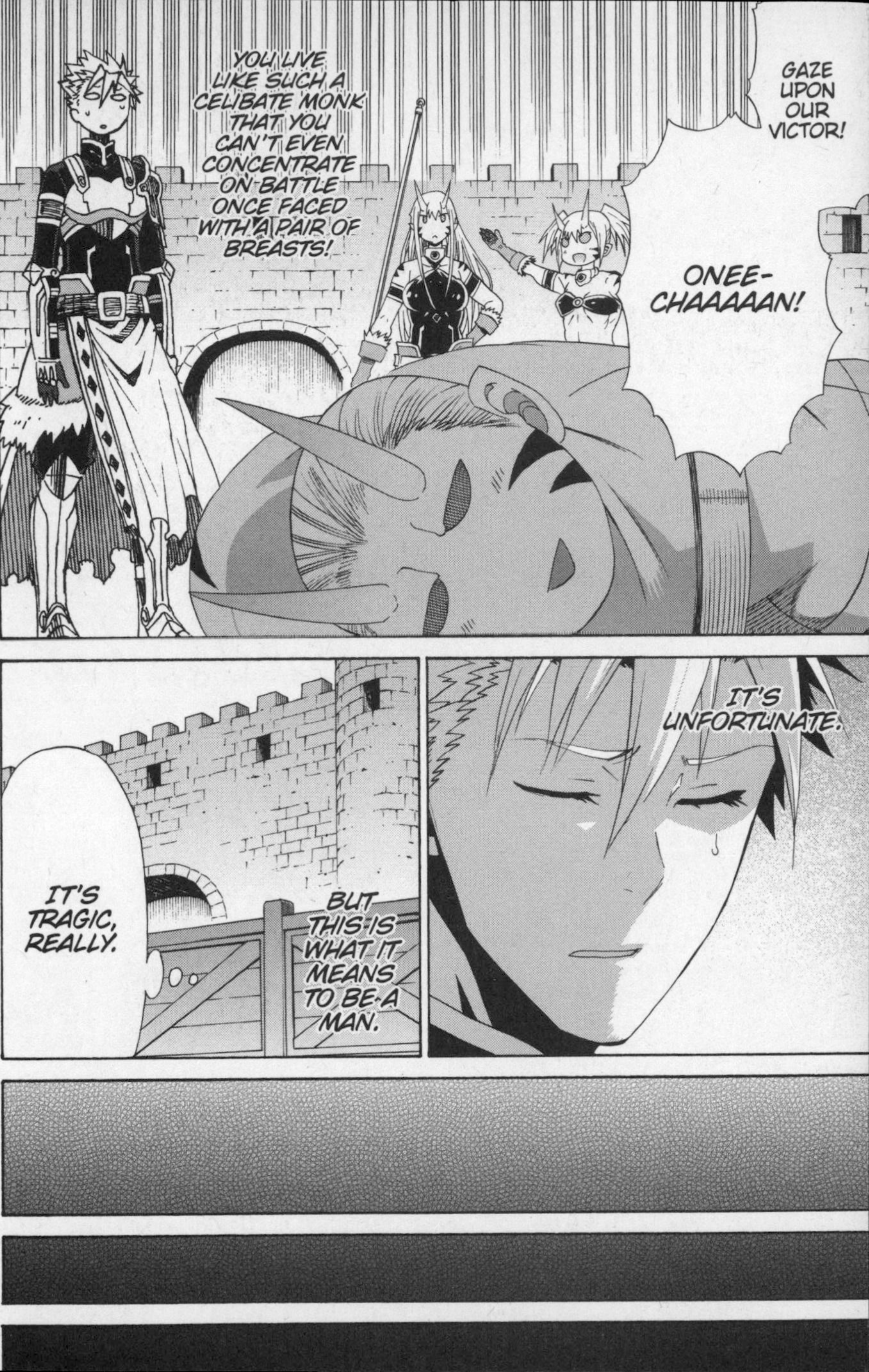
GAZE UPON OUR VICTOR!
ONEE-CHAAAAAN!
YOU LIVE LIKE SUCH A CELIBATE MONK THAT YOU CAN'T EVEN CONCENTRATE ON BATTLE ONCE FACED WITH A PAIR OF BREASTS!
IT'S UNFORTUNATE.
BUT THIS IS WHAT IT MEANS TO BE A MAN.
IT'S TRAGIC, REALLY.

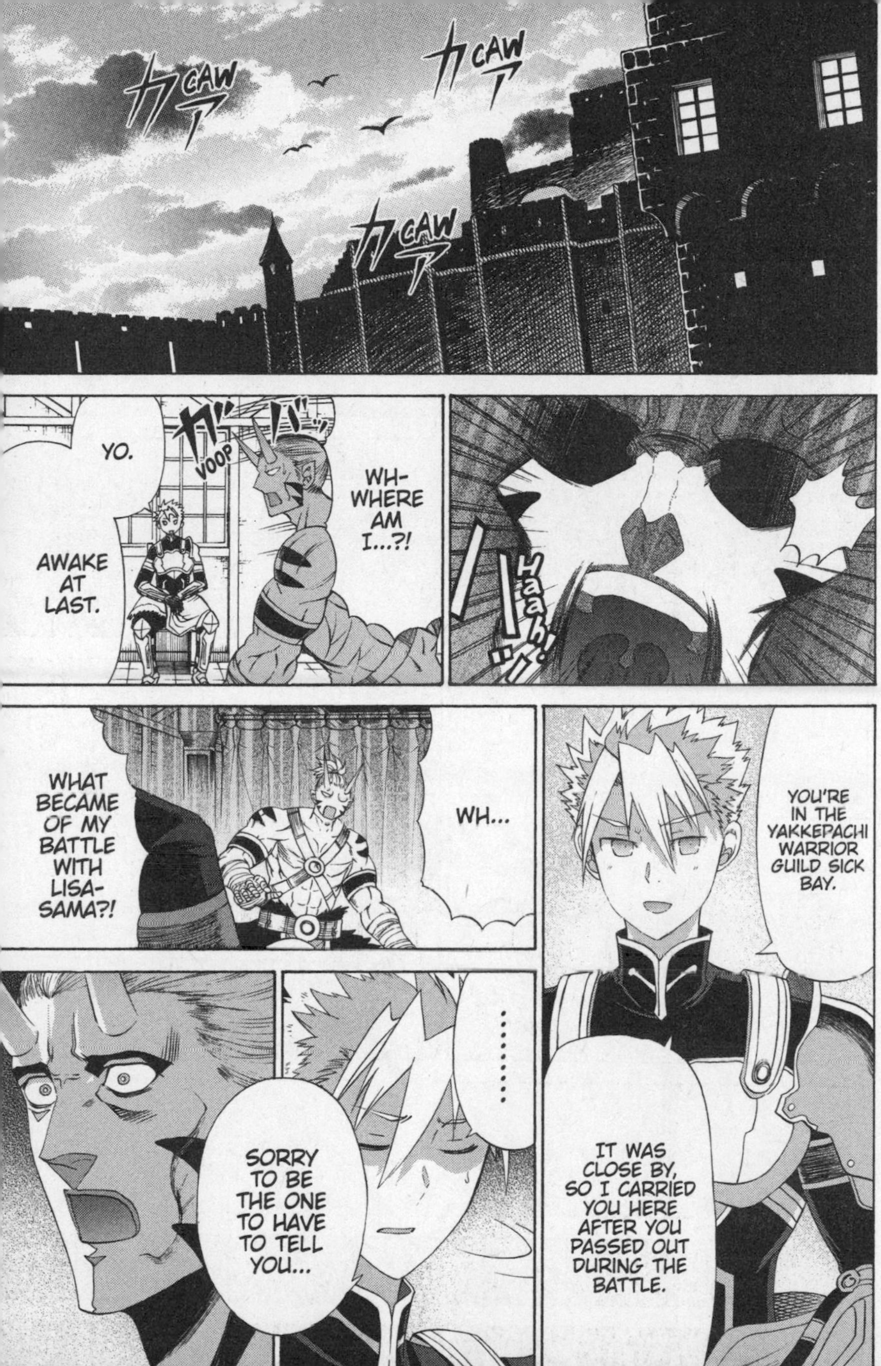

CAW
CAW
CAW
Haah!
WH- WHERE AM I...?!
VOOP
YO.
AWAKE AT LAST.
YOU'RE IN THE YAKKEPACHI WARRIOR GUILD SICK BAY.
IT WAS CLOSE BY, SO I CARRIED YOU HERE AFTER YOU PASSED OUT DURING THE BATTLE.
WH...
WHAT BECAME OF MY BATTLE WITH LISA-SAMA?!
......
SORRY TO BE THE ONE TO HAVE TO TELL YOU...

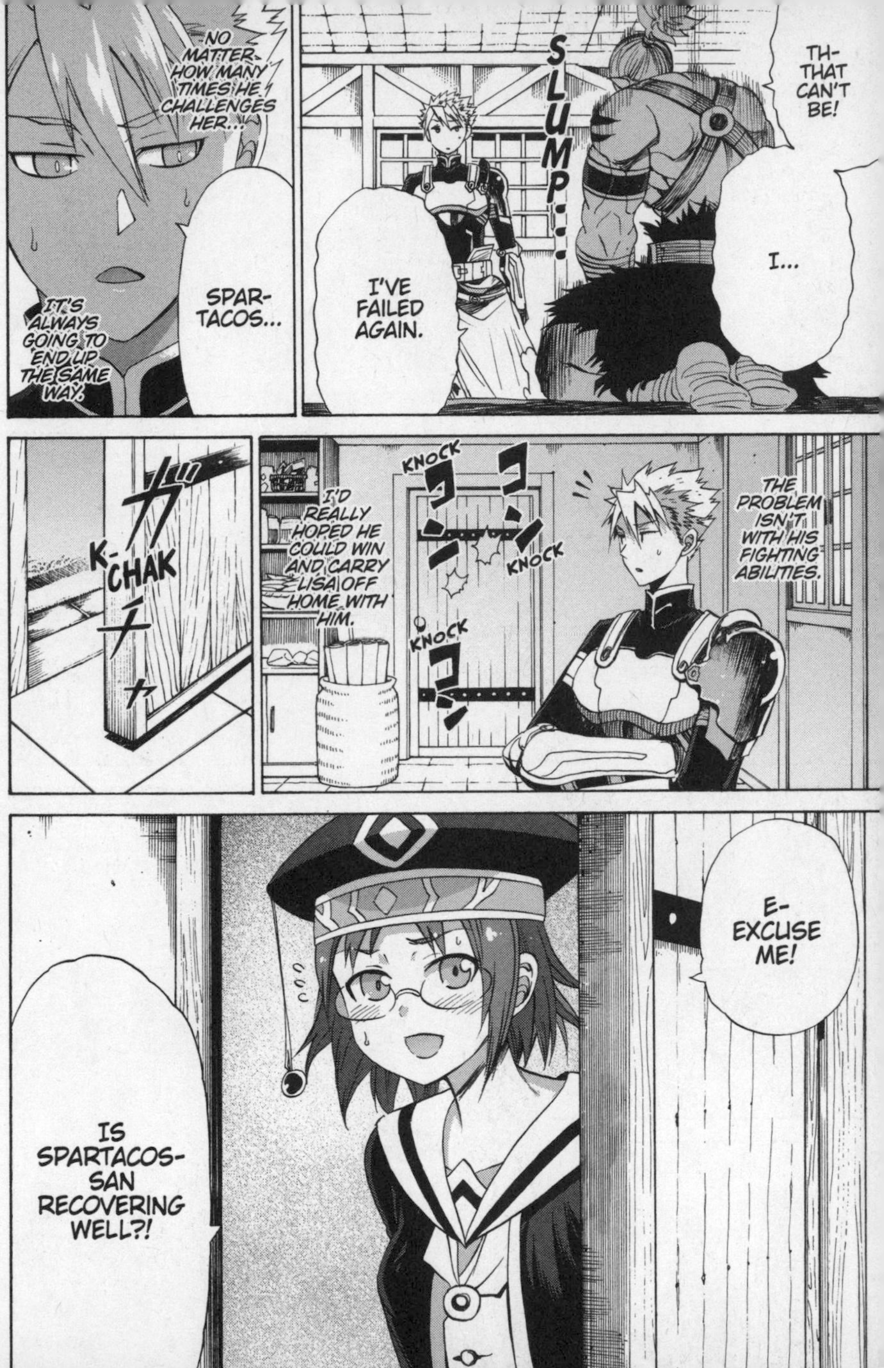
TH-THAT CAN'T BE!
SLUMP...
I...
I'VE FAILED AGAIN.
NO MATTER HOW MANY TIMES HE CHALLENGES HER...
SPAR-TACOS...
IT'S ALWAYS GOING TO END UP THE SAME WAY.
THE PROBLEM ISN'T WITH HIS FIGHTING ABILITIES.
KNOCK
KNOCK
KNOCK
I'D REALLY HOPED HE COULD WIN AND CARRY LISA OFF HOME WITH HIM.
K-CHAK
E-EXCUSE ME!
IS SPARTACOS-SAN RECOVERING WELL?!

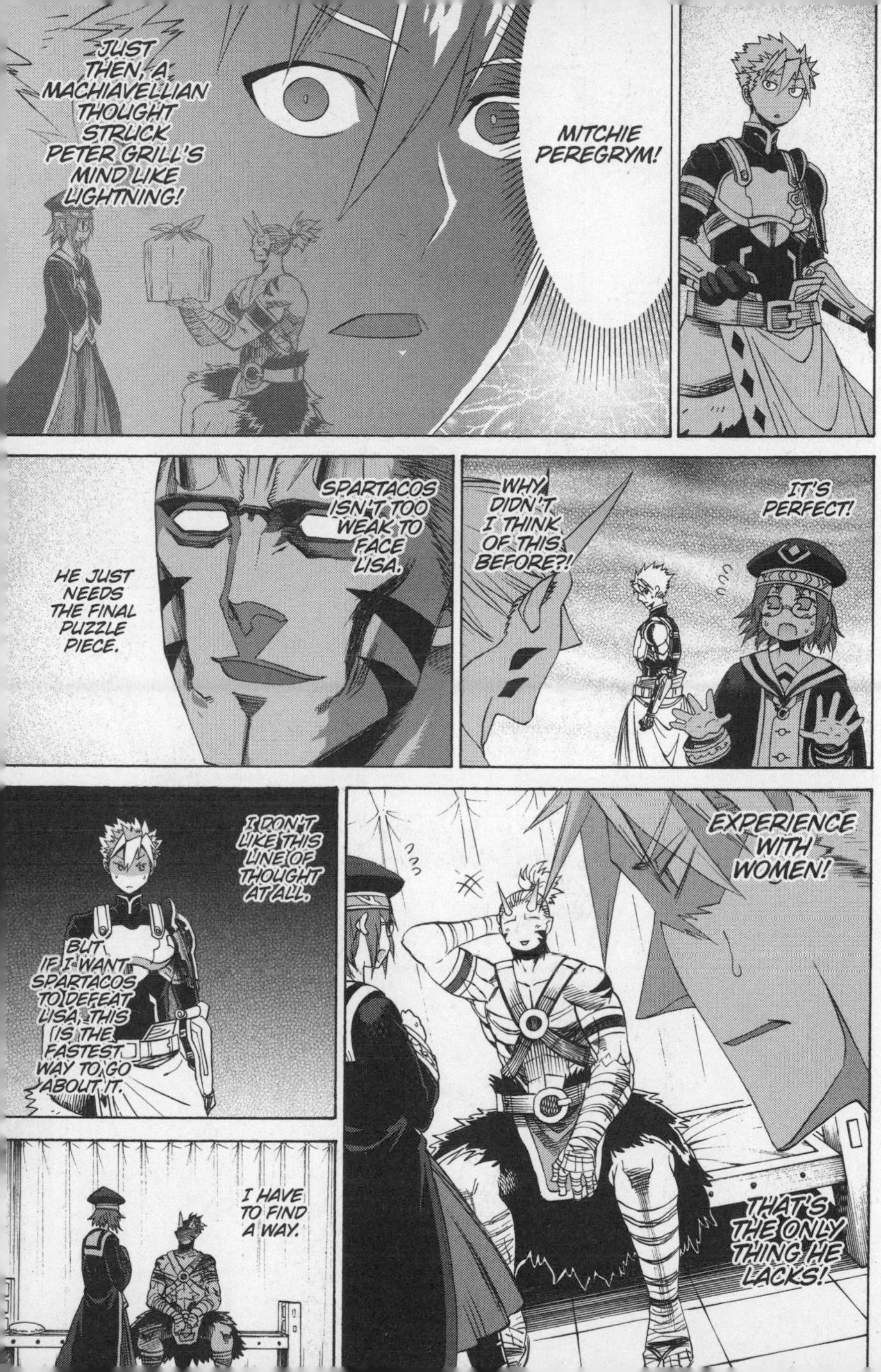
JUST THEN, A MACHIAVELLIAN THOUGHT STRUCK PETER GRILL'S MIND LIKE LIGHTNING!
MITCHIE PEREGRYM!
IT'S PERFECT!
WHY DIDN'T I THINK OF THIS BEFORE?!
SPARTACOS ISN'T TOO WEAK TO FACE LISA.
HE JUST NEEDS THE FINAL PUZZLE PIECE.
EXPERIENCE WITH WOMEN!
THAT'S THE ONLY THING HE LACKS!
I DON'T LIKE THIS LINE OF THOUGHT AT ALL.
BUT IF I WANT SPARTACOS TO DEFEAT LISA, THIS IS THE FASTEST WAY TO GO ABOUT IT.
I HAVE TO FIND A WAY.

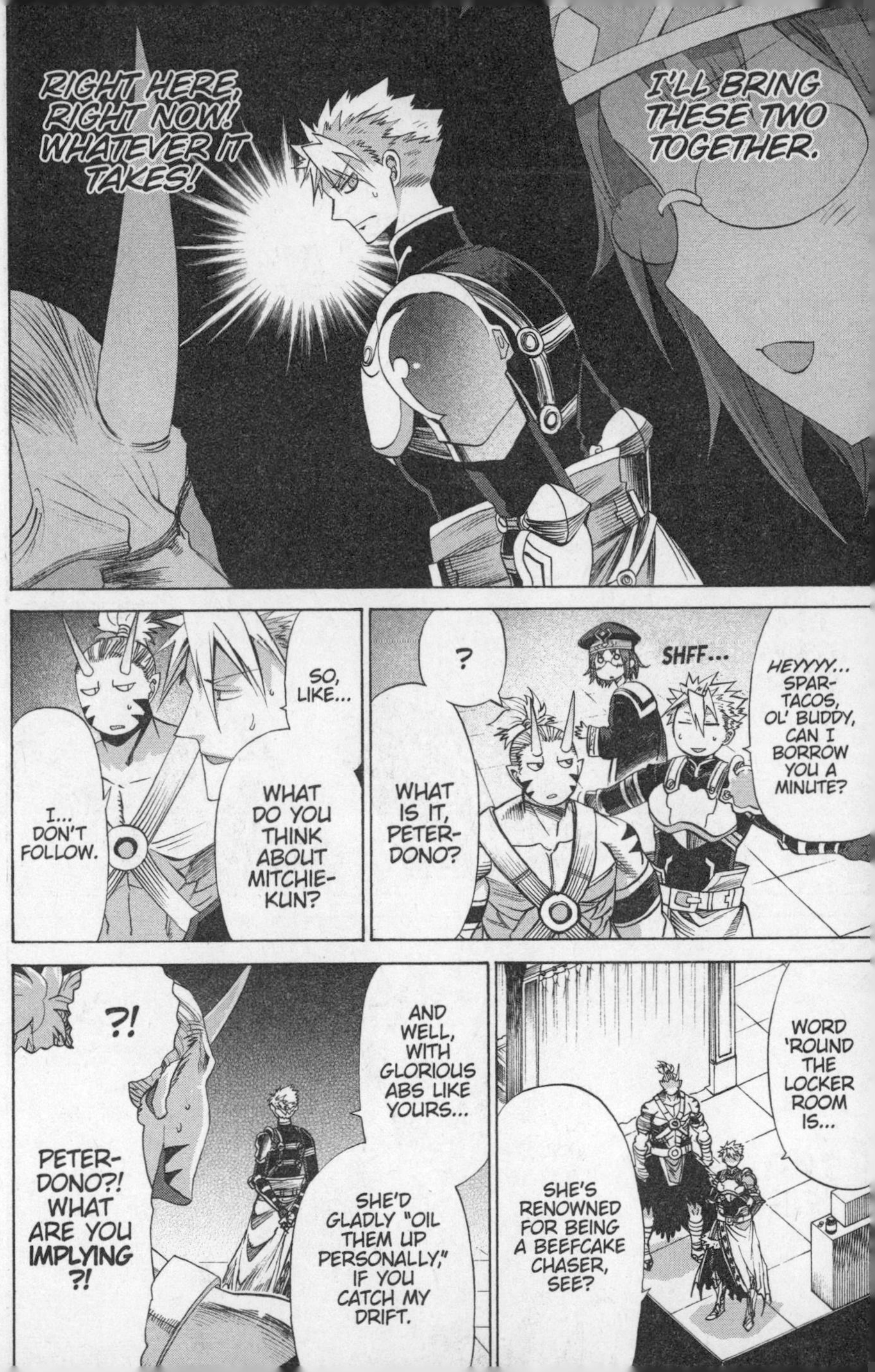
I'LL BRING THESE TWO TOGETHER.
RIGHT HERE, RIGHT NOW! WHATEVER IT TAKES!
HEYYYY... SPAR-TACOS, OL' BUDDY, CAN I BORROW YOU A MINUTE?
SHFF...
?
WHAT IS IT, PETER-DONO?
SO, LIKE...
WHAT DO YOU THINK ABOUT MITCHIE-KUN?
I... DON'T FOLLOW.
WORD 'ROUND THE LOCKER ROOM IS...
SHE'S RENOWNED FOR BEING A BEEFCAKE CHASER, SEE?
AND WELL, WITH GLORIOUS ABS LIKE YOURS...
SHE'D GLADLY "OIL THEM UP PERSONALLY," IF YOU CATCH MY DRIFT.
?!
PETER-DONO?! WHAT ARE YOU IMPLYING?!

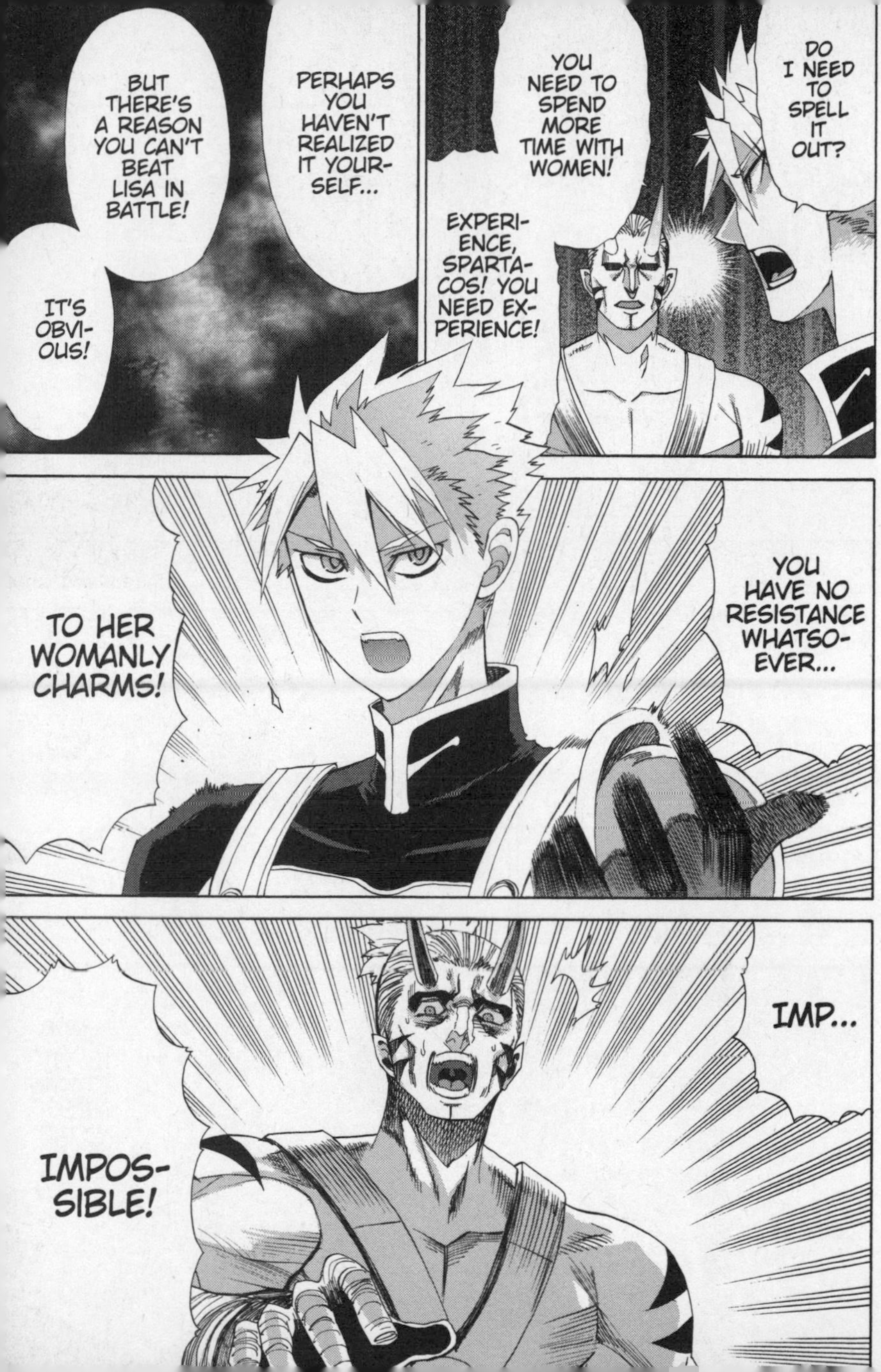
DO I NEED TO SPELL IT OUT?
YOU NEED TO SPEND MORE TIME WITH WOMEN!
EXPERIENCE, SPARTACOS! YOU NEED EXPERIENCE!
PERHAPS YOU HAVEN'T REALIZED IT YOURSELF...
BUT THERE'S A REASON YOU CAN'T BEAT LISA IN BATTLE!
IT'S OBVIOUS!
YOU HAVE NO RESISTANCE WHATSOEVER...
TO HER WOMANLY CHARMS!
IMP...
IMPOSSIBLE!

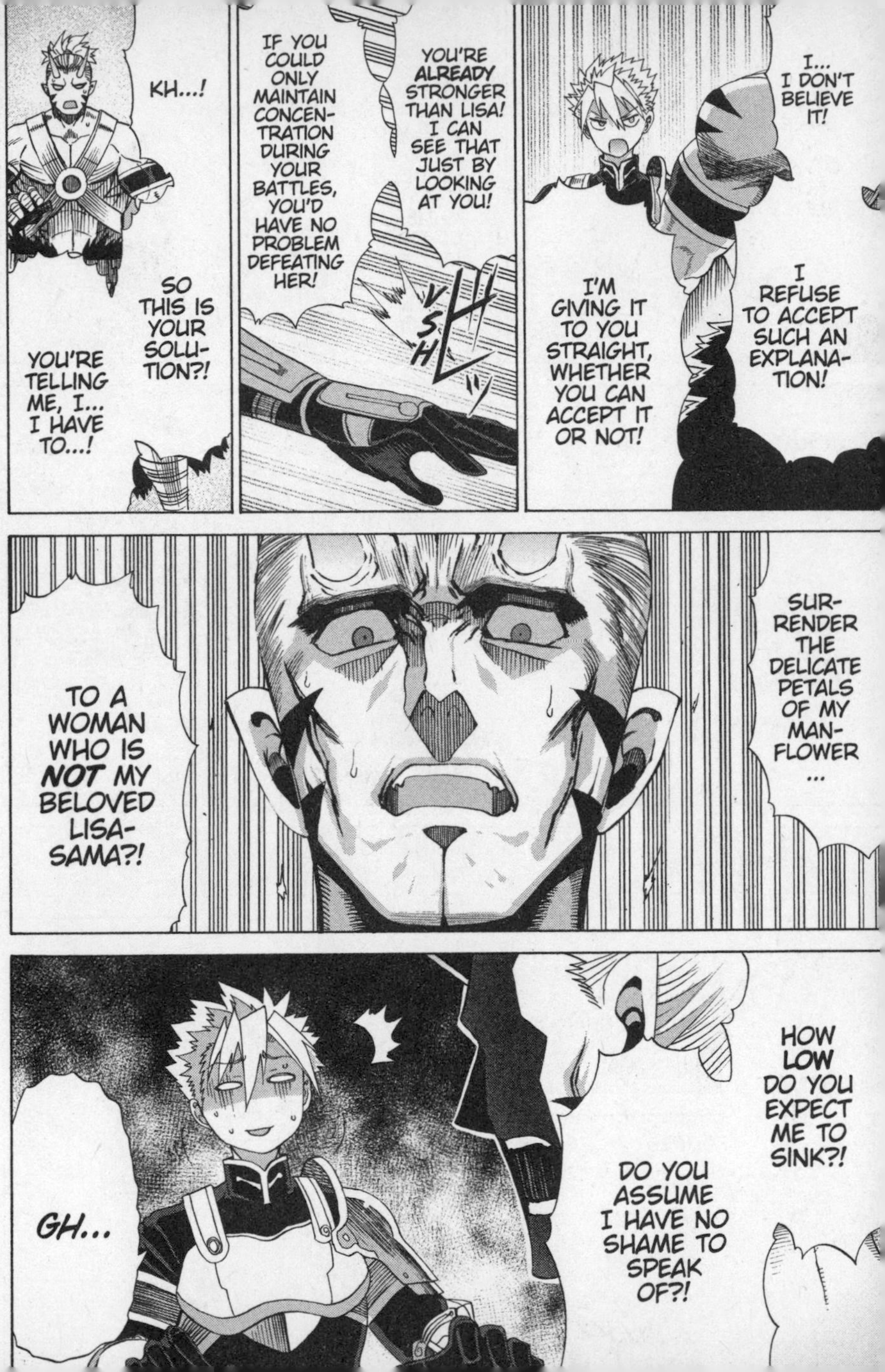
I... I DON'T BELIEVE IT!
I REFUSE TO ACCEPT SUCH AN EXPLANATION!
I'M GIVING IT TO YOU STRAIGHT, WHETHER YOU CAN ACCEPT IT OR NOT!
YOU'RE **ALREADY** STRONGER THAN LISA! I CAN SEE THAT JUST BY LOOKING AT YOU!
IF YOU COULD ONLY MAINTAIN CONCENTRATION DURING YOUR BATTLES, YOU'D HAVE NO PROBLEM DEFEATING HER!
VSH
KH...!
SO THIS IS YOUR SOLUTION?!
YOU'RE TELLING ME, I... I HAVE TO...!
SURRENDER THE DELICATE PETALS OF MY MAN-FLOWER...
TO A WOMAN WHO IS ***NOT*** MY BELOVED LISA-SAMA?!
HOW **LOW** DO YOU EXPECT ME TO SINK?!
DO YOU ASSUME I HAVE NO SHAME TO SPEAK OF?!
GH...

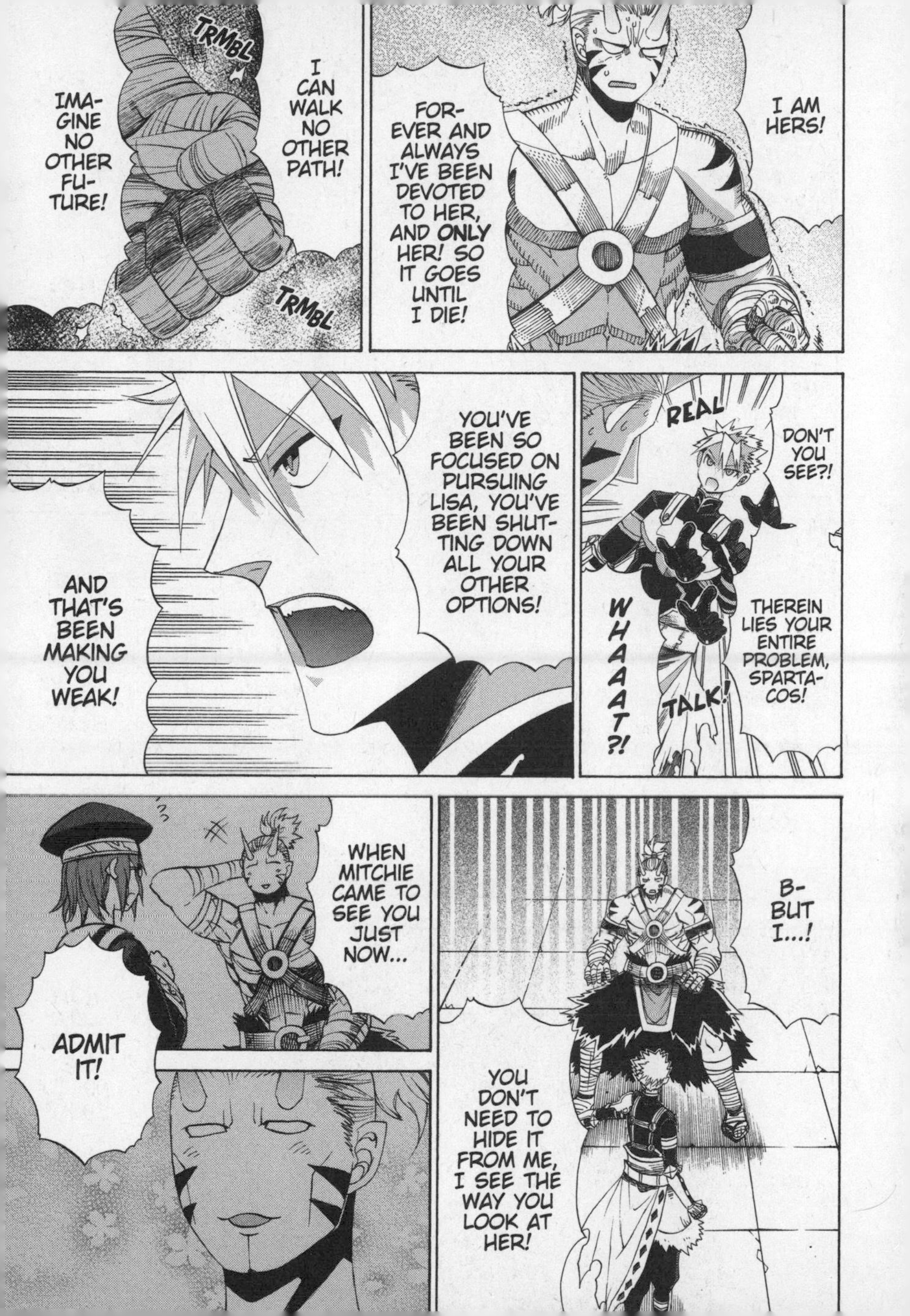
I AM HERS!
FOREVER AND ALWAYS I'VE BEEN DEVOTED TO HER, AND ONLY HER! SO IT GOES UNTIL I DIE!
I CAN WALK NO OTHER PATH!
TRMBL
IMAGINE NO OTHER FUTURE!
TRMBL
REAL
DON'T YOU SEE?!
TALK!
THEREIN LIES YOUR ENTIRE PROBLEM, SPARTACOS!
WHAAAAT?!
YOU'VE BEEN SO FOCUSED ON PURSUING LISA, YOU'VE BEEN SHUTTING DOWN ALL YOUR OTHER OPTIONS!
AND THAT'S BEEN MAKING YOU WEAK!
B-BUT I...!
YOU DON'T NEED TO HIDE IT FROM ME, I SEE THE WAY YOU LOOK AT HER!
WHEN MITCHIE CAME TO SEE YOU JUST NOW...
ADMIT IT!

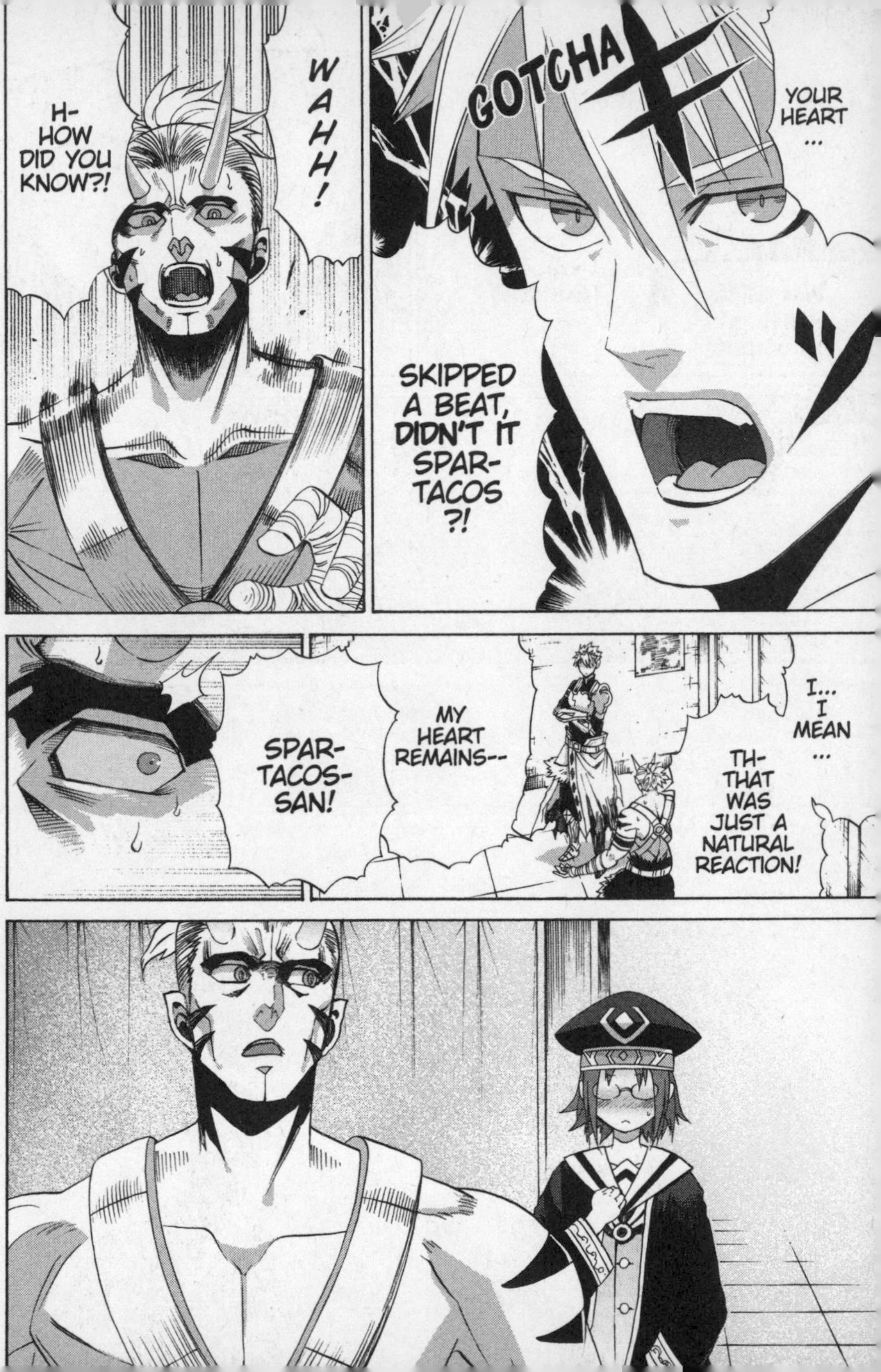
GOTCHA
YOUR HEART ...
SKIPPED A BEAT, DIDN'T IT SPAR-TACOS?!
WAHH!
H-HOW DID YOU KNOW?!
I... I MEAN ...
TH-THAT WAS JUST A NATURAL REACTION!
MY HEART REMAINS--
SPAR-TACOS-SAN!

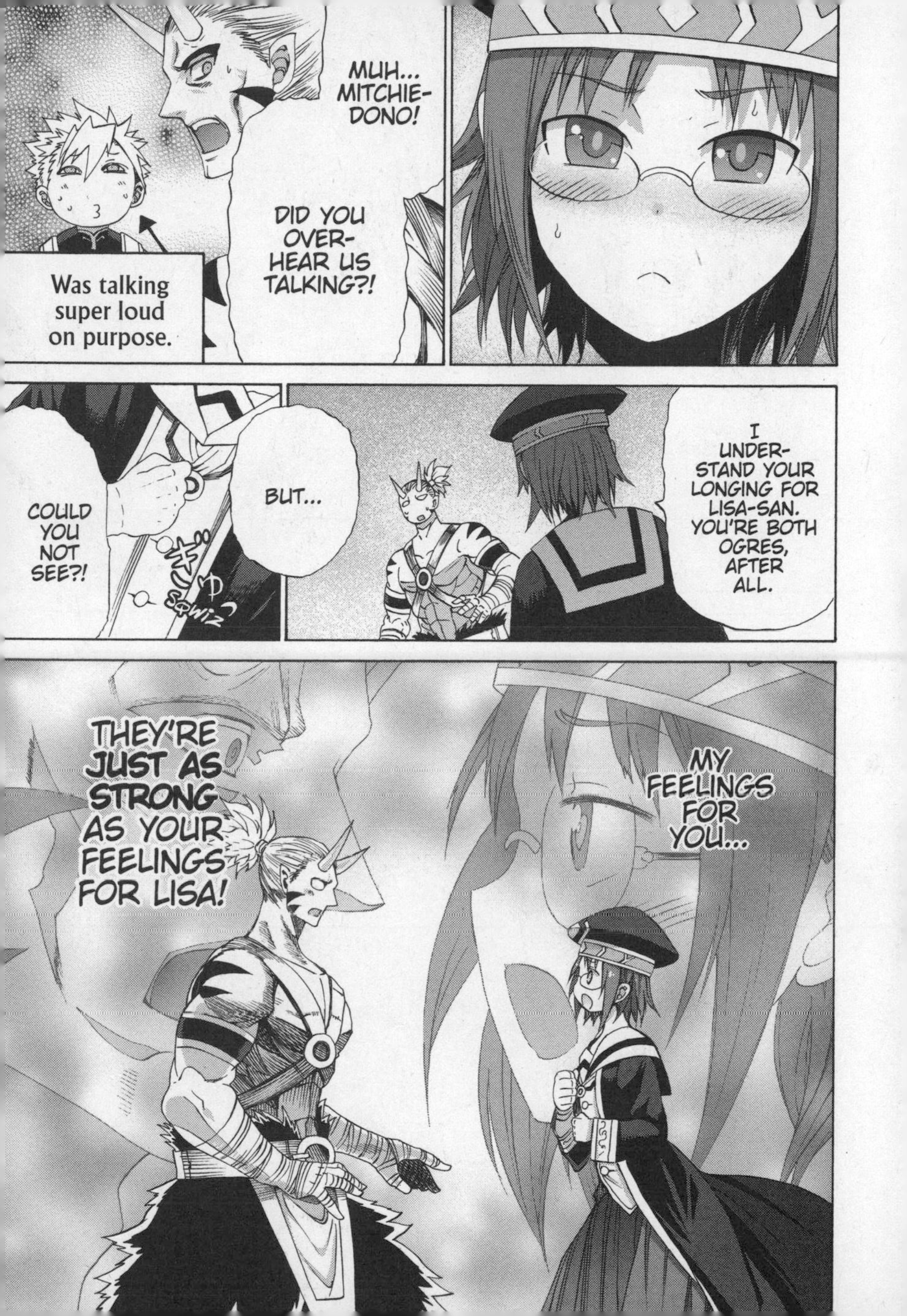
MUH... MITCHIE-DONO!
DID YOU OVER-HEAR US TALKING?!
Was talking super loud on purpose.
I UNDER-STAND YOUR LONGING FOR LISA-SAN. YOU'RE BOTH OGRES, AFTER ALL.
BUT...
COULD YOU NOT SEE?!
Sqwiz
MY FEELINGS FOR YOU...
THEY'RE JUST AS STRONG AS YOUR FEELINGS FOR LISA!

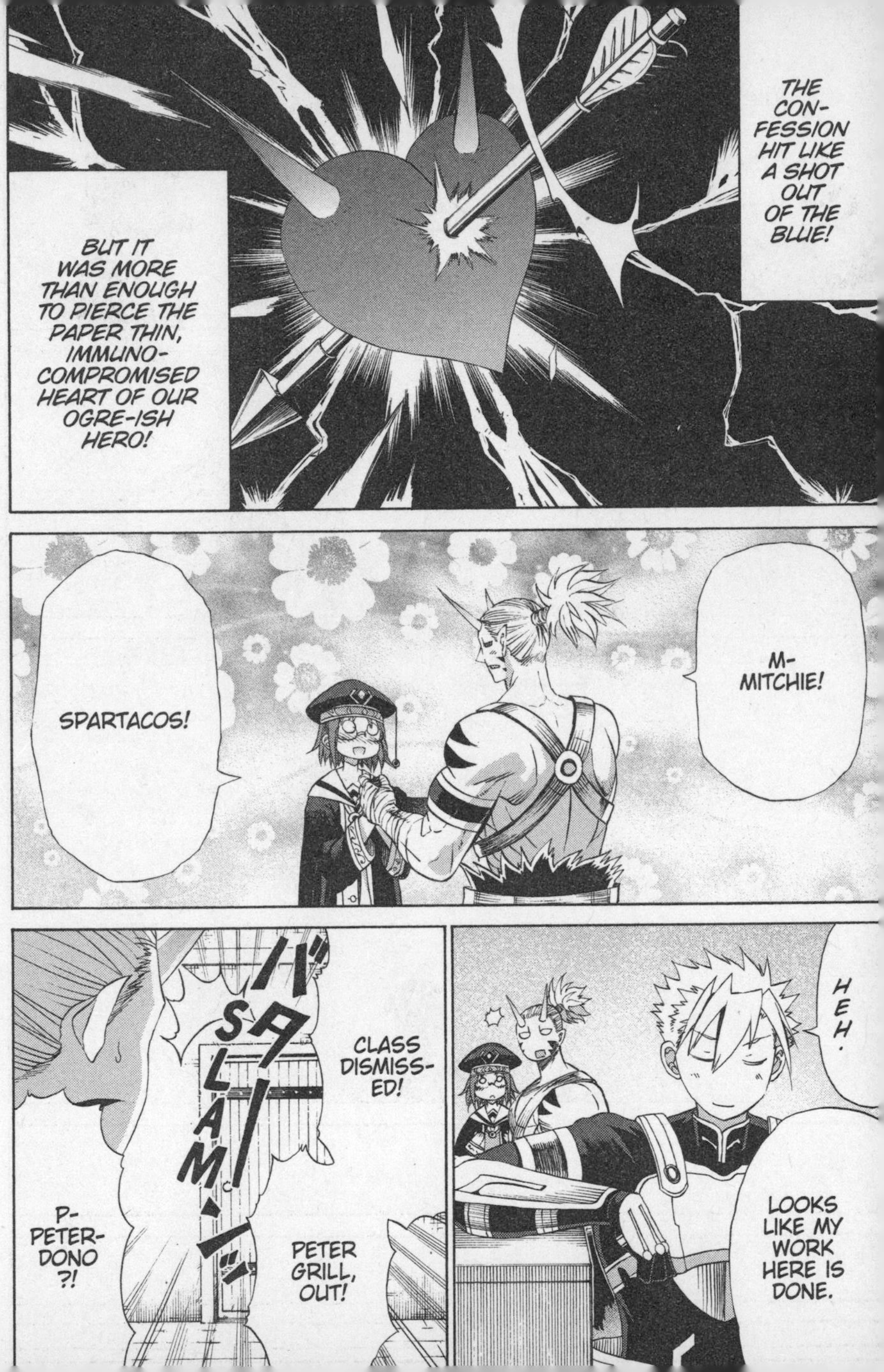
THE CON-FESSION HIT LIKE A SHOT OUT OF THE BLUE!
BUT IT WAS MORE THAN ENOUGH TO PIERCE THE PAPER THIN, IMMUNO-COMPROMISED HEART OF OUR OGRE-ISH HERO!
M-MITCHIE!
SPARTACOS!
HEH.
LOOKS LIKE MY WORK HERE IS DONE.
CLASS DISMISS-ED!
バ
SLAM
PETER GRILL, OUT!
P-PETER-DONO ?!

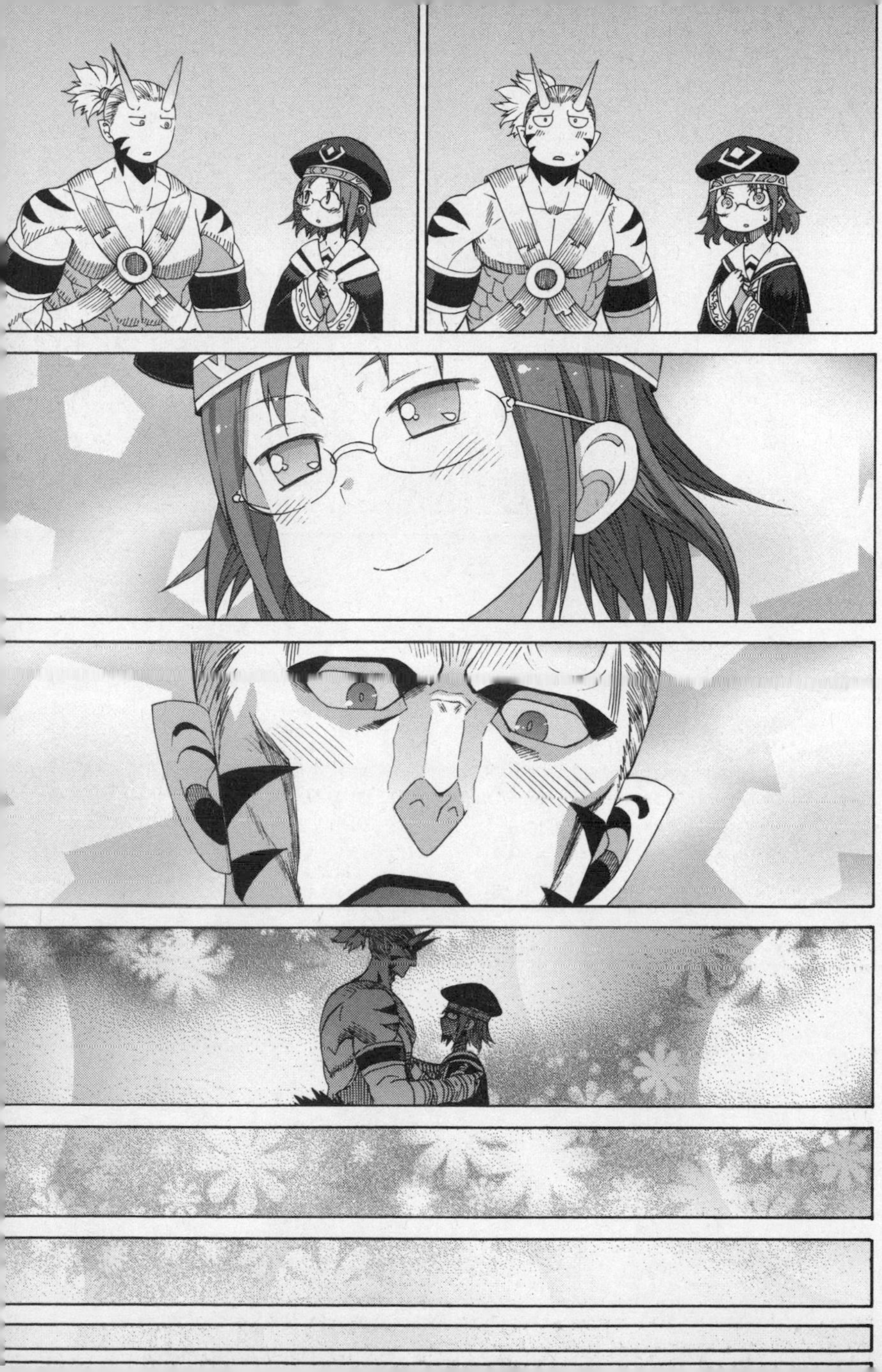

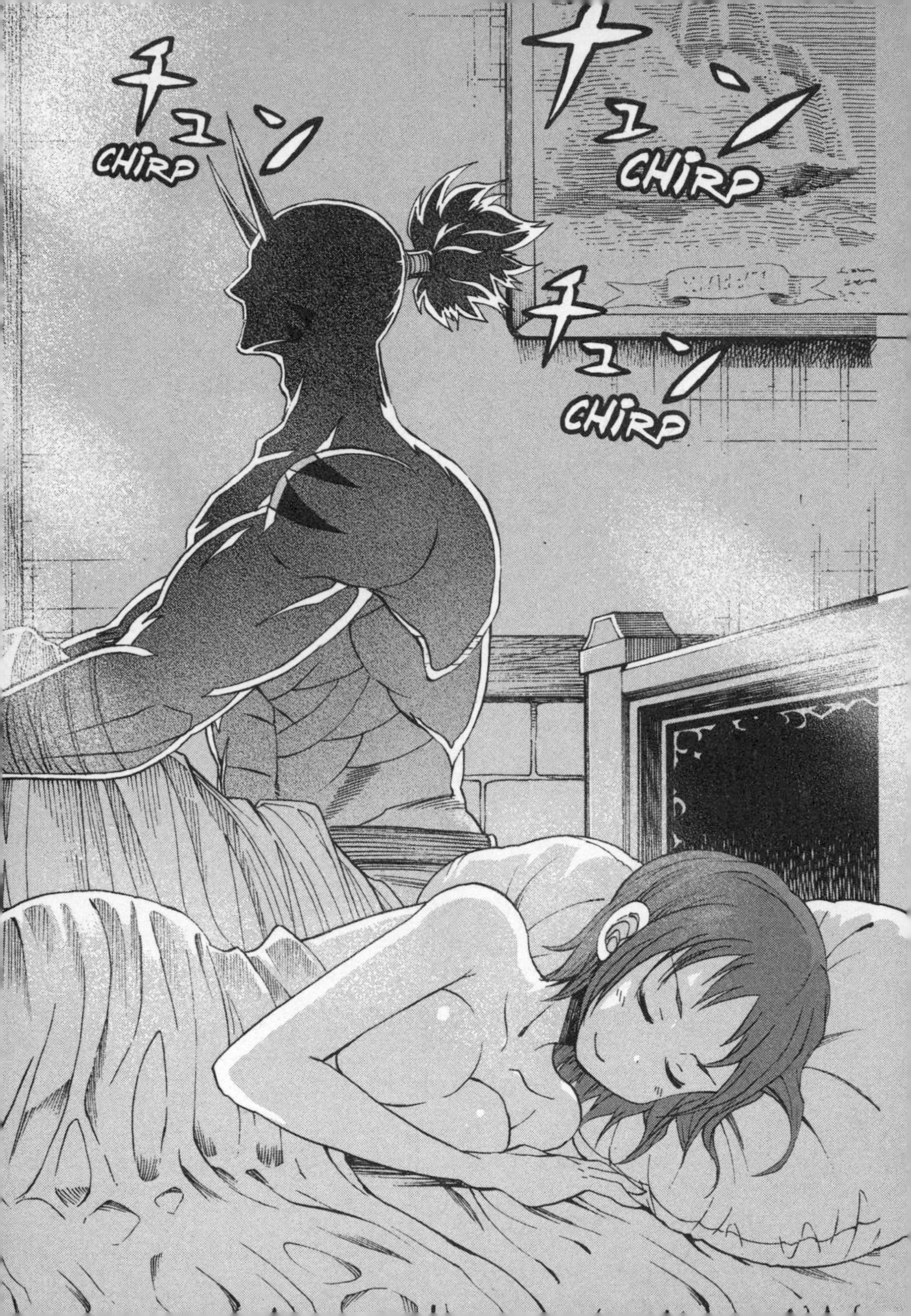
チュン
CHIRP
チュン
CHIRP
チュン
CHIRP

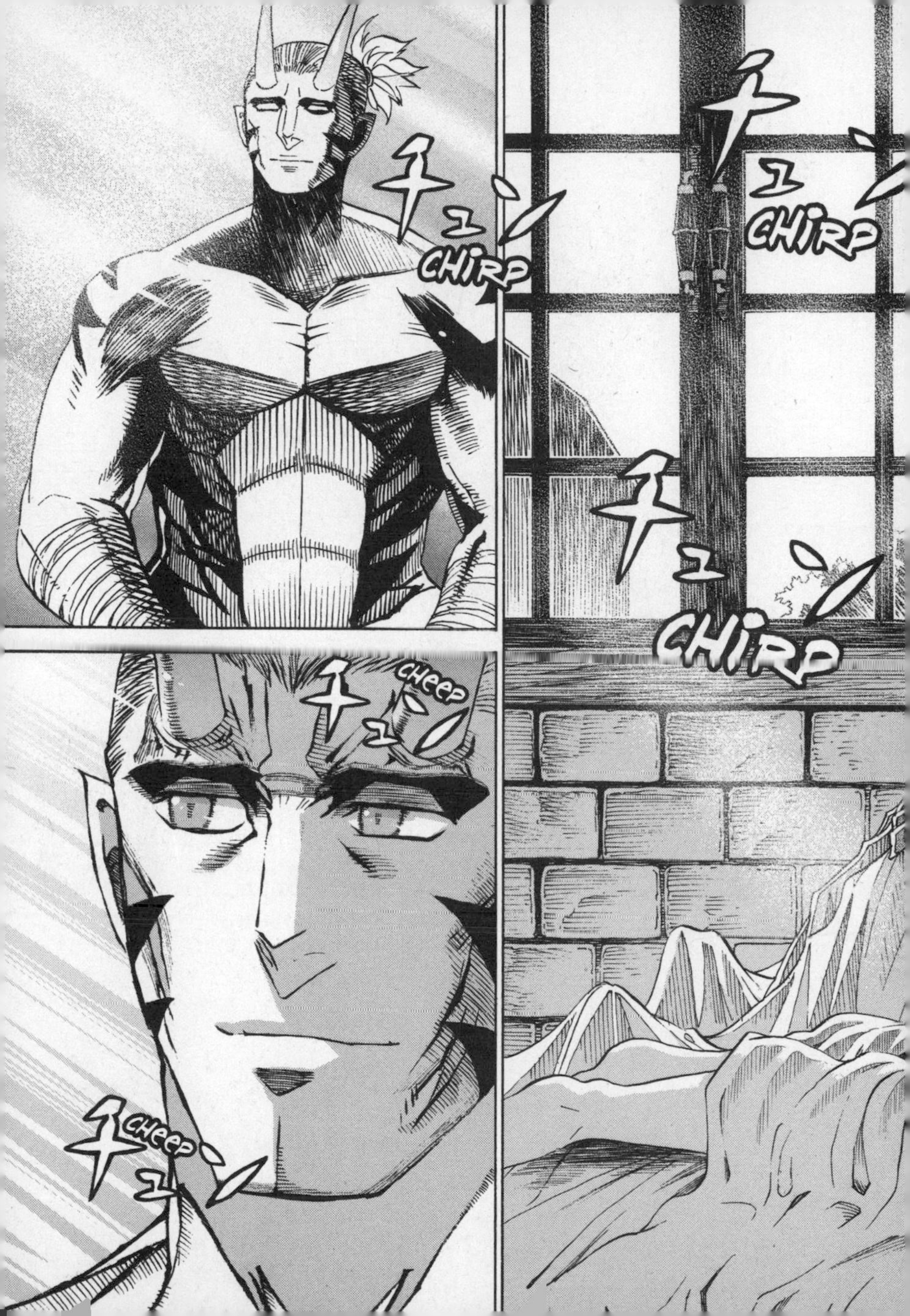
チュ
CHIRP
チュ
CHIRP
チュ
CHIRP
チュ
CHEEP
チュ
CHEEP

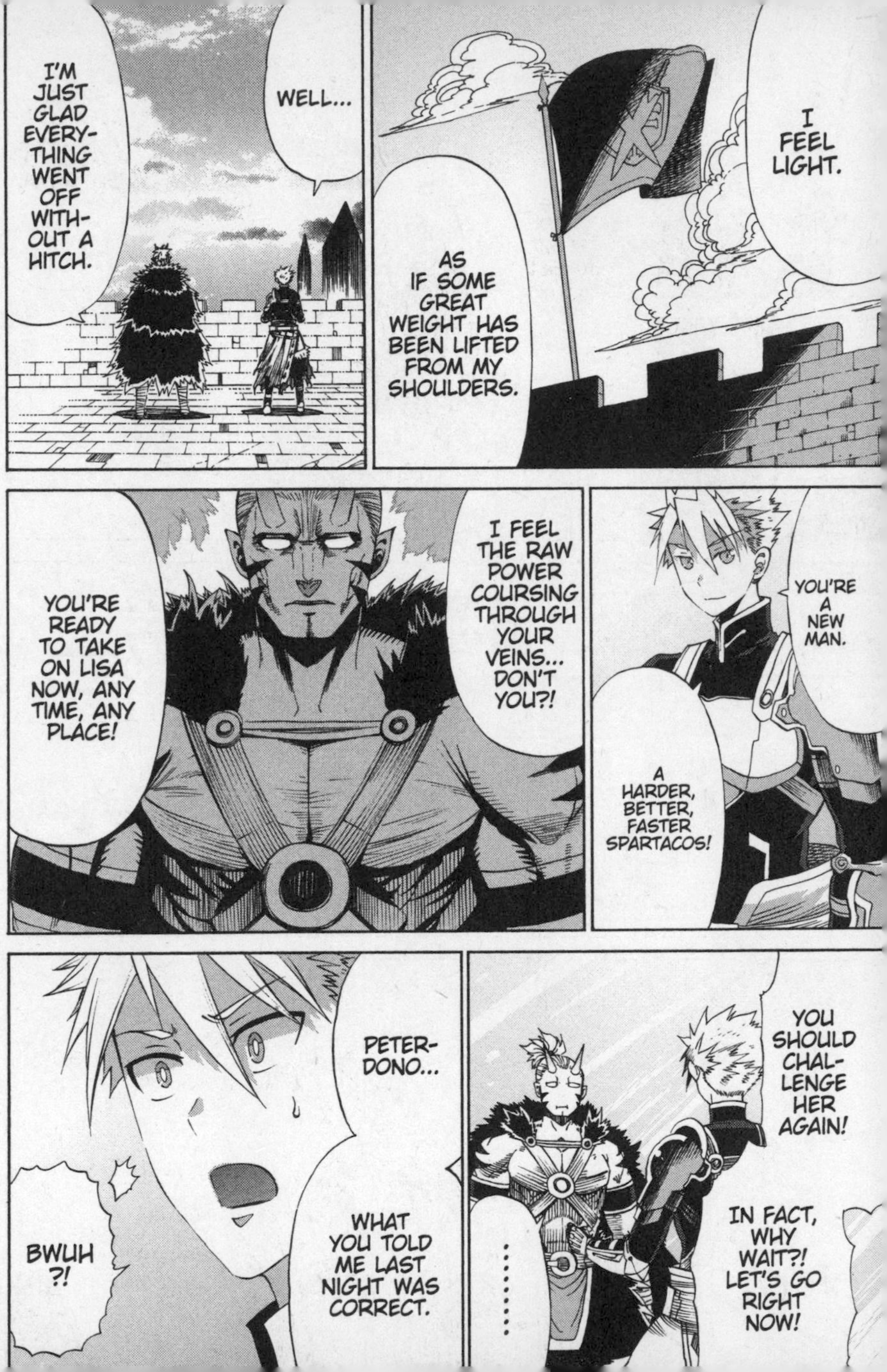
I FEEL LIGHT.
AS IF SOME GREAT WEIGHT HAS BEEN LIFTED FROM MY SHOULDERS.
WELL...
I'M JUST GLAD EVERYTHING WENT OFF WITHOUT A HITCH.
YOU'RE A NEW MAN.
A HARDER, BETTER, FASTER SPARTACOS!
I FEEL THE RAW POWER COURSING THROUGH YOUR VEINS... DON'T YOU?!
YOU'RE READY TO TAKE ON LISA NOW, ANY TIME, ANY PLACE!
YOU SHOULD CHALLENGE HER AGAIN!
IN FACT, WHY WAIT?! LET'S GO RIGHT NOW!
......
PETER-DONO...
WHAT YOU TOLD ME LAST NIGHT WAS CORRECT.
BWUH?!

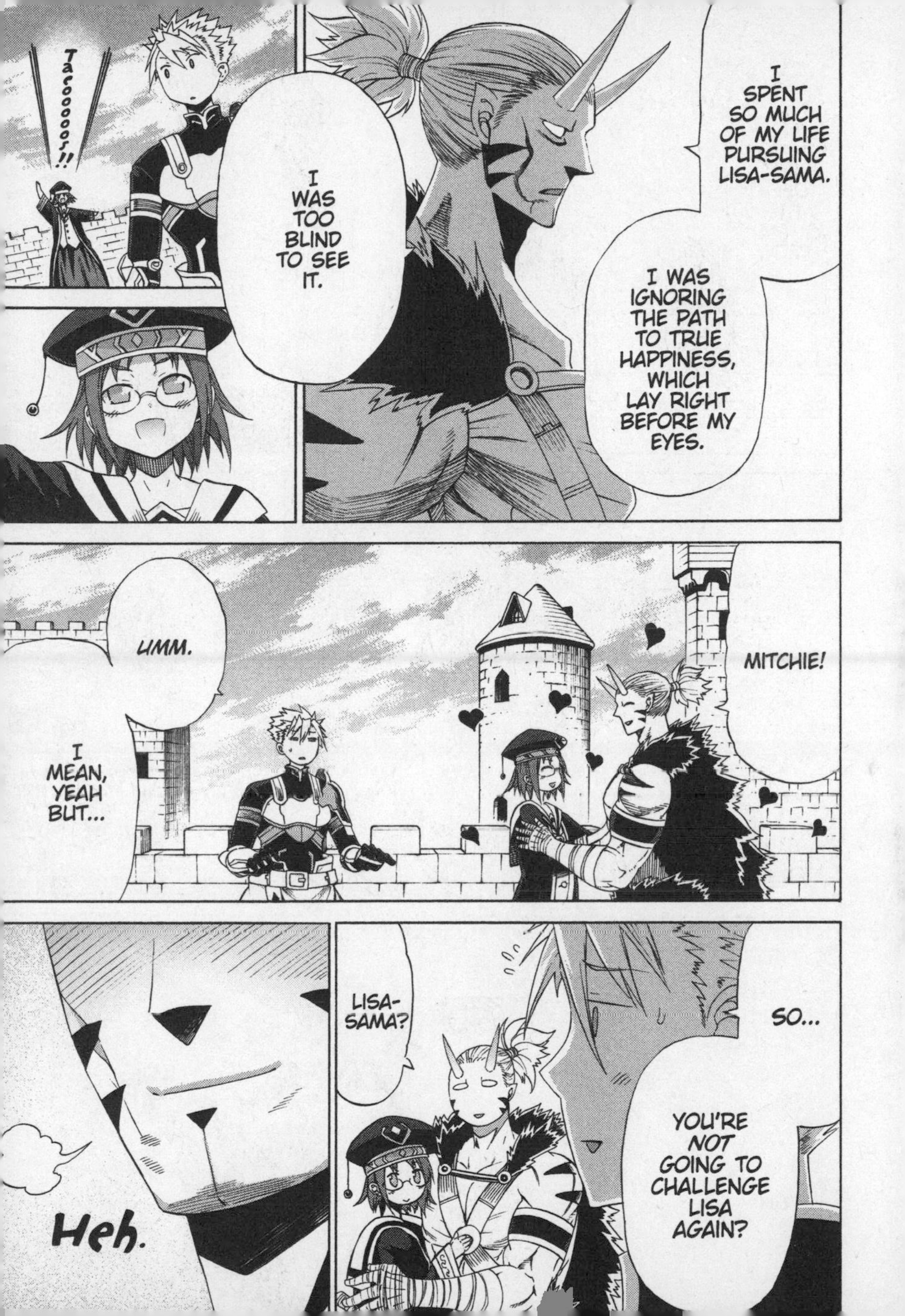
I SPENT SO MUCH OF MY LIFE PURSUING LISA-SAMA.
I WAS IGNORING THE PATH TO TRUE HAPPINESS, WHICH LAY RIGHT BEFORE MY EYES.
I WAS TOO BLIND TO SEE IT.
Tacooooos!!
MITCHIE!
UMM.
I MEAN, YEAH BUT...
SO...
YOU'RE NOT GOING TO CHALLENGE LISA AGAIN?
LISA-SAMA?
Heh.

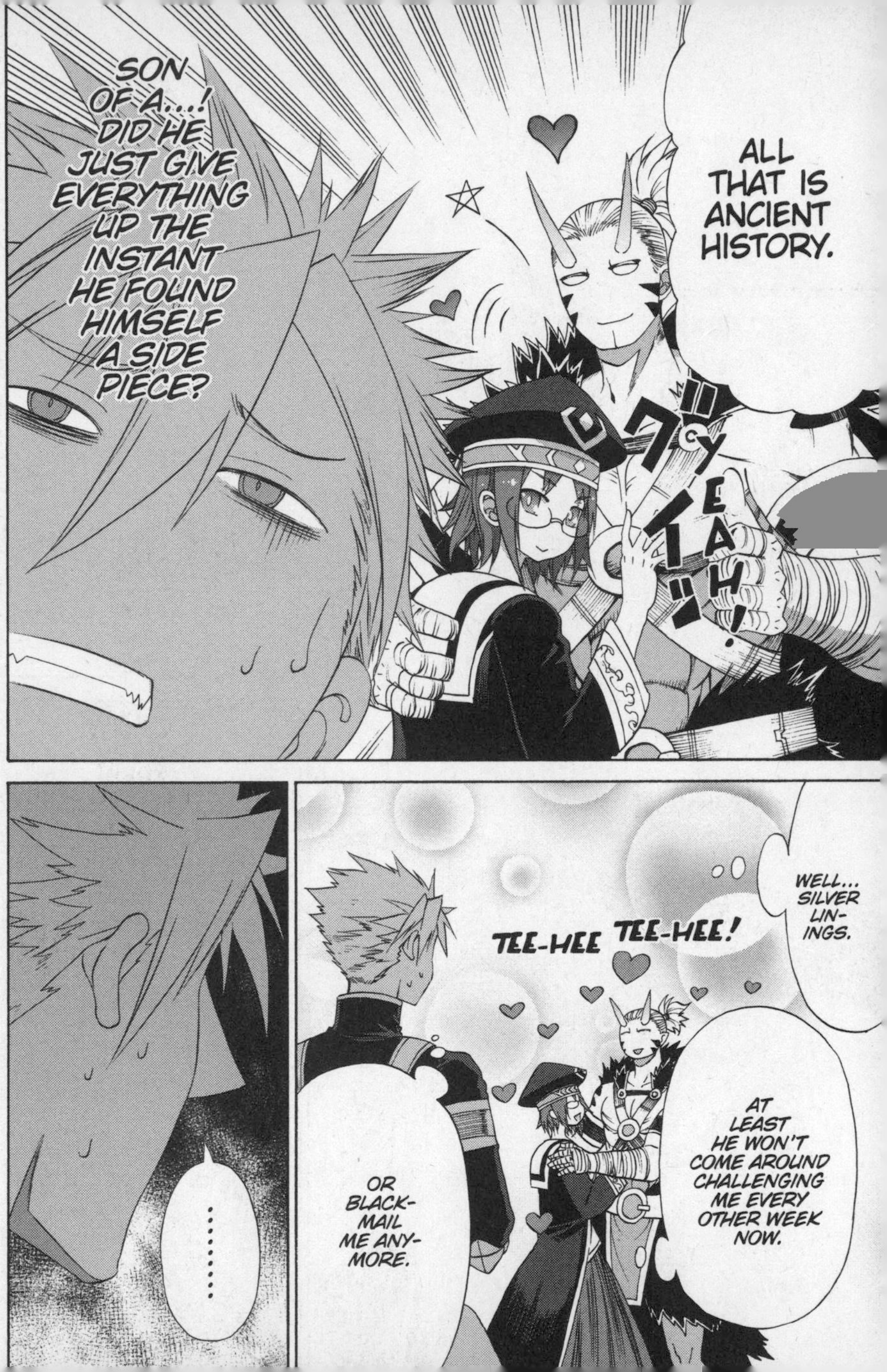

ALL THAT IS ANCIENT HISTORY.
CYEAH!
SON OF A...! DID HE JUST GIVE EVERYTHING UP THE INSTANT HE FOUND HIMSELF A SIDE PIECE?
WELL... SILVER LIN-INGS.
TEE-HEE TEE-HEE!
AT LEAST HE WON'T COME AROUND CHALLENGING ME EVERY OTHER WEEK NOW.
OR BLACK-MAIL ME ANY-MORE.
....

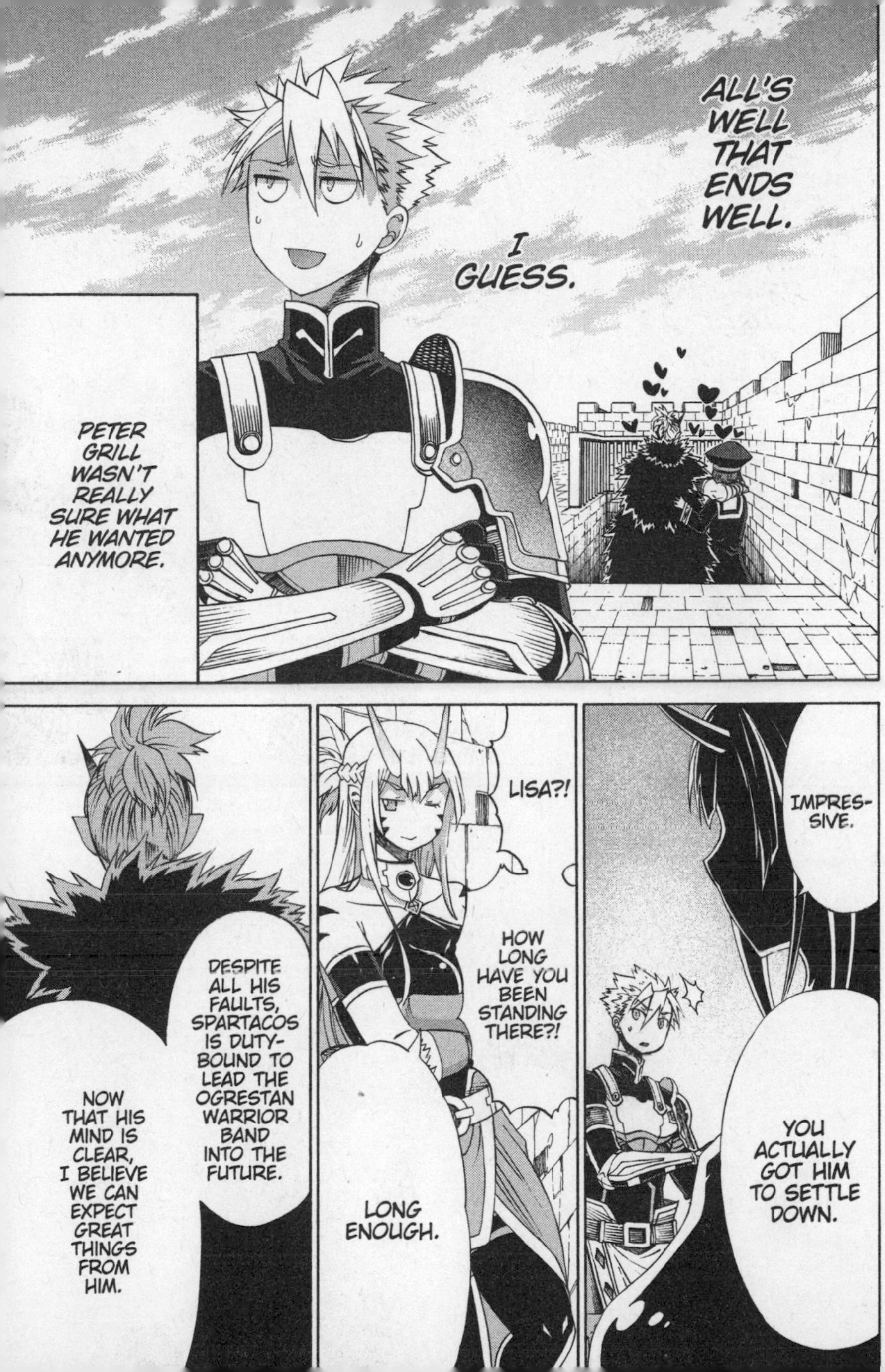
ALL'S WELL THAT ENDS WELL.
I GUESS.
PETER GRILL WASN'T REALLY SURE WHAT HE WANTED ANYMORE.
IMPRES-SIVE.
YOU ACTUALLY GOT HIM TO SETTLE DOWN.
LISA?!
HOW LONG HAVE YOU BEEN STANDING THERE?!
LONG ENOUGH.
DESPITE ALL HIS FAULTS, SPARTACOS IS DUTY-BOUND TO LEAD THE OGRESTAN WARRIOR BAND INTO THE FUTURE.
NOW THAT HIS MIND IS CLEAR, I BELIEVE WE CAN EXPECT GREAT THINGS FROM HIM.

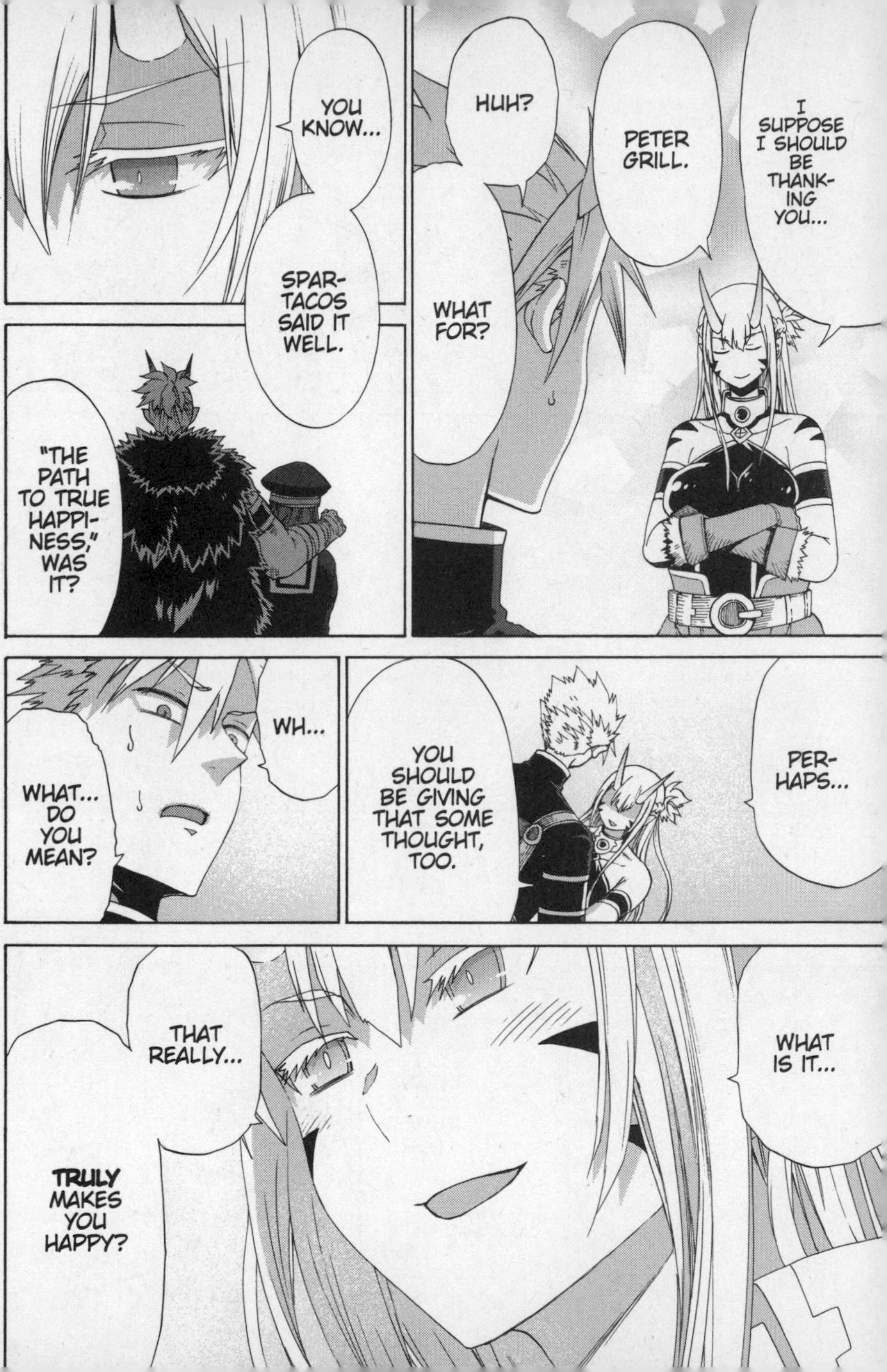
I SUPPOSE I SHOULD BE THANKING YOU...
PETER GRILL.
HUH?
WHAT FOR?
YOU KNOW...
SPAR-TACOS SAID IT WELL.
"THE PATH TO TRUE HAPPI-NESS," WAS IT?
PER-HAPS...
YOU SHOULD BE GIVING THAT SOME THOUGHT, TOO.
WH...
WHAT... DO YOU MEAN?
WHAT IS IT...
THAT REALLY...
TRULY MAKES YOU HAPPY?

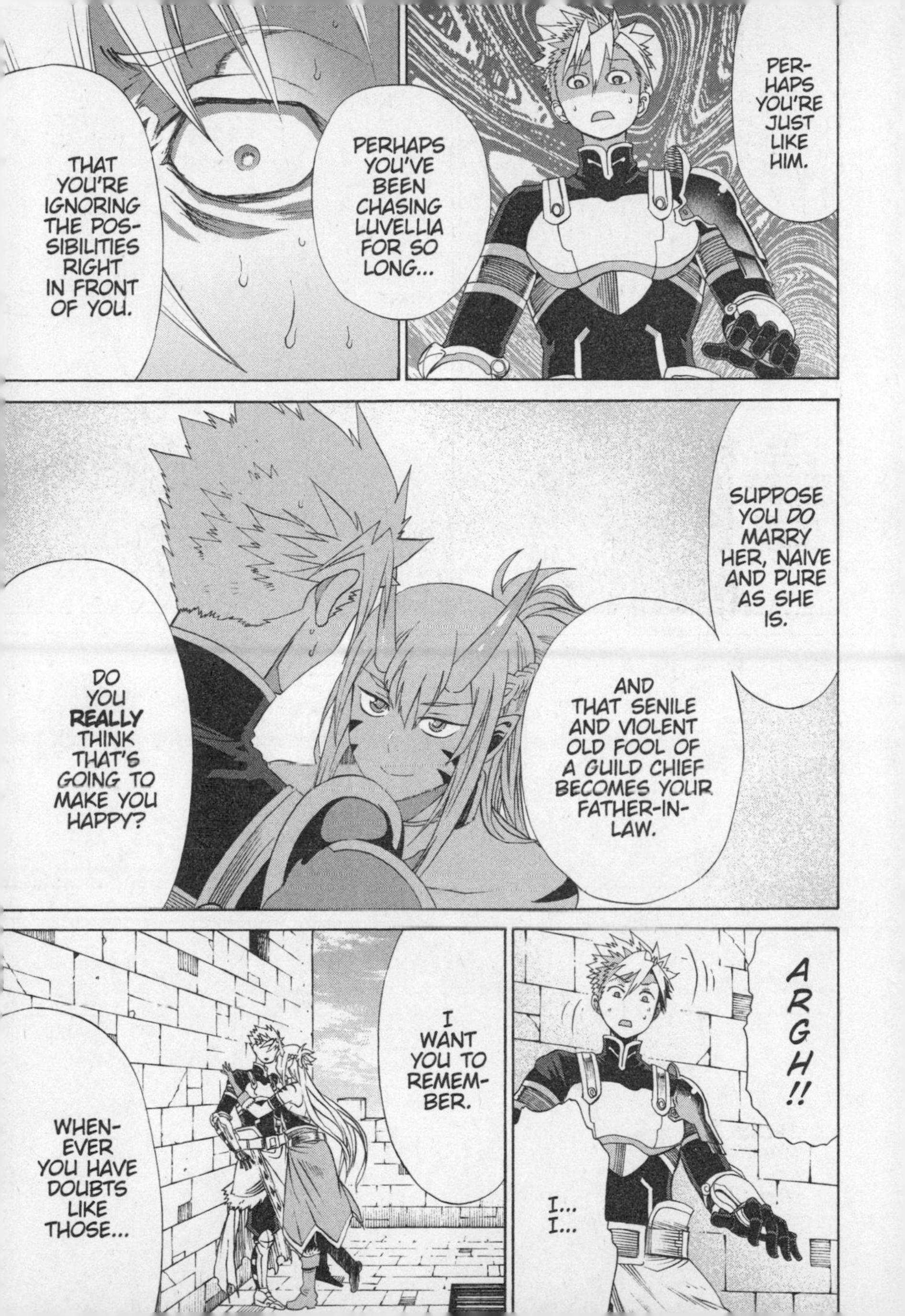
PERHAPS YOU'RE JUST LIKE HIM.
PERHAPS YOU'VE BEEN CHASING LUVELLIA FOR SO LONG...
THAT YOU'RE IGNORING THE POSSIBILITIES RIGHT IN FRONT OF YOU.
SUPPOSE YOU *DO* MARRY HER, NAIVE AND PURE AS SHE IS.
AND THAT SENILE AND VIOLENT OLD FOOL OF A GUILD CHIEF BECOMES YOUR FATHER-IN-LAW.
DO YOU **REALLY** THINK THAT'S GOING TO MAKE YOU HAPPY?
ARGH!!
I... I...
I WANT YOU TO REMEMBER.
WHENEVER YOU HAVE DOUBTS LIKE THOSE...

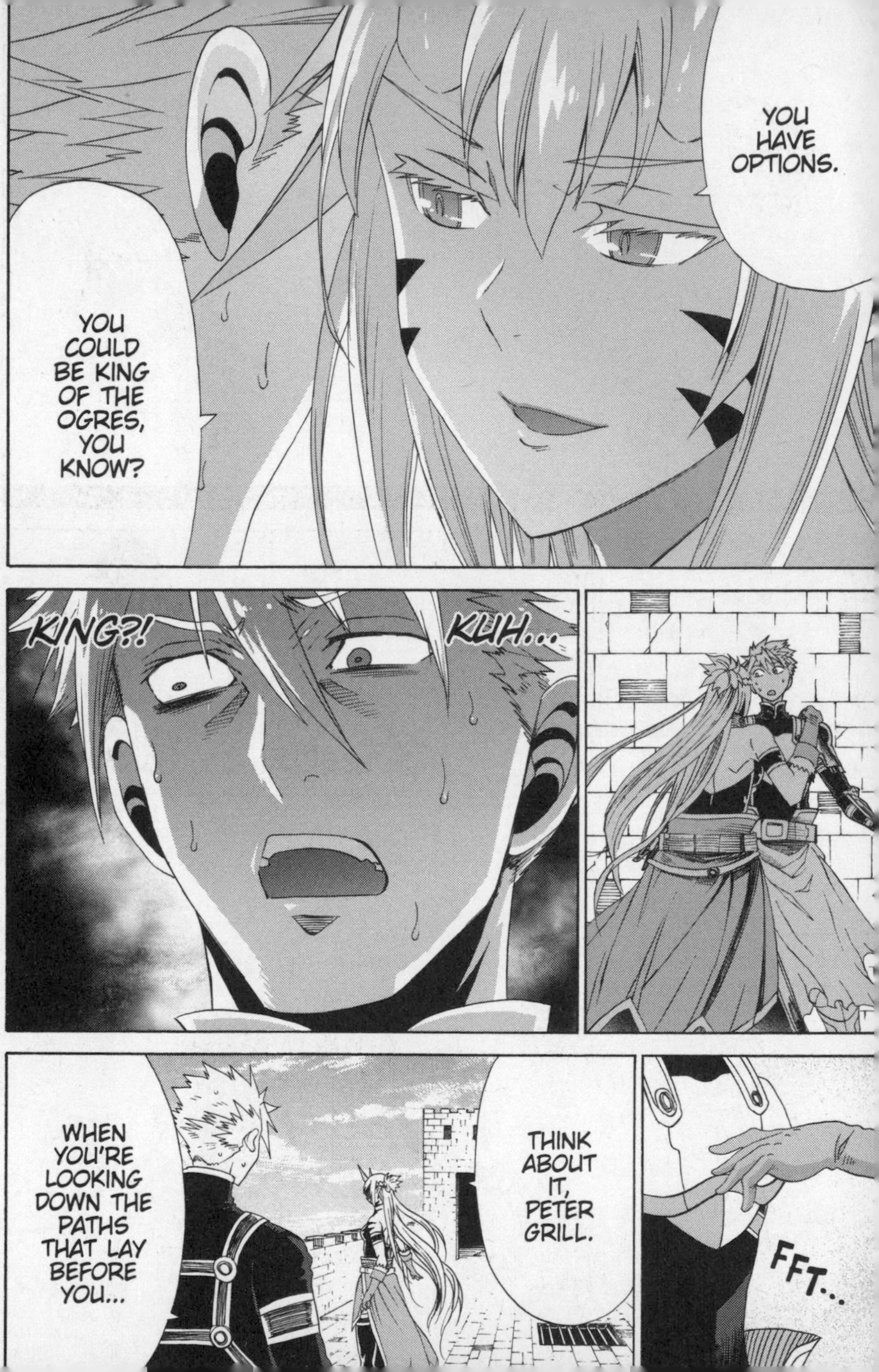
YOU HAVE OPTIONS.
YOU COULD BE KING OF THE OGRES, YOU KNOW?
KUH...
KING?!
FFT...
THINK ABOUT IT, PETER GRILL.
WHEN YOU'RE LOOKING DOWN THE PATHS THAT LAY BEFORE YOU...

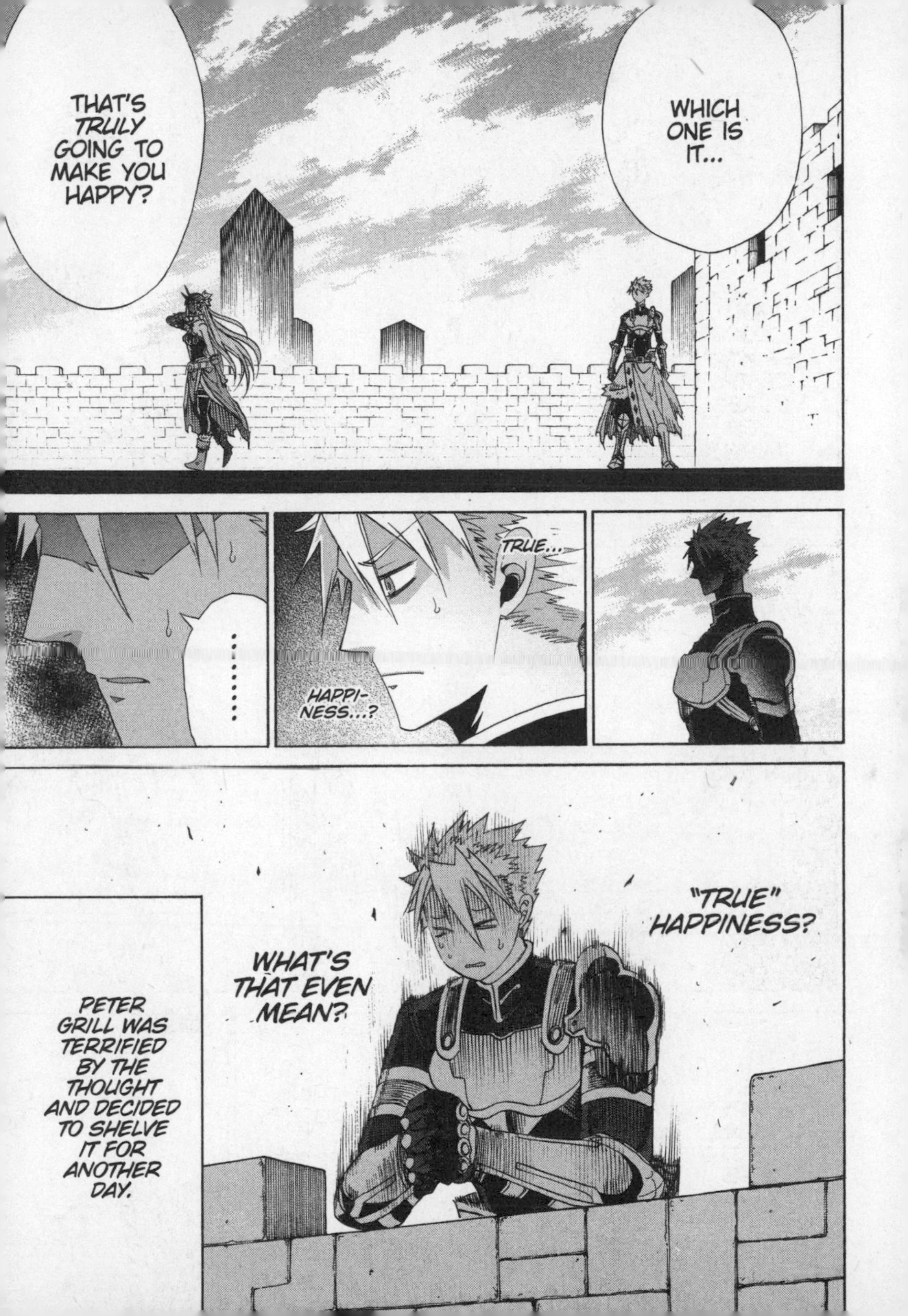
WHICH ONE IS IT...
THAT'S TRULY GOING TO MAKE YOU HAPPY?
TRUE...
HAPPINESS...?
......
"TRUE" HAPPINESS?
WHAT'S THAT EVEN MEAN?
PETER GRILL WAS TERRIFIED BY THE THOUGHT AND DECIDED TO SHELVE IT FOR ANOTHER DAY.

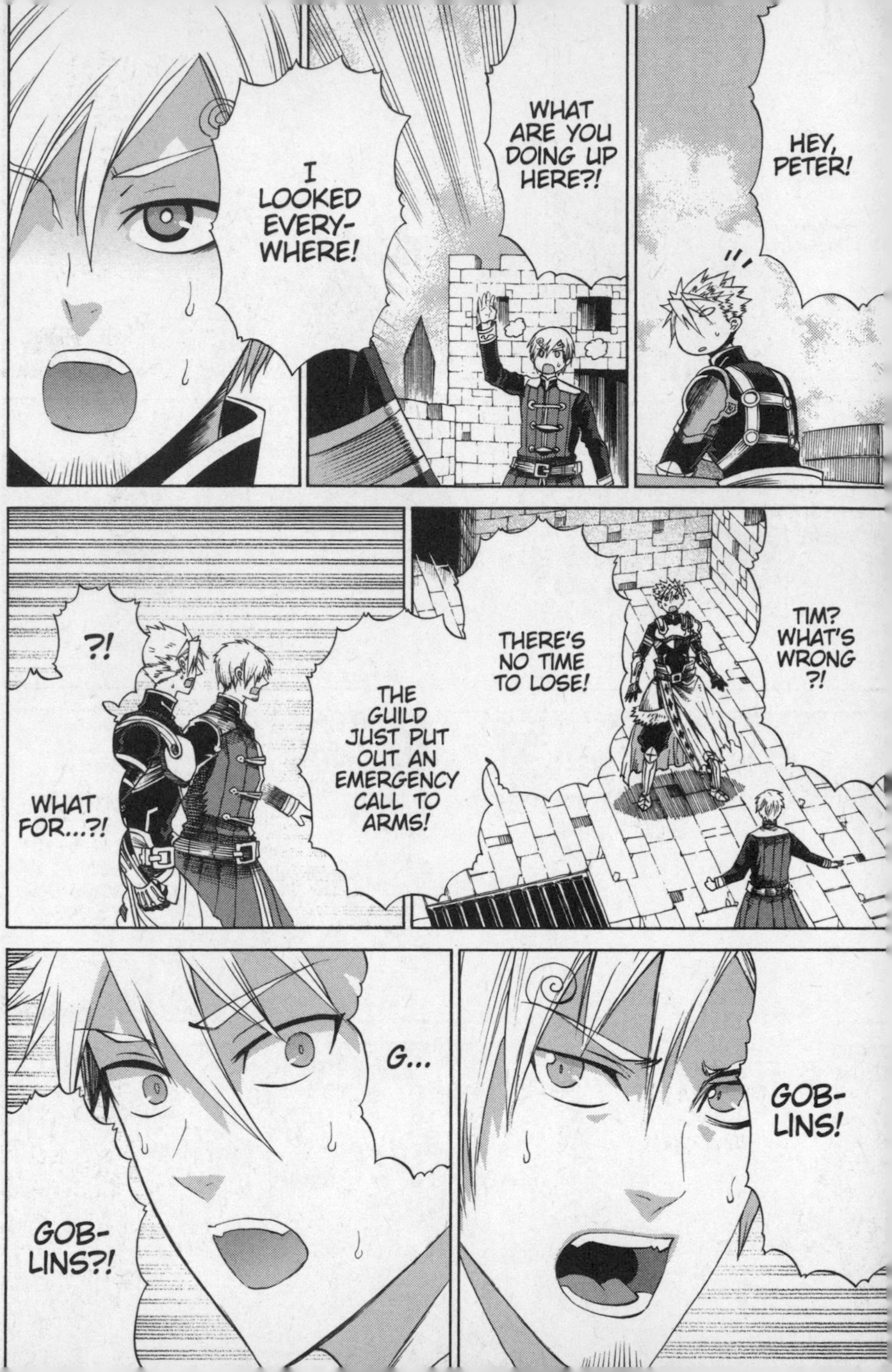
HEY, PETER!
WHAT ARE YOU DOING UP HERE?!
I LOOKED EVERY-WHERE!
TIM? WHAT'S WRONG ?!
THERE'S NO TIME TO LOSE!
THE GUILD JUST PUT OUT AN EMERGENCY CALL TO ARMS!
?!
WHAT FOR...?!
GOB-LINS!
G...
GOB-LINS?!

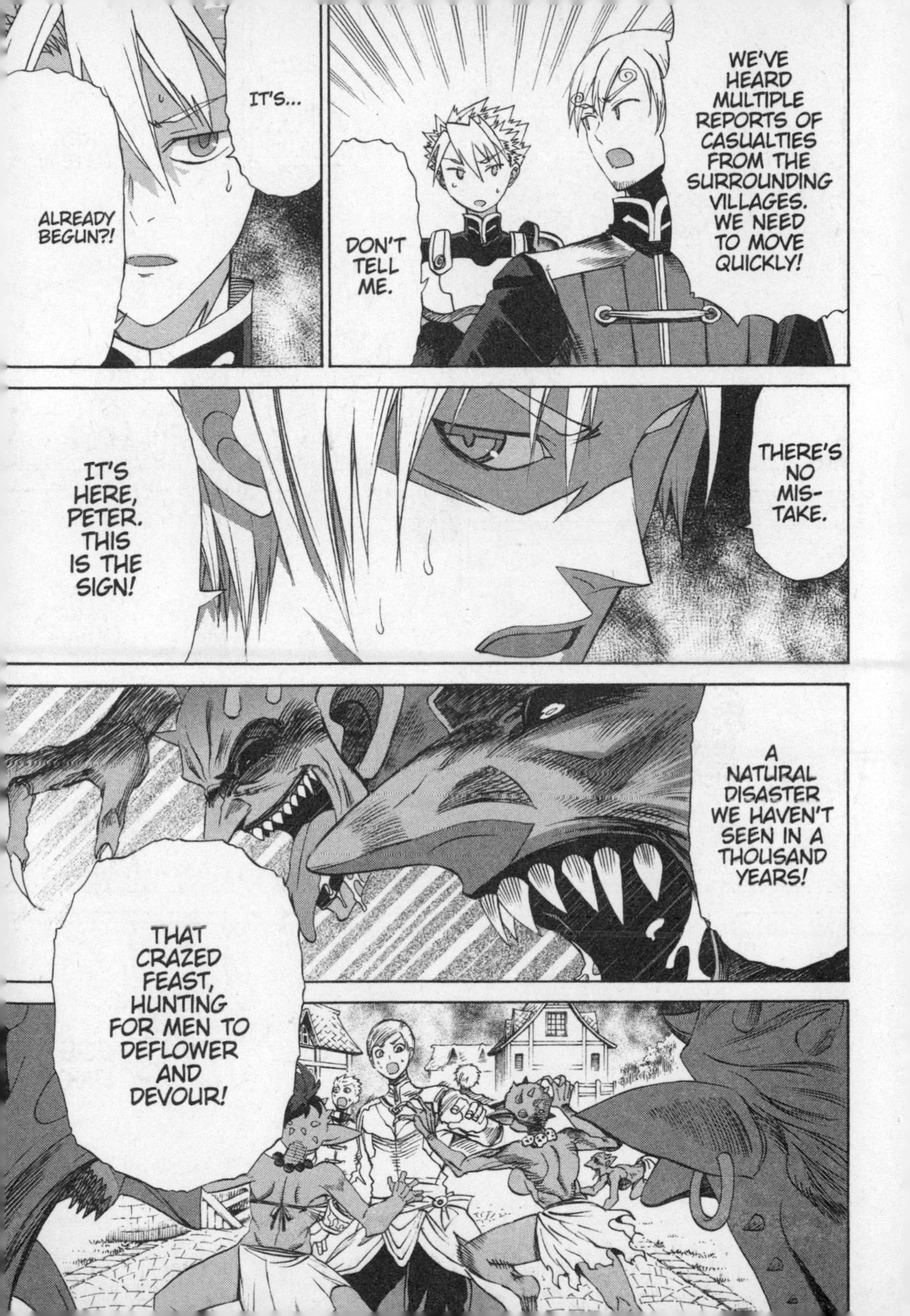
WE'VE HEARD MULTIPLE REPORTS OF CASUALTIES FROM THE SURROUNDING VILLAGES. WE NEED TO MOVE QUICKLY!
DON'T TELL ME.
IT'S...
ALREADY BEGUN?!
THERE'S NO MIS-TAKE.
IT'S HERE, PETER. THIS IS THE SIGN!
A NATURAL DISASTER WE HAVEN'T SEEN IN A THOUSAND YEARS!
THAT CRAZED FEAST, HUNTING FOR MEN TO DEFLOWER AND DEVOUR!

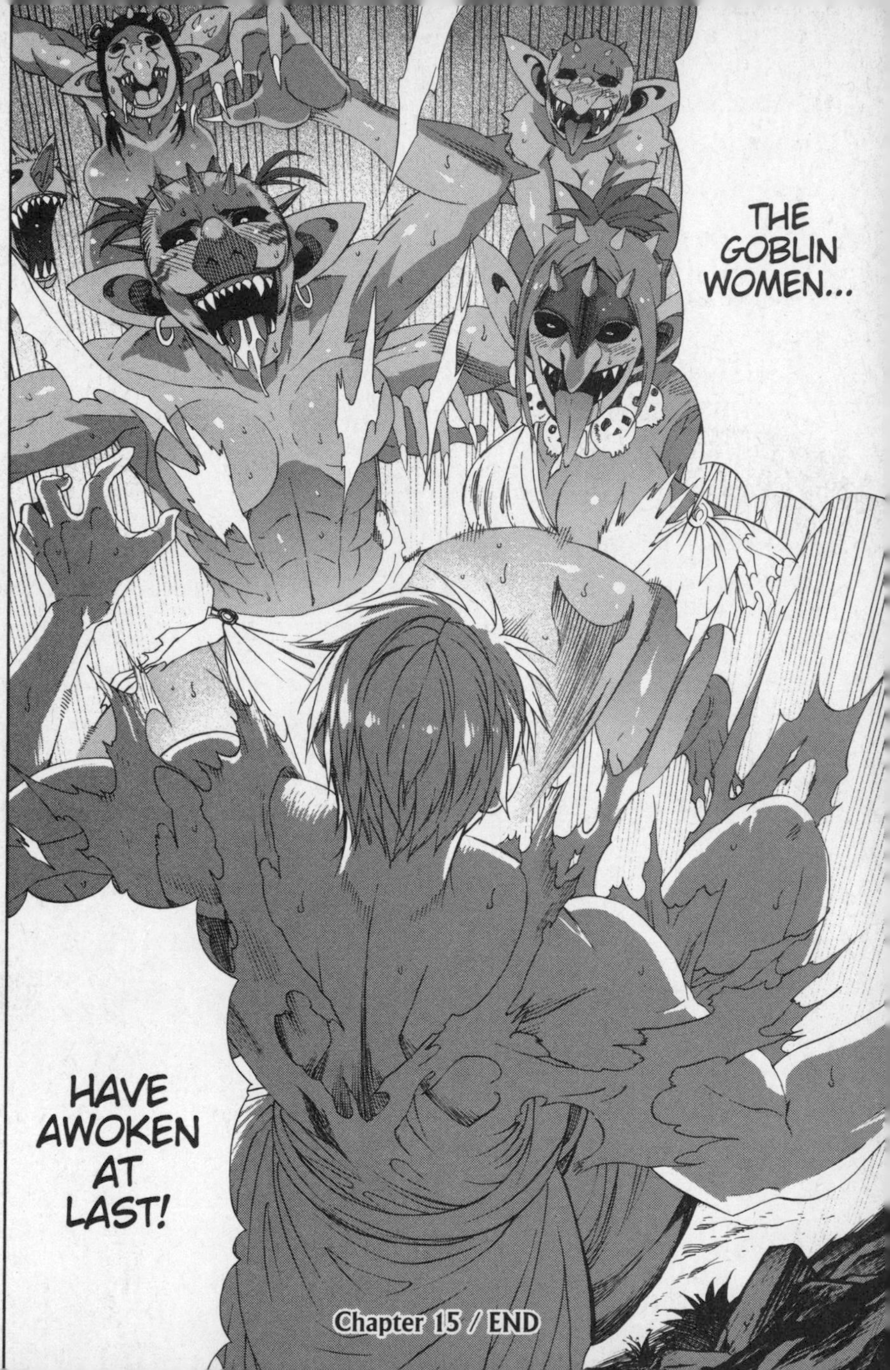
THE GOBLIN WOMEN...
HAVE AWOKEN AT LAST!
Chapter 15 / END

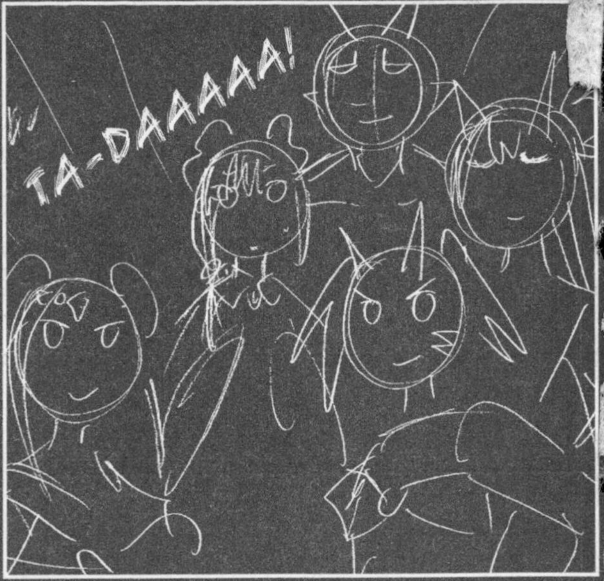
TA-DAAAAAA!

The strongest man on Earth and his merry band set out to battle the goblin threat!!

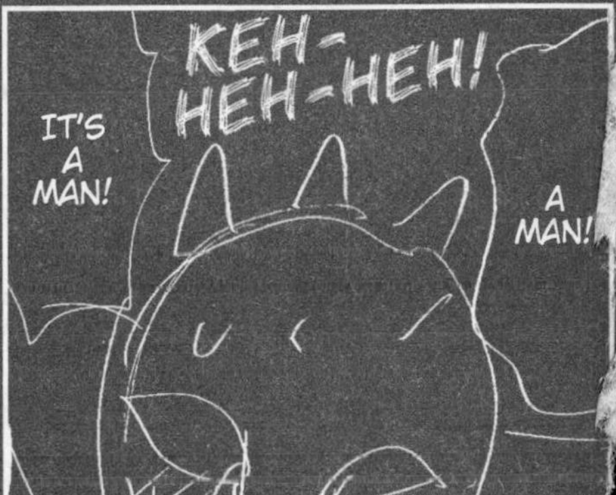
KEH-HEH-HEH!
IT'S A MAN!
A MAN!

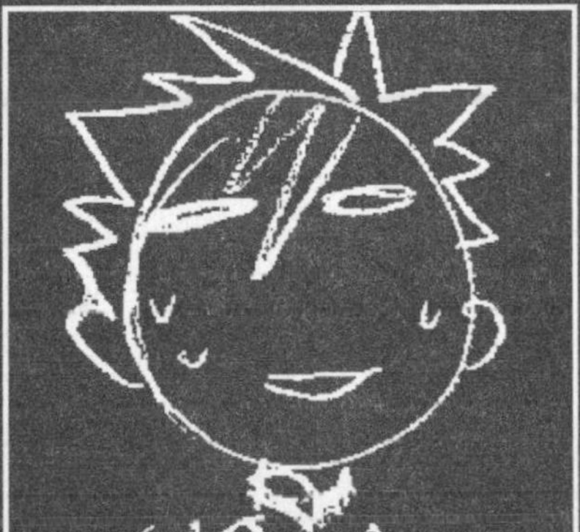

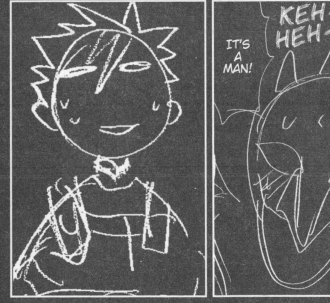

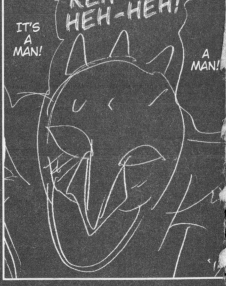

Peter Grill and the Philosopher's Time
Volume Four— Coming soon!!!

SEVEN SEAS ENTERTAINMENT PRESENTS

PETER GRILL
AND THE PHILOSOPHER'S TIME
story and art by **DAISUKE HIYAMA**   **VOLUME 3**

TRANSLATION
Ben Trethewey

ADAPTATION
David Lumsdon

LETTERING
Simone Harrison

COVER DESIGN
Nicky Lim
(LOGO) **Kris Aubin**

PROOFREADING
Dawn Davis
Janet Houck

EDITOR
Elise Kelsey

PREPRESS TECHNICIAN
Rhiannon Rasmussen-Silverstein

PRODUCTION MANAGER
Lissa Pattillo

MANAGING EDITOR
Julie Davis

ASSOCIATE PUBLISHER
Adam Arnold

PUBLISHER
Jason DeAngelis

PETER GRILL AND THE PHILOSOPHER'S TIME VOL. 3
© Daisuke Hiyama 2017
All rights reserved.
First published in Japan in 2019 by Futabasha Publishers Ltd., Tokyo.
English version published by Seven Seas Entertainment.
Under license from Futabasha Publishers Ltd.

Seven Seas press and purchase enquiries can be sent to Marketing Manager
Lianne Sentar at press@gomanga.com. Information regarding the distribution
and purchase of digital editions is available from Digital Manager CK Russell
at digital@gomanga.com.

Seven Seas and the Seven Seas logo are trademarks of
Seven Seas Entertainment. All rights reserved.

ISBN: 978-1-64505-849-6

Printed in Canada

First Printing: December 2020

10 9 8 7 6 5 4 3 2 1

FOLLOW US ONLINE: *www.sevenseasentertainment.com*

READING DIRECTIONS

This book reads from *right to left*, Japanese style.
If this is your first time reading manga, you start
reading from the top right panel on each page and
take it from there. If you get lost, just follow the
numbered diagram here. It may seem backwards at
first, but you'll get the hang of it! Have fun!!

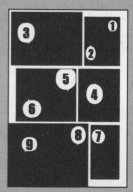